THE

EVADER

An American Airman's Eight Months with the Dutch Underground

By

Harry A. Dolph
(Harry A. Clark)

EAKIN PRESS ★ Austin, Texas

FIRST EDITION

Copyright © 1991
By Harry A. Dolph

Published in the United States of America
By Eakin Press
An Imprint of Eakin Publications, Inc.
P.O. Drawer 90159 ★ Austin, TX 78709-0159

ISBN 0-89015-795-2

Library of Congress Cataloging-in-Publication Data

Dolph, Harry A.
    The evader : an American airman's eight months with the Dutch underground / by Harry A.
Dolph.
        p.   cm.
    Includes bibliographical references and index.
    ISBN 0-89015-795-2 : $18.95
    1. Dolph, Harry A. 2. World War, 1939–1945 — Underground movements — Netherlands.
3. World War, 1939–1945 — Personal narratives, American. 4. Escapes — Netherlands —
History — 20th century. 5. United States. Army Air Forces — Biography. I. Title.
D802.N4D65   1990
940.53'492 — dc20
                                                                                            90-44651
                                                                                                CIP

Dedicated to my wife,
Patricia,
who was the driving force to put it on paper.

Also dedicated to Peter and Mimi,
without whom there never would have been a book,
AND
Oom Joop, who lost his only son,
AND
George and Niko, two of the best,
AND
Ernst Scheufele,
without whom there never would have been a story to write,
AND
To the eight who died in the Wig-Wam
AND
To Johnny Capps, lifelong friend and comrade,
AND
The five who didn't make it.

Harry A. Clark, staff sergeant.

Foreword

The Eighth Air Force was the largest air force in the world ever committed to a single theater flying combat missions from one base area (England) for nearly three years. Before the war ended, 350,000 Americans served in the 8AF. Over 26,000 died in that struggle, equal to the combined losses of all other USAAF units (more than the number who died in the U.S. Navy in WWII).

The crew I was honored to serve on as pilot had the distinction of leading the group on the two worst missions of the 466th Bomb Group: Mission #6 to Brunswick, 8 April 1944 (6 a/c lost); and Mission #106 to Vechta, Germany, 15 August 1944 (4 a/c lost).

On 15 August 1944, our crew flew its twenty-fifth mission — only five more for us. We were flying in 592U, later named *Black Cat*. This was the first mission for this aircraft. We also flew it on our last mission (1 November 1944). It was the last plane lost by the 466BG, on 21 April 1945.

The reader may be interested in knowing that the Archer Crew flew its first misssion on 3 June 1944. Due to that later start, they had thirty-five missions to fly (the rules were changed after we began in February). On 15 August they were on their thirty-third and thirty-fourth mission, with only one or two more to go.

The Archer Crew in *True Love* were in the second 466BG section of seven aircraft; a number of ships had aborted. Jim Fawver was flying *Biff-Bam* in the lead of this section with John Jacobowitz as command pilot. At about 1250 hours about fifteen or twenty ME-109s came through the formation, hitting this second section and knocking down four planes with 20mm cannon fire in one pass. But that story belongs to Harry Dolph.

It is my great pleasure to introduce you to this book. Just remember that there never was such an air war before, never since and likely never again. When you read of the events recounted by Harry, just remember that his experience was unique, shared by only a very few Americans. Good reading.

JOHN H. WOOLNOUGH
President, 466th Bomb Group Association, Inc.

Preface

What's in a name? Let me tell you. My name while I was in the service of my country was Harry A. Clark.

I was named Harry Arthur Dolph, Jr., after my father, who divorced my mother before she learned to properly put diapers on me. She put our belongings in a suitcase and moved to nearby Jackson, Michigan, rented a small flat, and took in washing to earn money.

By the time I was four she was earning $65 a week, much more than the average working man's salary of $15 a week. She had married a boxer by the name of Clicky Clark who, when he wasn't training for a fight, was a full-time alcoholic. His favorite pastime was beating me. My mother usually sported a black eye or a split lip. During his drunkenness, he often threatened her life.

One night, in a blind rage, he stabbed her in the stomach. Blood spurted from the wound and the doctors proclaimed she was lucky to be alive. Upon our arrival home from the hospital, he pushed her in the back door of the house then hit her, knocking her to the kitchen floor. Then he kicked her in the stomach. My mother struggled to her feet, went to her bedroom, and returned with a .38 police special revolver. Her first shot hit him in the upper arm and the second grazed his ear as he bolted out the front door. She emptied the gun at him as he ran up the street, then she fainted.

I called the ambulance but the police arrived before it did. At the hospital she was sewn up again and given transfusions. The police found blood on the walk in front of our house. Clicky disappeared from Michigan and our lives.

Next she met a bootlegger by the name of George Welch and she became one of the biggest bootleggers in Jackson. Her main clientele consisted of the "good ol' boys" from city hall and members of the police and sheriff's department. The only time she was raided, I was raided! I was twelve years old and was serving customers when it happened. The deputies broke in the front and back doors. The following day she paid a five-dollar fine to the "good ol' boys," and that was the end of it.

I discovered I was not wanted by my mother. I became a liability to her and was treated badly. She wore the most fashionable clothes and was very popular among the opposite sex.

I wasn't a good student and my grades proved that fact. School counselors suggested I be given some psychological help. They checked my IQ (125), gave me a physical, and discovered I was anemic. The shrinks determined there was nothing wrong with me a little TLC wouldn't cure.

More often than not, my mother referred to me as "my brat," and I was left to shift for myself. I might add, I wasn't the cleanest kid on the block either. I had a lot of opportunities to go bad, but for some reason I never took that final step over the edge.

Finally, the juvenile authorities took me away from her. My father, who had remarried, was notified and was awarded my legal custody. I moved with him to Flint, Michigan, in September 1931. Five months after I moved in with him, he died in Hurley Hospital of bronchial pneumonia.

The inspiration my father gave me during those five months was the only motivation I ever had in my life. He was an artist, more of a cartoonist really, but he brought out some latent talents in me I never knew I had. In many ways my father was truly a wonderful man, and to this day I miss him. I've probably made a martyr of him because of his untimely death at the age of thirty-two. Nevertheless, because of him I was on the honor roll from the day he died until my senior year at Central High School in Lansing, Michigan, in 1936.

After my father's death, I moved back with my mother. All the big money she had made bootlegging was gone. I graduated from high school a month before I turned seventeen and was still a runt. I was an honor student until the last half of my senior year — when I discovered girls. After graduation, I went with my grandfather, who had a sideshow, and traveled with carnivals and fairs from April until late October. The season I was with him was an education in itself.

I returned to Lansing with $110 hidden in various parts of my clothing. Finding that my mother had pulled up stakes and moved, I joined the Civilian Conservation Corps. I was sent to CCC Camp St. Martin in the upper peninsula of Michigan, where I became a sign painter and worked on a survey crew as a chainman. My wages were $30 a month. I received eight and the other twenty-two went to my mother (after they found her in California). Six months after I joined, I was honorably discharged and promptly joined my mother in LA.

I got a job at the Peerless Laundry on the corner of Slauson and Main streets, within walking distance of our house. I earned $18 a week, while my mother made $22.

I made a down payment on a 1930 Ford with the money I had earned in the Civilian Conservation Corps and saved from the carnival. The "in" place to go on Saturday nights was Bessie Clark's school of dancing in Inglewood, highly chaperoned and no alcohol allowed. You either abided by Bessie's rules or went elsewhere. It was a great place to learn all the latest dance steps. Her regular students mingled with those of us who paid the two-bits to get in. Olympic greats Marjorie Gestring and Sammy Lee (high divers) and Marie McDonald (Hollywood starlet) were among the regulars.

One Saturday I met Lois Oakley, a newcomer to Inglewood from Kansas. Her family moved to California because her father found work as a jeweler. Shyly, she asked if I would dance with her. I was flattered because she was so petite and beautiful. She had long black hair, an olive complexion, and was the most gorgeous girl I had ever seen. She was barely five feet tall, and though she couldn't dance too well she held on to me, giving me an occasional squeeze while trying to learn the jitterbug. A week later we were going steady and a month later she could dance circles around any girl I knew. We entered many dance contests at the big piers — Santa Monica and Venice, as well as the Palladium in Hollywood — and won or placed in all of them. We were deeply in love and planned to be married on December 29, 1938, the day she died of cancer.

I almost lost my IQ. I think I did go off the deep end for a while. I lost my job, my car, and most of my friends. I was furious because I didn't have guts enough to kill myself.

I wrote to my grandmother in Michigan and told her what had happened. She wrote and told me to get my tail to Kalamazoo. I hitchhiked and rode freight trains, but ten days later I was at her door, dirty, broke, and miserable. Within a week she had me straightened out. In retrospect, moving away from LA and the circle of friends Lois and I moved in probably was as much of a cure as anything. It took most of my life before I stopped comparing other women to her.

My cousin Bobby Lillie lived in Kalamazoo. At his suggestion we enlisted in the Civilian Conservation Corps and were sent to a CCC camp in the western part of the upper peninsula, the coldest hell-hole I've ever seen. The barracks stoves were inadequate for heating. We worked outside in temperatures as low as forty-five below.

The infirmary and half the barracks were full of young men suffering from frostbite and frozen limbs. The commanding officer of the camp lived off the jug and couldn't care less about those placed in his trust. One night in February, 120 of us went over the hill to desert en masse. I returned to California the same way I had traveled to Michigan — by thumbing it and riding freight trains.

War news was everywhere. I stayed with my mother and applied for jobs at every defense plant in Southern California. I was only 5'6 and weighed about a hundred pounds. I was baby-faced and looked like a junior high student. In addition, I had no viable working skills. Men with elementary school educations were hired on the spot and I'd be passed by. I tried to enlist in the army, navy, coast guard, and even the merchant marine; however, I couldn't meet their minimum weight requirements and they wouldn't waive them. The Marine Corps told me to come back "when I had grown up." There were posters asking for men to join the Civilian Conservation Corps, but I was afraid to apply because I had gone over the hill in Michigan.

A month after I had been back in California, getting more and more discouraged, my mother made the suggestion that would change my life: "If you can't find a job at the defense plants and can't get into the service, why don't you go back into the Civilian Conservation Corps and enlist under the name of Harry A. Clark? My name is Clark. And since you wouldn't know anybody, who would ever know the difference?"

I made one last attempt at the four branches of the service and was turned down again because I hadn't gained a pound.

So, Harry Arthur Clark joined the Civilian Conservation Corps. No identification was needed. No birth certificate, no high school diploma. Nothing but "Sign here!"

I was sent to CCC Camp Pine Grove in California. Later, I did a favor for an inspecting officer and he got me transferred to the motor pool in Sacramento, chauffeuring inspection officers and driving ambulances. It was the cushiest job in the CCC.

Some army recruiters came to the motor pool and waved the flag. Since I was already in the CCC it was just a matter of transferring into the Army Air Corps with no credentials needed.

So what's in a name? More than you'll ever know. It kept me from getting a commission, and it kept me in a state of anxiety for seven years. But another name would protect me in an unforgettable eight-month period — as a member of the Dutch underground during the war.

ONE

T hey were both armed with Schmeisser A-38 machine guns held by straps around their necks. They were talking excitedly and somewhere the word *"fraulein"* filtered through their guttural gibberish. Their blue-gray uniforms were unkempt and their knee-length boots were dusty. The straps on their helmets swayed back and forth with every step.

Four hours earlier, our bomber had been shot down in flames by ME-109 Messerschmitts of the Luftwaffe over Holland. Johnny had saved my life by buckling on my parachute; it saved my life when I bailed out. The delayed jump kept me from being captured by the waiting German troops and, luckily, I was able to outwit the enemy soldiers once I was on the ground.

The floor of the forest was covered with rolling sand dunes, many ten feet high. The woods had a thick growth of long-needled pines about thirty feet high. Many of them grew in clusters. A wide path ran into the woods, and the three-foot-deep ditch in which I was hiding ran along beside it. Despite my fears and the pain from my burns, I had fallen asleep. Now alien voices awakened me. I heard the sound of the intruders swishing through the sand before I caught sight of them. I gripped my .45 Colt Automatic, removed it from its holster, pulled the hammer back, and took it off safety.

There they were. Two enlisted men of the Luftwaffe, neither more than twenty years old, were searching the sides of the path as

1

they inched closer to my hiding place.

Well, I thought, *if they spot me, I'm ready for them!*

I ducked down as low as I could but still kept them in sight. An icy chill numbed me and my hair stood on end. When they were twenty feet away, the taller one stopped in his tracks and looked straight at me. He spun around, grabbing his machine gun with both hands, and took dead aim at me. He yelled loudly to his partner as he did so.

My Colt barked four times as I came up out of the ditch shooting. They fell almost simultaneously as the German's weapon fired harmlessly over my head. One soldier fell backward and the other crumpled on the path opposite me. Blood spurted upward from the hole my slug had made in the taller man's neck. His helmet fell on the path, a bloody gaping hole in it; the chin strap still swung back and forth. The other German was hit in the center of his chest. He lay there, a pool of blood forming under his dead body. Occasionally he kicked his feet and jerked his arms. His weapon lay on the ground beside him. There were two fresh clips of ammo for the Schmeisser in his belt. I holstered my .45, took the ammo clips, and hung his Schmeisser over my shoulder by its strap.

The noise that a .45 makes is enough to raise the dead. With the German airfield less than a mile away, my first impulse was to get away. I ran deeper into the forest until I was exhausted, then walked until I caught my breath. I did this over and over until I came to the edge of the forest a half hour later. When I looked out over the terrain I saw nothing but open fields. It looked uninhabited: no farm machinery, no animals, only open fields of weeds.

Afraid of being seen, I went back into the woods and sat down against a small tree. I dropped my arsenal of weapons on the ground beside me and tried to take stock of my situation.

I couldn't believe I had killed another human being. Oh sure, when we laid a string of bombs on a target they took lives. But this was different. I had come face to face with two of the enemy and didn't hesitate to pull the trigger. I looked at the German's Schmeisser beside me and remembered the look on his face when he aimed his weapon at me. *He was actually going to shoot me!* I thought. *He really was! My God, they were too young to shave!*

I told myself to put it behind me. I wished Johnny were there. Then my thoughts turned back to early morning . . .

"Archer's crew!" yelled the officer of the day. "Hit the deck. Three a.m. Come on, rise and shine! Last call!"

The blinding flash of the overhead lights took the sleep out of me long before his booming voice did. It was an honest-to-God relief when he stopped flipping the light switch off and on. He slammed the door behind him when he left.

"Aw shit," I said aloud. I had been dreaming the same fairy tale we all dream of when we're in that deep sleep, that land of impossibilities. Only this one had been brunette, beautiful, and endowed with all the attributes necessary to form the perfect female specimen. Nothing had been impossible as far as my dream had progressed. But thanks to the OD, now I'd go through life without knowing the outcome of my fantasy. Somehow it seemed important at the moment. All I could think to say was, "Thanks for nothin', you loud-mouthed jerk!"

The rest of the crew began to stir, so I rubbed the sand from my eyes and put on my pants. "Come on, Johnny, get your ass outta bed," I said, kicking the bunk.

I got my shaving kit and walked across the road to the community latrine and washroom. It was filling rapidly, but I found an empty sink. As I started to shave, Johnny joined me. After we shaved and brushed some of the moss off our teeth, we went back and made our beds.

He was born John Marvin Capps and hailed from Dexter, Missouri. As soon as we met we became close buddies, almost like brothers. Orders were cut putting together combat crews at the 18th Replacement Wing located at the fairgrounds next to Salt Lake City's airport. We were sent by train to Gowen Field near Boise, Idaho, for transition training. Our pilot walked the train from one end to the other amid the turmoil of hundreds of rowdy, noisy GIs until he found all of us. Then we were joined together for the first time.

At Gowen Field we were introduced to the B-24 Liberator bomber, a huge, four-engine monstrosity. We soon learned its main function was to develop hydraulic leaks and cause the bombers to abort from the easiest training missions. Unlike its older brother, the B-17, whose systems were all electric, only two of our turrets were electric. If the number-three engine, which drove the hydraulic pumps, wasn't fired up first, nothing else worked. Many funny cartoons were passed around about the airplane. They were not funny to those of us who risked our necks in them. Only a B-24 man could speak adversely

3

about the airplane. Fisticuffs broke out when B-17 Flying Fortress crews belittled it.

During our eight weeks of indoctrination, bonds grew stronger among the crew members. Much depended upon teamwork and each other's judgment. We learned to rely on one another completely. On this day, August 15, 1944, Johnny Capps would save my life.

We dressed, donned our leather A-2 jackets, and hiked the short quarter-mile to the mess hall in the inky darkness.

Johnny was a couple of inches taller than I and outweighed me by twenty-five pounds. He had wavy, dark brown hair and spoke with a Missouri drawl. Everybody liked him. Although he wasn't a fighter, he might be drawn into a pugilistic debate on a controversial subject if it was important. He was an admitted heartbreaker, as attested to by the ladies in his hometown and later by those in other cities where he had been stationed.

"You're a goddamned miniature Greek Adonis," Bart once said.

"How big was Adonis?" Johnny asked.

In Boise, during the 1943 Christmas season, we went to a photographer to have portraits made for our mothers. When we went back to get them, a huge two-by-three-foot picture of Johnny was elaborately framed and put on display in the photographer's window. He gave Johnny $25 to allow him to display it and overcharged me almost the same amount. When the war was over, he sent the picture in a new frame to Johnny's mother. I never had a dime refunded to me.

If a man can say he loved another man, then I can honestly say I loved Johnny for the friend he was to me.

As we headed for breakfast, we were joined by other crews. Occasionally I could see the glow of a cigarette. The well-traveled roadway was uneven and rough. I stumbled and almost fell.

"Goddamn it!" I said, as Johnny grabbed my arm.

"You're a clumsy fart, Knobby. Look where you're walking."

"You can't see your hand in front of your face and you tell me to watch where I'm walking?" I grumbled, limping slightly. Then we both laughed when he tripped over a bump.

The still morning air was fresh and clean and smelled good. It was a quiet time for crews going on a mission, each man deep in his own thoughts. What conversation there was sounded muffled. In the distance, the roar of an engine came to life, the final effort of a conscientious crew chief giving his charge a last check. Probably it was the

4

tenth time before turning it over to its crew for the dangers they would face. It felt good to be alive.

In July 1944 we had finished our first twenty-five missions. We were ordered to take ten days of rest and recreation (R&R) at an air force facility in southwestern England or take a ten-day furlough. Johnny and I took the furlough and caught a train to Glasgow, Scotland. After an overnight trip we stayed in Glasgow for eight days. The Allied soldiers who had been waiting for the invasion of Europe had long since gone, thus sacrificing the huge city to two lonely GIs on a ten-day furlough.

We met two gorgeous waitresses at the Taj Majal restaurant, and during our furlough we were inseparable. There was a shortage of soap in the British Isles. Johnny said that if he ever found a girl with clean heels, he'd marry her. We had found two of them. We were a pair of reluctant GIs to go back to flying combat. Of course, he never married the girl with clean heels from Scotland. But we aimed to go back to Glasgow when we finished our tour.

"I figure we'll finish up within three, four days tops. Maybe even have our thirty-five by this weekend," I said as we reached the mess hall.

"Well, I hope you're right. I'm ready to go to Scotland!"

All of England observed the blackout regulations. In the distance I could see a flickering of light caused by a piece of canvas nailed over the doorway of the mess hall. When a man entered, the light seemed to flicker. We set our sights on the doorway and were happy to find there were only about twenty-five guys ahead of us. We took our place in line and listened to the same old crap.

"Wonder where it'll be today?"

"Oh yeah, what'd she say?"

"How many missions you got in?"

"Did you fly yesterday? We hit a Jerry airfield at Dole/Tavaux. We got so much shit shot at us you'd have thought we were over Germany instead of France."

"So goddamned much flak you could walk on it."

"Yeah, Joe got a 'Dear John' from his wife yesterday. She's screwin' somebody else. Pilot sez he ain't fit to live with himself, let alone fly. Had the flight surgeon ground him."

"We had so goddamned many holes in our airplane. I counted eighty-one just from the inside alone."

5

"Christ, I'll be glad to get on oxygen. I'm so goddamned hung-over."

The mess line moved quickly. Soon the steaming pans of food were in front of us and the cook filled our trays.

"Same ol' crap," I said.

"You don't have to eat it, Sarge," the good-natured cook said with a wide grin on his face. "But if you don't, you'll be one hungry bastard by the time you get back."

It was important to complain about the food to the cooks. Breakfast was the same as most other mornings. Today we had fresh eggs, greasy bacon, fried potatoes, oatmeal, milk made from a powder, and our choice of tomato or orange juice. When you consider what the cooks had to work with, they were really magicians. On occasion we had "shit on the shingle" — my very favorite breakfast. It consisted of creamed fried hamburger over dry toast. I loved it. And thank God for the coffee.

Those in our crew were considered "old-timers" by the majority of the crews. On this day we'd be flying our thirty-third mission over enemy territory. After this one and two more we'd forget flying bombing missions. We could go home and train crews, volunteer for another tour of duty with the Eighth or Fifteenth Air Force, or train for the Air/Sea Rescue boats and pick up survivors from downed aircraft in the English Channel. There were secret missions with the Carpetbaggers, such as dropping canisters of weapons to underground organizations in the occupied area of Europe as well as dropping pamphlets, food, and Allied agents. Some of the missions were to Sweden and Switzerland. It was rumored they picked up interned airmen and returned them to England. These missions were top secret. Only a few very select B-24 crews participated.

Our 466th Group was comparatively new to the ETO. It flew its first mission on March 22, 1944; the twenty-fifth, and our first, mission was flown on May 5, 1944. The mission was to bomb a V-1 launching sight at Sottevast, France. Our lead navigator misjudged the location of the target by twenty miles. As a result we bombed a long road and a farmer's barn. The mission was a "no-ball" and we didn't get credit for it. We waited until May 8 for our indoctrination to fire when we bombed Brunswick, Germany. We really got our taste of war, after being pounced on by FW-190s, ME-109s, and heavy flak.

We hit our target right on the button.

In the United States, while waiting to be sent overseas, we met B-17 crews who had completed their twenty-five. It was only natural for us to ask how bad it really was. They were extremely honest in their interpretation of the air war over Nazi Germany.

"It's tough! Widow-makin', goddamned missions! Fighters! Flak! Shit, wait'll you see 'em! ME-109s, FW-190s, ME-210s, and now Jerry's got some new fighters waitin' to shoot yer ass outta the sky! Heavy flak . . . Fire . . . Fun? Shit, just wait!"

Somehow we figured they were exaggerating, wanting us to think they were heroes. It made us wave the flag all the more in our eagerness to get overseas and bomb the Nazis.

After we had flown the first few missions, we could attest to their honesty. Then Eighth Air Force Headquarters decided we had fighter protection most of the way to our targets. Chances of our being shot down by enemy aircraft had diminished somewhat. They tacked on five more missions. Now we had to fly thirty.

"So, okay," we thought, "what the hell's another five?"

Later, rumor had it that a high-ranking general officer flew a milk-run (not a difficult one) over the Pas-de-Calais area on the coast of France. He decided the mission was so easy, he tacked on still another five, increasing our tour of duty to thirty-five. On the day he made his decision we had flown twenty-six. If we hadn't taken our ten days R&R, we'd have been through before the orders were changed.

On the day the thirty-five order came down, a crew had just finished their thirtieth and, as was the custom, was allowed to land last, buzzing the field in a victory celebration. This particular pilot mowed the lawn with his props. When they learned they had another five to do, one of the waist gunners went to the hospital and threw stones at it, breaking several windows before he was subdued by the orderlies. He was sent under sedation to the psycho unit near London and then to the United States. The extra five missions drove him over the edge. The rest of the crew, with a replacement gunner, flew their additional five missions and went back to the States unscathed. Many crew members teetered on that invisible edge.

In my opinion, adding the additional five missions wasn't helpful to the war effort. Replacement crews and airplanes came to the ETO on a regular basis. The GAF (German Air Force) was dying, as was their war effort. They'd last eight months more.

Our crew had missions thrown at us so fast we were never given time to get the rest needed to fight the stress and fatigue of constant combat flying. We flew our thirty-three between May 8 and August 15, a total of ninety-eight days (or about one every three days). Some crews who had been with the Group since its inception were only on their twenty-fifth, and we were almost through.

On the other side of the coin, the war-weary crews were very sure of themselves. "It couldn't happen to me," was their by-word. We had no doubt that Archer's crew would make it through the war. We fought against being too cocky, but the tension and stress were there, especially in our later missions.

I was the armorer-gunner for the crew. My gun position was at the left waist window. When our plane was assigned to us, the ground crew-chief had already dubbed the bird *Stardust*. When it was new, Hoagie Carmichael, the genius who wrote the song by the same name, christened the plane with a pint of "bitters" (English beer). The crew-chief, using red and yellow paint, which was the only paint available at the time, created a huge yellow comet with a tail on each side of the nose of the plane. In eighteen-inch-high red letters he emblazoned the airplane's name. The B-24H was painted OD (olive drab) with red vertical stabilizers and a white band running through the center of them. The letter "S" was centered in the white band. The serial number of the bomber was 42-49202S. We flew *Stardust* on all our missions except our last.

Our airfield was located eight miles northwest of Norwich and southwest of a small village called Weston-Longville. We were close to the village of Attlebridge. Our tower call sign was CLETI. The good English people took us into their homes and hearts. We became a part of the community, something that couldn't be avoided. They did many fine things for us and would take little or no compensation for their kind acts.

Our commanding officer had been Col. Arthur J. Pierce ever since the 466th was formed back in the States. The Group was known as "Colonel Pierce's Flying Deck," with a trump assigned to each of the four squadrons. The 786th's trump was hearts.

As soon as breakfast was over, the six enlisted men of our crew went to the briefing room en masse. A huge quonset hut housed the briefing room. It could hold all the crews on the base at one time. A platform covered one end of the room upon which a desk and five metal chairs were neatly arranged for the brass. Behind the stage on the wall was a huge white cloth sheet. Behind that was the operations map, showing us our target. In no time at all, the room was full.

Bart Philo, sitting on my left, nudged me. "Gonna be a big one today," he said in a low voice.

Willie Lowen, sitting next to him, answered. "The last time you said that we didn't even get credit for the mission."

"Shit," said Bob Lehman, "I've got five pounds in my pocket right now that says we're gonna go to Big-B sure as hell!"

Before any of us could consider calling his bet, the door on the side of the building opened and Col. Luther J. Fairbanks, our new base CO, entered with his aides. Colonel Pierce had recently been promoted to the job of plans officer at Eighth Air Force Headquarters.

Somebody shouted, "Tenshun!"

Once on the platform, the new CO faced us.

"At ease," he said, sitting down in the center chair.

Most of us didn't have time to get to our feet anyway. The briefing officer, Major Marshall, opened the session. "Men, we've been waiting six months for this operation," he began, "and today we're gonna take a good crack at the GAF. We are going to Luftwaffe airfields in the ETO in squadron strength. We'll kick hell out of twenty-five of the ones that give us the most trouble. Both the Eighth and Ninth Air Forces will participate. We'll bomb their planes, their revetments, their runways. We'll post-hole their airfields and hit 'em where they live! Our particular target has the new Messerschmitt MT-163s with rocket or jet engines. A lot of them are based at Vechta. G-2 tells us this new type airplane's only mission is to cut off our route in and out of Germany. So far, they haven't changed their tactics. They've been attacking our formations from six o'clock high, so you tailgunners and top turret gunners stay on your toes. Once you're attacked, get 'em in your sights quick because they won't be there long. No short bursts. Give 'em a long lead and keep your triggers down. Shoot the living hell out of 'em."

The curtain was pulled away, disclosing the operations map. Our target was east of Holland about a hundred miles. A red ribbon pinned on the map followed our route to and from the target.

This was the 466th Group's 106th combat mission.

The briefing officer continued, pointer in hand. "We'll be escorted by P-51s all the way in and out of the target area. We expect some problems from German fighters over the target and there'll be some flak, but no more than a dozen guns. Our big problem will be the fighters. Our target is this airfield near Vechta, Germany," he said, using the pointer. "There are several military installations in the area and we're after everything. There's going to be a hell of a lot of airplanes in the sky, so help your pilots keep an eye out for them!

"We leave the Wash and make landfall on the enemy coast over the island of Rottumerplaat on the coast of Holland." His pointer showed us the way, slowly moving along the red ribbon. "Then we'll fly over the coast of Holland and at Warfum, just south of Winschoted, we head into Germany. It's a straight shot to the IP [initial point] just east of Lethen then another sharp right turn from the target after we unload. We'll go around Quackenbruk and head for home over the Zuider Zee in Holland. The first section will drop five-hundred and thousand pounders. The second section will drop five-hundred pounders and frags. Take off at 0700 hours. Good luck!"

When the sheet had been dropped, exposing the target of the day, a sigh of relief went up from the crews. Vechta was only a short run into Germany and should be an easy mission, especially with fighter support all the way in and out. The older men — me included — felt the hair stand out on the backs of our necks when told we would go in at squadron strength, for the secret of success in daylight bombing was in the number of bombers. Each airplane had ten .50-caliber machine guns, eight of them duals, firing from four turrets. The enemy was aware they couldn't all be fired at the same time, but there were always some that could. Flying in squadron strength (twelve airplanes) gave us the firepower of 120 .50-caliber machine guns. A minimum of four to six guns per airplane could return fire at the enemy and sometimes more. This would be a far more inviting target to the enemy than a group of bombers (four squadrons), with 480 guns and a minimum of 192 to 288 capable of returning fire. My fear was that when the GAF discovered we were in squadron strength, they'd have a field day. If they launched their new MT-163s, they'd blast us and be gone before we ever knew what hit us.

Shut up! I said to myself. *Let's see what else they have to say.*

Our new CO was next to speak. "As the major explained, we've never done this before. But, Division is of the opinion that German fighter strength has been badly weakened by lack of parts and fuel. G-2 thinks the GAF will keep the Luftwaffe in reserve to protect really big targets such as Frankfurt, Big B, Munich, and so on." He paused long enough to take a drink from his coffee mug. "Give 'em hell, and good luck to all of you! See you when you get back."

The ribbon was removed from the map and the sheet replaced, doubling as a screen for the overhead projector. We were shown photographs of the target that were less than twenty-four hours old. The runway, a ribbon of concrete about a mile long, ran through a large, open space in a forest. On the east side of the field, hidden in the trees, were the revetments which held the secret new airplanes. On the other side of the runway were the shops, billets, and headquarters area for the air base.

We were further informed that the mission would be a waltz. Instead, it would be the dance of death.

Our navigators had a separate meeting. They received information pertinent to the navigation of the mission. Later, when we met at the airplane before takeoff, we'd compare notes and each of us would be as well informed as the other.

We piled onto a waiting truck. It took us to the equipment shack. Dawn was breaking on the eastern horizon, and though the sun had not yet made an appearance it was starting to get light.

"Well, this is the first time I was ever wrong . . . almost!" Bob Lehman said. "I'm glad I'm only right ninety-nine percent of the time. It'd be hell to be perfect."

We laughed at the comedian of our crew. Not because he was particularly funny, but more from relief that he was wrong about us going to a big one. We all thought the mission should be a milk-run.

We were assigned lockers in which we kept our flying gear. The parachute riggers also lived in the equipment shack. I unlocked my locker and removed my flight bag, making sure my flak vest was still inside. I hung up my A-2 jacket, my pride and joy, with a replica of *Stardust* on the back. Single silver bombs were painted underneath, one for each mission we had flown — thirty-two in all. I pulled on my heated flight suit, a glorified pair of coveralls with zippers all over them, and put on the suspenders. I exchanged my shoes for heated booties and plugged the wire into my pants, then my sheepskin-lined flying boots. Next came the heated jacket, the electrical connections to be made later.

Into my flight bag went the following: heated outer gloves, silk inner gloves, scarf, helmet, goggles, an under-helmet the Red Cross ladies had knitted, an oxygen mask, throat mike, an extra box of .45 ammo for my pistol, a Mae West life jacket, and finally my parachute harness. I put my Ray Ban sunglasses into the upper pocket of the flight suit and zipped them in. The shoulder holster went over my jacket, and I made sure the ammo clip for my Colt .45 was loaded and stuck it into the weapon. As I put my fleece-lined jacket and pants into the bag, I checked to make sure I didn't have anything of a personal nature. Only two packs of Camels and two books of matches were on me. I put my wallet and a couple of personal letters on the top shelf, slid the combination padlock in place, and locked the locker.

At the counter, S.Sgt. Pete Rosenberg gave me my repacked chest pack parachute. We turned them in after every mission. The riggers, who lived in the equipment shack, checked them for holes and on every other flight repacked them carefully. Often, while being inspected, they removed pieces of flak and even spent rounds of German ammunition. They had boxes full of the stuff. Since damage is difficult to spot, the repacking process was the only sure way to guarantee they were a hundred percent operable. We appreciated their efforts.

Rosenberg tossed me an escape kit. "Got French francs in this one!" he said.

I stuck it in a pocket of the flying suit and zipped it in.

"Remember," he said, as I was going back to my locker, *"Oui oui* is pronounced *wee wee* and it don't mean no no in gay Paree!"

"I won't forget." I smiled at his last minute humor.

Johnny was waiting for me. We took our flight bags outside and waited for the rest of the crew, then climbed on the rear end of a truck to ride to our revetment.

The overcast was breaking up as the first rays of the morning sun came up. Along the way we saw ground crews preflighting their Liberators for the mission. *Laiden Maiden, Nobody's Baby, Biff Bam,* and *True Love* were among them. The truck pulled into our revetment but instead of *Stardust,* the airplane I had seen in the distance, *True Love* was in its place.

Our ground crew chief, M.Sgt. Rudy Hess, was waiting.

"What the hell is this?" Willie asked as he jumped off the truck, unhappy at the sight of the strange airplane. He faced the crew chief, who stood a good foot taller than Willie. "I thought we had an agreement that if we couldn't fly our own plane you'd tell me in time so I could check the replacement out. I ain't never seen this airplane before!"

"I had to change number three on *Stardust,*" he exclaimed almost apologetically. "A piece of flak went through a cylinder and another piece chewed up the blower on number four. I tried but I couldn't get her back on line today. *True Love* is a reserve airplane and a good one. I checked it from one end to the other. *Stardust* will be ready to fly tomorrow, I promise."

Three days previously, we had bombed an airfield in France at Mourmelon. Returning to base, we ran into some heavy flak and lost our number-three engine. The flak went into the engine and it quit cold. Our pilot feathered the prop, but number four turned sour so he pulled back the RPM and coaxed the B-24 home. Number four quit on the downwind leg and he had to feather it too. We landed with number one and number two turning with no difficulty. It was a bad mission. We watched another plane from our group go down. Everybody on board was killed.

I looked at the serial number of *True Love*: 41-29449-D. I will remember it all my life.

Well, I guess this is our bird for today, I thought, walking over to the plane. I crawled under its belly and up through the rear bomb bay door into the back end. I stepped around the supports for the ball turret and went to the waist position. I laid my bag under the ammo belt. The single .50-caliber, hand-held Browning machine gun was clean and lightly oiled.

I went into the bomb bays and noted we were carrying a mixed load: two 1,000-pounders and six 500-pounders. Their nose and tail fuses were installed with the arming wires in place, one end through the hole in the fuse on the bombs and the other securely fastened to the bomb rack itself. When the bombs were released, the arming wires, attached to the bomb racks, were pulled from the fuses, allowing the tiny propellers to rotate and unscrew themselves from the fuses. As the entire mechanism fell away, the firing pins were exposed, arming the bombs.

I checked each bomb and, satisfied, went up on the flight deck and then down into the bombardier's station to check the bomb release mechanism. It was properly set so that the 1,000-pounders fell first to be followed by the six 500-pounders in rotation, first from one side and then the other in mini-second intervals. I retraced my steps, went back to the waist, and looked at both guns again. Everything checked out.

I removed the parachute harness from my bag. It was a new "quick-release" type developed by the RAF. The four harness straps, two over each shoulder and two from between the legs, snapped into a round metal disk about three or four inches in diameter. To get out of it, one had to give the disk a quarter turn and hit it with the palm of a hand. The straps were then released and we could fall freely.

In the past we never carried personal weapons when we flew. However, after the invasion on June 6, we were instructed to carry our .45 Colt pistols and fifty extra rounds of ammunition with us at all times. If we went down in a combat zone, we were further instructed to join the first Allied soldier and fight the enemy until relieved by proper authority.

The sun was up and warmed the morning. The whole crew was relaxed, lying on the cement floor of the revetment. When I finished preflighting, I got out of the airplane and joined the others. I lit a Camel, took a long drag, and inhaled deeply. The last cigarette before a mission was always the best. There would be no more smokes until we were off oxygen and home from the mission.

"It's a pretty old plane," Bart said to Willie.

"Not too bad. It looks like it's in pretty good shape. It's a newer plane than *Stardust*."

"Well," I suggested, "let's not get any new holes in it. Let's bring it home just the way we took it. Okay?"

"I remember seeing this old bird using parachutes for brakes when it was landing not too long ago. The hydraulics musta been shot up," Bob Lehman offered.

On this mission there were four other enlisted crew members besides Johnny and me.

T.Sgt. Willie Lowen hailed from Ponca City, Oklahoma, and was our flight engineer. He was about the size of an underweight jockey. He was married and one of the few guys who didn't cheat on his wife. Willie loved to fly in the ball turret. A house painter by trade, he worked in his father's established business. He was a good gunner.

S.Sgt. Bart Philo from Fruitvale, Michigan, was the assistant engineer. He stood 6'2 in his stocking feet. He flew all his missions in the upper gun turret. A farmer and a Swede, he was single and didn't run around much with the ladies. After the war he planned on going back home to "do a little farmin'." He was an excellent marksman with any gun on the plane, but a dead shot in the upper turret.

T.Sgt. Donald McCarty, a native of Terre Haute, Indiana, was the radio operator. His hair was the color of copper. He was single and a ladies' man. He flew the right waist-gun position and was pretty good with the hand-held .50-caliber. Don wanted to go into broadcasting after the war. His problem was the best kept secret of our crew: He got airsick! The flight surgeon would have grounded him had he

14

known. Don kept a collection of gallon tin cans, which he retrieved from the mess hall. On each flight he brought one on board. Once we were airborne, he'd go into the bomb bay and vomit in the can. Afterwards, he'd set the can on the bomb bay doors so that when they opened, the first thing to fall out was the can. It was a well-known fact that I wanted to rename our plane *"McCarty's Puke,"* but nobody would go along with me. Especially Don.

S.Sgt. Bob Lehman, from Ada, Oklahoma, was our nose-turret gunner and the best shot from any position on the crew. He flew all his missions in the same position. He was about 5'8 and had coal-black hair and eyes. His smooth, hairless skin and peach fuzz on his cheeks was characteristic of his Cherokee blood. He joined the Army Air Corps upon graduation from high school. He was a brawler and loved to fistfight, but still had some of the finest qualities I've ever seen in a man.

Johnny was a staff sergeant, our tail-gunner, and a good shot. Though they were never confirmed, I know of at least four planes he either shot down or participated in shooting down.

Willie looked at his watch and thought of the 0700 takeoff. "Okay, guys," he said, "let's run the props through." We went to the airplane and walked the four propellers through about five full revolutions apiece, lubricating the cylinder walls so they would crank easier when they were started.

It was 0645 hours. Takeoff in fifteen minutes, and the officers hadn't even come to the revetment yet. *Damn,* I thought. *It seems we always have tougher missions when we're late gettin' off.*

"Maybe the mission has been scrubbed," McCarty said, hopefully, probably thinking the same thing I was.

Several minutes later, a Jeep drove into the revetment, the three officers sprawled on it. Our pilot, straddling the hood, jumped off as the Jeep braked to a stop. He misjudged the speed of the vehicle, and if Philo had not grabbed him he would have fallen on his face. His flight bag slid along the revetment floor and his cap fell at my feet. He pulled himself together, laughed at his clumsy effort to alight gracefully, and watched as the other officers got out of the Jeep more conventionally.

I picked up his hat and put it on my head.

"Mornin', fellas," our leader said. "It's a beautiful day!"

"Howdy," we all chimed in.

"Jack," I said, "you're gonna break your ass if you don't watch

15

those acrobatics gettin' off that Jeep. You almost crashed, and we haven't even taken off yet!"

He looked at us with a sheepish grin while holding his arms out in a gesture of despair as the Jeep tore out of the revetment. "So, I get a few days' rest," he commented.

"Oh great!" I said loudly. "Then you can finish your missions with another crew, 'cause we'll be home by then."

I pulled his cap down. It slid over my ears.

Johnny laughed. "Knobby, you're gonna have to grow a lil' more head to fit into that one."

I was about to direct more remarks to our good-natured pilot, but a staff car pulled into the revetment. I took the cap off my head and put it behind me. The driver got out and opened the back door. A first lieutenant dressed in flight gear emerged from the seat. The driver opened the trunk and removed the officer's flight bag and a chest pack parachute, then gently set them down. He saluted and drove away.

Jack grabbed his hat from me as he walked by to meet the newcomer. Under his breath he said, "We'll finish this later," and added with a grin, "you little fart!"

He shook hands with the officer. "This is Lieutenant Leslie, our squadron gunnery officer. The lieutenant is coming along to observe the effectiveness of our bombing."

With that, Jack and the newcomer walked to the airplane.

"I wonder why Jack didn't tell you Leslie is coming along to observe those new German planes?" Norm Peck asked. "You were told about them at briefing, weren't you?"

"Yeah," Johnny answered. "They're either rockets or jets, and they were built just to give us trouble."

Norm opened his navigator's case. "Okay, you guys, here's the dope on them. Messerschmitt is manufacturing them. It's a model MT-163. It's got a thirty-foot wing span and is only twenty feet long. It can fly under its own power for ten minutes, maybe eight, they're not really sure. It can climb a mile a minute or faster, has a pair of twenty- or thirty-five-millimeter cannons in its nose or wings. It likes to hit us from six o'clock high and has no landing gear. It uses a dolly for takeoff and jettisons it. Lands on skids after its fuel has been depleted. G-2 says there are forty or fifty in the Vechta area."

Norm looked at each one of us individually, then added, "For God's sake, keep your eyes peeled for these little bastards today. I'd hate to see any of you guys get your asses shot off."

We all looked at each other, for Norm was always noncommittal about his feelings as far as danger was concerned. For the first time I thought, *Maybe this isn't going to be a milk-run . . .*

We had only the three officers on our crew. Some time ago, they removed bombardiers from air crews. Instead, they used the navigator to hit the toggle switch that released the bombs. We dubbed him "Tog-a-leer," a name he didn't much like.

1st Lt. Norman Peck, the navigator, was from Brooklyn, New York. He was absolutely tops in his job. Norm was a Jew and was uncomfortable when he thought of getting shot down and captured by the Germans. Rumor had it that the Krauts despised Jews and treated them badly in POW camps. The closer we got to the end of our missions, the more stress he was under. Flying missions was bad enough, but with this added burden it was twice as tough on him. His real name had been Norman Pecker but some kindly Brooklyn judge understood his request and changed his name legally before he joined.

1st Lt. John S. Archer, Jr., our pilot and aircraft commander, hailed from Cleveland, Ohio, and insisted we call him Jack in the air and privately. He was married with a brand new baby. Our crew was confident in his ability as a pilot. He had brought us home from some real bummers. There were no formalities on the crew, nor would he allow any. Each of us had a different name and that was the way he wanted us to address each other on the intercom. His main objective was to complete the thirty-five and fulfill his obligation to the crew.

1st Lt. Thomas L. Bell was our copilot. A non-Mormon, he came from Salt Lake City, Utah, and was unhappy in his marriage. The crew had as much confidence in him flying the plane as they did in Jack. He loved life and having a good time. I guess Johnny and I fit his mold better than the others, and the three of us would frequently become real hell-raisers if the occasion called for it. He was in no hurry to go home — even planned to fly another tour of duty when we were finished.

1st Lt. Doyle Stegall had been our bombardier and flew with us on our first ten missions. He was married, from Tyler, Texas. He was such a good bombardier that when they formed the Pathfinder squadrons, he was immediately trained for the job, using a new radar-aimed bombsight. Finally, he was transferred to a different squadron in the 466th. We missed him and would make him buy us a drink whenever we saw him in town.

"Okay, guys, let's get on board," Jack yelled to us.

17

I took a last drag on the Camel and stepped on it. We boarded the Liberator and returned to the waist position. I retrieved my jacket and hooked up the electrical connection. I strapped on my shoulder holster and gun, then the Mae West and finally the parachute harness. Donning my helmet, goggles, throat mike, and oxygen mask, I hooked up to the plane's systems and was set to go.

Almost at once, Tommy called on the intercom. "Let's check the intercom."

Each of us answered in rotation.

"Okay, relax fellas. Be sure and check your oxygen regulators and heated suits." The intercom went dead.

I leaned out the waist window and Johnny joined me. "Christ, it's a beautiful day," I said.

"Yeah, it sure is," he answered.

Jack started number three. I looked at my watch. It was 0715 hours. Another late start. We should already have been fifteen minutes into the mission. It was only a short distance to the continent, though. Maybe it would be okay.

The pilot started numbers one, two, and four. He ran the engines up individually to 2100 RPM and checked both mags (magnetos) on each engine. Satisfied, he released the binders (brakes) and eased the big bomber onto the taxiway, where we took our place in line. We were number six for takeoff.

Altogether there were twenty-four Liberators waiting to go. Ninety-six props were spinning, reflecting the early morning sunlight. A hundred and twenty thousand horsepower was driving those props. It was an awesome, spectacular sight. In an all-out effort, with sixty of us in line and 240 props spinning, a full 300,000 horsepower drove them.

We waited for the first plane to line up on the runway and go. After holding for ten minutes, an officer walked down the line of planes and told the pilots to shut down their engines. There would be a slight delay. Suddenly, it became quiet as the engines stopped and the props became idle.

"Well, time for a little shut-eye," I said. I removed my helmet and lay down on the floor, leaning against my flight bag.

"The mission will probably be scrubbed," Johnny said.

I closed my eyes and was awakened as number three started again. I was wet with perspiration. Johnny was standing in the waist window and I joined him. My watch said 0855. I had slept an hour and a half.

18

Maybe the mission was on after all, or would we taxi back to the revetment?

As I looked out the waist window, I saw a green-green flare. The mission was on! Only red-red would have scrubbed it.

1st Lt. John H. Woolnough was the mission leader and the first to take off. He was flying a different airplane. I saw his *Gruesome Goose* being repaired in the revetment. He pulled off the taxiway onto the main runway. The tower flashed him a green light, and he throttled up the four Pratt and Whitney engines and released his brakes. The Liberator rolled down the runway, increasing its speed until the nose lifted, launching the heavily laden airplane into the early morning sky. At 500 feet, he began a slow left turn toward the east, climbing steadily through the morning sky. The B-24 disappeared from view on the northeast side of the field, still climbing. By then, two more of our squadron had taken off to follow him.

At last, it was our turn. Jack slowly inched *True Love* onto the runway and lined up for takeoff. He locked the nose wheel and closed the cowl flaps. All our eyes were on the tower when it flashed us the green light. Our engines roared in unison as the throttles were shoved all the way to the stops. Forty-eight hundred horsepower came to life, spilling its might into the outstretched blades of the props, forcing them to bite into the cool morning air and propel the giant airplane faster and faster down the runway. As I stood watching from my waist window, holding on to my gun mount, I saw the bomb bay doors close. Then as the end of the runway grew closer, Jack pulled back on the yoke and the plane responded, leaping into the air gracefully. Once clear of the runway, the wheels retracted outward into the wheel wells. He gently touched the brakes to stop the wheels' rotation.

We flew past the end of the runway and started our left turn, still climbing. Slowly, the flaps were retracted back into the wings. Now we were in our normal flying attitude and continued our turn to the left. We hit the prop wash of a plane that had taken off before us, causing *True Love* to buffet in the air. Jack quickly righted the Liberator and we flew northward.

We passed over the coastal village of Weybourne, out over the "Wash," just north of East Anglia. We were at 8,000 over Weybourne. About twenty miles further, all eyes were scanning the sky for our forming airplane. The sky was filled with Liberators from other groups as well as our own, moving in a slow, counterclockwise circle. We finally located our quarry far above us and off to the right.

"*Ready and Willing* at three o'clock," Tommy said.

19

"Roger . . . thanks," Jack replied.

We continued to climb in the big circle, keeping our eyes on the forming airplane. When we reached altitude, we'd form on the right off Woolnough and lead the high right element.

One of our planes headed home with a feathered prop.

I watched McCarty stick his head in the bomb bay and vomit into his can. Then he unzipped his pants and relieved himself. He placed the can on the bomb bay door gently, then went back to the flight deck, smiling.

"Twelve thousand. Let's have an oxygen check," said Tommy.

Again we checked our systems and reported in unison. From now on our conversation would have to be on the intercom.

The *Ready and Willing* was painted white with red lightning bolts running the length of the fuselage and the breadth of the wings. It was covered with lights making it easy to find on our early morning missions when we took off in the darkness. The heroic airplane had flown the bulk of its missions with the Fifteenth Air Force against the Ploesti Oil Fields in Romania. Badly shot up, it was scheduled for the scrap heap when our group requisitioned it for spare parts. Then it was completely rebuilt, its bomb bays converted into cargo space. It was used as the work-horse for our group, traveling the length and breadth of the United Kingdom.

Our squadron formation was a diamond shape with three planes on each corner. The three on the right flew a little higher and the three on the left flew slightly lower. The remaining three, or "Coffin Corner," flew lower than all the others. This way none of the aircraft disturbed the other's air and could fly smoothly. At group strength the same formation applied, except there was a squadron in each corner of the diamond. When a division or a wing formed, with group strength on each corner, it comprised a lot of airplanes. When an "all-out" effort was called, and the entire Eighth Air Force showed up with a couple of thousand assorted airplanes of different sizes, it was an amazing sight to see. Still, the same formation applied.

The most airplanes I ever saw in the air at one time was on D-Day, the sixth of June, over the beaches of France. The sea was peppered with warships firing their huge guns. We were the last group of bombers to hit the beach. We dropped bombs at 6:20 A.M. and flew two missions that day. The second was a low-level attack on a bridge on the Cherbourg peninsula.

Our toughest mission was to Munich, Germany, on one of the four we flew to that particular target. We had just turned on the IP

20

headed for our target, a factory which produced airplane parts. The flak was extremely heavy and the sky was black from it. The German flak shot several holes in the plane and hit number-four engine, which quit cold and belched flames. Tommy feathered the prop and hit the fire extinguisher, dousing the fire. But to maintain speed, we had to lose altitude. When the group dropped its bombs they fell all around us. How they missed our airplane, I'll never know. I saw the props on the fuses of a 1,000-pounder still unscrewing itself as it fell past my waist window. Afterward, the formation left us. Norm gave Jack a heading for Attlebridge and we headed for home. We continued to lose altitude until we were at 17,000 feet. We seemed to be able to hold that altitude okay. We were alone in the sky.

An hour later, a pursuit plane homed in on us. "Don't shoot, it's a P-51," Johnny yelled into the intercom.

The "little brother," as we affectionately called them, tucked himself under our right wing and stayed there all the way to our base. Sometimes he flew with his gear down and flaps about halfway extended; the rest of the time he had his flaps all the way down and his wheels retracted so that he could fly at our slow speed.

Upon landing back at the base, the P-51 followed us in. The pilot was 1st Lt. Robert H. Smith. He had three enemy fighters to his credit and had only been in the ETO for a few weeks. He told us he flew on the edge of a stall in order to stay under our wing. He gassed up and left, buzzing our field wide open at about ten feet altitude.

Afterward, our pilot received both criticism and praise for bringing *Stardust* home. The debriefing officer praised us, and the squadron commander said we shouldn't have risked our lives in the long flight over enemy territory. We were told we should have gone to Switzerland for the duration. Now, as we began our fateful mission, I was wishing we had.

We were in position for about twenty minutes when the *Ready and Willing*, shooting flares from the top of the airplane, peeled off from the formation. It lost altitude rapidly as it headed for home. We headed east toward Germany.

From this moment on, my life as I had known it was over. I would never again be the happy, carefree, immature boy I had been. I would be thrown into uncontrollable circumstances, into a situation that would be unbelievable to anyone who hasn't lived it. Within a month, I would mature to someone twice my age. Within eight months, I would live another lifetime.

TWO

F lying at 25,000 feet altitude with each pair of eyes glued on the open mass of nothingness, probing the sky for airplanes, friendly or unfriendly, watching for a malfunction in the engines or airframe and listening to the endless drone of the four propellers were all part of the job. We fought the urge to catnap and let our minds wander. Most of the time the earth below was cloud-covered, invisible; all that remained was a mass of hypnotic, horizonless emptiness.

We couldn't smoke for lack of oxygen. On long missions, we opened a box of K-rations and unfastened our oxygen masks to take bites, chewing the food inside the mask. We had no water, for it froze quickly in the forty to sixty-five below zero temperatures. When we dropped our bombs, they fell away into the sea of cotton, and we never knew the results. When nothing happened during the mission — as we waited silently beside our guns, the waist windows open, frigid air blasting our faces — it was miserable and boring.

Sometimes a couple of idiots in different planes tried to be comedians at their waist positions, making obscene gestures at each other. The game they made out of their idiocy detracted from the seriousness of their job. Soon, obsessed with their own stupidity, they would no longer be effective to watch the sky, and the two positions were lost to the safety of the mission.

Flying became exciting when there were individual acts of heroism and courage, or when we'd have a particularly good bomb run on a clear day and could see what we hit. We became charged up and didn't think about food, cigarettes, or water. When a battle-damaged airplane joined our formation and we gave him all the moral support we could muster, we believed we played a part in helping him back to England and safety. The adrenalin flowed heavily during air battles with the Luftwaffe flying their deadly Messerschmitts and Focke Wulfs, especially if they had a bad day and we had a good one. It was exciting to watch the little bastards spin in, on fire, with their pilots bailing out.

Fear was always present. Our baptism by fire was our first mission. Then on later missions, fear came in watching a close friend's B-24 go down on fire as far as the eye could see. Straining our eyes for that parachute that never appeared. Watching a Liberator blow up and disintegrate in the air, then, out of that huge explosion of black smoke and falling debris, the twisted, mangled bodies falling. It was the end for all of them and but for the Grace of God, it could very well have been us. When your airplane has a hole big enough to drive a Jeep through and the flames are gutting the inside, you look at your buddies in distress and they look at you with pleading eyes. When it's your time to go, my friend, then it's your time to go! *That* is fear!

The Luftwaffe were not attacking our formations as often as they previously did. Occasionally, about ten of them would make a single pass through a formation then leave as fast as they came. It was nothing like the first several missions we flew, when fifty or sixty would batter the formation time and time again. We thought that perhaps the Luftwaffe had a shortage of fuel for their airplanes. It had been a long time since the GAF had singled out our plane for an attack. But there was no shortage of flak! We were always taking evasive action to get out of the stuff.

I looked at the tail. Johnny's turret was moving back and forth. He was watching every inch of sky he could see. Willie, in the ball-turret, was making semicircular sweeps, doing his job. I was the only one at the waist window and wondered why McCarty hadn't come back to man his gun. I took turns looking out both windows, watching the sky on both sides.

This could get to be old crap, I thought, *especially after we make landfall.*

"Jack," I said into the intercom.

"Yeah, Knobby, what can I do for you?" he came back.

"Willie's in the ball and Johnny's in the tail. I'm watching both windows. When's McCarty coming back here?"

There was a moment of silence.

"Knobby, hold it down till we make landfall. Lieutenant Leslie will come back and man Mac's gun. Okay?"

"Roger," I replied and moved back to the other window.

For the next half hour I watched both sides of the plane.

Norm came on the intercom and said, "Holland just ahead!"

I pulled my goggles down and stuck my head out into the slipstream. We were going to cross onto the continent just north of the Frisian Islands. I didn't know then I'd be spending Thanksgiving on one of them.

The mainland of Holland was clearly visible when a flare went up from Woolnough's plane. The two squadrons began to separate, each taking its own heading to the target.

Just before we got over the islands, some small, hour-glass-shaped puffs of black smoke appeared off our right wing.

"Flak at three o'clock level," Tommy said calmly.

The black puffs kept getting larger and closer as the German anti-aircraft crews zeroed in on us. Finally, the lead plane took a more northerly heading. The flak guns shot at the empty sky.

The landscape unfolded beneath us like a huge painting being unrolled from a giant spool. The picture was ever-changing and lush, with green and brown checkerboard designs. Sometimes we would see a train, but that was rare for our pursuit planes made short work of them.

The long, white, steamy contrails flowed behind each of our engines and followed each plane like a long highway we had just traveled over. These were caused by the freezing moist air flowing through the hot finned cylinders of our engines and the still hotter exhaust stacks of our superchargers. The moisture condensed and resulted in the contrails of water vapors. From the ground they looked like long, white trails of smoke. Depending on our altitude, sometimes the airplanes themselves couldn't be seen, but the steamy white lines in the sky were readily visible. Like the airplane that was making them, the vapor trails soon disappeared over the horizon, and neither was no more.

Suddenly, our left wingman fell back from formation. He feathered his number-four prop and moments later peeled off, losing altitude quickly, winging his way back to Attlebridge. Our other wingman snuggled in a little closer.

24

"Jack, did you see our wingman abort?" I asked.

"Roger, Knobby. Lieutenant Leslie is coming back now. Help him hook up."

"Gotcha," I replied.

Moments later, Lieutenant Leslie joined me in the waist with an emergency oxygen bottle. He uncoupled it and snapped into the main oxygen supply. I chuckled to myself as he awkwardly plugged into the intercom and electrical system.

"Do you know how to operate the gun?" I asked.

"Yes, Sergeant, I graduated from Las Vegas Aerial Gunnery School," he replied.

With the knowledge that he was indeed a genuine gunner, the crew could now rest at ease. What really surprised me was when he put his parachute on the floor under the window, lay down with his head on it, and fell asleep almost immediately.

Again I watched both sides of the airplane. I had done it before. I'd have to be careful not to step on him.

I went back and forth, scanning the sky. The drone of the engines was almost hypnotic. I was so accustomed to the synchronized roar I didn't pay attention to it anymore.

The Army Air Force had been good to me and for me. I hated real responsibility and the problems life could offer. My only real responsibility not connected to the air force was making regular monthly payments on my Ford back home. I lived from payday to payday, like ninety-five percent of all the guys I knew. At the end of the month, when cash got low, we signed chits at the NCO club for cigarettes.

We had a life of frivolity, and flying was the only job that really mattered. We were very conscious of the seriousness of it. Nothing else mattered. We had a "live today and die tomorrow" attitude, although none of us would admit it. We all had our share of the ladies, and they seemed to enjoy our frivolity as much as we did. None of us were alcoholics, but we did like to tip the suds frequently. I'm not saying we'd never change. We all would when our environment did. But during those times, flying combat or even flying stateside, there were many close calls in the air. Our attitudes never changed.

"Jack, we're ten minutes from the IP," Peck announced.

"That's a Roger, Norm," the pilot answered.

Lieutenant Leslie, awakened by the voices on the intercom, came to life. He stood up, looked out the waist window, stretched his arms, and spoke to me. "Everything okay, Sarge?"

25

I nodded my head. I wanted to thank him for watching his side of the airplane from his prone position, but I didn't.

"We're almost there so we'd better keep our eyes open."

"Yes, sir, we're twenty minutes from the target," I replied.

"Waist, cut the chatter," Jack cut in. "Keep your eyes open! We've got some little brothers straight ahead and some more off to the right about two o'clock. Look up about two thousand and you'll spot 'em."

I'd been watching the same P-38 Lightnings for the last fifteen minutes. There were about thirty of them, in formation and zigzagging across the sky, giving us good protection up front and high, in the same location from where German fighters usually came at us. As we approached the IP they left us, racing out of sight at twice our speed. They weren't P-51s, as we had been told at the briefing.

The landscape continued to unfold beneath us; tiny villages and an occasional bomb crater came into view.

"That's Lethen ahead and off to the left," Norm said with an air of excitement in his voice. "We turn in four minutes."

"Roger," Jack replied quietly.

I glanced out Lieutenant Leslie's waist window. Ahead, off to the left, was a good-sized town. As we flew past, I could see the town square and the beauty of the village. I wondered if the people were watching us. The railroad tracks had a big crater in them just as they entered the town. No railroad cars were visible; however, being the experts they were at camouflage, it was possible there was a whole train down there and we couldn't see it.

Five miles past the town we made a corrective turn to the left at our IP and headed to the northeast. When we leveled off we were headed straight for our target near Vechta. The entire crew was alert with eyes on the sky.

The conversation on the intercom was between Archer, Peck, and Tommy Bell. Unless there was an emergency, the rest of the crew stayed off the system. I could visualize Norm turning on the switch of the bomb release, lifting the safety cover of the triggering device, his finger ready to toggle the bombs. The success of the mission depended entirely upon the lead airplane. The first bomb to leave the bomb bay was a smoke bomb. It left a trail of white smoke from the moment of release until it hit the target five miles below. When the other airplanes came to the cloud of smoke, they toggled their bombs. Theoretically, all our bombs would fall on the target in the same pattern as the lead plane if the bombardier did a good job with his Norden. If he missed, we all missed.

A few minutes later, Peck came back on.

"Okay, Jack, Vechta is about eleven o'clock and ten miles ahead. The target is dead ahead at twelve o'clock about eight miles ahead. It's a good bomb run, no cloud clutter, CAVU [ceiling and visibility unlimited] all the way."

"Roger, Norm, I can see the clearing and the runway in the middle of the woods. Crew, watch for those new planes!"

"Flak at ten o'clock," said Tommy nonchalantly.

I looked out the waist window. There they were, as advertised, about ten o'clock, those familiar, hour-glass-shaped puffs of black smoke. They were coming closer now that we were holding a steady course on the bomb run.

"Bomb bay doors open," yelled Peck.

The big airplane shuddered as the freezing air rushed into the bomb bays and on into waist through the open door.

I saw McCarty's puke can fall from the bomb bay. Our wingman opened his bomb bay doors. We threw pieces of chaffe, small pieces of lead or tinfoil similar to that used on Christmas trees, out the waist windows. If the German antiaircraft guns were radar-aimed, as most of them were, the chaffe disrupted their radar by throwing a false echo on the screen and screwing it up as an aiming instrument. They would shoot all over the sky, and only the lucky hits would get through and score on the bomber flow.

The flak was heavy. A few bursts were within the flow of bombers. There would be a lot of damage to the Liberators today. I hoped nobody would be wounded or sent home in a box.

Our right wingman took a hit in his number-one engine, and the resulting explosion blew his entire engine cowling off. The propeller spun out of control momentarily until the copilot feathered it and stopped the churning. The engine spewed flames. Immediately, the Liberator dropped back from formation as the flames grew more intense, a stream of black smoke belching over the top of the wing. The smoke turned white as the copilot turned on the internal fire extinguisher. Moments later, the fire was out and the smoking stopped. But the plane kept losing altitude. Attlebridge was a long way off, and he was in a lot of trouble.

Now *True Love* was alone. Both our wingmen had aborted. We were indeed a "sitting duck." When the bomb run was over, Jack would probably slip down beside one of the other echelons for more protection. Right now, however, we watched our lead plane.

He dropped the smoke bomb along with his regular load. They fell one at a time in perfect synchronization. Instantly, we dropped our load. They fell without a hitch as our airplane rose slightly in the air, relieved of two and a half tons of bombs. I watched as they fell, the tiny propellers spinning off, exposing the firing pins. The lethal messengers of death and destruction were headed straight for the target, disappearing from view, merging with the terrain below. Next we would pass over the airfield.

The bombs were bursting all over the target area. It looked as though we wiped out the entire runway. The forest on each side of it exploded, disintegrating in giant balls of fire and black smoke. Huge pyrotechnical displays were everywhere. Rockets streaming white smoke flew in all directions blown from the ammunition dumps. Red and orange explosions with black smoke erupted from the middle of them. On the right side of the runway I could see some twin-engine airplanes — definitely a new design. Some of them were on fire and exploding, throwing fiery debris in all directions. There was another huge explosion, a big one, near the end of the runway. No doubt their fuel storage dump was on fire. It grew bigger as the black smoke rose rapidly into the atmosphere. The airfield was in shambles. As far as I could tell, all our bombs had fallen on the target.

I looked for our aborted wingman. He was a quarter of a mile behind us and at least 3,000 feet lower. He had dropped his bomb load. Even as I watched, he peeled off and headed for Attlebridge. Another sitting duck.

We flew over Vechta, made a sharp right turn, and leveled off — headed straight for Attlebridge and the end of our thirty-third mission. There was no activity from the ground. The flak guns had stopped firing at us.

As I looked out my waist window, I could see the huge column of smoke rising almost to our altitude. New explosions from the airfield were plainly visible, some small and some with great intensity. If any of the enemy died as a result of this action, I would never know it and really didn't care. I couldn't feel their terror as the bombs exploded around them, see their blood, hear their screams, or feel their pain. I would never know the aching in the hearts of their families over the loss of their loved ones.

Sound ruthless? You bet your life it does. We were bombing their military targets to preserve our own safety on future missions. It was the job my country had chosen for me to do in that stinking war. Each bomb that left our bomb bays had permanently etched on it, in my mind, a father and his child, and I silently dedicated the destruction our bombs made to them.

It happened after we completed our first ten missions. As a reward our crew got a three-day pass and went to London. It was the only pass we ever got. We were happy to get a few days off from flying.

We had it in mind to meet some friendly ladies and tip a few mild and bitters in the local pubs and maybe find some romance. It was to be a fun-filled weekend, and we'd just been paid.

We got good accommodations just off Piccadilly Circus in an old but modern hotel. After we checked in, Johnny and I decided to walk around and see a little bit of London. We walked about a mile, flirting with girls and looking in shop windows, when the air-raid sirens sounded. Strangely, nobody ran for the tube (subway) or shelters. Instead, all eyes turned skyward.

Soon we could hear it. The noise sounded like my mother's Hoover vacuum cleaner running over the bare wooden floor with the brushes beating on it. Then we saw it. The V-1 buzz-bomb came into view at no more than 2,000 feet in the air. It passed in front of us about a mile away, going from our left to right at an angle. The engine shut off and the bomb went into a steep dive. There was a tremendous explosion when it disappeared among the rooftops of several buildings. The windows and the street rattled from the concussion; debris flew into the air from the direction of the explosion, then slowly floated back to earth. We decided to see how much damage the bomb had done.

The V-1 had exploded in the street in front of the rows of houses. The hundred-foot crater dug up the street, exposing all the underground pipes, wires, and sewer lines. Water was streaming from the broken mains. Although it only took us a few minutes to get there, the local fire department, police, air raid wardens, and English soldiers were already busy searching the rubble for survivors. At least twenty houses were completely destroyed, and probably another twenty were questionable as to whether they could be lived in again. A row of bodies, with torn flesh and shredded, bloody clothing, lay in a cleared area by the street. More were being added steadily. Blood, guts, screams and moans filled the street. It was terrible. The medics were treating others awaiting ambulances on the sidewalk.

A London bobby approached us. "If you Yanks would like to lend a hand, we'd appreciate it. If not, quit gawking and clear the hell out of here so we can get the job done."

I apologized for our inconsideration and asked what we could do. In no time we were with the others, clearing rubble until our hands were bloodied. We worked until they were satisfied there was nobody left alive in the carnage. I have never worked so tirelessly or been so unconcerned about my personal well-being, despite all the scratches and digs in my skin, as I was during those several hours in London. I know I've never moved so many stones and pieces of wood in my life and probably never will again. All the houses were built of brick and stone and many of them had steel fabricating. Regardless of the excellent construction, many of them were leveled or almost so. There wasn't an upright wall in the area nor an unbroken pane of glass within a ten-block area. At least forty bodies had been laid beside the road. They had been taken to a morgue or funeral home by the time we were finished. Ambulances took another hundred to hospitals. As we worked, an additional three buzz-bombs hit London, none of them more than a mile away.

There was a dead man, in his early twenties, with his dead son, I presume, clutched in his arms. He was bloody from head to toe and his guts were strewn out on the sidewalk beside him. His dead eyes stared back at me as if he were trying to say something to me. The child had a gaping hole where his head was supposed to be; blood still oozed from the severed arteries in his neck. His little battered head was barely connected to his torso by a few threads of flesh and muscle. It was to those two I made my dedication, "Goddamn the Nazi bastards!"

Our nicely tailored uniforms were dirty, bloody, and stained. The bobby we had talked to previously thanked us and took our names. We caught a taxi, placed newspapers on the seat so we wouldn't soil them, and went back to our hotel. We must have been a sight when we walked into the lobby, for all eyes turned to look at us. The bell captain, a small, very thin-faced chap with a jutting chin and cheery eyes, greeted us. In his Cockney accent he asked, "You Yanks been in a bad one, eh? What was it, a bloody buzz-bomb?"

"Yeah," Johnny said as he escorted us to our room.

"Well," he said, "let's get your clothes off and see if I can't get

30

some of that muck cleaned off them. You can't be seen running around like that, now can you?"

We undressed. The bell captain took our clothes, socks, underwear, shoes, and even our neckties. Then Johnny and I took a bath, shaved, and put on some clean underwear and a clean shirt. Since our spare pants didn't constitute a uniform, we couldn't leave the room. We figured we'd be lucky if we had our clothes back by Sunday, the last day of our pass.

The bell captain returned with four bottles of cold beer and a first-aid kit. We put iodine on the scratches and covered the worst with small bandages. The beer really hit the spot.

Two hours later, there was a knock on the door. The bell captain stood in the doorway with our uniforms. They looked like they just came from the cleaners. Our shoes were polished and everything had been washed and ironed — even the socks! The man had the proudest smile on his face I have ever seen. He wouldn't let us pay him or even take a tip.

"No sir, Yank. Not a bloody shilling!" he said. "You do for my people and I'll do for you!" He waved his hand in the air as he spoke, then left with a beautiful grin on his face.

The bomb run was over; we had done our job. I had no feelings one way or the other for the people down below. Their sons and fathers and husbands did the same job we were doing. The Germans started the war. They were responsible. They had to answer for their indiscriminate killing with buzz-bombs.

Chatter began on the intercom. I heard Bob say, "They'll have a hell of a time taking off from that runway for a while."

"We're over Holland, fellas," Norm interrupted. "We're crossing the border now. I estimate the North Sea in thirty minutes. Our present altitude is twenty-five thousand two hundred."

We were still flying alone on the high right of the formation. I was surprised Jack hadn't dropped down to another echelon or the lead pilot, John Woolnough, hadn't signaled one of his wingmen to join us. I imagined there would be quite a discussion about it among the brass once we landed, and rightly so. I meant to ask about it at debriefing.

Oberlieutenant Ernst Scheufele, squadron commander of the JG5

31

Hunter squadron, pushed the throttle of his Messerschmitt ME-109G to its stops as the little fighter plane sped down the runway and took off from his base at Sachaeu, Germany. Quickly he climbed and headed north to the forming area over Muretz Lake just south of Rostock. He looked over his shoulder and saw the eighteen ME-109s of his command obediently following him to the planned altitude of 7,000 meters.

He joined up with the ten planes of JG53, Maj. Franz Gotz's squadron, and when JG5 joined them, the entire group of twenty-nine fighters headed south on a heading of 190 degrees.

Twenty-year-old Ernst Scheufele had proven himself in combat with twelve victories, most of them P-39 Aircobra type airplanes shot down on the Russian front. He had been a member of the Hitler Youth until he began his flight training on his eighteenth birthday. He was faithful to the Nazi cause and was willing to give his life for the leaders of his country. After the Russians came closer to his airbase at Petsamo, Finland, he was promoted and transferred to Sachaeu. Once he was back in his fatherland, he found out about the slaughter of the Jews. His respected leaders had become a bunch of criminals, especially the SS and the SD. He discovered these men were murdering the citizens of captured nations — Poland, France, Belgium, and even neutral Holland. After that, Lieutenant Scheufele fought only for self-preservation.

After the two squadrons flew over Kassel, Germany, they dropped their 300-liter auxiliary fuel tanks and headed west-northwest on a heading of 285 degrees into Holland. It was Scheufele's first flight over the lowlands.

In the distance, Major Gotz saw what appeared to be glittering water. As he came closer to it, he saw a flight of B-24 Liberator bombers heading westward. Unhesitatingly, he lowered the nose of his ME-109 and aimed at the group of bombers, firing both his 13mm machine guns and his 20 mm cannon at the bomber flow.

JG5, headed by Scheufele, was two minutes behind Major Gotz and when he was in position, led his squadron to attack the enemy. He singled out a lone Liberator flying on the high right, which was slowly turning away from his group, and took dead aim. He watched as the wing on the B-24 burst into flames and huge holes appeared in the after sections of the fuselage.

Bob Lehman shrieked into the intercom: "Bandits! Bandits! Twelve o'clock high!"

I stuck my head out the waist window and looked at the sky in front of us. At least ten Messerschmitt ME-109 fighters tore through our formation with all their guns blazing. At Bob's first warning I threw a fresh .50-caliber into the chamber of my machine gun and fired at the little bastards as they came screaming past. I could see the markings on their planes and the helmeted heads of their pilots. I could feel the vibration from our four turrets as they answered the Germans' fire. I watched the enemy airplanes as they made a one-eighty down low in back of the formation. Then they came back at us, shooting at our formation again. Lieutenant Leslie started shooting too.

Johnny, who had the best opportunity, didn't waste it. He met fire with fire, shooting short but deadly bursts with those twin fifties. Willie, in the ball-turret, just held the triggers down and sprayed .50-caliber slugs at them. The ME-109s were coming into the formation one at a time. They were taking careful aim at the Liberators, and of course, the "sitting duck" got the brunt of their attention. A lone ME-109 came into our formation and hung on his tail after firing at the B-24 just to the left and below us. While he was in that suspended position, I got off at least five or six good bursts of twenty rounds apiece while he hung there stationary in my sights. His cowling flew off into the slip-stream, breaking apart as it hit the horizontal stabilizer of the small plane. He showed me his belly and peeled off, diving to a lower altitude. I kept shooting. Small black puffs of smoke erupted from his engine before I lost sight of him.

Bob sounded off again: "Here come some more of them from twelve o'clock high. There's a lot of 'em, guys. I think we got 'em mad at us!"

At once there was a tremendous explosion within our airplane and I felt myself going into that land of Morpheus. It was a wonderful feeling. I was drifting in oblivion to fulfill the end of my dream from which I had been so rudely awakened that morning, and by God, I *would* find out what happened! I was reaching out for that beautiful brunette with the big . . .

"Come on, Knobby, wake up. Goddamn it, wake up! Get up, Harry, get up now!" I heard Johnny's screaming voice first, then opened my eyes to see him leaning over me. He was snapping my parachute onto my harness. I was lying on the floor next to the bulkhead near his tail-turret. My head was spinning and he was shaking the hell out of me.

He screamed at me again, louder this time. "Come on, Knobby! We gotta bail out! Get your goddamned ass up!" His oxygen mask was hanging on his helmet without an oxygen line attached to it.

I came out of my daze long enough to understand him. I looked at my waist position where my gun had been. It was gone! In its place was a hole big enough to drive a Jeep through — no exaggeration. Fire belched through the bomb bays back into the rear of the fuselage where we were. In spite of all this, with Johnny's help, I got to my feet. At once it seemed there was no confusion. Willie and Lieutenant Leslie had their parachutes buckled on, as we had trained to do a thousand times. Practice was paying off. I went to the escape hatch on the floor and pulled it open, snapping it in place. I checked my parachute, making sure it was snapped securely. I took a last look over my shoulder.

Lined up in back of me were Johnny, Willie, McCarty, and Lieutenant Leslie.

I didn't hesitate. I jumped out of the burning aircraft feet first. The wind caught my feet and turned me over several times before my body straightened out and I fell on my back, slowly rotating clockwise. We had been trained to make a delayed jump if we bailed out from a high altitude. That way we would get away from enemy action, away from the dangers of the fire in our own plane and any resulting loss of control or explosion by our own aircraft. Also, at a lower altitude, there was no dependency on oxygen and we would be clear-headed. So, I made the delayed jump and counted for thirty seconds before I reached for the rip cord. I counted, "Twenty-eight one-thousand, twenty-nine one-thousand, thirty one-thousand." With my right hand I reached for the handle of the rip cord. It wasn't there!

My story could have ended there. But I looked down at the parachute, turned it over as much as I could, and discovered the handle was on the right side. My parachute was snapped on upside down! No matter. I uttered a silent prayer and pulled the rip cord with my left hand.

That beautiful parachute blossomed over my head with barely a jerk. However, the flap which is supposed to be on the bottom slapped me in the face so hard it bruised my cheek and forehead, stunning me for a moment. I tucked the flap down under my harness and looked up at that glorious white circle of silk. I thanked God and Sergeant Rosenberg that it worked.

Our airplane, now far above me and a few miles distant, was

going down in a flat spin, something I didn't think it could do. It was entirely engulfed in flames and completely out of control. When it got to a lower altitude, perhaps four or five miles from me, it exploded in midair and disintegrated into thousands of pieces. There were two different groups of four parachutes each. Small, tiny white spots in the sky far above me hadn't made the delayed jump. I was hoping there would be ten survivors, but I counted only eight other chutes. Which one of the crew failed to make it? After the explosion of our airplane, it made no difference. Whoever was on board would never know what hit him.

Then I saw two more B-24s going down off to the southwest. I couldn't see any parachutes from either one of them. Then I saw yet another B-24 headed earthward and burning badly. It was too far for me to see if there were any parachutes. That made four B-24s the enemy had shot down today that I could see. Where the hell was our fighter protection? I scanned the sky.

The remaining planes of our squadron were going westward, far above me. Even as I looked, they disappeared.

I looked at the ground again. There was a very tiny village with a church steeple sticking up through the trees. I estimated I was still at eight or maybe ten thousand feet altitude. Directly beneath me was an airfield. I could see a lot of activity and two airplanes on the runway, their propellers turning. They were ME-109s! My God, I was going to land on a German airfield!

As soon as Ernst Scheufele's squadron of ME109s passed through the bomber flow, he heard the terrifying words come over his radio: "Lightnings! Lightnings!" His red fuel light had come on, indicating he had less than ten minutes of fuel remaining, so he headed toward earth, followed by a wingman, and landed on the friendly airfield below. He later learned it was Havelte.

He stopped on the runway in front of the tower and, along with the pilot of the other ME109, ran toward a building beside it. As they ran, a Lightning passed low over the field, ignored the two ME109s sitting on the runway, and fired at them as they hit the dirt. They ran to the small building where two Luftwaffe men and two Dutch girls were hiding under a table. Forty-five minutes later, after they had coffee, they refueled their Messerschmitts and flew back to their base at Sachaeu.

What an exciting, wonderful ride it is in a parachute. I loved it!
We had been told our heavy flying boots would come off when the parachute snapped open. Wrong. It didn't happen. Then, for the first
time, I noticed part of my heated suit was smoldering. My head felt
like it was burning too. I jerked my helmet off as well as the woolen
under-helmet. They had both been on fire and were smoldering. The
leather top of my helmet had the top burned out of it. I threw both of
them as far away from the parachute as I could, and to my utter amazement they fell at the same speed as I did. Not only that, but they
stayed in exactly the same spot where I had thrown them. It was eerie.
The arms of my heated suit were both smoldering, so I beat on them
with my hands until they stopped burning.

Thus engrossed with putting out my fires, I failed to notice the
ME-109 coming straight at me, firing his two 7.9mm machine guns.
Some of the bullets penetrated the canopy of my parachute and severed
two shroud lines. He flew past me, not missing me by more than the
wingspan of his airplane. His engine roared loudly as he passed by so
close. I was so busy watching him to check his next move that I failed
to notice he had more problems than I. A greater roar filled my ear as
an American P-38 flew past me in exactly the same spot going full out.
He was on the Messerschmitt's tail and started shooting the moment
he cleared my chute. I turned my head to watch as they broke into a
steep climb. The German tried to make a turn and fall off the top of his
climb but at that very moment caught a full burst of .50-calibers from
the P-38. It filled the Kraut plane with lead and a small explosion,
more of a puff really, enclosed the German with fire. The flaming ME-
109 stalled out, then flipped into a spin from which he never recovered. He crashed in the deep forest about two miles away with a tremendous explosion and a huge ball of fire. Black smoke marked the
German's grave. The P-38 followed him down, then peeled off and
went looking for more ME-109s.

The entire episode took only a few seconds but seemingly it lasted
for hours. When I looked at the holes in my parachute, I was grateful
to be alive. Three times in the last five minutes my life had been put
on the line and I wasn't even on the ground. I never knew the Luftwaffe shot at airmen in their parachutes. Why the Nazi bastard shot
at me, I'll never know. It was quite evident I was going to land on his
lousy airfield and I'd be captured at once. Nevertheless, this guy had
shot at me point-blank.

I wanted to shake the hand of that P-38 jockey and buy him the best drink in the ETO. He deserved it.

Then, that fast, the sky filled with P-38s. They strafed the airfield and everything that moved. Lt. James L. Wallace of the 479th fighter group took a long run at the antiaircraft gun emplacement just east of the airfield, firing all his guns in the dive. The Germans returned his fire with machine guns and 20 or 35mm cannon and got the best of him for the P-38 rolled over on its back and crashed upside down into the gun positions, taking a lot of Nazis with him. It almost looked suicidal, but of course it wasn't. The pilot never pulled back on the throttles once he was in his deadly dive. There was a tremendous explosion and a huge ball of fire. Of course, the courageous pilot died before he crashed. What a waste of men and machines.

The things I saw coming down in my parachute were fantastic. It was almost like watching a giant motion picture screen. The drama of war unfolded before my eyes: the planes crashing, the explosions and the parachutes; the flames, smoke, more explosions, gunfire from the antiaircraft cannons, as well as machine guns and 20mm cannon. The noise was unbelievable. I felt the concussion of every explosive charge and it held me spellbound. I was a captive audience. The scene I witnessed was impossible, yet there it was unfolding before me. The real hell of the air war was indeed a frightening, horrible experience. But watching those sights is an experience I was privileged to see and I'll never forget them.

The German runway loomed beneath me. I thought I'd land in the middle of it. I could see that it was paved with red paving bricks. They must have used a million of them. As I drifted nearer the runway, the ground winds started blowing me away from it toward a large clump of trees about 150 feet away.

Well, I thought, *at least the Germans won't have far to come for me.*

For the first time I noticed my gloves were smoldering. In fact, they were almost burned off the backs of my hands. I tore them off and threw them as far away as I could. My hands, now exposed to the air, stung badly for I pulled off some skin too. The ground winds continued to blow me away from the runway. For the first time, the thought of evading capture entered my mind, but I was fairly certain it would only be a matter of minutes before German troops would be there. They were probably already in the trees with their guns trained on me. But looking around, the only Germans I could see were a group running across a field a quarter of a mile away and they weren't even looking my way.

About 500 feet off the ground I could see I was coming down much faster than I thought. I crashed through the trees and put my arms over my face, the limbs breaking my fall until I came to a stop, still hanging in my harness and my feet a scant six inches from the ground. The parachute blossomed over the entire group of trees, its white canopy marking my location.

I turned the swivel release on my parachute and hit it with the palm of my hand. I fell the remaining few inches from the harness. My left rib cage hurt badly and hurt especially when the holster carrying my .45 Colt Automatic rubbed against it. Probably when my chute opened, the gun had slapped down and bruised me. I looked at the weapon and cursed myself for not using it on the ME-109 when he was shooting at me. I couldn't have missed.

Immediately, I started walking through the trees toward the runway. I estimated I was no more than half a mile from the flak gun, for there was a column of smoke rising from the crashed P-38. As I walked, I realized the situation I was in with more clarity than when I was watching the countryside and the events taking place around me. I had some sore ribs and was burned a little. I had no wounds or broken bones except maybe a rib or two. I was in pretty good shape for what I had been through. I started to cry. I should have been rejoicing that I was still alive!

I stopped and sat down in a small indentation in the sand. It was covered with underbrush and weeds. The tears kept coming. I got down on my knees and talked to God, thanking Him for my deliverance. At that moment, I believe He was listening. Aloud, I thanked Him for sparing my life and asked for His guidance. It was the only time in my life I prayed for myself and my own well-being, and I did it from my heart. I believe I felt the presence of God. Afterwards, I knew what I was going to do. With God's help, I would try to evade capture.

Through the trees, I could see the runway. After taking off my Mae West and scarf, I reversed my direction, almost returning to my parachute. Then I walked toward the open field which separated the forest from me. It was only a few minutes before I reached the clearing. Another 200 yards would put me in a huge forest thick with lush pine trees. It looked like a good place to hide. The village I had seen with the church spire was on the other side of the woods. The terrain was sandy, much like beach sand except it was peppered with long pine needles. The land was dotted with rolling dunes some six to eight feet high.

I looked in the air. There were still five parachutes, small white dots in the sky, at least a mile high. They would land about a half-mile west of me and much nearer to the Germans who would be waiting for them. I set off across the clearing with my heart in my throat. To my left, perhaps a quarter of a mile away, I watched the group of twenty or thirty German troops which I had seen from my parachute walking in the same direction I was, parallel to me and going in the direction where the earthbound parachutes would land.

Then they spotted me.

"Halt! Halt!" They yelled at the top of their lungs.

"Halt! Halt!" I yelled back at them, just as loud. I waved my arms crazily.

Their uniforms and my heated suit were about the same color, especially at a distance. So I kept walking and waving my arms.

The ruse worked. They waved back, yelled something to me in German, then continued walking across the field in the same direction they had been when they first saw me. What a deal! I was scared to death but kept waving at them dutifully. I thanked God for helping me pull off a bluff like that.

I continued walking and kept edging away from them until I came to the edge of the forest. The dunes were generally much higher there, some as high as ten or twelve feet.

I headed for a small road off to the right leading into the woods.

"Hey, American!" said a voice in broken English, no more than twenty feet in back of me.

My heart almost stopped as I spun around, reaching for my gun.

THREE

I turned toward the voice. My heart was in my mouth, my pistol in my hand.

Atop a sand dune, three men in civilian clothing had been watching the plight of the American airplanes and parachutists. One of the men came off the dune, scattering sand with his wooden shoes. He was in his fifties, heavy-set, and badly in need of a shave. He had graying hair and a broad smile on his well-lined face. His eyes seemed to twinkle. He was dressed in a badly soiled and tattered suit.

As he approached me, he took off his visored cap and held out his hand. I shook it. Before he had a chance to speak, I said, "I'm an American airman, can you help me?"

"Hello, American!" he replied in a thick, guttural accent. "Was that you in the parachute over there?"

"Yes that was me," I replied anxiously. "I've got to get away from here. The German soldiers are very close!"

"Ya, I know. They are after the other parachutes. You fooled them good . . . they thought you were one of them." He laughed. I nodded and turned to walk in the direction of the road leading into the forest.

He took my arm as I turned to leave. "We'll help you," he said.

"Go down that road about three hundred meters and lay down in the ditch. We'll be along soon."

Grateful, I turned around and made a hasty retreat. When I got to the road I discovered it was more of a path as I followed it into the woods. *What the hell is a meter?* I asked myself. I had never learned the metric system either in school or the air force. So I walked about 500 yards until I came to a good place in the ditch with a solid growth of underbrush. I crawled into it and lay down, pulling the brush around me as best I could. I removed my pistol from its holster, pulled the slide back, loaded the weapon, and put it on safety. Then I lay on my back so I could watch the path.

My every instinct told me to run farther away as fast as I could. I began to think that trying to escape was stupid. If I had surrendered, I'd at least be with Johnny and the rest of the crew. I'd probably be captured anyway, maybe even killed.

My hand tightened on the grip of my pistol when I heard voices. The three Dutchmen, their arms loaded with brush, came up the path looking for me. Carefully, they placed the brush around me until they were satisfied I couldn't be seen.

"Lay very still and be quiet," the big Dutchman said, looking at their job with approval. "I hope you're not caught. We will come back tomorrow to see if you are still free. Good luck."

I looked at my watch for the first time as the three of them went back down the path. It was 1:30 P.M. on a beautiful sunny day. The events of the last hour had me so shook up that I began to tremble. I fell into a troubled sleep and woke up at 4:30. I put my gun back in its holster and closed my eyes, hoping I was dreaming. But it was all too real.

The top of my head and the back of both hands were tender and sore from my burns. My hands were badly blistered, but I could move them. I could smell my singed hair. It stunk badly. I decided to leave my hiding place long enough to relieve myself. Instead, I opened my eyes wide when I heard voices.

In spite of my fears and the pain from my burns, alien voices in the distance awakened me completely. I gripped the butt of my pistol and removed it from its holster and waited.

Well, I thought, *if they spot me I'm ready.*

The two Germans had machine guns held by straps around their necks and when the tallest one aimed at me, I shot him and then the other one. I retrieved one of the Schmeissers and the ammo clips and ran to the farthest edge of the forest. I was on the run but didn't know where to run. I was hungry and thirsty but settled for a Camel. I took a long drag on the cigarette. In the distance I heard the German troops singing "Lily Marlene." They sang it beautifully.

Daylight was fading and it was quiet as death. I climbed to the top of a sand dune, where I had an unobstructed view, and when it was almost dark I felt I had my bearings. I decided to cross the open field and go to the church. I put the two ammo clips in my belt, slung the Schmeisser over my shoulder, and came down off the dune. I could still see the outline of the church spire against the sky some miles away. I set out, walked a quarter of a mile, stumbling frequently in the darkness, and suddenly plunged downward three feet. Stopping momentarily, I then slid another five feet into water over my head. The Schmeisser slid off my shoulder and the two ammo clips fell to the bottom.

I stood in water up to my neck and caught my breath. Though it wasn't cold, it was a severe shock, probably as much from surprise as anything else. The first thing I did was try to locate the weapons I had dropped with my feet. The bottom was deep mud. When I thought I felt something with my foot, I dove down only to find it was a stone. My .45, thank God, was snapped securely in its holster. With much difficulty, I found a place I could crawl out of the stream and onto the bank. I was soaked to the skin and felt chilled. I decided to get back to the forest and take a better look the next day.

By the time I got back, I was chilled to the bone and shivering. I climbed to the top of the highest dune I could see in the darkness and took off my wet heated suit and boots. The night air was warmer. Long after midnight, I dozed off and slept restlessly. By dawn I was awakened by the sound of voices. I was sure it was the Germans. Instead, it was two Dutchmen walking on the path a hundred yards distant. They were followed almost at once by two more headed in the same direction. I picked up my wet clothes and slid down off the dune, crossed the path, and hid in back of another dune.

Many men were on their way to work. At last, I saw the three men who had helped me the day before. I started for the path and as soon as they saw me, they followed me back to the sand dune.

"American! Are you all right?" asked the one who spoke English.

"Yes, I'm fine. But I had some trouble last night."

"I can see. Your clothes are wet."

"I fell into a stream trying to cross the field to get to the church."

"There are several streams and a canal between here and the village. Let's move further away from the path so we can talk."

We walked about 200 yards and sat down. He opened the sack he was carrying and gave me some sandwiches wrapped in paper. He also gave me a bottle of hot tea. I wolfed down two of the sandwiches and half the tea. He gave me two small bags of tobacco and some cigarette papers. I accepted them and rolled a cigarette. I got out a pack of Camels which were not wet because of their cellophane wrapper. I gave each of them a couple of cigarettes and they put them in their pockets.

"What's your name?" I asked the big man who spoke English.

"You can call me Karl. It's not my real name, but in this kind of a situation it's better if you don't know my real name."

"My name is Harry Clark," I said.

"It's much too dangerous for you to stay here!" Karl said. "As soon as we leave, you walk deeper into the woods. The Germans are looking for you everywhere. Don't let anybody see you. Some Dutchmen are called 'Landwatchers' and they are bad. Two German soldiers were found dead near the ditch where we hid you. They think you killed them or they were killed in the air raid yesterday. We will meet you here on this spot a little after five o'clock tonight when we are finished working. If you can't get back or get lost, we will be here in the morning, okay?"

I nodded to him.

As I had been eating my cheese sandwiches, Karl talked to me. He called the German airfield Vliegveld Havelte. The big church was located in the middle of the town.

"Were you heading for that church last night?" he asked.

I nodded in the affirmative, for my mouth was full of food.

"It's a good thing you didn't make it. The Dominee of the church is married to a German national and many think he is a Landwatcher. He wouldn't have helped you. Instead you would be in German hands right now. He is not a good man, Harry. Stay away from that church." He gave me the bag of food. Then he and his friends went down the path to their jobs.

I remembered the escape kit in my hip pocket. I had carried it unopened for thirty-two missions, and now I had reason to use it. On the exterior of the OD (olive drab) waterproof bag was printed in red letters, ESCAPE KIT — MARK IV. It had a sealed flap which grudgingly gave way to my constant tugging. I opened it carefully, not wanting to lose any of its contents in the sand. It contained three maps, each about thirty inches square, made of silk and printed on both sides. They cov-

43

ered the entire area in which we flew our missions. There was also a tiny compass, a chocolate bar, a few sticks of gum, cigarettes, matches, several thousand French francs, and some lesser items that were useless to me.

I located the map of Holland and found Havelte. It was about five miles north of a bigger city called Meppel and close to another big town called Steenwijk. I thought it was pretty smart to put the maps on cloth; they wouldn't crinkle or make any noise when opened and could be stuffed in a pocket.

Carefully, I folded the maps and put everything back. I ate the chocolate bar, lit one of the cigarettes, and tried to decide where to go. Afterwards I put the compass in my pocket.

I dug a shallow hole in the sand and put my heated suit and boots in it, carefully making note of the location. I decided to head in the direction of Havelte and then go south to Meppel if everything was clear. Through a small clearing in the trees, I saw the German runway and some buildings. I thought I was miles from Vliegveld Havelte. Staying hidden in the woods and circling the clearing, I got close to the runway again. The troops were working, clearing the wreckage of several burned-out buildings and repairing others damaged by our strafing P-38s. The wrecked P-38 was partly loaded on the back of a truck, with one of its tail sections hanging over the end. There was no other activity.

I started walking back into the woods and five minutes later started to go over a small rise when I heard voices with the familiar guttural accent. I dropped to the ground and froze. An engine started. My curiosity got the best of me, so I went up the small rise on all fours. When I reached the top I raised my head high enough to look on the other side and discovered it was a revetment for the German ME-109s. Inside, mechanics were working feverishly on some battle damage to a rudder of one of the planes. It was almost shot away. The engine noise was from a big truck leaving with soldiers in the back. I lay very still, almost hypnotized, watching their activity. How long I stayed I don't know, but I felt as if I were in a trance. I finally came to my senses and remembered where I was — and that these were the bad guys.

Retreating back down the hill on all fours, I finally became lost to view among the trees. I saw three more revetments. After bypassing two of them, I looked into the third. It contained four parked trucks and nothing else. From my vantage point, however, on top of the rear of the revetment, I got a better look at the buildings on the other side of the runway. There were two wrecked and shot-up ME-109s lying on their bellies and a third had one of its wheels down and the other retracted. Its wing was bent grotesquely, sticking straight up. All three were being dismantled and loaded onto trucks parked nearby. Most likely they were being stripped of machinery and instrumentation, for they would never fly again. Some of the workers wore uniform coveralls and others civilian clothes. None of them appeared to be overworked. I looked down to the end of the runway, opposite the end where I came down, and saw a huge gasoline storage tank with camouflaged netting stretched over it. A guard stood nearby.

I was fascinated watching the enemy at work. They were less than a city block from me. The buildings were just on the other side of the runway. I pulled myself together and got away quietly, carefully circling back and forth, on the alert for anything.

Miles away, it seemed, I came to a road that was about eight feet wide and was paved with the same red bricks as the runway. On the other side were open fields and a few homes. I kept inside the forest and followed the road toward Havelte for perhaps an hour, when the wooded area ended abruptly. There were a few miles of open fields between me and my objective and no way to get to the other side except by crossing the fields. I reversed my direction. After walking almost two hours, long after the road had became a path and then vanished completely, I heard voices and the sound of new activity ahead. This time I had my bearings and knew it wasn't Vliegveld Havelte, which had to be at least three miles away.

Again, the forest ended abruptly to a manmade clearing. As I watched, I could see at least a hundred and perhaps two hundred Dutchmen working with hand tools, mostly shovels and picks. They were constructing a new runway. Some German officers were huddled together a few hundred feet away. The sight of those uniforms gave me cause for alarm, so I turned back, deeper into the woods. Later, I enjoyed my sandwiches and tea. I had no trouble keeping our rendezvous at the appointed time. A little after 5:00 they joined me. Karl, with a big smile on his face, put his arm around my shoulder and walked with me. We headed back toward the construction site.

"We must not talk too loud for the forest has ears," he said.

"How did you learn to speak English as well as you do?" I wondered.

"Before the war I worked for Standard Oil Company on a tanker ship. I traveled to America all the time. Sometimes we go through the canal to the west coast of the USA. Once I was going to marry a lady in New York. But I traveled so much I lost her and she married another man." He sighed as he thought back to the affair and held out his arms in a gesture of despair. "I left the sea for a year, lived in New York on the east side, and went to night school to learn English. I worked in the shipyard during the day. When my visa expired, I went back to sea." He looked at me and winked. "Now that I have a new American friend perhaps I'll come to the USA and see you after the war. Okay?"

"After the war, you can come and stay with me whenever you want. I live in Los Angeles, California."

"Oh ya?" he replied excitedly. "Wilmington. I have been there a hundred times. All the seamen get drunk and fuck the ladies in Wilmington. The police are good men — they never put us in jail. They always took us back to our ships. Ya, Wilmington is one helluva good place."

We talked as we walked. He told me that all the men, himself included, were forced to work for the Germans. He was lucky to be able to live with his family. He followed the rules set down by the Germans except when it involved the underground. He said he was not a member. "But," he declared, "I am a good Nederlander and would die before I would betray them!" He lit a cigarette. "Men from the Resistance or somebody who takes care of pilots will be in touch with me soon, another day or two."

We walked a couple of miles and stopped. "This is where you stay tonight," he said.

One of his friends had walked ahead and came back with some blankets and another bag of food, which they had evidently hidden on their way to work that morning.

"This will be a safe place unless the Germans search the woods. Then, no place is safe. We'll come back in the morning." He took the bag and bottles I had been carrying with him and waved goodbye as the three of them headed for home.

Again I had some cheese sandwiches and cold tea.

Just before dark I was sitting on the blanket, smoking a cigarette. Three deer walked within twenty-five feet of me, one as close as ten. They were all females. When they saw me, they stopped eating and stood completely motionless for several minutes, staring at me with their big brown eyes. Then, unafraid, they serenely continued grazing

46

and slowly made their way through the forest. What a contrast between war and peace.

My burns were really painful. The backs of my hands were especially sore, but my head was tender too. *I wonder if you get the Purple Heart for burns too?* I mused. I was wounded once before but didn't get a medal. I would have to check on that when I got back.

On our second mission to Munich, we bombed a marshaling yard where trains were made up. The flak was the worst I'd ever seen. Just after we released our bombs, I was standing at the waist window when I felt a stinging sensation in my left thigh. I rubbed it with my hand and felt a hole. My heated suit and my gloved hand were covered with blood. I looked at the offended area and discovered a hole in each leg of the fabric, one about an inch wide and the other about two inches wide.

I screamed into the intercom, "I'm hit, I'm hit!"

Don McCarty, on the other waist gun, turned around and saw the blood. Acting quickly, he disconnected his outlets, went to the bulkhead, and got the first-aid kit. He reconnected his outlets and removed two bandages, wrapping them tightly over the holes in the heated suit. Willie Lowen came up out of the ball-turret and got the mummy-bag. With the bandage securely in place, both of them gently lifted me into the mummy-bag and Don snapped it closed. He made me lay down, put my head on my parachute, and tried to make me comfortable.

"Does it hurt much?" he queried.

"My pecker, Don, I think I got my pecker shot off! It burns like hell!" I complained.

"Take it easy," he said sympathetically.

He dug into the first-aid kit and found the morphine. After unwrapping the tube, he removed the needle cover and stuck it in my arm, right through the heated suit. I could barely feel the needle as he squeezed the narcotic into my arm.

Five minutes later, feeling wonderful, I was ready to make the flight back to Attlebridge without benefit of the airplane.

Three hours later, on our final approach into Attlebridge, Bart Philo loaded the Very Pistol and shot a pair of red-red flares out of the top of the plane, signifying to the ground personnel we had wounded on board. Jack made the smoothest landing he ever made in his life. The medics took me out through the bomb bay doors and carried the stretcher to a waiting ambulance. In no time I was in the hospital, lying on the operating table.

When the flight surgeon saw the location of my wound, he cut away the bandages and pulled my pants down over my feet. He was assisted by five nurses and two orderlies. The morphine was wearing off and I was trying to remember the last time I had sex, for that would probably be the last time in my life. I firmly believed my penis had surely been blown into a million pieces.

I looked down. My God, was all that blood mine? The next time I tried to look, my shoulders were held flat on the table by a huge nurse who tipped the scales at least 300 pounds and maybe more. With a hand on each of my shoulders, she kept repeating, "There, there." I could feel the doctor cutting away and finally they pulled something else down over my feet. Now I was really exposed and again, I tried to look to see if any of it was left. "There, there," she said. Her hands weighed at least a ton apiece and I couldn't budge. Then she bent over me so she could see my wound, her breasts straddling my face. I was suffocating but couldn't move her to catch a breath of air. Luckily for me, she straightened up and I could breathe again. I felt them cleaning the area and washing away the blood.

Oh God, I thought, *how many stitches? Maybe they'll find enough of it to sew it back on me.*

The flight surgeon signaled my 300-pound nemesis to refrain from crushing me. She removed her hands and left the operating room.

"Sergeant, you're a lucky bastard. Just another inch or two and you'd squat to pee for the rest of your life!" He turned to the orderly. "Put a band-aid on it and mark him duty." He left the operating room chuckling to himself.

At last I could get up on my elbow and look. It was the happiest moment of my life, for my shriveled pecker was still a part of me. There was a small nick in the head of it and another on my left thigh. My right thigh had a four-inch-long surface cut which looked more like a welt. The blood had stopped. I was the only one who felt sorry for me. The orderly did the doctor's bidding and put band-aids on the offended areas.

The orderly smiled and said, "So many of you fly-boys get shot in the dick. You guys ought to start a club or something."

My big nurse came in with a bathrobe and slippers and helped me sit up on the table.

"These will get you back to your barracks. Do you think you can

48

make it?" she asked. I said that I could and she left.

When I went outside, the crew was waiting for me. They had to humiliate me further, each of them volunteering to do my lovemaking for me. I had to expose my wound in broad daylight as they roared with laughter. Many other spectators joined in the fun, including some nurses. I hope they were nurses.

It was hard to live down, but I was the only one in the barracks with a bathrobe and slippers or who had been wounded in action.

After pondering about my burns, I put the blanket on the ground, lay on half of it, and covered myself with the other half. I slept like a baby. Up at the crack of dawn, I finished off the sandwiches and cold tea.

Karl brought a sack and removed some civilian clothes. He asked me to put them on. I explained that if I was ever captured wearing civilian clothes I would be shot as a spy.

"What makes you think they wouldn't shoot you anyway, uniform or not? They are mad as hell at you and want you any way they can get you, dead or alive. They think you shot two of them. The Boche are searching for you everywhere. It's not safe for you . . . especially today. You'll thank me for it later, wait and see."

For the first time since the war started, I put on civvies. Coat, trousers, shirt, visored cap, and leather shoes — which all fit. The only things I took with me were my tobacco, matches, and cigarette papers. I put my flight suit, pistol, and boots inside a cotton bag. Karl handed me a paper bag. "Your lunch," he said.

On the way to the construction site, we stopped near some huge boulders beside the path. They hid my stuff in them.

"Your uniform is well hidden," Karl told me.

"So, what am I going to do today?" I asked.

"You're going to shovel dirt with the rest of us!"

So, on August 17, 1944, I went to work for Herr Adolph Schikelgruber Hitler, helping to build a new runway for his ME-109s.

There was a small toolhouse near the edge of the construction site. The Dutchman handing out the tools looked at me and winked as he gave me a long-handled shovel. He said something I didn't understand, so I just nodded and walked away with Karl. At least 200 of us worked on the runway. I saw no soldiers.

The construction methods were primitive. The runway was about a mile long and less than 200 feet wide. It was paved with red paving bricks, and was about a third completed. Karl told me the Germans wanted to extend the runway. There were only three hand-operated concrete mixers run by small gasoline motors. It would be a long time before this field would be operational.

All day long we stayed in a small group. About an hour after we started working, two companies of German soldiers, perhaps 300 strong, marched into the work area near the edge of the forest. Most of them were armed with rifles, their bayonets fixed in place. Others had Schmeissers slung across their chests. At a point about in the middle of the runway, their sergeant brought them to a halt. They separated into a long line with perhaps twenty-five feet between each man. Satisfied, the noncom blew a whistle. The soldiers entered the woods and disappeared quickly. Karl smiled.

"Tell me, my good American friend, how do those civilian clothes fit now? A little better perhaps?" He pointed toward the woods. "They will search every inch of the forest for you. They think perhaps you are wounded or dead and want to find your body to close the chapter on you. And, my friend, this is but one company looking for you. There are others back there by Vliegveld Havelte. You see, old Karl knows what he's talking about!"

"I'm grateful," I said. "Even the shovel fits better now." I had the urge to cry out, *Hey fellas, I'm over here!*

As the day wore on, I sweated a great deal — probably more from anxiety than manual labor. Several German officers came to the job site at different times during the day and passed as close as ten feet from me. Their only interest was the workers' progress.

Just before 5:00 in the afternoon, the German troops came out of the field. They looked tired and sat down as soon as they arrived. When their sergeant emerged, they got into formation and he marched them toward Vliegveld Havelte.

At exactly 5:00 we turned in our tools and headed into the woods. We retrieved the bag containing my belongings from behind the boulders. I put my flying suit on immediately and strapped on my gun. When I took off my cap, a small portion of my scalp and hair which was stuck to it came off also. It bled, so Karl took out a well-soiled handkerchief and wiped the blood off my face. I had to laugh when he said, "A little nose juice won't hurt it at all."

The bald spot on my head where the scalp and hair pulled off would always remain. Today it is a constant reminder of the day I assisted the Germans in their war effort.

"Harry, my friend, you must trust me from now on. Tomorrow the underground will move you to a safe place. We are waiting for a man now. I don't know who he is, but a password has been arranged. He will take you to another place in the woods for tonight. You must leave your pistol and holster with me, for you cannot carry it on the open road. Later, perhaps, it will be returned to you. I don't know where he is taking you but it is a prearranged meeting place. When he leaves you there, stay there and don't move around. About four tomorrow afternoon you will be picked up. Do you understand?"

I assured him I did.

"This man is your lifeline and he is a member of the underground. So do what he says, understand?" I nodded affirmatively.

The other Dutchmen shook hands with me and said in broken English, "Goodbye, Harry," then disappeared in the trees. I took off my gun and gave it to Karl. He put it in his lunch sack.

"Thank you for trusting me," he said.

Moments later, a man I didn't recognize approached us from within the forest. I motioned to Karl and he turned around.

"*Aardappelen!* (Potatoes!)," said the stranger.

They shook hands. "*Aardappelen,*" Karl said.

He faced me. "*Dag,*" he said.

"Hello," I replied.

Karl and the stranger entered into a short conversation, then Karl spoke to me. "He speaks no English. Do what he wants, and stay where he puts you."

I offered him the cloth sack with the rest of the food in it and the civilian clothes. He waved them off. "Keep them. You can't travel on the roads in your uniform."

Then facing me, he put his arms around me in a friendly embrace and kissed me on each cheek. I put my arms around him and patted him on the back.

"Tell me," he whispered, "did you kill the two Germans?"

"Yes," I said, still in his embrace.

"Good! God bless you. I hope you get home to your family."

"Will I see you again?"

"God willing," he answered, picking up the sack and throwing it over his shoulder. He walked in the same direction as his two companions. Without looking back, he waved his hand.

I liked this warm and friendly man with a big heart. He was very

51

brave and I felt I owed him my life. But all he wanted to do was help another fellow human being in distress. He had done all he could for me, and now he was gone.

We walked quickly and quietly through the deep sand and occasionally my guide looked back to be sure I was following him. At times he would stop and listen for a moment, but he never said anything. He seemed to know exactly where he was going. About two miles further into the forest we came upon a downed Focke Wulf FW-190 pursuit plane. It appeared the plane had come down in the only open spot in the forest, where there wasn't room enough to land. It was on its wheels. Obviously, it was a recent wreck, for the cannons and machine guns were still intact in the wings. It was obvious, too, that nobody had come near it since the crash. There was evidence of machine gun holes around the tail section, but other than that it looked ready to fly. We circled the FW-190, giving it a wide berth. There were no guards posted nearby.

My guide stopped and listened. We bent down low as we passed the fallen aircraft. I followed his every move. Once satisfied there were no guards, we took off through the forest in the same general direction we had been going before for at least two miles, until we came to a posted area. There were white signs with the word "VERBOTEN" in red on them. Underneath was a stenciled skull and crossbones in black. They were nailed to the trees at fifty-foot intervals. I was fearful we were going into a minefield, but the Dutchman kept walking straight ahead.

After a mile, he slowed. We stopped beside a dense clump of bushes some twenty-five feet in diameter. He pointed to it and indicated I was to hide underneath. He put his finger to his lips to let me know I should be quiet. Taking my arm, he pointed to my watch, put his finger on the three, and whispered in unknown words. I knew he was telling me that somebody would be there at 3:00 the next day. I nodded in the affirmative, so he'd know I understood.

He had a smile on his face, and I shook hands with him. Then he walked away and the forest swallowed him up instantly.

It was a warm, balmy evening. Just before dark, I slid into the bushes, found a fairly open spot near the center, and stretched out. When total darkness set in, it was the most foreboding place I have ever been in. Every noise put me on edge. I was well hidden. To find me, someone would have had to walk through the thick branches, and that was impossible.

As the sun's rays filtered through the trees, I felt reborn. When it was fully light I crept out of my hiding place and walked about fifty yards and watered a small pine tree. I had no idea where I was. I ate the last half of a cheese sandwich and drank the rest of the cold tea. I tried to visualize what was in store for me next. *Yeah, what's in store for me?* I thought. *I'm not even supposed to be here. I'm liable to be shot by some trigger-happy German soldier. And come to think of it, I'm liable to be shot by these guys from the underground. This is a heavy load for me to tote! My life is on the line and I don't want to lose it! I wonder if it hurts the soul to be killed or if the only pain is the pain in the body? Now that's a poser!*

I pictured the Resistance people who were coming to get me. I saw some pretty tough hombres, armed to the teeth and ready to kill at a moment's notice. I began to think I never should have tried to evade. I wished I was fearlessly brave like the guys in the movies, who would fight to the death and all that crap. *No use kidding . . . you ain't no John Wayne and don't forget it!* I told myself.

The day was long and hot. I was my own worst enemy. I did my best to shake my lousy thoughts. Looking at my watch constantly, I was amazed how slowly the hands moved across the dial. I was hungry and thirsty. I got back in the clump of bushes and lay down in the sand. *I'd give my soul if I had my gun back. If the underground people aren't here by four o'clock, I'm gonna leave here, walk in a straight line for the airfield, and give myself up,* I thought. *No use playing this game. It's making a mental wreck out of me.*

At fifteen after the hour I made a firm decision. "If nobody comes by five o'clock I really will walk back to Vliegveld Havelte and turn myself in." The tricks my mind was playing on me were ridiculous. I had convinced myself that anything was possible now. I even considered it possible that Karl had changed his mind or had been captured by the Krauts, who forced him to talk.

"Is anybody there?" an American voice called out quietly, shaking me back to reality.

Frightened to the point of almost shattering my sanity, I lay flat on my belly, watching in the direction from which the voice had come. Then I saw them! Three men dressed in suits were pushing bicycles through the deep sand with some difficulty. Their eyes were searching everywhere as they approached the area where I lay.

The man leading the others, handsome and young, probably in his early twenties, repeated the query again in excellent English.

"Is anybody there?"

I mustered all the courage I could. In spite of the fact I was thoroughly terrorized and knowing full well that within the next few seconds I could be lying on the floor of the forest dead, I got to my knees and came out of the bushes, stood up and faced them. They didn't point a gun at me and I didn't speak. It was the bravest thing I have ever done in my life.

Their leader spoke. "Are you an American?"

"Yes," I replied.

"I'll bet you've really been sweating us out, haven't you?"

"You can say that again," I answered.

He came forward and shook hands with me.

"Are you an American?" I asked.

"No, I'm Dutch. I've helped so many of your countrymen I've picked up your accent."

"You've been to the United States, though, haven't you?"

"Nope, I've lived in Holland all my life and never been out of Europe. Are you armed?"

"No, I gave my gun and holster to Karl."

"How long have you been in the woods?"

"Counting the day I was shot down, this is my fourth day. I was shot down on the fifteenth."

"Can you ride a bicycle?"

"Of course," I replied.

"I was told you had civilian clothes. Do you?"

"Yes," I said, pointing to the bushes. "Do you want me to put them on?"

"Please do."

He walked back to the other two men who had remained in the background. They talked in Dutch while I changed my clothes. One of the Dutchmen took his bicycle and left.

I emptied the pockets of my flying clothes and put all my worldly possessions in my pockets. I left the Ray-Bans because the lens was cracked. I left my OD socks on; they were the only ones I had. I was tying my shoes when the Dutchman returned.

"We are members of the Dutch Resistance," he said. "We'll take you to a safe place to stay temporarily while we make arrangements to start you on the escape route back to Allied control. We are all armed. If we run into trouble with the Germans we intend to use our weapons. Do you have any objections?"

I told him I didn't. I wished I had my .45 — it was a good equalizer in an argument. I got up, put my flying clothes in the sack, and gave it to him.

He threw it back into the bushes where I had slept.

"Do you have any questions before we start?"

"Yeah, what's your name? Mine's Harry."

"Pete," he replied. "Do you like beer?"

"You bet!" I answered.

He picked up his bicycle. "Okay, let's get started."

We came to a small clearing and stopped for a few minutes waiting for the third man to come back. When he did, he waved for us to proceed.

Next we came to a small dirt trail on the edge of the forest. I sat on the back of Pete's bicycle and we started out. The trail widened into a small road, paved with brick cobbles. It was much easier after that. Thirty minutes later, the road came to a dead end at a main road. We turned left and traveled another mile. We stopped at a small building beside the road. They leaned their bicycles against it.

"Don't talk once we're inside," Pete said.

Inside the small beer garden several people were sitting at tables, drinking beer and talking. They paid no attention to us as we entered. The proprietor brought four glasses of delicious beer and put them on the table. I could have put away a dozen glasses just to satisfy my thirst. A few minutes later, when our beer was gone, the proprietor waved to us as we left. Outside, there were now four bicycles instead of three. We rode in pairs. Pete and I led the way, with the others fifty feet in back of us.

"We'll be going through the town of Steenwijk," Pete said. "There are a lot of German barracks in the town. There's a downed B-24 bomber by the church. It might be yours. The crew was buried in the churchyard by some of the people who live here."

"How many did they bury?" I asked.

"I don't know. If it's your plane, I'll find out for you."

It took very little effort to ride the bicycle, and we kept up a pretty good speed. The road we traveled was beautiful. In the distance I could see a church steeple. There were farms and fields, but no animals. When I asked about it, Pete told me the Germans had confiscated the livestock and sent the animals to Germany. Forests were abundant, both large and small. The land was flat with many canals and streams. No crops were growing in the fields. Most of the houses and barns had thatched roofs. Some of the houses had the barns attached to them. Everybody wore wooden shoes. Pete told me nobody wore leather shoes out in the country.

As we neared Steenwijk, trees took shape on each side of the road and soon we were riding through a tunnel formed by the trees. What a beautiful place this must be during peace time. I hoped I could come back someday to see it.

"We didn't have any problems when we came through Steenwijk a few hours ago, so don't worry about the Germans," Pete said.

As we rode along, it became evident that this was a big Nazi garrison. Their barracks were small, gray, wooden buildings set back from the road and surrounded with barbed wire. I looked at my OD socks and realized I shouldn't have worn any socks at all. I felt like I had American flags wrapped around my ankles.

"Their motor pool," Pete said, nodding in the direction of some trucks and armored vehicles behind a high barbed wire fence.

The further into Steenwijk we rode, the more German soldiers we saw — not only walking on the sides of the road but in the compounds. We pedaled down the road, through the middle of the German troops, with no problem at all. Pete nodded to several of them and they smiled, returning his friendly gestures. At first I was terrified. I did my best to shake off the inner urge to ride faster and get away from this dangerous situation. But, fortunately, because of Pete's self-assurance, I was able to contain myself. Actually, it was more like a Sunday ride in the park. Nobody paid any attention to us.

Were they really looking for an evading American airman? I learned a lesson through Pete: "It's safer to sit in the middle of the German army than be stopped by a single patrol."

We came to the wreck of the B-24 about 300 yards in back of a church. It was painted OD, and the fuselage of the Liberator was burned to the ground. The props were bent and the tail sections intact. White circles were painted on them. The plane's origin was unknown to me. There couldn't have been a lot to bury, from the looks of the airplane.

I thought of Johnny buckling on my parachute. I owed him my life and I hoped he was all right. "Wow!" I said aloud. It came out before I could even think about it. I guess I said it more to bring me back to reality than to make a remark about the burned and twisted remains of the American bomber.

Pete kept a pretty close watch on me as we passed the downed aircraft. I think he knew what was going on in my mind and was watching my reaction. We kept on pedaling.

After we went through Steenwijk the road turned in a south-easterly direction beside a canal. There were many canal boats tied to the sides. Small, picturesque drawbridges crossed the canal frequently. We passed two sets of locks. There were no towns between Steenwijk and Meppel.

The sun was almost setting when we reached the outskirts. I was tired from riding the bicycle. Our two Dutch friends passed by and led the way into town. They separated, each taking a different route. We slowed our speed inside the town. My muscles were grateful for the relief.

Meppel was a small town, much smaller than my map had led me to believe. We went over the bridge of a canal and rode toward the center of town. It was clean and almost deserted. The houses were built close together or shared a common wall. I saw a few people walking or riding their bikes in the distance. No vehicles were around, besides a parked truck and a police car coming down the street.

The officer waved to Pete. I didn't see a single German. We rode together side by side through the center of the town and perhaps five blocks past. We turned to the left on Weerdstraat, a small neighborhood street with houses lining both sides. We stopped in front of number 51 and rolled our bicycles around to the side of the house. We went back to the front. A woman opened the door and said, in very broken English, "Come in."

The foyer was small. On the left were stairs leading to a second floor. The hall to the right led to the rear of the house, where the kitchen was located. We followed the woman to the kitchen. Two young women got to their feet as we entered.

Holding the arm of the older woman who let us in, Pete said, "This is mevrouw de Groot. She owns the house. And this is Jelly, who works in an office in Meppel. And this," he said, putting his arm around her waist, "is my fiancée, Mimi de Jong." He introduced the three women with a great deal of respect. "Mimi speaks a little English and so does Jelly, at least enough so you can understand. Mevrouw de Groot can only say 'hello.' This will be your new home for the time being. Now you have met the important people, so please sit down at the table."

Mimi interrupted. "Harry, are you hungry?"

"Well," I was embarrassed.

"When was the last time you ate?"

"Yesterday noon."

"Peter, I told you to take some food with you." She looked at me. "Forgive him, sometimes he is not very thoughtful."

Mimi spoke in Dutch to the older woman. It was like pushing a button for the old lady, and Mimi went into motion. Jelly excused herself and went upstairs. I could detect a somewhat unfriendly attitude or a fear of being in the presence of an American. In no time at all, I sat down to my first Dutch meal: boiled potatoes, cabbage, bread and spread, and some hot tea. It was wonderful. I was so hungry I would have eaten anything. They watched as I put the food away.

I thanked them for the meal, then for the first time it dawned on me that I must have smelled like something out of a pig sty. I hadn't washed or shaved for four days. I hadn't even combed my hair.

"I'm sorry," I said. "I'm not too clean. It's been four days since I washed myself."

Pete laughed. "Yeah, we know, but now that you've got something on your inside, we'll get the dirt off the outside." I followed him upstairs to the toilet. There was a commode, a wash basin with cold water, and nothing else.

"The women will fix you a tub of water in the kitchen."

I went into the toilet and relieved myself. There was no soap, so I just rinsed my hands in the cold water. When I came out, Pete showed me a small front bedroom where I would sleep.

"They'll have your bath ready soon. I'll find some clean clothes for you, I won't be gone long." He went downstairs.

A few minutes later, Mimi called me. There was a wash tub in the middle of the kitchen floor half full of warm water. A bar of brown soap, two towels, and a robe were left on a chair. The woman of the house was gone, and Mimi closed the door as she left. I stripped and stood in the tub. I washed my hair, causing my scalp to bleed again, then washed the rest of my body from the top down. Once I finished, the water was filthy. I dried myself with the towels and put on the bathrobe.

When I finished, I called for Mimi. She was there in an instant. When she saw the blood on my head and face, she got some clean water from the stove and cleaned the burn, wiping it dry with another clean towel.

"How bad is the burn?" I asked her.

"It's not bad. Be careful and it will heal in a few days."

"Where shall I empty the bath water?" I asked.

58

"Don't worry about it. Peter will empty it when he gets back. Go upstairs and relax till he gets here."

He wasn't gone long. When he returned, he had a pair of pants, clean socks, a shirt, and a pair of BVDs. He also gave me a razor and used blades, toothpaste, and a new toothbrush. He called to Mimi to bring up some warm water, which she poured into the bowl in the bathroom. The blades were about as sharp as a butter knife. Pete showed me how to hone a blade in a water tumbler to put an edge on it. It took a half hour to shave the stubble, and most of that was pulled out rather than shaved off. My face burned from the ordeal. I brushed my teeth three times then put on the clothes. They were too big for me but they were clean. I felt great.

I went back down to the kitchen. Mimi poured all of us tea and had cut some bread into squares. Mimi had a long-toothed comb and combed my hair for me, showing Pete the burns. She suggested that she comb my hair for me until my burns healed.

They were curious about me as a stranger. I talked for half an hour about the United States and England.

Finally Pete said, "We have an eight o'clock curfew, you know. Everyone must be home by then. I don't have to observe it for I work for the Germans. Mimi does too." He changed the subject. "You are very fortunate to be fair-complexioned because you look very Dutch." He smiled. "What is your ancestry?"

"German, Dutch, and English," I replied. "My father was third-generation German."

"I knew you had some good Dutch blood running through your veins," he said, grinning.

He saw me looking at the decor of the kitchen. "The house is typical of most houses in Holland," he said. "This is a very safe house too. We will not expose you to the neighbors, but if anybody does come to the house unexpected, just act as if you are deaf and dumb. The Dutch word is *'doofstom.'* We've decided to keep you here until we see what is going to happen in the war. It's only a matter of time till the Allies cross the Rhine. When they make their way north, you'll be liberated."

"The most important thing for you to remember is to stay away from the windows so you won't be seen from the street!" Mimi added.

"Okay," I said as we lit a cigarette.

"You must be as Dutch as we can make you. You will dress as we do and learn some of our language. You'll have an identity card exactly like ours. A photographer will come here tomorrow and take your photograph for the card. Carry it with you at all times. There will be some other cards to prove your identity too. A different man will come to the house to measure you for clothing that will fit you. Oh yes, Harry, don't scatter your belongings around the house or even your room. Keep them together. If we move you in a hurry, nothing will be left behind to identify you. If you need something and I can provide it, I will. I see you smoke, so I'll bring cigarettes." He handed me a half-empty pack of Dutch cigarettes and a box of wooden matches. "These will carry you over till tomorrow."

Pete was in the military service when the Germans bombed Rotterdam and conquered their country. Captured, like all the military, he was taken prisoner. Two weeks later the Germans set the military prisoners free and told them to go home. There was an option to join the NSB (National Socialistische Bewegig) as a member of the Nazi party and the German army. Twenty-five thousand Dutch, thinking the German military was invincible, did join. Pete was from Rotterdam and so was Mimi. He had an official position working for the Germans. His job was to find smugglers, aliens, or unsavory individuals who would be detrimental to the good of Holland and to find people so qualified to do tasks for the Germans. Those people were exempt from working in defenses and were given special privileges by the Germans. His job called for him to know everybody. Since he was a personable and likable young man, he fit the mold very well. When he heard that a high-ranking German officer for the Reich Labor Department was coming to Meppel and needed a dependable secretary, he recommended Mimi. She came to Meppel and was put to work. She assisted Pete with his paperwork and was the personal secretary for the officer. They were trusted completely.

Neither Pete nor Mimi were German collaborators. Everybody knew it but the Germans. They were both in an excellent position to get information from the inside of the German hierarchy and pass it on to the Dutch Resistance as well as American Expeditionary Forces (AEF) headquarters in London. They both spoke excellent German with hardly a trace of accent, in addition to French and English. This was the result of their formal education.

He told me many of his friends died at the hands of the SD (Sicherheitsdienst) and the Green Police (Grune Polizei). The SD, he said, were as bad as or worse than the hated SS (Hitler's Elite Guard) and had no concern for human life. Many of the SD were Dutchmen who, by thinking they were on the winning side, became traitors to their own country. They had the power to treat their neighbors badly and were even worse than the Germans. Pete told me that these bad Dutchmen never killed their victims unless they had been tortured to death's door beforehand. The relatives who claimed the tortured broken bodies of these victims were unable to recognize what remained of them.

He told me of the food and fuel shortage in the big cities such as Rotterdam, Amsterdam, and the Hague.

"If the country isn't liberated before winter sets in," he said, "and especially if it's a long, cold winter, the people in these cities will die by the thousands of starvation and freezing. Especially the very young and the very old. The Germans have moved everything to Germany — the machinery from our factories, all our automobiles and trucks, our farm animals, and now they're taking our bicycles unless we have a special permit. The bells from our churches have been melted down, and any other metal they can use has been sent to their fatherland to make armament.

"I know you noticed the lack of men on our streets. You spent some time in the forest and know they are building a new runway. All the men working on it are forced labor and if they resist the Germans, they are either shot on the spot or sent to concentration camps and never heard from again. The Germans make it very clear to us that they will fight their own wars with their own people but the captured peoples will do the labor to help them win their war!"

I learned that many policemen were Nazi collaborators and sympathized with their captors and their cause. Pete knew who the "good" and the "bad" policemen were. Some of them were members of the Dutch Resistance and worked with policemen who were members of the dreaded SD. It was the job of the SD to try to infiltrate the Resistance. Pete had to know who was who.

"In the smaller towns and villages," he said, "especially farther north, there is a better chance for survival because the population is small and they are farming communities. Food is more plentiful, especially potatoes, turnips, cabbage, carrots, all the tubers. Meat is practically nonexistent. There is no sugar, coffee, tea, salt, pepper, and the like. The tea we drink is made from herbs and dandelions. It's a credit to the women who have concocted the brew. Somehow tobacco trickles into the country. We bag it like your American Bull Durham or Duke's Mixture. The paper to roll the cigarettes is harder to get than the tobacco. A lot of people are growing tobacco but it's really

61

strong. Ready-made cigarettes are impossible to find. I get mine from the Germans. That's what you're smoking now!"

He told me the Dutch Resistance had about 25,000 partially armed members. In recent months many canisters of weapons were dropped by the RAF and Americans. This was a risky business too. The Germans knew it was going on and were especially watchful for suspect drop zones. Sometimes they'd get a tip from an infiltrator. In these cases there were many dead patriots, and Allied weapons meant for the Dutch fell into German hands. Captured Dutchmen participating in these drops were never seen or heard from again for they were handed over to the SD.

It was hard for me to believe the gruesome facts. He told me the various methods of torture the Nazis used on their victims. I couldn't understand how a human being could bring himself to do these things — enemy or not.

Pete said he had helped between 100 and 150 American and British flyers who had been shot down in the Netherlands. He had given each of them identity papers, clothing, food, and a safe place to stay before he sent them on a newly established escape route which he referred to as the "Comet Line" (an underground railroad). This route took the airmen by bus, bicycle, train, walking, or any other form of transportation from Holland to Belgium, then to France and finally over the Pyrenees Mountains into Spain, a neutral country. There they fell into British hands and were flown from Gibraltar back to England.

Evaders never flew combat in the same theater of operations once they were returned to safety. Usually they were sent back to the United States and became instructors.

According to Pete, his success ratio was about ninety percent. The airmen who were caught were captured only because they didn't follow instructions. Those who did were free men in a very short time, anywhere from a few days to a few months. Of course, the invasion had started, so the Comet Line was no more. However, the underground took the flyers close to the Allied lines and let them wait for the Allies to overrun their positions.

It's a fact. For every flyer who made it back to Allied hands, at least one member of the underground, somewhere along the line, gave his or her life obtaining that flyer's freedom.

This man, Pieter Jan van den Hurk, was the bravest man I had ever known. During the course of our conversation he told me, "I had my pistol trained on you when we first met in the woods. My opening remark to you, 'I'll bet you've really been sweating us out, haven't you?' would only have been understood by an American. It's strictly 'Yankee slang!' No other nationality would have answered it correctly. If you would have answered it any other way or not answered, I'd have considered you were the enemy trying to infiltrate. I would have dealt with you accordingly."

"You mean you would have shot me?" I asked unbelievingly.

"Deader than hell!" He was as serious as he could be. "Harry, there's no room for mistakes in this game we play with the Nazis! I knew there was an American downed in the vicinity of Havelte. In fact, it was rumored there were two of you. When your whereabouts became definite, under the watchful eye of Karl, who saw you in your parachute, I gave orders indirectly to him how I wanted the situation handled. Though I have never met Karl, he did his job and we picked you up. Now you are reasonably safe."

I told Pete some of my experiences in the woods. He didn't know I had joined the Dutch workforce until I told him. When I told him the soldiers searched the woods for me, he didn't like it.

"Too much of a risk," he said. "I always pick up my flyers because I speak English with an American accent and I know your slang. I always screen the flyers. If I make a mistake and lose my life for it, it's my fault and I can't blame anybody else."

We talked for the better part of an hour. I yawned a couple of times and apologized for doing so. Pete led me up the stairs to my room.

"Remember the windows," he said, "and have good dreams." He shook my hand firmly. "Welcome to Holland!"

FOUR

I have never slept as soundly or felt as secure as I did that night in Meppel. The glaring sun pierced my eyes between a fold in the curtain or I would have slept longer.

Reluctantly, I looked at my watch and got up. I shaved, washed, and carefully combed my hair, but my scalp started to bleed. The house was quiet so I went downstairs only to find mevrouw de Groot waiting for me. She took me to the kitchen and I sat down at the table.

She had on an attractive blue dress and a white apron. Her deep blue eyes were her finest asset; her hair was salt-and-pepper gray. She had a constant half-smile on her face. I felt stupid for I could not understand what she said to me. She prepared my breakfast (which I was to discover was the standard first meal of the day) of bread, cheese, and a cup of tea. After I ate, I pushed my chair back to leave, but she put her hand on my shoulder.

"Harry," she said, with an impish smile on her face. She moved some dishes aside in the sideboard and retrieved a large jar of marmalade. With my knife she spread a generous portion of it on a piece of bread. She replaced the marmalade and held her finger up to her lips so I wouldn't tell her secret. After she refilled my cup with tea, she sat down and joined me.

Later, I went into the parlor and found some Dutch magazines and took a few of them upstairs. The pictures amazed me. They were all propaganda with displays of the Nazi occupation, boasting of German good deeds.

Mimi came home and called to me. I went downstairs to meet mijnheer Horlich, a man in his forties. He had piercing blue eyes, a receding hairline, and finely chiseled features on a well-defined ashen face. His black eyebrows were thick and bushy. His hands, almost effeminate, were hairless with long, endless fingers. He appeared to be frightened and had an abused look on his face, one of constant pain. I shook his hand and found it to be cold and clammy. I took care not to grip too tightly.

He set up a cherrywood tripod and attached a beautiful cherrywood box camera to it. He handed me a freshly ironed shirt, a coat, and necktie. I put them on. As I sat in front of a white sheet held up at the corners by Mimi and Jelly, the morning sunlight streamed through the kitchen window, and he took several pictures of me.

"No smiles, Harry, just somber pictures!" Mimi instructed. I stopped smiling and mijnheer Horlich got his pictures. He left hurriedly, unsatisfied with his efforts.

Later, Pete brought a short, fat man who measured me for clothes. He also left hurriedly when he was through.

"The man is a Jew and was very uncomfortable. The SD would like to get their hands on him. Before the war he owned the biggest clothing store in Rotterdam."

Pete bent over the stairs in the foyer. "I want to show you something." He lifted on the bottom step. The first five stairs were on a hinge and raised upward. Underneath it, two men could hide comfortably. He dropped the stairs back in place.

"If you ever have to hide, you know where it is!"

We ate lunch and the women left for work. Pete and I were left alone at the kitchen table. He handed me a piece of paper.

"I'd like for you to fill this out, please." The questionnaire asked for a lot of military information. We learned early in boot camp to give only our name, rank, and serial number if we were captured by the enemy. But this wasn't the enemy, so I wasn't sure how to handle it. I asked Pete why he needed it.

"The next time I'm in touch with London, I'll be able to give them more positive information about you." I looked at the paper. Perhaps it was my A-2 training that made me suspicious. I started at the top. Name, rank, serial number. That would be simple. But then other questions followed. Group and squadron? Location of airfield in

England? Type of aircraft I flew? My position on the plane? Target when shot down? How shot down (fighters, mechanical, flak, etc.)? Names of crewmen and their positions? Type and weights of bombs dropped? Injured or wounded? Family name and address in the USA? Occupation of family? Married or single? Children's names? Contacts made in the underground?

There were also some qualifying questions: What is a P-38 called? A P-47? A Mustang? An Aircobra? A Warhawk? And so on.

Perhaps when the war was over, he wanted to contact those he helped during the war. If that was the case, I would gladly give him any personal information he wanted.

He knew when and where I was shot down, my name, the kind of airplane I was flying in, and my only contact in the woods. He knew nothing more about me. I blamed my suspicions on "stinkin' thinkin' " and completed the questionnaire.

That evening the little man who measured me came back to the house with a large bag and a suitcase. Pete showed him upstairs. The man brought a suit, an extra pair of pants, three pullover shirts, two neckties and a red and black pullover sweater. The suitcase contained an overcoat and a pair of black leather oxfords. The clothes were all new. Pete nodded to him and he left.

Both pairs of pants were five inches too long, but Mimi made quick work of shortening them. By the time I went to bed all my clothes fit. Pete brought me a new razor with three new blades. They lasted for eight months. He gave me some toothpaste and another new toothbrush. Included in his gifts were six bags of tobacco with several packs of cigarette papers and half a dozen packs of German cigarettes. A week before I would have scoffed at the gifts. What a difference a day makes!

One day while Mimi and mevrouw de Groot were changing the bed linens, Mimi called to me to look out the back window of the house. On a small rise in the land was a red brick school consisting of several large buildings. The Germans had put up a ten-foot wire mesh fence and topped it off with rings of coiled barbed wire. It had been renovated for use as the headquarters and billeting area for the local German army. The troops — SS, SD, Grune Polizei, Wiermacht, and some uniformed women — were billeted there. At night, bright lights illuminated the place.

Small watchtowers were erected on the roofs of the buildings with sentries posted twenty-four hours a day. I estimated there were 300 troops living there. During the day, each of them did an hour of close-order drill. It was highly regimented, more so than their American counterparts. In my opinion, and of course I was biased, our American troops could outmarch them any time, any place, and on any given day. The Germans wore loose-fitting, baggy uniforms which looked dirty even when they were clean. Their trousers had no semblance of a crease. They wore knee-length boots which were cumbersome and dull. American soldiers are the only troops in the world who go into battle wearing fatigues (coveralls). All other armies wear uniforms in battle.

After spending an hour marching, the final five minutes were spent doing the "goose-step." It was hilarious. I couldn't see how each marcher kept from kicking the man in front of him in the butt. I watched them so much I tagged those I recognized with nicknames. My favorite was "Sergeant Major Fitzenheimer." He was tall and skinny and unlike the others. It was obvious his uniform was professionally tailored. His boots shined as if they were made of patent leather. The crease in his trousers would cut a piece of paper. His chest was adorned with several medals, ribbons, and other badges befitting the chest of a war hero or a general. It indicated he spent enough time in battle to earn him easy duty with the army of occupation. A strict taskmaster, the slightest miscue from any of his troops invited a real ass chewing and he was an expert at it. Then the offending soldier continued to do laps around the parade rounds after his counterparts were inside resting. The sergeant major stayed with his charge, counting the laps. His daily demonstrations of the goose-step were the highlight of my day. With his legs rigid, his feet extended and toes pointing outward, he'd lift his legs and feet waist-high, exactly ninety degrees from his erect stance with each step. He covered at least three and a half feet with every step. I tried it. All I got for my efforts were leg cramps.

Occasionally, women would take over the parade grounds. Pete told me they were not German girls but were Dutch. Like the bad Dutchmen who joined the Germans, these girls had joined forces with the Nazis and "serviced" their troops. He knew of no female German troops in the Netherlands.

On August 24, Pete came home with a box. Mevrouw de Groot's twelve-year-old daughter was with us for the occasion of Mimi's birthday. Once seated at the kitchen table, Pete opened the box with somewhat of a flair and produced creme-puffs, chocolate eclairs, and some real Dutch chocolate candy.

"Happy birthday, Mimi!" he shouted, laughing.

Mimi, with tears in her eyes, put her arms around him and kissed him on the mouth. It was the only time I ever saw any outward sign of affection between them. The goodies were shared equally. We ate slowly, savoring each morsel until its flavor dissipated from our tastebuds. I sang "Happy Birthday" to Mimi in English. There was lots of laughter; we all had a good time.

My education to learn some Dutch began in earnest. The first few words came easy: *mesh, vork, lapel* — knife, fork, and spoon; *dag* or *goode dag* — hello; *lucifer* — match; *Veltrushten, schlap laker* or *goode nacht* — goodnight; *radio* — radio, only with a broad "a." My first sentence was *"Tis niet donker van avond, tis moi licht"* (It's not dark this evening, it's nice and light). I picked up a few words every day.

Pete lived on the other side of Meppel but came to see Mimi and check on me almost daily. Occasionally he'd be gone for a day or sometimes two. He never offered any explanation of where he'd been. Once in a while Mimi would tell me about his activities. Mostly he was looking after the needs of other downed airmen. He was a leader of the Dutch Resistance and was very busy. I thoroughly enjoyed Mimi's company and we joked a lot. I taught her some English too. Jelly was more reserved and distant, almost afraid to be around me. If I entered the room, she'd go to her room. I liked to talk with Pete. He was intelligent and inquisitive, making our conversations interesting.

One Saturday he said, "Well, Harry, how'd you like to go to church tomorrow? You have a new suit of clothes and you could show them off to all the girls in Meppel."

"It's fine with me if you think it's safe."

"Well, not only do I think it's safe but I think it's high time. You need some fresh air. Church will be a good outing. Perhaps we can go swimming later in the day. How's that?"

Mimi awakened me in the morning. "The tub is waiting in the kitchen. Hurry so we can eat," she said.

I hurried down to the kitchen and took a quick bath. I looked in the mirror after I shaved and dressed. I was a spiffy-looking dude! My hair was neatly combed now that my scalp didn't bleed every time I combed it. I went downstairs to find everybody sitting at the kitchen table eating breakfast. We agreed we were a pretty fine-looking group. We drank a toast with our tea.

After we finished, the women cleared the table and Pete talked to me. "If we have a 'situation' remember this — the Germans can't speak Dutch any better than you. They may know more words but that's all. I know both languages sound alike to you, but they don't talk alike. Act as if you are deaf and dumb whenever I introduce you. I'm armed and so are several of my friends who are also going to church. I want you to walk about fifty meters behind us for the women's protection. I know you understand why."

Thirty minutes later we left the house and walked to church.

There were many German soldiers on the streets, all of them armed with rifles slung over their shoulders. Some of them passed by without giving us so much as a glance while others nodded in greeting. They traveled in groups of two or more. I tried to spot Pete's comrades but couldn't even find a good candidate. Many of Pete and Mimi's acquaintances exchanged nods on the way. A couple of them spoke to me and I said *"Dag,"* but kept on walking. It felt wonderful to be outside again. Pete was right, I needed the air.

At church we were warmly greeted by the minister. I merely nodded my head when Pete introduced me. We went to our seats and I spent the next hour listening to a sermon I didn't understand. I had no idea what denomination the church was. When the services were over, we went out on the sidewalk. Pete and Mimi talked with some of their friends. Mevrouw de Groot left with some women and we started to walk home.

Two German soldiers passed by Pete and Mimi. As they neared me, the shorter of the two took out a pack of cigarettes. He put his hand on my arm and stopped me, choosing his words carefully in Dutch. The only word I understood was *"lucifer."* I took out my matches, lit one, and held it to his cigarette. I looked at the soldier's face as I held the match. He was no more than twenty and had a terrible scar on his forehead. Red dots lined each side of the scar where the sutures had been recently taken out. He puffed on the cigarette until it was lit, then blew out the match. Smiling, he patted me on the back as he took a single cigarette from his package and gave it to me.

"Me danks," he said, walking away, while holding up a forefinger in a gesture of a salute. I watched the German as he turned on his heel and hurried to catch up to his friend, now some fifty feet away. I lit the cigarette and returned the matches to my pocket.

The German was polite and a handsome lad. He seemed to be carefree and out for a good time, much like an American soldier. For the first time in my life I was eye to eye with the enemy. Not once did he look back, so I continued on my way.

Pete and Mimi had stopped. She soon left him and continued walking alone as he stood in the middle of the sidewalk with his hand in his right coat pocket. When the episode was over, we all continued on our way to 51 Weerdstraat. I was proud of the way I had handled my encounter with the soldier.

Once we were safely home, Pete took me by both shoulders.

"How did you know what he wanted?"

"One of the first words Mimi taught me was *'lucifer.'* It's the only word I understood from the soldier."

"What other words did you teach Harry?" Pete asked her.

I interrupted. "I want to show you something." I took the matches from my pocket and gave them to Pete. They were American book matches which were unheard of in Europe. They advertised a good American five-cent cigar. I used them because they didn't take up as much room in my pocket as box matches did.

Pete shook his head in disbelief and put them in his pocket.

When mevrouw de Groot came home, she and Mimi reached into her magic kitchen and prepared a wonderful Sunday dinner. She brought a small portion of roast beef from her friends. Pete said grace over the food and thanked God for our good fortune.

Later in the afternoon we went swimming. We followed the same procedure as before. It was a pretty August day, and the whole world seemed at peace. There were many women and children on the streets. We rode through town, turned on a side street and then again to the outskirts of town. Finally reaching a big canal, we saw at least a hundred Dutchmen swimming. Some people were on the grassy banks of the canal as others splashed in the water. Everybody was having a good time.

We laid our bicycles on the ground and took off our clothes. Mimi had managed to dig up a pair of trunks for me. Pete, letting out a loud yell, took a long run at the water and jumped in butt first, making a tremendous splash. He didn't hit bottom so I followed suit and dived in. After the initial shock from the cold water, my body became accustomed to it.

The swimmers were of all ages. Two of the couples were at least seventy-five and were having as much fun as the youngsters. There were young people with their children, some of them only babies still in diapers. This was my first experience with Dutch immodesty, for often the men or boys got out of the water, walked a few feet from the canal, and relieved themselves. I never saw the women do it. Oh well, we swam in the water anyway.

Pete introduced me to several of his friends and I merely nodded. One of them was a sweet young thing named Sue, who was about twenty. Suddenly, I noticed Sue was swimming beside me.

"I know you are an American pilot. I heard all about you." She spoke almost flawless English.

I said nothing and swam away from her.

"The least you could do is talk to me," she said.

I gave her a deaf/mute smile and swam back toward Pete.

The girl came alongside me again and looked at me very closely before she spoke.

"You're not being very nice to me, you know."

She got out of the water and glared at me. Then she walked toward Pete and Mimi. As I approached, Pete jumped back in.

"What's the matter, Harry, got a problem?" He laughed without waiting for my reply. "Sue is the daughter of a good friend of mine. He shouldn't have told his family about you, but since he has it'll be all right to talk to her. Don't let anybody hear you speaking English, though." He winked at me.

Sue was an exceptionally beautiful girl with long blond hair, big blue eyes, perfect teeth, and a flawless complexion. She was well-endowed and proud of it. As she walked, all the men on the canal thoroughly enjoyed the display. Her brief suit exposed more than her cleavage. We swam away.

She told me she was waiting to go to college in Groningen. In spite of the German occupation, she had managed to finish high school. She wanted to be a veterinarian and was dead serious about it. She loved Americans and had met some pilots before, but only for a moment.

"Now that we have met," she proclaimed, "we can spend all kinds of time together. I live just a few blocks from mevrouw de Groot. I'll visit you. You can tell me all about America and I can learn to speak better English. Okay, Harry?" she asked.

"Okay," I replied.

"I'm not a virgin, you know," she confessed. "I was raped by two German soldiers when I was seventeen. Of course, I told my parents and was placed in the doctor's care. My father tried to find the identity of the soldiers, but when he confronted their commanding officer he was informed it was an internal affair. I have never seen them again but I have looked for them. Probably I wouldn't even be able to identify them now, it's been so long ago. Anyway, later, I met a boy about my own age in Meppel and we did it because he wanted me to. At first it wasn't any fun but after then I got so I liked it."

"You shouldn't tell me that." I couldn't believe my ears.

"I know it, but I like you and I want you to know all about me. What is the English word for it?"

"For what?" I asked.

"You know, what we did."

I stammered. "Sexual intercourse?"

"No, no, not that," she said, "I don't like those words at all. Let me see, we had it in school. Oh yes, fuck! That's the word, fuck!" she giggled. "Anyway, I like to fuck!"

"That word is vulgar!" I said. "It shouldn't be used by a nice girl like you. We say 'making love.' Do you understand?"

"All right, then, 'making love,' " she said. "Anyway, during the time we were f — er ah, making love, I missed my monthly period and stopped seeing him. I really didn't want to stop but I did. You know what that means when a girl misses her monthly period, don't you? It's frightening and scares hell out of you!"

"Well, I've never had a period," I said, laughing at her.

"Silly, of course you didn't — only girls do." She looked at me curiously for a moment then continued. "Later I met another boy but he didn't count because he was through before he even started and that spoiled it. Oh yes, I got my monthly late!"

"Why do you insist on telling me all this?" I asked.

"I already told you, I like you. That way if we decide we want to f — er, make love you'll know it's all right."

We had swum a goodly distance from the others and though we were not out of sight, there was nobody around us. The water became more shallow and we were able to stand on the bottom in water up to our necks.

"We'd better go back," I said.

"Why? There's no hurry and we can't talk in English around the others."

She brought her body close to mine and we kissed.

"There now, you can see I'm just a normal girl."

Slowly, we swam back up the canal toward the others. We held hands and sneaked underwater caresses all the way.

"I hope I see you again real soon," I said.

"Don't worry about that . . . you'll see me sooner than you think. Next time we'll make love," she said, squeezing me.

We joined Pete and Mimi, who had dressed. Sue and I got out of the water and toweled off. I put my clothes on over my wet trunks and quietly said goodbye to her.

"Don't say goodbye. We'll be together in a day or two."

Pete overheard her and smiled knowingly. He said to Sue, "You'll have to come and visit Harry when you have time."

"Thank you, Pieter, I'd like that very much."

On the way home we didn't see a German.

Later, lost in a daydream, I thought about my encounter. Sue knew a lot about me. The information had come from her father. It worried me that he would be that loose-lipped.

I was totally dependent on these people for my very existence. They seemed to enjoy doing things for me. They knew the risks but did it willingly, knowing full well the consequences if they were caught. I couldn't understand why. As for Pete and Mimi, I was grateful for all they did for me. I loved them as much as any man can love a brother and sister.

Monday, August 28, Pete brought my *persoonsbewijs* (identity card) card to me. He also gave me a *noodkaart* (food ration book) and my work card, which had been issued by the Germans. It was known as a *ken-kaarte.* Everything had been stolen from the Germans at one time or another. The documents were authentic. The regular Dutch and German stamps were affixed and countersigned with my signature and rubber-stamped in ink. My new name was Jan Veen. I memorized the other information. I was born September 19, 1916, in Olst. The ID was issued on May 12, 1944, in Langbrook, and I moved to 77 Darp Street in Meppel on May 12, 1944. I was a carpenter. I had no scars or marks. This was second-issue of my card for the words "TWEEDE EXEMPLAR" were typewritten on the face of the document. My photograph and my thumbprint were affixed, as well as my signature. There was a control number on the document too. My card number was L001472 and had been altered.

Pete stayed two days with me, waiting until very late before he went home. They were two good days. We talked about the Americans and what was going on in the United States and England. In turn, he taught me a lot about the little nation of Holland. They taught me a card game called *"Schopen."* We played often in the evenings. We enjoyed each other's company. Life couldn't have been better. I prayed it would continue.

Later that night, as I lay in my bed, I thought back to when I joined the Army Air Corps . . .

I had made buck sergeant three months after I got out of boot camp. I wanted to get on flying status, which was considered to be "hazardous duty." The fly-boys made half again as much as I. Also, I'd have a better chance for promotion.

A close friend, Sgt. Wayne Valentine, a flight engineer on a B-18, suggested I put in for a transfer to his squadron. They needed crews. So, with the help of his pilot and the squadron's adjutant, I got the transfer. The base flight surgeon gave me a two-day physical and I was placed on flying status. I spent most of my waking hours in the hangar, working on engines and doing maintenance work. I flew four hours a month to collect my flight pay, and that's all I flew.

I was stationed at March Field near Riverside, California. Most of our flights were to the Army Air Depot at McLelland Field in Sacramento to pick up or exchange parts. On occasion, Wayne and I would fly to McLelland together, especially if we were going to RON (remain overnight).

The new Boeing B-17s and Lockheed Lodestars started making an appearance at March. They all had British markings. We thought the B-17s were big until one day the new B-19 arrived at March on its maiden flight from Douglas Aircraft in Santa Monica. The cigar-chewing pilot, Major Oldham, greased the runway on its first landing. He gently taxied to the tarmac and shut it down. The plane never went into production, but so much was learned about airframe construction it became the forerunner of all the big airplanes. Each of the single tires on the main landing gear was eight feet in diameter and retracted into the wing. It was scrapped for salvage after the war.

Notice was posted that a new group was being formed to assist the Coast Guard flying coastal patrol. The new group would fly out of Mine's Field in Inglewood, California, only fifteen minutes from my mother's house. Wayne and I both stuck our names on the list and were notified the following day that we were to be transferred to Headquarters, Los Angeles Air Defense Wing, on the corner of 8th and Flower streets in downtown LA.

On Sunday morning, December 7, 1941, the Japanese bombed

Pearl Harbor. We were on patrol about twenty-five miles out at sea on our return leg from Watsonville, California. Upon landing we learned of the attack. We were at war with the Japs!

Mine's Field still exists today, only now it's called LAX (Los Angeles International Airport). The hangar we used was still in existence in 1989 on the south side of the field (an old wooden structure with a half-round roof).

Headquarters, Los Angeles Air Defense Wing, was contained in an eight-story building. (After the war it housed the Western Union.) It was a top-secret organization, manned by highly screened women volunteers. Supervisory personnel, all military people, wore civilian clothes and were called "mister." We were under threat of a court-martial if we divulged we were in the military to any of the women. Our group was attached to the Wing. When we were not flying, we pulled other duty under the supervision of Major Totten, the commanding officer and a Signal Corps West Pointer. In my mind he would have lost a popularity contest to a skunk!

The building contained members of the Signal Corps, who provided the communications; a unit of Field Artillery from Camp Hahn, who afforded security and camouflaged antiaircraft protection from the rooftop; and, of course, the Army Air Corps, whose job it was to coordinate and manage the entire operation of the Wing.

After Pearl Harbor, all military personnel were ordered to report to the Wing in full uniform. Major Totten advised us that if we wore civilian clothes again we'd be court-martialed. He appeared delighted to use any threat he could muster. The volunteers were startled to see we were servicemen, and many resigned at once. Others resigned because we were now a military target.

The Wing's main function was to keep surveillance on airplanes and watercraft in our area of responsibility in the United States. Ships and boats, particularly military ships and convoys, had to get clearance through the Wing before leaving port. We continued to maintain surveillance as long as the "bogey" was in our defense perimeter. The location of a bogey was transmitted to the Wing by telephone, radio, teletype, or from the hundreds of volunteer "spotters" located in the LA area. It was the Wing's responsibility to keep track of everything. If a bogey couldn't be identified from the ground, we would immediately scramble a squadron of pursuit planes to intercept it. When a plane flew out of our area of responsibility, the information was transferred to the next zone.

Fashioned somewhat after the Air Defense Command in England, huge maps, covering Los Angeles and the surrounding area, were transposed on thick pieces of plywood and set on a waist-high table like a giant jigsaw puzzle. The final thirty-five-by-sixty-foot map was exactly to scale. Our volunteers surrounded the map and used long-handled wooden rakes to move the markers on the map. Small toy ships or airplanes with a number-holding device designated a bogey and moved to new coordinates when they got word from the spotters or our new secret radar defense system. That way, the bogey would move across the map much the same as it did in the air or on the sea. Numbers lined the east and west coordinates marking the grid with the phonic alphabet on the north and south sides.

Overlooking the huge map was an elevated control room with eight-foot-square panes of glass across the entire front of it. Known as the "booth," it contained a maze of the newest and most sophisticated communications equipment known to the Signal Corps. It was manned by officers, of whom at least one was a full colonel — the controller. His job was to oversee the entire operation. If there had been an attack, the controller would call an intercept room in another part of the building. An officer, also a pilot, would guide the scrambled pursuit planes to the bogey. An enemy airplane never was spotted over LA, but thousands of bogeys were checked out during the war.

Though I wasn't an officer, I worked in an intercept room. It was serious work and I got good at it. Sometimes it was internal practice, but the pursuit squadrons complained they didn't get enough real practice and so we gave the pilots a chance to fly, scaring hell out of unsuspecting airline pilots whom we had designated as a bogey.

The officers and sergeants lived in the Ritz Hotel just across Eighth Street on Flower, about half a block from the Wing. The military took over about five or six floors. My room number was 1020 on the tenth floor.

After the United States declared war, all the volunteer women were given a higher security clearance. Many of them were dropped because they couldn't pass. About a month after war was declared, they put all duty pilots in the intercept rooms as part of their job. I did nothing but fly. Our schedules had been stepped up so we spent more time in the air.

One morning when I got back from a flight, my first sergeant told me to report to Major Spear. He gave the message to me privately and added seriously, "Don't tell anybody about this — that's an order."

I showered and shaved, dressed in a clean uniform, and, though I was pooped, reported to Major Spear. He was short and heavy-set with a rosy, round face and a black mustache which enveloped his upper lip. His uniform left a lot to be desired as far as neatness was concerned. He couldn't button his collar and pushed his tie up as far as it would go without choking himself. In spite of his weight he was very agile and moved quickly around the office. He was our A-2 (intelligence) officer for the Wing, but I had never seen him before.

He offered me an opportunity to work for him at the Wing, but he didn't tell me immediately what the job was. I told him I liked the job I already had. "Besides," I said, "I've grown used to getting my flight pay."

I thought no more about it until about a month later when the first sergeant told me to report back to him again.

Major Spear wasn't a stickler for military etiquette. He had me sit on the davenport as he sat in an overstuffed chair.

"How many people have you told about my offer?" he asked.

I thought before I answered. "I haven't told anybody, sir."

"I still want you to work for me," he said, touching a match to his half-smoked cigar. "If you work for me, you can remain on flying status, but on a more limited basis. You'll draw flight pay each month. How's that?"

I tried to think of a good answer. Before I could, he said, "We've got five hundred volunteers working here. All of them have to be monitored."

"You want me to spy on them?" I asked sarcastically.

"A hell of a lot better than them spying on you, Mister!" he answered angrily with a loud voice.

He was quiet for several moments as he regained his composure. He took a sip of water from the water fountain.

"Hell, son, I know how you feel. You'd not be a stool pigeon but, damn it, this operation has to be secure. This isn't for publication, but restricted information is leaking out of here by our ladies. We've got half a dozen suspects we think are sympathetic to the Axis. We caught one trying to get into our decoding room. She was working on the lock with a professional lock-pick. She thought it was the ladies room. She's still here. We watch her in and out of the building.

"And here's a surprise. We've had you under surveillance, and that's one of the reasons I want you to work for me. You could be very effective. The way you get along with the volunteers, bullshit with them, date them and so forth makes you an ideal candidate for the job. We know you like the girls and they seem to like you." He paused. "Believe me, you can do the job."

He talked to me for over an hour. He'd be my CO and I'd answer only to him. I'd be sent away to school to learn my duties. He described exactly what I'd do. At one time I almost told him my real name was Harry Arthur Dolph, Jr., but chickened out at the last minute. At his insistence I reluctantly agreed to apply for a "top secret security clearance," and I agreed to do it without being drunk or doped, knowing full well it would be the end of my military career. Major Spear was the most persuasive man I've ever met. To get the clearance meant the FBI would check me out completely. As soon as I was given a clean bill of health I'd.be sent to school. Upon my return I'd be assigned specific new duties and a new title.

I sat at the major's desk with the application for the clearance in my hand. An hour later, I gave him the completed application. *Goodbye, career,* I thought to myself.

He thanked me and told me he had "friends" who would help rush it through. "I want you with me soon as possible," he said.

After I left his office I began to tremble. Did I want to self-destruct? In my subconscious was I tired of living a lie and wanting to get this alias thing straightened out? In the back of my mind I thought maybe it would slip through and I'd get the clearance, but that was just wishful thinking. Somehow I really was glad it was coming to a head. I'd get a dishonorable discharge. Anyway, it was too late. I'd done it this time!

The next two weeks were the most miserable I ever spent in my life. I thought everybody was watching me. The only time I relaxed was when I was flying. On each flight, I fully expected the FBI to be waiting for me.

Sixteen days after I filled out the application, my first sergeant came to the hotel after I'd just returned from a flight.

"Spear wants to see you again," he said.

"Okay, thanks," I replied, knowing this was it — today my life would come to an end.

"What's going on? Are you an enemy agent or something?"

"No, I'm an all-American boy," I said. "I know somebody they're checking on. They probably want some more information."

"Oh, I knew it had to be something like that. Glad you got no problems, Sarge. Anyway, he wants to see ya."

I knocked on the door of Spear's office and went in. He was on the phone and waved me to the davenport and continued his conversation in muffled tones. His mood was serious and he was taking lots of notes. I was sure it was about me. Probably the FBI or OSS. My mind wandered. The major hung up the phone, picked up a file of papers, and with a toothy grin, shook hands with me.

"Here you are!" he said, handing the file to me.

It was more than a half-inch thick. My application was the second sheet in the file. I thumbed through it. It appeared the United States government had written to everybody in Los Angeles and other states too. The document attached to the application was stamped "TOP SE-CRET" across the top and bottom in red ink. HARRY ARTHUR CLARK, SSN 19000426, SERGEANT, ARMY AIR CORPS IS CLEARED TO HANDLE SECRET INFOR-MATION (or words to that effect).

"Jesus Christ!" I thought angrily. "Tojo and Hitler himself could both get a security clearance if this is an example of how thorough they are." I fully expected to be arrested. I was totally surprised I got the clearance, and it made me angry.

I boarded a C-47 the following morning at March Field. There were several of us on board but I believe I was the only one going to this particular school. It was an ATC flight and carried cargo as well as passengers. I went to Washington, D.C., for six weeks and trained for the job. They put me through the wringer, and I'll still respect the clearance I got and say no more about it. One of the jobs for which I was trained, because I could type, was coding and decoding messages on the cryptograph. It was and still is, I believe, one of the best kept secrets we have.

After returning to the Wing, I was briefed by Major Spear. I was not told nor did I ever ask who else worked for him. I couldn't have cared less.

My new job was public relations representative for the women volunteer workers. I had an office on the second floor. Once volunteers had been accepted for duty, I interviewed them and that became a part of their file. I briefed them about their job, their status, and the importance of keeping their work secret. After I interviewed them, they understood that any problems or complaints would be handled in my office by me. I had to interview every woman in the Wing, a chore that took well over six months. I listened to many job-oriented complaints from the ladies and did my best to resolve them, even change their job if necessary to make them more comfortable. Soon I was listening to their personal complaints.

Being a normal red-blooded boy, I dated quite a lot. On occasion, if our mutual needs required privacy, we shared my quarters at the Ritz or elsewhere. I never asked any of the women for information. Instead I listened and let them ask the questions. It was my job to be a good listener — especially to listen to questions regarding activities at the Wing. The only information I leaked out to the ladies (and I was under direct orders to do so) was that I coded and decoded most of the top secret messages, which I actually did.

Eventually I knew more about many of them than did their husbands or boyfriends or lovers. I had just finished interviewing the last of the permanent volunteers when a new volunteer by the name of Gwen Walters came to my office one morning. I briefed her, emphasizing the importance of secrecy. She was by far the most strikingly beautiful woman at the Wing. She had brown wavy hair, big brown eyes, and a fantastic figure. She was personable and friendly. She remarked that she would buy me a cup of coffee for being so helpful. Later I checked her file and found she was from LA, and had gone to UCLA but hadn't graduated. She was single and lived with her mother in Pasadena. Afterward, when we'd pass in the halls, she reminded me she still owed me a cup of coffee. All the GIs ogled her. She could have had her pick of anybody at the Wing.

One day when I got off duty, I headed for my hotel. I was hungry for I'd missed lunch. Gwen surprised me and took my arm.

"Hi there," she said, smiling.

"Oh, hi, Miss Walters," I replied. "How are things going?"

"My name is Gwen," she answered, "and things couldn't be better. How about that cup of coffee?"

"How about it?" I repeated. We went to the Ritz coffee shop and ordered coffee. We sat for an hour talking about our lives, our aims, and our desires. Finally, she looked at her watch.

"Oh, my God! I'm late for my appointment with the hairdresser." She picked up her purse. "Sorry I've got to run like this, but I have to pay for the appointment even if I don't keep it. See you tomorrow, okay?" She put a dollar on the table and left.

During the ensuing month, she was very friendly to me. She never gave another guy the time of day and I was flattered by her attention. I couldn't put my finger on her thinking.

One day I went in the teletype room just before her break.

"How about a cup of coffee?" I asked.

We went to the coffee room and sat down. I asked her to go to dinner with me after she got off work. To my utter amazement, she accepted my invitation and to my greater surprise asked me, "What took you so long to ask?"

"Well . . ." I stammered, "I didn't think you'd go."

"Why not?"

"Well, you're a damned good lookin' woman, and you could do a lot better than going out with the likes of me."

"You underestimate yourself, Harry. You could probably do a lot better than the likes of me. Don't sell yourself short. I think you're a damned attractive guy and I've been waiting a long time for you to ask me out." She looked straight into my eyes as she talked. Only when she had finished did she drop her eyes, seemingly embarrassed by speaking her mind that openly.

We met in front of the building when she got off work. I took her to a new restaurant on Flower Street. As we walked, she put her arm in mine. I felt ten feet tall!

We ate a leisurely meal, talking about all the good things in life. She was well versed on current events and could talk at length on any subject. Afterward, I walked her to her car. I opened the door and she slid in behind the wheel. As she rolled down the window to say goodnight, I stuck my head inside and kissed her on the lips. She didn't exactly return my kiss nor did she reject it either. She had a surprised look on her face as she drove off.

The following week she was quite formal with me. I supposed she acted that way because I kissed her. She cornered me on Friday.

"How about coming to my place Sunday for dinner? My mom's probably the best cook in Los Angeles."

Her invitation surprised me.

"Well," she asked again, "yes or no?"

"Of course," I stammered, "I'm just surprised."

"Why should you be?" she said, winking at me. "We're kissin' cousins, aren't we?"

"We are that!" I replied.

"Pick you up in front of your hotel at noon sharp, okay?"

It was a feast. Gwen and her mother looked a lot alike. She was widowed and very beautiful. When dinner was over, Gwen helped her clear the table and suggested we all go somewhere for an after-dinner drink. Her mother had a date later in the evening, and so she told us to go on without her.

At my suggestion, Gwen drove to the Ambassador Hotel on Wilshire. We found a comfortable booth and ordered drinks. For a change, I talked about myself: how much I loved flying, outdoor life, dancing, the work I was doing. All the time I was being careful not to divulge my real job. It was a delightful time. Gwen talked freely.

After our third drink, she said she needed some air.

"I'm getting a little woozy, I think," she said.

Outside, she locked her arm in mine and we walked down Wilshire a few blocks window shopping. Then we crossed over Wilshire and came back on the other side, until we came to the Brown Derby restaurant. The maitre d' pointed out special drawings and photographs adorning the walls of the famous restaurant. He wouldn't let me pay for our coffee because I was in uniform.

Later, we drove to Santa Monica. I parked the car under the palm trees on the cliffs overlooking the Pacific. It was dark and very balmy. The moon was shining on the water.

"Just like in the movies," she said.

It was very romantic. We started necking.

Later, when I turned the key to 1020 at the Ritz, she asked, "Does the government pay for your room here?"

It was a light question, but one that made my ears perk up. I didn't answer but kissed her instead.

She was a wonderful lover and later, as she lay in my arms, she let go with a barrage of questions I couldn't ignore. She almost ran the gamut!

What a disappointment . . .

I reported her to Major Spear the first thing in the morning after she went home. He wanted to know every question she asked. He pulled her confidential file and leafed through it.

"Her security check was excellent . . . cleared everything all right. Never been in trouble with the law or any agency. Went to UCLA, third-year law student, no degree. From a good family. Her friends seem okay and give her a clean bill of health."

"Wanna look?" he asked, offering her file to me.

"She was just too nosy," I said. "She asked me everything except how the cryptograph works." I thought a minute. "No sir, Major. There's more to this than meets the eye. I've talked to all the women in the place, but this is the first one who asked *all* the questions. She knows more than she should. I'd suggest a twenty-four-hour surveillance on her."

"Harry, I want to check some more — the FBI, OSS, you know. How about coming back after you close up shop? I might need your help, okay? Let's see, your shift is over at four, right?"

After work I returned to the major's office and knocked.

"Come in," his voice commanded.

Gwen Walters was comfortably seated on the davenport with her legs crossed, balancing a cup of coffee on her knee. She had a smile on her face. When I saw her, I turned to leave.

"Sit down, Harry," the major said.

I took a seat in a chair against the far wall.

He was reading a sheaf of papers. Finally, he looked at her.

"Are you sure?" he asked. She nodded in the affirmative.

"Harry, this is Gwen," he began, "but then you already know her, don't you? I want you to know that you got superior grades on your initial evaluation from G-2."

"Huh?" I said. "What in hell . . ." Then it hit me. I knew I'd been had. She had checked me out!

"Hold on, Harry. Let me finish!" the major said. He got to his feet. "Let me introduce you formally. This is Captain Gwen Walters, recently attached to our office by G-2 at March. She's here on·TDY [temporary duty]."

I tried to sneer at her and looked at her in disbelief.

"Why didn't you tell me . . ." I began.

Spear interrupted. "You know damned well she couldn't tell you anything any more than you could have if the situation were reversed. She followed her orders. Whatever else is involved between you two is your business. Now I know you can hold up in a stressful situation. That's my interest. Under normal circumstances, you'd never know you had been checked. Captain Walters requested . . . no, *insisted* that you be told."

"Well, I'll be damned," I said.

I really had been taken in and I resented it. Here I was, practically in love with her. I did my duty and reported her to the major, hoping against all hopes that her questions would prove to be innocent curiosity.

Spear continued. "Anyway, my boy, you got excellent marks in all categories and I'm damned proud to have you on my team."

Yeah, I thought, *I'll bet my grades were excellent in all categories.*

"Anything else, sir?" I asked. He waved his arm in a signal to dismiss me. I left the office quickly with Gwen right after me, closing the door behind her.

"Harry," she called, "wait up."

I stopped in my tracks and faced her.

"Yes, ma'am!" I replied as I would address a female officer.

"Now cut that shit out!" she said. "Do you think last night was just for kicks? What the hell do you think I do, sleep with every man I check?"

She was really angry and looked beautiful in her rage.

"Slow down," I said, "I knew I'd be checked. We learned that in school. I know too that the people who check us excel in the job. The fact that you fooled me so completely has me upset. You're very good at your job, Captain!"

"I told you to cut out that officer shit! I'm Gwen, goddamn it! I'm supposed to be good at my job, so now let's go eat because I need lots of energy. I'm going to screw your ears off tonight!"

I looked at her and was about to say something when she suddenly took my arm and steered me toward the elevator.

Gwen and I were deeply attracted to each other and through the efforts of Major Spear she continued working at the Wing undercover as a civilian volunteer. She was promoted to the rank of major shortly after that. Later she moved into the Ritz in a room adjoining mine. To my knowledge she never checked anybody else. Instead, she checked volunteers the same as I did. Eighteen months later, she was transferred to Washington, D.C., where she worked on some big stuff for the government. We wrote each other at least once a week, but usually every day.

I came back to reality. I wondered if Gwen knew I'd been shot down. The day we were shot down, I'd put her two most recent letters in my locker in the equipment shack.

On the evening of August 29, Pete came to the house and it was apparent he was upset. He spoke in Dutch to Mimi and mevrouw de Groot. This in itself was unusual. I went to my bedroom and figured if it had anything to do with me, he'd come and tell me. It was only a few minutes before he did.

He sat down on the lone chair.

"Harry, I'm afraid I have some bad news."

"I have to leave here for some reason or other," I said.

"The queen's birthday is the thirty-first of August, the day after tomorrow, and the Germans are going to have a *razzia* in Meppel. It's a national holiday and everybody will be off guard — a good situation for the Nazis to do their dirty work. I discovered this information about an hour ago."

A *razzia* was the worst thing that could happen to the community. Several German troops would converge on the city and ravage it. They would make house-to-house searches looking for anything contraband: weapons, Dutchmen between sixteen and sixty-five, Jews, food, radios, bicycles, artwork, old furniture of antique value, automobiles, motorcycles, trucks, underground publications, and especially evidence of the presence of Allied airmen. Books written in English gave cause for trouble. Pete said, "There are always people put to death during the raids. Others are sent to concentration camps in Germany and not heard from again. If an Allied airman is discovered hiding in a house, the family, men, women and children alike are lined up and unmercifully shot to death. Instant reprisal. Instant death to the inhabitants."

He continued. "We can't move you south because of the German activity in the area. Now a *razzia* is coming and, I'm sorry, Harry, but for the good of all concerned you'll have to be moved from Meppel. You might be safe in the hiding place under the stairs, but if they found you it would be a tragedy for all the women. I hope you understand why you must go." He stood up. "We will move you the first thing in the morning. That will give me the rest of the night to find a safe house for you."

He left and closed the door behind him.

"Well, now what?" I asked, but no answers came. There was a soft knock on the door. It was Mimi.

"May I come in please?" she asked.

"Of course," I said, sitting up on the side of the bed.

"Mevrouw de Groot and I both want you to know, Harry, we hate to see you go. You are welcome to stay under normal circumstances. Jelly, mevrouw de Groot, and I like to have you here with us. But a *razzia* . . ." She made a face and shrugged her shoulders.

"You have no idea what it's like. Afterwards, when the problems have been put out of our minds, we can bring you back."

"Thanks, Mimi," I said. "I want you to know how much I appreciate what you have done for me. When this damned war is over we can all get together again and really get to know each other."

She bent over and kissed me on the cheek. There were tears in her eyes. "I hope you get back to America all right," she said as she went out the door. "Oh yes, I almost forgot," she said, "Sue wanted to come see you. She was coming to see you on the queen's birthday. Is there anything you want me to tell her?"

"Yeah, tell her I loved swimming with her."

Later, I got up from the bed and undressed. The room was in total darkness. I pulled the shade back from the window and looked out on the street below. It was just as dark outside and I could see nothing. I went to bed and closed my eyes.

Pete came in very early the next morning. I lit a candle and went to the bathroom to shave, dress, and comb my hair. My burns had long since healed. I got my belongings and put them in the suitcase. After I checked the room carefully, I took the suitcase down to the foyer and walked into the kitchen. Pete was sitting at the table talking to Mimi. I joined them.

"Did you find a place for me to stay?" I asked cheerfully.

Pete put his arm around my shoulder. "A policeman is going to pick us up. He will drive us a short distance to the north."

"Good," I said. I smiled at him even though I wanted to cry. "I guess I won't have to ride a bicycle this time, huh?"

"No, we are taking you about twenty kilometers north of here to a town called Diever. It's just north of where you were shot down. The place you are going to stay is in the forest. This is an extremely safe place and has been used by the underground for several years. It's a hole in the ground. It's built among the sand dunes and is made to look like a sand dune. I understand you can stand right beside the place and never know it's there, it's such a masterful job of camouflage. There are between eight and ten men living there now. I'll bring another American airman to stay with you in a couple of weeks."

Mevrouw de Groot interrupted Pete and put breakfast on the table. I felt like a condemned man being served his last meal.

Mevrouw de Groot bent over and kissed me on the cheek then shook hands. She left the kitchen hurriedly, crying.

Pete and Mimi were talking in Dutch. From what I could gather, she didn't like the idea of my going back into the forest to live in the ground. She never challenged Pete, but I was sure she was upset and speaking her mind.

I hated to leave Meppel. I had a wonderful time there and was treated royally by everybody. I would have liked to see Sue again for obvious reasons.

Shortly, there was a knock at the door. Pete welcomed a uniformed policeman. He was a very handsome man and made himself at home in the kitchen helping himself to a cup of tea. He was armed with a holstered pistol on his belt.

"Harry, this is Temmingh. He's a good friend but he doesn't understand English. We had better get going," Pete said.

I kissed Mimi on the cheek.

Temmingh went out first. It was still dark. He turned and nodded. I got in the back seat with my suitcase. Pete got in the passenger seat as the policeman started the car.

As we started down the street, I looked out the back window. There was the dim outline of three figures standing in my upstairs bedroom window, waving. I waved back, then turned around to face the road in front.

God bless all of them! I thought.

FIVE

M y mind went back to Sue and our brief encounter as we drove past the canal where she and I had gone swimming. The countryside was beautiful in the early morning mist. We drove north, parallel to the canal on the same two-lane brick road which we had traversed coming to Meppel. We passed a German patrol, pushing their bicycles. There were several barges docked on the sides of the canal but no activity on them.

Ten miles north of Meppel, the car started to lose power. Temmingh pulled over to the side of the road. Since very little gasoline was available to the civilian population, a charcoal-burning unit was bolted to the front of the vehicle. It developed methane gases which were extracted from the charcoal and fed into the cylinders through the carburetor-like device as if it were gasoline. When the engine started to run rough or lose power, an external crank was turned to stir the charcoal and get the gases flowing again. Temmingh inserted the crank and turned it briskly. The engine smoothed out. We continued on our way.

Close to Havelte, we encountered many Luftwaffe troops in groups of two or three on the shoulder of the road pushing their bicycles. Occasionally, they would wave at Temmingh and he would return their greetings enthusiastically. The morning was bright and sunny. Everything was lush and green.

"Look in the air off to the right," Pete said.

An ME-109 was coming into the airfield at Havelte, the hated crosses emblazoned on the wings and fuselage. It roared over the car about 200 feet high. Karl would be coming to work in a few minutes. It was almost 7:00 A.M.

Temmingh turned sharply to the left on a dirt road. There was a sign which read "DIEVER 2KM" with an arrow. To the northwest was a huge forest. As we entered the small village, I noted the population couldn't be more than 500 or so.

It was a rural town, for the townspeople — without exception — wore wooden shoes. The village was quaint and rustic. The only man I saw was about seventy. Several villagers waved at Temmingh. We turned right into a smaller street, went two blocks, and drove into the driveway of a small, red brick cottage. He parked the car in back. We followed the policeman into the house, where his wife greeted us warmly.

Pete introduced her. "This is Fenna, Temmingh's wife," he said, "and this is Jan Veen, an American pilot."

Fenna was a strikingly pretty woman. She was twenty-three, very robust, and spoke no English. She had blond hair, blue eyes, and her flowered dress was freshly ironed. Her hands were rough from hard work. I liked her eyes and her obvious good manners.

She seated us at the kitchen table, served bread and cheese, and poured tea into antique tea cups. She was most gracious. Pete and the policeman got up from the table.

"Well, Harry, it's time for us to say goodbye," Pete said. "Temmingh will take me back to Meppel and finish his day's work. I have much to do to prepare for the *razzia* tomorrow. When he returns from work tonight, he will take you to the forest. In the meantime, mevrouw Temmingh will take care of you." He looked at her and smiled. "I'll see you real soon," he whispered in my ear as he embraced me, patting my back. We shook hands. "Take good care of yourself," he said. It was the last time I ever saw him.

Temmingh returned late that evening. He parked the car in back and came in with a broad smile on his face. He and his wife talked happily together. I wondered when we were going to leave for the woods. An hour later Fenna, carrying a solitary candle, motioned for me to follow her. We went to a spare bedroom in the back of the house. She pulled the covers down on the bed, indicating I was going to spend the night there. Smiling, she said, *"goode nacht,"* and closed the door. I

89

blew out the candle, undressed, and crawled into the feather tick bed. It was more like floating on a cloud than lying in bed.

Despite my comfort, I slept a troubled sleep and had nightmares throughout the night. Perhaps it was the lack of communication with my mentors. I was so completely unaccustomed to their ways and was more uncomfortable than when I had left the woods two weeks before. Perhaps I distrusted my situation. I considered crawling out a window and going on my own. I kept waking up in a cold sweat from my lousy dreams. Finally, I rolled over and fell into a deep sleep.

I was awakened by Temmingh shaking my shoulder. He had a re-assuring smile on his face, but when he left the room my heart was pounding. I went to the toilet, shaved, and dressed. I took my suitcase to the kitchen and sat at the table as Fenna ladled steaming oatmeal into a bowl and placed a small glass of milk on the table along with the usual fare. Even without sugar, the porridge was delicious. After breakfast Temmingh said a prayer, got up from the table, then mo-tioned for me to follow him.

We picked up some boxes of food and carried them to the car. It took a long time to start the engine. When it did, Fenna took my hand and shook it, saying, "*Vaarwel,* Jan Veen."

We backed down the driveway into the street. A mile west of the village, he turned onto a small one-lane road that led into the forest. A mile into the woods, he pulled over and parked. I got out of the car into what proved to be a carbon copy of the woods I stayed in near Havelte. The thought of it sickened me, for this was going to be my home for only God knew how long! The pines were larger and more dense. The dunes were a little bigger, but it was still the same sand and filled with the same pine needles. Inwardly, I was crying my heart out.

Temmingh gave my suitcase to me and placed a box of food on top. He took the other two boxes and led the way. I stayed in his path as we walked perhaps a quarter of a mile deeper into the forest. Finally, we stopped and put the boxes down.

I lay my suitcase on end and sat down on it. The policeman sat on the ground cross-legged. Silently, we rolled cigarettes and touched a match to them. Conversation was useless.

"Hello, American pilot!"

The voice came from in back of me and I actually wet my pants! I spun around and there, less than ten feet away, framed in a three-by-four-foot hole in the side of a sand dune, was a boy of sixteen or seventeen, grinning from ear to ear.

"I'm Franz! Welcome to the Wig-Wam!" he said in English.

Still very much frightened from the unanticipated greeting, I couldn't believe I was so close to my new home. My heart was pumping so fast I was fearful it would jump out of my chest. Though I regained my composure, it pissed me off when the boy continued to laugh. When he saw my displeasure, he stopped.

"I'm sorry," he said, "I thought Temmingh told you where you were." His accent was thick and guttural. Temmingh continued to laugh and said something to Franz in Dutch and they both laughed again. Franz was about my height but a little heavier. He had a round face, straight brown hair, and sparkling deep blue eyes. He wore wooden shoes. He took my suitcase and box of food and carried them into the entrance.

"Come on in," he invited. "What is your name?"

"Jan Veen," I said, deciding to use my Dutch alias.

The Wig-Wam had three different areas. The main room was fifteen by twelve feet. The floor was dirt but the ceiling and walls were reinforced with logs six to eight inches in diameter and set very close together. They supported the roof and were sunk in to the floor around the sides. The ceiling was seven feet high throughout the entire structure. Shelves were attached to the walls and held books, memorabilia, playing cards, shoeboxes, and magazines. Ventilation came through a vent in the center of the ceiling. The table in the middle of the room had a moveable bench on each side. Personal effects were hung from pegs on the walls.

To the left of the entry was a smaller room, perhaps four by eight feet, containing a larder and a small cooking stove. There was some firewood stored along the wall. A stovepipe chimney was set into the wall. If the stove was not in use, the stovepipe was retracted, unseen from the outside.

To the right of the main room were the sleeping facilities. It was a "stepped-up" affair. The room itself was some ten by fifteen feet with an emergency exit at the far end. The men slept on the ledge, side by side, allowing little more than two feet per man if everybody stayed overnight. Occasionally, the men placed their lives in jeopardy and stayed with their families or were away for extended periods doing work for the underground.

Franz said, "Make yourself at home. I am alone for now but seven others live here too. You and I will make nine. Everybody is doing errands but we will all be here by nightfall."

Temmingh brought in the other boxes of food and laid them on the table. He shook hands and left, waving goodbye. Franz and I went outside and Franz closed the door behind us, then filled the seams with sand. We watched Temmingh disappear in the trees.

Franz told me he learned what English he knew in the public schools and from an English woman who lived in Diever.

Outside, I looked at this masterpiece of camouflage. It was just another sand dune. The sand floor of the forest was dimpled with natural marks in the sand, so footprints didn't show. I walked around the place. Nothing hinted of its existence. The roof was solid enough to walk on and the vent well-camouflaged.

"Don't leave cigarette butts, paper, or any other materials laying around. What one of us does to jeopardize our safety will risk the lives of us all," Franz instructed.

We went 200 meters from the place, sat in the sand, and I rolled a cigarette.

Well, I thought, *I'm back in the woods, no better off than the first day I was shot down. From the lap of luxury in Meppel to this again.* I felt alone, rejected, and abandoned. I would miss Pete and Mimi. I wondered how Johnny was doing.

"I understand another American pilot is coming and that will make ten of us," Franz said. "That is the most who can live here. The three Egginh brothers have a farm close by. Every day they do their chores and sleep here unless there is danger from the Germans. They also carry water to us. A Jewish doctor built the Wig-Wam from materials gathered in other parts of the woods. The Nazis want to get their hands on him but they never will. He stays here every night. My father stays here all the time. He seldom leaves. Today he is home with my mother and two sisters. He will return by six this evening.

"Two of the men have escaped from forced labor. They do dirty work for the Resistance and are away most of the time. I have to hide because I am sixteen and supposed to work in the defenses. The end of the war is not far off. When we were asked by the underground to keep you with us, we took a vote. You are very dangerous to have here, you know. If the Germans find you, we will all be shot with no questions asked! The vote was eight to zero. We know many Allied airmen have lost their lives fighting for our liberation. Now, in a small way, we feel honored to help you. We will do all we can to keep you safe. We all get along very well together. Occasionally there is a disagreement. We are under a lot of stress. But there has never been a friendship lost in the Wig-Wam. Several men who didn't fit the mold were asked to leave. I am the only one who speaks English. If there is anything you want to know, I'll help you if I can. I will teach you to speak Dutch so you can understand us, okay?"

"Okay," I said and shook his hand.

"Franz," I started. "Er, ah, where do you go when you have to go to the toilet?"

"Come with me," he said, laughing. We went back in the Wig-Wam. There he retrieved a long-handled shovel and an old, half-used magazine. We walked about 500 feet into the woods.

"Dig your own hole and fill it back up."

Politely, he walked about a hundred feet back toward the Wig-Wam and leaned against a tree with his back to me.

Afterwards he said, "It's important to go at least two hundred meters away, even if you only have to pee, for when the sun shines all day long an odor comes from it. A good rain neutralizes everything, but then our footprints show on the wet sand. We know the Germans have heard about the Wig-Wam. If they searched the woods and caught scent of the urine, they would certainly look further. The hiding place is four years old and there have always been people here. We hope it will be safe till the end of the war."

We walked back toward the Wig-Wam. A few minutes later he laughed. "We passed the place two hundred meters back. You will need a guide whenever you go out until you get used to the surroundings."

I was still looking for the entrance when he reached down in the sand and opened the door.

"Do you know how to play *Schopen?*" he asked.

We played cards until the Egginh brothers returned. They joined us in our card game. Two more men arrived. Their names were Gunninh and Voss, and they were loners. They didn't speak and, after seeing us, went back outside again.

Shortly after they left, a middle-aged man came in. He was short with a thin, gaunt face and deep-set blue eyes.

"Harry!" he said, smiling at me.

His smile was contagious. I grinned at him. "Who are you?"

"This is my father," Franz interrupted. "He doesn't speak a word of English. He only learned your name yesterday."

93

"Tell him for me that he speaks my name like an American."

Translating for his father, I discovered he was "Oom Joop" (Uncle Joe), a friend of Temmingh. He was a *schilder* (painter) by trade and excelled in his profession. After the war he would tell me his real name. He wanted me to know I was welcome at the Wig-Wam and, further, that a few of the men living there were Jews and wanted by the German SS more than I was. I was not to think I was placing anybody in jeopardy, for that was the case long before my arrival. Nobody kept weapons in the Wig-Wam.

Oom Joop was a gem! He had a Kris-Kringle kind of twinkle in his eyes and a constant smile on his face. He was the authority in the Wig-Wam. When a question arose, it was Oom Joop who gave the answer and the others heeded his decisions. I was glad he seemed to take a liking to me.

The first evening I was there, Dolf started a small fire in the stove, boiled cabbages and potatoes, and made a huge pot of tea. Then he doused the fire. Franz set the table with a clean, ironed tablecloth, silverware, and cups. When the food was placed on the table, we bowed our heads as Dolf read a verse from the Bible. The candle-lit atmosphere lent an aura of godliness during the meal. The food was very good. When supper was over, he read another verse from the Good Book and the table was cleared. Dolf did the dishes too.

We went outside, each of us pairing off with another, going in different directions. Franz, Oom Joop, and I went into the forest about 300 yards and found a good place to sit. I rolled a cigarette and Oom Joop filled his pipe. He held a match for me, then held it to his pipe until it had a cherry-red glow coming from within the bowl. He took a long draw and inhaled it deeply, letting the smoke filter out through his nostrils. Franz stayed upwind from us. He hated the smell of tobacco. We sat a long time, Franz translating, until well after dark.

When we approached the Wig-Wam it was pitch dark. Looking up through the pines, a few stars were visible, but there were many dark clouds rolling in from the west. The outline of the dunes was visible from the moonlight reflecting off the clouds.

Franz reached down into the sand and opened the door, an impossible task to me. No light escaped from the interior, even though many candles were burning. Some of the men were reading, and others had gone to bed. The doctor and Dolf played cards.

"*Slaap lekker, jongens* (Sleep well, youngsters)," said Oom Joop before going to bed.

"Goodnight," I said, understanding him.

Soon Franz and I joined the others in the sleeping room. It was close quarters. I slept comfortably on the straw mattress.

Life in the Wig-Wam became routine. I asked Oom Joop for a pencil and paper, thinking it would be a good idea to keep a log of the events in my life since August 15. He wouldn't let me keep the writing implements in the Wig-Wam for obvious reasons. He brought a gallon can with a top which fit well enough to render it watertight. When I finished writing, I put the paper and pencil in the can and Oom Joop buried it somewhere in the woods.

I asked Temmingh about the *razzia* in Meppel. He avoided the question, so I stopped asking him about it. When I asked about Pete and Mimi, he always said, "They send their best regards."

Franz, translating Temmingh, told me later that neither he nor his father ever heard of a *razzia* in Meppel. It aroused his curiosity, so Oom Joop decided to check into it.

My Dutch improved daily. Franz was a good teacher. I could converse a little with everybody if they kept their grammar on a simple level.

I liked to be alone once in a while. After I was able to find my bearings back to the Wig-Wam, I'd wander off and sit against a tree or lay down in the forest and let my mind wander. About two weeks after arriving at the Wig-Wam, I found a cozy place in the woods I liked. It was well-protected on all sides by dunes and I was comfortable when I went there. On this day, I lay down and thought about Los Angeles . . .

Los Angeles and Gwen. After she had been in Washington, D.C., for several months, I saw her only once. We wrote regularly. I had a hard time finding a new life for myself; I was so accustomed to her and her ways.

One night a group of us went to Pan Pacific Auditorium to iceskate. I was a pretty good skater, having come from the cold country. A cute little gal cut in front of me and, being a smart-ass, I skated as fast as I could. But instead of cutting in front of her, as I intended to do, I hit her pretty hard and we both went down, skidding across the ice until we hit the boards on the side. She gave me the kind of a look I had coming to me. I apologized but she wouldn't accept it. We were married six weeks later in Las Vegas.

We rented a small furnished apartment on Sunset Boulevard just west of Figueroa, within walking distance of the Wing. The marriage was a great success for eight months. I used to tease her, saying she married me to get even for slamming her into the boards the night we met. She worked for North American Aviation, earning five times more than I did.

There were some reports of an unidentified trio of parachutists landing on the ridge between Los Angeles and Bakersfield. I drove Major Spear to the area in an official car. An AT-11 observation plane flew us over the area for about three hours at different altitudes, but we could find no evidence of the landing. We drove back to Los Angeles. I was particularly anxious to get home because my wife, who was a good cook, promised to cook my favorite meal of chuck roast and all the trimmings for dinner. When I got to the apartment, I knocked on the door. I had forgotten my key.

She opened the door. A navy chief was sitting on the sofa. She introduced him as a friend from her hometown in Nebraska. I shook hands with him and sat down to be sociable. My wife sat next to the chief and their conversation continued for at least a half hour about the "good old days in Nebraska." They completely ignored me, so I went into the kitchenette. There I saw several dirty plates in the kitchen sink and the bone from the roast. My appetite for that meal was whetted to the point where I thought I was starving. Now it was a cinch it was in the chief's belly.

"Is there any roast left?" I inquired calmly when I went back into the living room.

"I think there might be enough to make a sandwich in the refrigerator," she answered but made no effort to make it for me.

I got to my feet and shook hands with the navy. "I'm glad I met you," I said, "and I hope you enjoyed the meal!"

I closed the door behind me, went across Sunset to a bar, and proceeded to get plastered. It was easy to do on my empty stomach, especially since I wasn't much of a drinker. The bartender steered me home at 2:00 in the morning. When I staggered in the door, the navy was gone and she was in bed.

Something went out of our marriage after that. Perhaps it was because of my immaturity or possibly jealousy, I don't know. But the fact that I was left out of the conversation and the fact that the good-lookin' chief ate my dinner didn't help matters much either. She didn't speak to me for three days and when she did, she never talked about the incident. Later, I discovered he really was from her hometown and at one time they had dated.

So, in June of 1943, I got tired of the grind at the Wing and decided I wanted to fly in the fighting war. I applied for Officer's Candidate School, got all my recommendations, and sent them in. While I was waiting for orders to see if I was accepted or not, I requested a transfer to Las Vegas Aerial Gunnery School, located about ten miles north of Las Vegas (now Nellis Air Force Base). The day I left, Major Spear was furious at me for transferring. But there was nothing he could do about it, I thought.

My wife stayed in Los Angeles and continued with her job at North American Aviation. She came to Las Vegas to see me once. Six weeks later I earned my Gunner's Wings and was transferred to Lowery Field near Denver, Colorado. There I went to school and became an armorer. My wife quit her job and joined me. She stayed with me eight weeks until I graduated with honors and was sent to Valley Forge, Pennsylvania, an aviation cadet for officer training. I stayed there four weeks then went to Yale University in New Haven, Connecticut, for the final phase. My wife joined me in New Haven.

Discipline was strict and the hazing for the first two weeks was rough. I wanted to graduate and was the best cadet in the corps. We had many celebrities at Yale. Maj. Glenn Miller and his orchestra were stationed there and played during our meals, whenever we marched, and at retreat in the evening. Cpl. Tony Martin was our singing instructor, and Cpl. Broderick Crawford was a drill instructor for the enlisted personnel. They were very close friends.

When we finished our training and were ready to graduate, I was told to report to the provost marshal's office. He was a chicken colonel who told me I would not be graduating with the rest of my class because of an investigation being conducted by A-2 at Los Angeles Air Defense Wing. Upon completion of the investigation, I would either be given my commission or my sergeant stripes and be reassigned. Of course, I wanted to know why I was being investigated. All he would offer was that my clearance for classified information had been suspended and all officer candidates had to have a top secret security clearance.

"But, sir, I have a top secret security clearance," I said. "I've had it for two years, working with A-2 in Los Angeles as well as being the Wing cryptographer."

"It's up to the Wing in Los Angeles. That's all, Mister."

I graduated with my class but wasn't commissioned. I pinned Bill Alexander's bars on his shoulders. He was from Topeka. The ceremony was brief and solemn, and I was almost a broken man because I wasn't an officer.

My new duties at Yale, pending the outcome of the investigation, were instructing cadets in two classes. Daily, I made the trip to the provost marshal's office to see if there was any change in my status. They wouldn't allow me to correspond or talk to Major Spear per his request. The major was having the last word and my hands were tied. I instructed for a month, then went to the provost marshal and requested to be reassigned. Two days later my orders came. I reported to Salt Lake City at the 18th Replacement Wing for crew assignment. My pregnant wife went home to Nebraska.

Our crew was put together and sent by train to Gowen Field at Boise, Idaho. The crew was so compatible, though we hadn't met before, we were sure we had been hand-picked. Our CO at Gowen was Col. John (Killer) Kane of the Fifteenth Air Force. He had led the forty-eight planes of the 98th Pyramiders Group on the first Ploesti Oil Field raid in Rumania. He earned the Congressional Medal of Honor for his heroism in this action. In appearance, he was a gruff officer who barked instead of talked. As far as I was concerned, the sky blue star-spangled ribbon, which he proudly wore over his heart, entitled him to act or talk any goddamned way he wanted.

Jack Archer, our pilot, had only transition training in a B-24 bomber (checked out for landings and takeoffs only). He had almost no stick time in the pilot's seat and had never flown without an instructor pilot sitting in the right seat. We flew a lot of night cross-country flights as well as our normal daytime missions. Doyle Stegall, our bombardier, got a lot of practice with the Norden bombsight dropping hundred-pound practice bombs, one at a time, from 25,000 feet, on a huge round, lighted target painted on the desert floor. We practiced bail-out drills, ditching procedure, and injured airman procedure. We were on the honor system and voluntarily drilled ourselves until we had them down pat. We flew so many mock cross-country missions, I can't remember all of them. I know we wiped out Salt Lake, Seattle, Spokane, Vancouver, Cheyenne, Portland, and Olympia, Washington! We worked hard at our jobs, preparing ourselves as a team. Once we finished transition training, we were as ready as any crew in the Army Air Force.

Boise, Idaho, was a city that opened its heart to the airmen from both Gowen Field and Mountain Home Air Base. There was a good-natured rivalry between the two airbases but seldom any outright hostility. Our hangout was the Music Box Lounge.

One of the crews with whom we shared our barracks were killed on a night flight. They perished in a fiery crash when they hit a mountain. They never had a chance to get out of the B-24 and never knew what hit them. Knowing them as well as we did, it was a terrible blow. The night before the bodies were shipped to their various homes for burial, a memorial service was held at a church in Boise. The ten flag-draped coffins were lined up, side by side, making instant believers of all of us.

When the services were over, we went to the Music Box and chug-a-lugged ourselves into oblivion on Coors beer and Seagram's Five Crown. We weren't the only crew to do so. It got awful drunk out there that night. The stag ladies who were present at the Music Box stayed stag. On this night, the men from Gowen Field ignored anything in a skirt. Long after the incident, the young ladies of Boise learned that airmen were drawn into mourning when they lost some of their own. But for the Grace of God . . .

On April 10, 1944, we flew our final checks and were sent by rail to Topeka, Kansas, for assignment and to find out if we were going to the Pacific or the European Theater of Operations. We were assigned a brand new B-24H Liberator. We were also given as many passes as we wanted and spent all our time off in Topeka.

The waiting was rough. None of us wanted to go to the Pacific. We wanted to go to England, where there was some real action and living conditions were better. When we completed twenty-five missions, we could come back to the States. We had positive thoughts about our chances in combat. Nobody doubted we would survive our tour of duty. We thought we spent so much extra time training that we were really ready, much more so than other crews, and could live through anything the Germans threw at us.

We were elated when the crew assignments were posted. We were assigned to the 466th Bomb Group in Attlebridge, England. The Eighth Air Force! The ETO! The plum had been picked!

Topeka was a hell of a town. I do believe there was something in the water to make the ladies so unselfishly patriotic! They gave of themselves to the absolute fullest. Our lives were made that much better during our final days in the States.

We usually hung around the White City Ballroom, located on a golf course between the airbase and Topeka. On one particular night, a chicken colonel accompanied by officers of lesser rank was drinking and ogling the girls. The colonel was a thin man, small of stature, bald-headed, and at least sixty years old.

One of the local girls, who hung around with McCarty, had enormous breasts and huge brown eyes. Her name was Jerri. She had joined us late. The crew was feeling pretty good from sipping Coors. Somebody dared Jerri to put the make on the old colonel. She was not one to turn down a dare, so she asked the old boy to dance. He got to his feet as quickly as age and booze would allow, then proceeded to pat every part of her anatomy as he continually excused himself for stepping on her feet. Watching the amorous old man constantly patting Jerri's behind started the crew laughing, much to the chagrin of the officers at his table.

Finally, Jerri came back to the table and picked up her purse and glass of Coors. She gave us a wink and with a smile on her face proclaimed, "See ya later, fellas. I'm gonna screw the old boy's ears off!" She marched out the door with him, arm in arm, both of them teetering.

As soon as they left, Johnny, Bob Lehman, Tommy Bell, and I followed. We fully expected them to get a cab for a motel. Instead, they staggered across the golf course and disappeared over a small rise near the eighteenth green. Carefully, we crawled up to the top of the rise just in time to see her taking off her panties. The windows from the brightly lit ballroom engulfed the area with light. The old boy mounted her quickly. She pushed her legs straight up in the air then wrapped them around his rump. The activity continued only for a few moments, during which time she had to help him considerably because he kept falling off. Finally, she started to moan and then hollered and let out a hell of a scream as they ended the session. From her gyrations, she acted like he was the greatest she ever had. During the entire time, the old man hung on for dear life. When they were through, the colonel just kind of slid off and rolled over on his back, his manly pride quickly shriveled until it faded away into nothingness. With her help and the colonel mustering all his remaining strength, he got to his feet and pulled up his underwear and pants.

The colonel was straightening his tie as they walked through the door of the White City Ballroom. He had a silly grin on his face, not knowing that his fly was still unzipped and his shirttail was hanging through it.

We were back at our table when they returned. Jerri saw him to his table then joined us.

"Well, did you get the job done?" I asked her.

"You know damned well I did. The old boy was pretty good!"

We roared with laughter.

"We watched from the hill near the green," Bob said.

"I know it," she grinned, "that's why I put on a good show."

We all chipped in and raised a little over twenty bucks then gave it to her. She picked up the money and looked at it.

"Waitress," she yelled, "I want a round of drinks for these two tables." She looked at us. "This ain't whore money is it?"

"No, it's a tip for some damned good entertainment!" someone said.

Our new B-24 had only eleven hours on the airframe. As a crew, we flew it around Topeka, got most of the kinks out of it, then took a couple of cross-countries. We added twenty-five new hours on the airframe before Jack said it was ready. The ground crew put two huge neoprene fuel cells in the bomb bays. They held an additional 800 gallons of 100-octane gasoline. They also ran fuel transfer lines so we could transfer into the main system. Willie and I spent a day learning how to operate the fuel transfer system since Bart Philo was ill. When we were ready for takeoff, we had a 4,000-mile range plus reserve for our flight. It was a comfortable margin.

On April 20, 1944, we took off in our new airplane. We had our personal gear stowed next to the fuel cells in the bomb bays. Our destination was Bangor, Maine. The weather was CAVU (ceiling and visibility unlimited). We took off from Topeka with a VFR (visual flight rules) clearance and flew straight to Terre Haute, Indiana, where we buzzed Don McCarty's house. His family came out in the street and waved. Then we flew to Cleveland, Ohio, Jack's hometown. He buzzed — and I do mean buzzed — his old high school. So many panes of glass were broken in the windows, they evacuated the school! Somewhere among the evacuated students, standing in the middle of the football field, was Jack's proud brother. The kids were waving at us, for they knew who was flying the Liberator.

When Jack put the plane down on the deck to buzz, Tommy aggravated the assault by putting the props in high pitch. The vibration they set up broke several windows in business establishments and homes too. Jack then turned his attention to his parents' house and buzzed it. His wife, baby, and parents were in the front yard. The neighbors had been forewarned he was coming. We made three separate passes at the house. He decided he'd better clear out of Cleveland before somebody got our numbers. If we had to pay for all the glass and damage, we would be paying until we were old and gray.

Later, in England, the FAA (Federal Aeronautics Administration) came to our base and questioned the entire crew about the incident. We played stupid — just about as stupid as it was to question us in the first place. Later, the city fathers sent Jack an official letter of protest signed by the mayor. Jack would, according to the mayor, have to answer the charges and pay for the damages.

We landed at Bangor, Maine, just before dusk. Early the next morning we took off and landed at Goose Bay, Labrador, during a severe thunderstorm. The ground crew towed our plane to a hangar, where the fuel cells were rechecked. Later, on the ramp, they were filled with hundred-octane gasoline. Our main tanks were topped off too. The B-24 was ready to cross the Atlantic.

The airfield was shared jointly by American and Canadian forces. The Canadian airmen were a great bunch of guys who wouldn't let us spend a nickel for beer. Instead, they dug into their own pockets for the refreshments. There was no personnel separation between the two nations on the field, and everybody comingled as comrades.

The following afternoon, after a long briefing on ditching procedure, survival in a raft, and overseas flight procedure, we prepared the plane for takeoff to Iceland, our longest leg of the flight and all over water. The weather was perfect for celestial navigation. After Willie and I checked the fuel cells to make sure they would be emptied first, the crew boarded the Liberator and we took off for Reykjavik, Iceland, nonstop. It was a night flight and turned dark shortly after takeoff. After his first fix with the sextant, Norm corrected our heading by a mere five degrees. Another half hour passed and he corrected two degrees. We held the course for two hours before he corrected again, following the great circle route. He gave new headings every thirty minutes. It was a moonless night and pitch black. We couldn't see the water, the ground, or anything in the air. Finally, it dawned on me: "That's the North Atlantic down there!"

About halfway across, Jack picked up the homing beacon from Reykjavik. Instead of telling Norm, he let him continue navigating the course across the Atlantic. Jack stuck to every heading he gave him. They complied with the homing beacon all the way! It proved one thing: Our navigator knew his job! We were never off course. After that, the crew had a lot more respect and confidence in him. We were in the air about ten hours.

Upon landing, the Consolidated factory representatives removed the fuel cells and replaced the fuel lines to their normal status. I was surprised they removed the cells, but their representatives told us the next leg of our flight to Ireland was about four hours. We could fly that nonstop and back again if we had to on our regular tanks.

Then a storm came up and we were weathered in for two days. We had a mixture of rain, snow, sleet, and fog. The city of Reykjavik was off-limits so we stayed on base. The American Red Cross women were very kind to the flight crews, serving coffee, donuts, paper or pens, smiles, and everything else we wanted.

When we did get off the ground for Ireland, we flew through a beautiful cloudless sky without a bump in it. The storm had completely dissipated for our flight to Nutts Corner, Ireland. We watched the ocean beneath us and an occasional ship as we drew closer to the islands. Near the Irish coast were literally hundreds of islands. It was such green country, checker-boarded with many hues of green and brown, purple and tan. We landed the airplane and it was promptly taken from us. We were informed it had to be modified for service in the ETO. Its armament had to be changed, special armor plating added, group and squadron identification painted on and assignment to a group in the Eighth or Fifteenth Air Force. It was a good airplane. We hated to lose it.

To celebrate our crossing, Norm Peck and I decided to journey into the local village and see the town. We checked out the pubs, tipped a few bitters (light warm beer), and went to a cinema where the aisles in the balcony were more like a ladder than stairs. I don't remember the movie, but I remember the occasion.

We were invited by a couple of the local lassies to their lodgings, where we were entertained with more bitters and tidbits, among other things. Hello Ireland!

The next day, hangover and all, the enlisted men of the crew were taken by bus to Greencastle. It was located just across the bay of Carlingford Lough from South Ireland, a neutral country.

We spent a solid week in extensive combat training. It was a crash course with both British and American instructors, guys who had flown their missions and knew what they were talking about. It was so interesting that the instructors kept our attention from morning until night. The things we learned that week in Ireland paid off many times later during our tour of duty. An entire day was devoted to evading capture.

When the training was over, we were shipped to Belfast by bus and stayed at a British base, where we were given passes to visit the town. I loved Belfast, the wonderful people, their warm hospitality and especially their dialect. We drank our share of Irish whiskey — the smoothest, easiest sippin' whiskey I ever had. The following day we went by ship to Scotland. It was a cold and miserable morning, the fog so thick your couldn't see the poop deck from the passenger deck. We docked at Prestwick and were whisked away to a British airfield.

The B-24 that picked us up was the most dolled up airplane I have ever seen in my life. It was a B-24D model, an older plane without a nose turret or any armament. The bomb bays had been sealed shut and a floor installed. There were jump seats along each side of the Liberator. It was, of course, the *Ready and Willing*. There were not enough seats for everybody, so we stood up for the takeoff. An hour later, still standing, we landed at Attlebridge, unscathed and in one piece.

A chicken colonel greeted us. We all popped to attention.

"Relax," he told us. "My name is Colonel Pierce." He gave us about a three-minute dissertation about the base, the civilians in the area, and our liberty town, Norwich. He seemed like a regular guy. "All I expect outta you guys is to get the job done the best you can, keep your ass in one piece, and go home after your twenty-five."

We arrived at Attlebridge on May 2, 1944. Our first mission would be on May 5. It was supposed to be to a V-1 launching installation near the Pas-de-Calais region of France. However, we bombed twenty miles away, missing our target completely, and never got credit for the mission. I was, I don't mind telling you, scared! It was frightening just looking down on occupied France for the first time. It was the only time I ever had that kind of fear while flying combat. Of course, I was scared many times — but never like on the first mission. The strange thing was, we never saw an enemy fighter or a single burst of flak.

I'll bet that French farmer was madder than hell when we bombed the long road and the barn beside it.

I was startled to wake up hearing a feminine voice. I looked at my watch. I'd been lying there two hours. I got to my knees and regained my senses. Then I heard her voice again. It came from over the dune where I had been resting. Slowly I stood up to see. There they were. Franz was holding the hand of a girl of fifteen or sixteen, and they were walking toward me.

"I know he's here someplace," he said to her in English.

"I still think you're fooling me," she replied.

"Jan," he called, "Jan Veen."

I stood up and walked to the top of the dune and looked down at them. When they spotted me, I walked down.

Franz introduced me. "Jan, this is my girlfriend Tina."

"I'm happy to know you," I said.

"Are you really an American pilot?" she asked, somewhat awe-stricken. She spoke better English than Franz did.

"Well, I'm from the United States of America," I answered proudly, "but in England they call me a Yank."

"Do you really fly bombers?" she asked.

"Yes, at least I did until a month ago when the Germans clipped my wings." (The old air force humor.)

"Do you really drop bombs on people?"

No humor there. That question sobered me up quickly. I answered her without a smile on my face. "No," I looked straight in her eyes. "We don't intentionally drop bombs on people. We drop bombs on factories producing war material for the Germans or V-1 buzz-bomb launching sites, submarine pens, bridges, marshaling yards for railroads, or anything that might help Germany in their war effort. Sometimes the bombs miss their target and people get killed. We don't want to kill civilians. We just want to stop the war. Do you understand?" She didn't answer but instead stared a hole right through me.

Finally she asked, "What is a buzz-bomb?"

I told her about the V-1s, finally telling her the story about the experience Johnny and I had in London. I told her how the Germans took deliberate aim on innocent women and children, killing them by the thousands.

Tina cried. I apologized for telling her the gory details.

When she calmed down, the three of us walked through the forest, talking about more current events and the problems Holland was having with the German army of occupation. We all agreed the war couldn't possibly last much longer.

I liked these two kids. We came to a big pine tree and with my pocketknife, carved our initials in it.

"When the war is over, we'll have a picnic right here!" Tina said.

I excused myself and left them alone. In the Wig-Wam I found Oom Joop had just finished brushing a coat of varnish on a piece of stained plywood about twelve by fifteen inches square. Two days later, he painted crossed flags on it, one American and one Dutch. Gold tassels were attached to the spear-tipped flag staffs. He took great pains and went into a lot of detail, shadowing in the folds of the flags. Underneath the flags he painted: "Amerika-Holland." Then underneath he painted the words "Een Dool," meaning America-Holland United! Through Franz he told me it was mine after the war.

Temmingh brought groceries later in the afternoon. He said he would bring another American pilot on his next trip. Pete, he said, was slowly bringing him closer to Diever and the Wig-Wam. He would join us within four days at the most.

Later that night I had a long talk with Franz about Tina. He said she never realized the Germans were doing the things I told her about. She had been taught that only the British and Americans killed civilians by bombing them from the air. This surprised me. Did other Dutchmen feel the same way as a result of German propaganda?

SIX

O n September 17, 1944, I met Jim Moulton, a B-17 tail-gunner from Albany, Oregon. It was 3:00 in the afternoon when I saw Temmingh, accompanied by a short, dark-complexioned man, approach, carrying boxes of groceries. I got up and met them. Jim smiled as he put the groceries down. Temmingh pointed to me.

"Harry," he said and pointed to his friend, "Jim."

"Hi, Jim," I said, happy to see him. "You're just the guy I've been waiting for!" We walked toward the Wig-Wam.

"Hi," he replied, "Christ am I glad to see you. I didn't believe Pete when he said there was another American here. Where in hell is this place anyway?" he asked, looking around.

"You ain't gonna believe this!" I said. Fifteen feet from the entrance I stopped. "Can't you find it? It's fifteen feet away." His eyes scanned the area. "Nope, I can't see it." Oom Joop opened the door. It startled Jim as much as it had me.

"Well, I'll be damned!" he said. "I can't believe it!" We went inside and I gave him the grand tour.

"Make yourself at home," Franz said. "It is your home now."

Temmingh and Oom Joop got the groceries and stowed them in the larder. Temmingh, always in a hurry, had no news and departed hurriedly. Franz and Oom Joop went outside, leaving us alone.

I talked first. I told him about myself during the time I had been shot down. I talked for half an hour. Then Jim talked. He told me he was single but engaged to a girl in his hometown and she was waiting for them to get married. Sometimes he worked in the forest as a lumberjack but mostly he worked in sawmills, a job he really liked. He never finished high school and had no intention of going back to school once he got home, even if Uncle Sam footed the bill. All he wanted to do was go home to the girl who was waiting for him. His crew had flown seven missions when they were shot down by flak two weeks before. All ten of his crew bailed out of their B-17 from about 5,000 feet. He had no idea where the others of his crew had come down and said he really didn't give a damn. I didn't question him about it.

Unlike my experience, a farmer hid him then contacted the Dutch Resistance. He wasn't burned or wounded and had all the comforts of home until he was moved. He had arrived in Diever that morning. He was glad to have somebody to talk to.

Jim was about 5'5, weighed about 150 pounds, and was solid muscle. He looked like a Mexican, with his dark black eyes, coal black hair, and dark complexion. He seemed calm and even-tempered. I liked him.

Later, I introduced him to the others as they returned. Franz took an immediate liking to Jim. He stayed near him most of the time. The three of us talked for hours, stopping only to eat supper. We talked until three in the morning.

The following day, September 18, Temmingh came to the Wig-Wam unexpectedly. Franz, Oom Joop, Jim, and I were the only ones there. The first thing to enter my mind was that there was trouble afoot. Instead, Franz translated, "The Allies parachuted into three towns — Neijmegen, Eindhoven, and Arnhem — and are across the Rhine River. Pete sends word for Harry and Jim to be ready to go south and meet up with your own soldiers."

Jim and I were probably the two happiest guys in all of Holland at that moment. We both grinned and shook hands, confident that Pete would be there for us in a day or two.

"I started to think this was the beginning of the end for me when I first saw the shit-hole we're staying in," Jim confided. "I hated coming to this place, living in a hole in the ground like a goddamned animal, depending on everybody else to exist —"

"Jim," I said, interrupting him, "I've been here almost three weeks. I don't feel like an animal nor do any of these people. I shave daily and keep my body clean. I eat regularly, get plenty of rest, and I'm grateful to them."

"Yeah," he replied, "but they get to go home once in a while and visit their families, taking a break from this. You know what I mean, back home we live in houses, sleep in beds, and — "

"Yeah, you're right," I interrupted again, "so did these people. Anyway, we're here and safe. For sure, it's just a little while longer." I wanted to drop the subject and did.

From that moment we lived in anticipation. We were both so excited at the prospect of leaving, heading south and meeting our own guys. We expected Pete to come for us at any time.

On the day Temmingh was supposed to come, he didn't. Franz assured us there had been other times when he came a day late. The following afternoon he came with three boxes of food. There was tobacco for both Jim and me. Franz translated Temmingh's words.

"Pete has gone south to get an eyewitness account of the situation. He is making contact with the group who runs the underground railroad. So far the Germans are kicking the hell out of the British at Arnhem. They'll probably win because they have thousands of troops and several Panzer divisions with tanks and heavy artillery. The fog is so heavy it is difficult to make visual contact with the enemy. The rotten weather has kept the Allied airplanes away and the Nazis are having their own way in the battle." I started to ask him a question. "That's all I know, except the casualties on both sides are tremendous! It's a slaughterhouse down there! Some of the Dutchmen who assisted the British have been put to death. I'll know more next time."

"What about the troops who landed at Neijmegen and Eindhoven?" I asked, with Franz translating for me.

"I don't know any more than I have already told you," he replied, shrugging his shoulders. He disappeared into the woods.

We were really let down so I took Jim aside. "I think it's about time we consider living where we are for a while. We're in good shape, safe, and not in the middle of a shooting war. The others, I'm sure, are more disappointed than we are."

Jim agreed, and the days continued to wear on.

When Temmingh came on his next regularly scheduled day, it was all over. Pete had returned from the south and gave an eyewitness account. The Germans had won a decisive victory. It cost them dearly in men and materiel. The bridge, which the English came to capture, was left intact, so the Germans could use it. All the Allied soldiers who parachuted into Arnhem were either killed, captured, or wounded. Nobody escaped.

There would be no trip south. The battles in Eindhoven and Neijmegen had been won by American and Canadian forces.

Not only were Jim and I downcast, but so was everybody else. The end of the war was so important to the Dutch. It's a wonder they lasted at all. They faced the enemy bravely, sometimes with a gun at their head, yet they endured. A ray of hope had presented itself. Sometimes I wondered how they maintained their sanity. The Dutch never took their existence for granted. They lived from day to day and were dependent upon the whims of the Nazis. I never met a Dutchman who'd wager a guilder that he'd still be alive the next day. The more I got to know them, the more I loved them. My heart went out to them.

Considering the way we felt, life went on normally.

On October 14 we were getting ready to go to bed when the door was jerked open and two strangers forced their way into the Wig-Wam. Nobody knew them! They laughed at our fright and said they had been watching us for several days. Their names, they said, were Niko and George. They knew there were two American pilots staying there and pointed to us. They said they were from an underground group in Friesland.

George, the shorter of the two, was about 5'6 with blond hair. His clear blue eyes were crossed but keenly alert. He was a powerfully built man. One of his front teeth was missing. He had a cocked .45 Colt Automatic in his belt. If it went off accidentally, he could forget about sex forever.

Niko was a direct opposite. He was perhaps 6'2 and 170 pounds of solid muscle. He had coal black, wavy hair and dark brown eyes. His face was thin and gaunt. A foreboding-looking man, his sinister eyes pierced right through you. He spoke high school English pretty well — not as good as Franz, but it was understandable. His eyes belied his constant smile. He had the look of a man never to be trusted.

They were both dressed in baggy, well-worn suits and wore faded neckties. Their mission was to tell the people in the Wig-Wam the danger of having Americans with them. They wanted Jim and me to accompany them to Friesland, where we would be safe.

Oom Joop was furious. He spoke loudly in a commanding voice to the two intruders. He waved his arms and at one point was ready to attack Niko. Finally, the argument ended when Oom Joop told them, "Get out of here and don't ever come back!"

110

They went. But Niko shouted over his shoulder as they left: "We'll be back, old man, just to show you just who is boss!"

Needless to say, everybody in the Wig-Wam was upset over the episode. Shortly after they departed, Oom Joop put on his coat and hat and left. It was about ten at night and I was fearful for his life out in the woods against that pair. Franz told me his father had gone to Temmingh's house to tell him.

"Don't worry, he can take care of himself," Franz said.

Everybody went to bed except me. I decided to wait until Oom Joop returned, for he was on the streets after curfew. I left a candle burning on the table beside me and I played solitaire. Next thing I knew, Dolf had his hand on my shoulder, waking me. It was daylight. I had gone to sleep with my head on the table. The candle had burned down to nothing.

I was the happiest one in the Wig-Wam when he returned at noon. Franz told us he slept at Temmingh's house.

"Temmingh," Franz translated, "is familiar with the two men from Friesland. They were snooping around in Diever and Havelte before their visit to us and are a part of an underground group in northern Friesland. Temmingh promised me he will check further and advise me as soon as he knows something. We're not to worry as far as them talking about the location of the Wig-Wam."

We ate lunch. Afterwards, as Franz was doing the dishes and cleaning up, Jim and I went outside and walked into the forest. Only this time we didn't stop walking. We walked for hours and went places we never knew existed. We walked to the northernmost edge of the woods which overlooked barren farmland. I could see the spire of a large church pointing skyward in the distance.

Finally, we sat down. "I hope we can find our way back," Jim said.

"I don't know if we should even go back," I replied.

Jim looked at me thoughtfully. "Maybe you're right!"

We talked at length about the situation we had made at the Wig-Wam. We rehashed the things Niko said. They made sense. He had the appearance of a vicious man but spoke in a soft, convincing voice. Engrossed in our thoughts, we continued to walk away from the safety of the Wig-Wam, staying within the boundaries of the huge forest. We were careful not to be seen or heard. In the final analysis, it was up to Jim and me whether or not to go with George and Niko. One thing was certain: We'd no longer be a burden to our friends. We felt that until we made a decision, we wouldn't go back at all — at least not yet.

We were both hungry and thirsty with no idea of how far we had wandered. We walked all afternoon, pausing only long enough to relieve ourselves or listen for alien sounds in the forest. Finally, we headed in the direction of the Wig-Wam and increased our pace. Several landmarks seemed familiar and we changed directions many times. At dusk we made a big observation: We were lost!

Close to the edge of the forest, with darkness falling, we found a small, cozy spot at the base of a huge sand dune with lots of pine needles and sat down. We talked quietly of our experiences in the air force. Jim and I had some pretty good laughs as we related some of the events in our lives.

Long after dark, our conversation was interrupted by the drone of airplanes high in the sky. We had heard them before; British bombers en route to a target in Germany. We climbed to the top of the dune, trying to spot them in the darkness. They were unloading bombs on Vliegveld Havelte, some four or five miles to the south. We saw the flak from the German 88s as it exploded in the air, saw their searchlights probing the blackness seeking out the bombers. The detonation of the bombs with loud explosions lit up the sky and shook the earth beneath us. The ground flashes of the antiaircraft guns completed the pyrotechnical display. The fires reflected off the base of the scattered clouds, flickering, causing the sky to come alive. As we watched, we could see an occasional British bomber as it ran through the beam of a searchlight.

"Fifteen thousand?" Jim asked, estimating their altitude.

"I don't think they're that high!" I replied.

A second wave of planes flew over and bombed the airstrip again, duplicating the bomb run of the first wave. This time they had the fires for an aiming point. They zeroed in and dropped their loads, causing tremendous explosions. Fireballs and black clouds of smoke rose into the sky, making the clouds even brighter than before. The flak exploded in the heavens but the bombers never wavered from their course. We couldn't see the airfield itself, but we knew we were witnessing a highly successful bombing mission. Once it was over, we sat on top of the dune for a long time, watching the reflections in the sky. None of the bombers went down. A few pieces of chaff fell around us.

One thing the raid did for us was pinpoint our location. We figured we were about a mile from the Wig-Wam. No use trying to find it in the dark. Even if we did go wandering in at this time of night, we'd frighten everybody to death. The night air wasn't balmy by any means, but it wasn't cold either. We came down off the dune and stayed put for the night.

I hardly slept at all. Every time I'd doze off, there would be another explosion at the airfield. I could feel the concussion from the blasts. At daylight we could still see clouds of black smoke rising. We started walking and once we were in familiar surroundings, we stopped and checked the area before going directly to it. The first people we saw were Franz and Oom Joop, who had a genuine look of relief on his face when he saw us.

Everybody had been looking for us all night long. They returned after the bombing of the airfield. They thought we had either been captured or George and Niko had somehow gotten their hands on us. Perhaps we wanted time to think about our situation, they said, but they were concerned because we didn't tell anybody of our plans. They decided they were going into the woods and find us or find out what happened to us. They wanted us to know that the things Niko had said didn't speak for our comrades. We were welcome to stay as long as we wanted. The vote was eight to zero.

Oom Joop didn't go back to the Wig-Wam with us but went off through the woods toward Diever. Franz told us he was going to Temmingh's house to tell him how George and Niko's visit had affected the Americans. He returned with Temmingh at his side. Dolf and his brothers were the only ones there besides Franz, Jim, and me. We sat around the table and talked. I understood some of what they were saying, but Franz translated for us.

"There is a lot of talk in town and even in some other towns about the 'onderdikershol' for hiding Jews and American pilots in the woods near Diever," Temmingh said. "It is only a matter of time until some Landwatcher or Nazi sympathizer hears the information and the NSB or Landwatchers start snooping. I don't think the Germans have heard any such talk or they would have already been looking. I know there are no extra troops or strangers in Diever. Only the normal three-man patrols go through town twice a day as always. Nobody knows the exact location of this place, and fewer still know for sure that it exists at all. I am sure nobody follows me when I come here. I know you are all usually careful in your movements. Be extremely cautious now. Lay low and keep the location of this place a secret." He smiled. "Harry and Jim must stay close and not travel in the forest at all. This is a hiding place, so keep yourselves hidden. The situation can become dangerous in a hurry. If there are any new developments, I will let you know before anything happens!"

With that bit of information, Temmingh left and went back to Diever. Somehow, he seemed older, shaking his head negatively.

Again, things settled down to a routine. It was boring. I wrote frequently and Oom Joop kept the document buried. The war seemed to be at an absolute standstill. We existed from day to day. I enjoyed talking to Oom Joop for he spoke simply, using grammar school Dutch, and I understood him perfectly. One day he told me I was like a son to him. It was a genuine compliment.

About two weeks later, six of us were playing cards just before bedtime. I was about to turn in when the door burst open and two German soldiers bolted in. One of them was carrying a Schmeisser machine gun slung across his chest and the other carried a pistol in his hand.

I didn't look at their faces, only at that Schmeisser machine gun aimed at me. I was frightened and thought it was the end of my life. The room hushed and our faces paled at the sight of them. Neither of them spoke as the other kept his Schmeisser on us. Then we recognized them. It was Niko and George!

Oom Joop screamed at them unmercifully! I never saw the man so angry! His face turned crimson and the veins in his neck protruded as he screamed. Why had they come looking like a pair of Nazis? He told them it was a rotten thing to do, scaring everybody. He demanded that they leave. This time they held their ground and stared at the group. George held the Schmeisser menacingly.

"Sit down, old man, I have something to say!"

There was a deafening silence. Nobody moved and nobody said a word. Finally, Niko spoke. "Oom Joop, it's only a matter of time till the Germans find and raid your hiding place. So great a secret can never be kept. Especially when you have Allied airmen hiding among you. Think about it, that's all! It makes sense doesn't it? We had no trouble finding the place and we didn't follow anybody to get here. In the north, the Americans will be safe. We have an organization to handle these situations. In my opinion it's a miracle the Nazis haven't already found you, for everybody talks about the *onderdikershol*. The Germans know there are Americans hiding in the area, and they want them."

Oom Joop settled down somewhat. Niko and George stood at the end of the table.

"There are Jews hiding here," Niko continued. "We can take them too. Our towns there are full of Jews. They are all safe. Please, think carefully of what I say. For your own well-being and that of the two pilots . . . think." His voice was convincing.

Franz continued translating as Niko talked. "If the Germans come and there are no Americans, probably all they would do is put you in a work camp and make you build defenses. If they find the pilots here, you know it's instant death!" He ran his finger across his throat. "If they find the Jews here, they'll be deported to the camps in Germany for the duration. Think about it!"

Niko and George turned to go. "We will be in touch with you soon. Remember, we have many safe houses where the pilots will be welcome." With a smile on his face, Niko threw both Jim and me a pack of tailor-made cigarettes and left the Wig-Wam, closing the door after them. We could hear them throwing sand around the seams of the door so the light wouldn't filter out.

There was dead silence both inside and outside.

Slowly the men, each with his own thoughts, went to bed. No words were spoken. It was eerie. Not even Jim and I spoke. After we went to bed I lay there a long time before I drifted off into a troubled sleep.

For the next two days, things returned to the boredom of our normal routine. Jim and I went outside only to go to the toilet. The weather had started to turn cold and the nights were cool. We huddled in our blankets around us to keep the chill out.

On the afternoon of October 29, Temmingh came on an unscheduled day. He informed us there were two Dutchmen, NSB'ers for sure, nosing around Diever. They were looking for a "friend" of theirs in the *onderdikershol* in the woods. He was sure the strangers were German spies. He informed us he had sent a message by courier to George and Niko to come for us. He had checked them out carefully and they were indeed members of a group in Friesland who did all their "dirty work."

We spent our last night in the Wig-Wam on October 29. We stayed up late, talking for the last time. Jim and I gave everybody our address but wouldn't take theirs in case we were captured. It was a sad evening, for these were friends.

The following morning, Jim and I packed our suitcases. Oom Joop wouldn't let us more than an arms length away. Franz had tears in his eyes. Finally, two of the Egginh brothers came for us and said they had prepared a temporary hiding place away from the Wig-Wam until somebody from the other group came. I asked Oom Joop to get rid of my writing. We were ready to go and shook hands all around. Oom Joop kissed me on both cheeks, then on the lips real hard. "God bless you, *jongen!*" he said in Dutch. Franz wrapped his arms around both Jim and me and cried unashamedly.

We gathered our suitcases, went outside and, without looking back, followed the two brothers in a new direction through the woods. Tears rolled down my cheeks and the cold morning air bit into them. Jim appeared to be elated we were leaving. For fifteen minutes we walked in the direction of Diever, then headed south through the woods until we came to an open field. There was a large house and barn half a mile away. Between the forest and the house, haystacks were scattered in a field, perhaps thirty or forty of them. We left the protection of the forest and walked through the field until Dolf stopped beside one of them. It was no different from any of the rest. He crawled on his hands and knees into a hollowed out area beneath it and motioned for us to follow. The space was small but almost high enough to stand in. The roof had been reinforced with willows and branches. On the straw floor were some blankets and magazines, pillows, and two decks of cards. There was a bag containing bread and Edam cheese. A bottle of milk and two more of water lay on the straw. The Egginhs had outdone themselves to provide for us. I thanked them and watched as they placed some hay around the entrance.

Dolf was satisfied the door couldn't be seen and they left.

Jim and I covered the straw floor with a blanket. We settled down in our eight-foot round living room.

"The Wig-Wam looks pretty good right now, doesn't it?"

"One place is as good as another when you've got to live like a goddamned animal," Jim replied.

"I wonder how long it will be before we're contacted?"

"Probably never," he mumbled.

"Hey, Jim," I said, "I'm not responsible for this situation. If you want to know the truth, I'm scared shitless. I think we've got a decision to make if nobody comes for us. How long shall we stay before we take off on our own? We've got all our stuff, you know, clothes and all. It's just a matter of 'how long'."

"Let's give it twenty-four hours. If we're captured, we'll be sent to a prisoner-of-war camp and be with other Americans. At least we'd know what we'd be doing for the rest of the war."

"Captured? What the hell do you mean captured?" I asked him angrily. "You're awful damned naive if you think the Germans will put us in a POW camp at this stage of the game! Hell, they know when you were shot down as well as you do. Since we're both wearing civilian clothes and since the only uniform we've got are our dog-tags, we'd be treated as spies. You know what happens to spies, don't you, Jim? They grind your balls into little pieces for about two days then put you out of your misery. Before you surrender to the enemy, you'd better weigh all the pros and cons pretty damned carefully!"

"Well, how long do you think we should wait?"

"At least a week," I replied without any hesitation, "providing we get food and keep ourselves alive."

"Bullshit!" he said loudly, almost angrily. "We have no warm water to clean up with. We can't shave. I'm even afraid to go out and take a leak." He pondered his statement for a moment then continued. "No, Harry, I'll tell you what. You stay your week. I'll give it forty-eight hours from right now and not a minute longer. Then I'm gone — with or without you!"

"That's your decision to make, Jim," I said.

"I guess we'll have to take a leak in the morning and hold it till it gets dark before we can take another one." He laughed then got serious again. "You know, Harry, we're in a bad situation. I guess you know that, don't you? I wish that damned farmer hadn't taken me in. I know I'd have been caught real soon." He looked me straight in the eyes. "I've got a gut feeling we'll never get out of this alive. We're trying to play cat-and-mouse with some expert cats! We're in shit up to our necks! Just think it over! I don't think you realize the trouble we're in! Your life ain't worth a plugged nickel right now! I'll take my chances. Mark my words, if I ever get a chance to turn myself in to the Germans I'll do it, I swear to God I'll do it! I just ain't gonna live like a god-damned animal burrowing in the ground the way we have been! Sometimes I don't think you value your life at all. You just go along with whatever they say. Why are you so goddamned trusting all the time? You talk about being naive? That'll be your downfall. Just wait and see!"

Jim finished his dissertation. I didn't interrupt him. I was surprised he was so bitter, especially against those who helped him. Some of the things he said were probably true, but who were we going to trust if not the people who were risking their necks to help us? Starting out on our own would be stupid. We'd be dead ducks. *No,* I thought, *I'll continue to trust these people.*

I said, "You may or may not be right, Jim. I agree we're in one hell of a jam and have to depend on help from our friends. It's best to trust them. They have seen me through two and a half months, and I'm not captured yet! I disagree with you when you say you think we'll be caught. Look, I'm a free man right now! I'll probably still be free tomorrow and I ain't seen a German for over two months. I'm not kidding myself that none of them are around. Our danger will start the first time we set foot outside this haystack to leave for good. Why, we'll have to sleep with one eye open, be on the lookout all the time, and worry all the time. We'd wonder when the next patrol is coming and how to handle it when they stop you. Who are the Landwatchers and who are the NSB? This isn't like walking down Main Street in Albany, Oregon. This is German-occupied enemy territory! The place is crawling with Nazi assholes trying to get their hands on us. You can leave anytime and you'll leave alone. This is a comfortable place. There's food and drink, I feel reasonably safe, and I'll bet a month's wages we're being watched right now by good Dutchmen! Think about *that,* Jim! I'm right, you know . . ."

I hated to force my opinion on anybody, especially him. He had his own life to live. But in my opinion he would be cheated out of the rest of it if he went on his own. He had a bad case of my old nemesis, "stinkin' thinkin'," but couldn't recognize it. He needed a chance to accustom himself to our new surroundings and was probably feeling sorry for himself. But then, so was I.

"What the hell," I said. "Let's play some cards and get this crap out of our heads, what do you say?"

"Right," he said and picked up the deck cards. "Name your poison!"

The cards were almost new. We played *Schopen* for a while then decided to play solitaire for a nickel for each card we turned up and five bucks if we beat Old Sol. We played alternately until we had to call the game because of darkness. Jim owed me $35 and I really needled him about it.

"Tomorrow," he said, "I'll rake your ass over the coals so bad you'll call all bets off!"

After it was completely dark we took a walk, keeping one eye on our haystack. We relieved ourselves and then sat down beside it, bathing in the moonlight for a couple of hours. We spoke in low voices and finally went back inside, laid on the straw, and covered up with the blankets, sticking a pillow under our heads.

We slept soundly all night and were awake at the break of dawn. I looked around outside before we went out and took our morning leak. It was foggy, so nobody could see us.

"Drain it good, Harry. You can't turn the faucet on again till to-night."

We took advantage of the fog and stayed outside for a while to stretch our legs. The moisture in the air got our clothes so damp, we went inside. We ate bread, cheese, and drank some water, then put the remaining food back in the sack and laid it aside.

Then, out of nowhere, a young girl of perhaps fourteen or fifteen stuck her head in the opening of the haystack.

"*Dag!*" she said happily, smiling at us.

She placed a bag inside and left the place as quickly as she had appeared. I looked outside to see where she had gone but the fog had swallowed her up. Inside the bag was warm tea, hot oatmeal, and a bottle of milk. There were two bowls, spoons, and two cups. We ate another breakfast and really stuffed our guts.

After we finished, I leaned back on my elbow and rolled a ciga-rette. I inhaled the smoke deeply and relaxed. Jim was doing pretty much the same thing.

"Hell, Jim, this ain't so bad," I said.

He didn't answer but he had a satisfied look on his face.

The solitaire went on all day, each of us taking turns and playing like we were out for blood. We made a pact. This was a debt of honor. When we were liberated, the loser would settle up as soon as he had the money in his pocket. We also decided we would never change the stakes because if we raised the limit, the loser probably could never af-ford to pay up. So the game remained the same. At lunch time, Jim owed me $53. When we ate cheese sandwiches for supper, it was $90. When it got too dark to play anymore and we were both dizzy from looking at the spots, he had lowered his debt to $80.

The last thing he said when we bedded down for the night was, "I've got it turned around now, tomorrow you'll owe me."

It was the first indication that he wouldn't be leaving.

But there would be no tomorrow. At least, not for cards.

Just after I went to sleep, I was awakened by the sound of voices and the shuffle of footsteps in the field. I stuck my head out into the darkness and saw two shapes moving around in the field checking the haystacks. The moon was bright so I could see they weren't Germans. I recognized Niko and George.

"What are you looking outside for?" Jim asked.

"It's George and Niko," I replied, "they're looking under every haystack for us. Do you want to go with them?"

"We could do a hell of a lot worse!" he answered. "At least we'll be on the move and go to a safe place where we can relax."

"I think you're a dreamer, but if that's what you want."

Boldly, I crawled out from under the haystack and walked toward the two figures with Jim right behind me.

"George! Niko! Over here!" I said in a loud whisper.

They turned around when they heard me. "Hello Americans!" Niko said in a loud voice, unafraid of being overheard. They were dressed in the same suits they had worn in the Wig-Wam. George carried a small bag.

We walked them back to our haystack and the four of us went inside. There was barely enough room. George removed a small candle from his coat pocket and lit it with a match.

"Don't worry about the candlelight," Niko said. "There are no Germans within ten kilometers. We have a plan. The German patrol goes by here in two hours. Afterwards, we will walk the rest of the night, staying in the forest. We will go to a village called Hoornsterzwaag, in Friesland. If for some reason we get separated, head for Hoornsterzwaag and we will know when you are within ten kilometers of the village! Remember the name of the village and try not to forget it, 'Hoornsterzwaag.' It isn't too far, but we will travel by night and rest during the day. We will leave in three hours. Okay?"

When we didn't answer him, George blew out the candle and put it back in his pocket. "Now let's get some sleep," he said.

Somehow they didn't seem so sinister. Again, two Dutchmen were risking their lives for us. Evidently they had permission from the local group or they wouldn't have known where we were. Niko had proposed a journey, which in his mind was a safe one. Somehow they seemed different. I fell asleep without knowing it.

When I woke up, I struck a match and looked at my watch. We had been sleeping almost three hours. I woke the others and told them the time. I was rested but felt reluctant to leave the security of the haystack. Jim and I divided the remaining food and put it in our suitcases then went outside.

"Remember, now," Niko said in a low voice, "if we get separated, the name of the town is 'Hoornsterzwaag.' Got it?"

Both Jim and I repeated, "Hoornsterzwaag."

George took the lead, followed by Jim. Niko and I brought up the rear. We stayed within the confines of the forest and headed east toward Diever. Circling the town, we came to a main road heading north-south. We went north, walking along the side of it for about a mile, then we went into the woods and paralleled the road.

An hour before sunrise we came to Hoogersmilde and circled the village. Shortly we came to a different highway leading northwest. We stayed in the woods as the forest thinned somewhat, crossing some small open fields but staying parallel to the northwest road. We came to another forest and entered it. It was tough walking in the woods in the dark. There was very little moonlight. The Dutchmen seemed to have a sixth sense and never stumbled, but I tripped constantly and fell three times. Jim did the same thing. Every kilometer or so we stopped to regroup and listen for alien noises. George walked fast. When we stopped we had a chance to catch our breath. We climbed fences and forded small streams. One of them was deep enough to soak my crotch and made walking just that much more miserable.

As dawn was breaking in the east, the wooded area suddenly came to an end. We were a hundred yards deep into the forest beside the road with nothing but open fields before us. There were a few houses with barns in the distance. If we continued on our present course, we would be exposed. Niko and George decided we would stay where we were for the day. If there was any movement by Germans on the road, we could see them.

I found a place to settle in with plenty of pine needles. There were lots of bushes between me and the road, but I could see the road from under the bushes. I opened my suitcase and got into some dry clothes then laid the wet ones on the ground to dry. After I ate some of the cheese and bread, I stretched out on the ground. I didn't even remember going to sleep, nor could I recall the nightmares, but they must have been bad. When I woke up, I was wringing wet with sweat. I took off my coat and loosened my shirt. George was sleeping, leaning against a tree with his back to the road. Jim was lying about ten feet in back of him. Niko was concealed in some bushes near the road, watching in both directions. I watched him for a while then went back to sleep.

Later, when I awakened, Niko was bending over me, his finger held to his lips. Jim, fully awake, was lying in the same place with his

121

head raised, looking in the direction Niko was pointing. A company of German soldiers, led by a chauffeured staff car, its convertible top down and a German officer in the back seat, was coming down the road in our direction. They were no more than a quarter of a mile away, heading south. The soldiers were marching and armed with rifles slung on their shoulders, their eyes glued on the road ahead. They marched past our place of concealment like troops on review. Their calf-high, hob-nailed boots echoed a scraping sound in unison as they went by. As the staff car passed, I was fascinated by the Nazi officer. His legs were crossed, a cigarette in an apparent well-manicured hand hung limply over the side of the vehicle. He sat comfortably in the corner of the back seat, busily engaged in reading a novel, which he held in his other hand. He paid no attention to his charges or his surroundings; the smile on his face reflected the contents of the novel. The black cross on the side of the car and the officer's arrogance irked me. I wanted to yank his ass out!

We didn't move for at least ten minutes after the troops marched down the road. I turned to say something to Niko and saw that both he and George had their pistols in their hands. Again, I wished I had my Colt .45. I never realized how much security a gun can give.

There was more activity on the road. George and Niko had not moved, so I stayed put. A German patrol came into view, pushing their bicycles and heading north. They were laughing, talking, and paying little attention to their surroundings. Putting their bicycles down on the road, they crossed to our side. The three of them unbuttoned their pants and took a leak. Then they went back to the bicycles and rolled a cigarette. Each of them had a Schmeisser slung across his chest. Their helmets were strapped on the bicycle luggage carriers. Their uniforms were green rather than the blue-gray of the regulars. Soon they mounted their bicycles and headed up the road.

Niko, for the first time, moved away from me. He went back to the road where I saw him when I first woke up. We were all wide awake. My clothes were dry so I put them in my suitcase. It was half an hour before Niko returned.

"How come their uniforms were a different color?" I asked.

"They are the *Grune Polizei* (Green Police)," he replied. "They are bad Germans. Sometimes Dutchmen, NSB'ers, and the Landwatchers ride with them. Only the SS troops and the SD are worse, so we stay clear of them. The regular German patrols are not so bad. Usually, they won't even stop us. They had little peckers, didn't they?" he said, laughing.

"Yeah, especially the one in the middle," I replied. "It was so small he used both hands so it didn't slip back in his pants."

All four of us laughed after Niko translated to George.

Shortly afterward we heard the sound of heavy trucks from the south. In no time they rumbled past us. It was quite a convoy. First came two motorcycles with sidecars and an armed soldier in one of them. Then came two large trucks loaded with German soldiers; after that, a huge semi with a canvas-covered object on it. After it passed we saw the four fins of the rocket. Two fuel trucks followed and then a command car. Three of these convoys passed by within twenty minutes.

Jim looked at me. "I'm glad we're seeing them up close here instead of on the receiving end in England."

"Those are V-2 rockets," said Niko. "I heard they can go all the way to New York."

Christ, I thought, *I hope they can't.*

We saw German trucks twice more. Women and older men on bicycles traveled slowly while others walked to their destinations. Two men, both in their thirties and obviously ill at ease on the open road, sped toward the north on their bicycles. I hoped they didn't overtake the rockets. Fifty feet from us, two young women got off their bicycles, pulled down their bloomers, and relieved themselves in the road. They were talking and giggling happily. They pulled up their bloomers and rode on.

Just before dark, we started walking again. It was much easier because we were in level, open fields.

"How far have we come, Niko?" I asked.

"About twenty kilometers, but closer to thirty if you consider the extra walking around we did. It's still over thirty kilometers to Hoornsterzwaag but we won't walk all the way. A town called Oosterwolde is five kilometers up the road. We have many friends there and we'll get some bicycles. I know travel on the road is more of a risk, but we can get there sooner."

An hour later, it was completely dark. There had been no movement on the road. I could see the faint outline of a church steeple against the darkened sky to the right.

Niko saw me looking at it. "Oosterwolde," he said, pointing with his finger. We walked past the turnoff into town. The village was

123

as big as Meppel. We came upon a large grove of trees with dense underbrush on the left side of the road. The brush afforded good cover, so we moved into it and sat down.

The two Dutchmen talked for about five minutes.

"George and I are going to the village," Niko said. "We know the town very well so we won't get caught. We will get the bicycles and be back in two hours. If we're not back, stay here. You are well hidden even in daylight. If we don't get back, we'll return tonight, okay?" We both nodded in the affirmative.

Without saying more, they disappeared silently in the darkness. A little later I said, "We're halfway to Hoornsterzwaag according to Niko. We've come twenty-five kilometers and have about the same distance in front of us."

Jim didn't answer. Finally I said, "Well, what do you think about all this now? Don't you kinda wish we were back with the guys in the Wig-Wam?"

"Hell no!" he retorted. "At least we're doing something, not just sitting around waiting for something to happen. As long as I get to a safe place, I don't care where it is as long as I'm not burrowed in the ground and I can stay till the war's over."

"You just might have left that place a couple of days ago, Jim."

George and Niko surprised us. They returned shortly, each of them pushing a bicycle. They laid them in the bushes where they couldn't be spotted from the road.

"There's two of them," said Niko, "now we go back for two more." He handed me a bag. "Food and drink for later in the day. It will last you both through tomorrow if we don't get back."

Jim and I stayed awake, talking in low tones about the good old days, until Niko and George came back, each one carrying a bicycle tied to his back. Niko also had a burlap bag around his neck hanging from a small rope. They put the bicycles with the others and almost dropped in their tracks, exhausted.

"*Phew!*" Niko sighed. "We saw some Germans in town and got cornered in for a while. They didn't see us, so when the coast was clear, rather than risk riding them, we carried them all the way here. Anyway, we are all together again." He lit a smoke. "I hope you haven't been sleeping so we can all sleep during the day. We have enough food to last for three days. When we get up, I have a little surprise for both of you. But let's get some sleep first." The sun was starting to rise in the east.

It was a long time before I finally dozed off. The sky was brilliant with a red sunrise. What was that old mariner's adage?

> Red skies at night,
> Sailors' delight.
> Red skies at morning,
> Sailors take warning!

I was tired and apprehensive. It seemed we were really out in the open. We weren't as well protected as we had been in the woods. What kind of surprise could Niko have for us?

I woke up at noon agitated as hell. The sun had been shining in my face and it felt sunburned. My eyes smarted from the penetrating rays. I shaded my face but it was a long time before the spots left my eyes. I thought I was the first to wake up and looked around. The road was deserted except for Niko crouched near a bush fifty yards away. I walked back in the brush and relieved myself, heaving a sigh of relief. I went back to Jim.

He opened his eyes and sat up.

I looked around before I spotted George. I woke him up.

Niko waved to me then came over where we were gathered.

"All clear?" I asked.

"All clear," he replied.

We ate some bread and cheese, then killed a bottle of milk.

Afterwards, George and Niko spent about an hour by the road checking every bicycle that went by. We saw no Germans.

Jim and I stayed in our clump of bushes until the Dutchmen returned, laughing at a private joke. Niko retrieved the bags they brought from Oosterwolde. He went to the four bicycles. After checking them over carefully, he gave each of us one. They tied the bags they had brought on the back of their bicycles. We did the same with our suitcases.

"Are you ready for your surprise?" Niko asked.

"What the hell could be a surprise out here?" Jim asked.

Niko grinned, "Jim, I have a nice surprise for you. See here?" He took out a holster with an almost new 7.65mm P-38 pistol in it and handed it to him. "Careful, now, it is loaded."

Then he said, "Harry, for you!" He gave me a 9mm German Luger in its holster along with two extra clips of ammunition. It was a carbon copy of the one he carried. It had a five-inch barrel and was brand new. I know it had never been fired. The wooden grips were so new you could smell the wood. It was a beautiful weapon.

"Take care of your guns," Niko said. "I hope the day never comes when you have to use them." George was beaming.

For the next half hour Niko explained the mechanism of the guns while George watched the road. We learned how to field strip and load them, put them on safety, and, most important, how to hide them. I always wanted a Luger, even back in the States, and now I had my own. The circumstances under which I got it made it exceptionally special. I took my bag off the bicycle and put the holster and one of the extra clips in my suitcase. I made certain there wasn't a round in the chamber, then stuck it in my belt and pulled my sweater down over it. I put the other clip of ammunition in my coat pocket.

Then we had a problem. Jim took his bag off his bicycle and put the gun, holster, and ammo clips in it.

"Jim," I said, "put the gun in your belt so you can use it."

"Bullshit!" he replied. "If the Germans catch me with a gun, especially a German gun, I'll be dead for sure!"

"It might make the difference between life and death for all of us!" Niko said angrily.

"I can get it if I have to. It's laying right on top of my clothes. Harry, you're not going to carry that Luger are you?"

"You're damned right I am. If we gotta fight, then I want to be ready to do my share!"

"You're crazy!" Jim said loudly. "Niko, if you want this god-damned gun back, just say so!" he glared, challenging him.

George stood watching the whole thing from a distance, keeping a smile on his face. He spoke to Niko then looked at Jim in disbelief. I got some of the words but not all of them. He told Niko to throw Jim's gun into the woods and let him go unarmed.

Again, the two of them went down by the road and sat down. Fully an hour passed before they came back. All memories of the confrontation were forgotten for the moment.

"The road has been deserted for over an hour. I think it's safe to leave for Hoornsterzwaag," Niko said. "Darkness will start to set in shortly, so let's get our bicycles and go. Jim, you and George will leave first. Harry and I will follow."

We walked single-file, pushing our bicycles. George got on his bicycle and Jim mounted his. The two of them, riding side by side, headed northwest. In just a few moments they rounded a curve and were out of sight.

126

Five minutes later, we headed up the road at a steady clip — not fast, just smooth and easy, making good time. My Luger felt reassuring in my belt, even though it was aimed at my testicles.

I saw the spire of another church off to the right. A road led into the village with a sign reading *"Donkerbroek."* Four kilometers further on we came to another village on the right.

"Wijnejewoude," Niko said. A moment later he said, "We turn in three kilometers for Hoornsterzwaag."

We didn't pay much attention to anything after that. We picked up speed, anxious for the turn-off to our destination.

"Halt . . . Halt . . ." A voice boomed from in back of us!

At first I thought it was Jim. But that wasn't Jim's voice!

The voice boomed again: *"Halt!"*

I looked over my shoulder. A German patrol was about fifty feet in back of us. They were all huge men. Their leader was halfway between us, trying to catch up. Again he yelled loudly, *"Halt!"*

SEVEN

W hen I heard the word "Halt" and saw the Germans, I knew all was lost. Only the leader, a sergeant, carried a Schmeisser. The others carried regular-issue Mauser rifles slung over their shoulders. We got off our bicycles and Niko laid his down on the road. He whispered, "Let me do *all* the talking. Stay here!"

He approached the sergeant who stood by his bicycle. Niko didn't appear nervous and acted as if he were checked by patrols daily. He neared the sergeant, smiling. "Good day, Sergeant."

I understood the German as he asked for identity cards. Niko gave him his. He looked at the card carefully and motioned for me to come forward. I laid down my bicycle and he eyed me carefully as I approached. I gave the big German my card. The sergeant said something to me that I didn't understand.

Niko interrupted, saying a word I understood, *"Doofstoom."*

The German spoke to me again. If I were indeed *doofstoom* I'd better play the part. I hung my head limply and held out my hands in a gesture of despair.

"It's not on his identity card. It should be right here on his card, it should say *doofstoom* right here," he said, pointing to my card. He spoke very poor Dutch and I understood him. Peter was right; they didn't speak Dutch any better than I.

"It is the second issue of the card, sir," Niko said most respectfully. "No doubt the officials neglected to transfer all the information from his old card."

"This matter will have to be cleared with my captain."

"But it is the second issue of the card for Jan," pleaded Niko. "Sergeant, Jan's mother is gravely ill in Drachten and after we visit her," Niko lied, his face getting red, "we will go to the Drachten office and have the card corrected."

The German thought a moment, then shook his head. *"Nein!"* he yelled over Niko's objections. "Better get it taken care of now. Then when you are controlled again, there will be no problems."

Again the German spoke to me, softly at first, then yelling as he shook his fist. I hung my head and looked afraid. I stared at Niko in despair, an unanswered plea for help. The German turned his bicycle around. "To Oosterwolde!" he screamed, waving his arm.

As we returned to our bicycles, Niko whispered, "We will have to fight our way out of this. Do you have your gun?"

I nodded in the affirmative.

"Be ready when I tell you, okay?" Again I nodded.

We headed back the way we had come, at about the same speed. The Germans followed about fifty yards back.

We traveled a kilometer when a German truck came up the road toward us. Many soldiers were in the rear end. Both the truck and the patrol stopped. The sergeant ordered us to halt. He spoke to an officer riding in the front and a moment later the sergeant returned and ordered his men to get in the truck. He handed Niko our identity cards.

"Continue on to Oosterwolde," he said. "Report to Captain Kurtner and request a correction. Your papers are in order so there will be no problem. Good luck to both of you." Then he added, "I hope Jan's mother recovers."

He handed his bicycle up to the soldiers and climbed in himself. The truck went up the road, leaving Niko and me standing alone in the middle of it. The soldiers waved, and we waved back!

As soon as the truck rounded the curve, we followed in the same direction. Niko translated his conversation with the sergeant, which I hadn't understood.

He smiled at me. "If that was the Grune Polizei, either we or they would have been dead by now! The soldiers do not make good policemen. I can argue with them and get away with it. In fact, I believe they would have corrected your identity card in Oosterwolde and we could have pulled off the bluff. Anyway, we will never know because we won't wait to find out. I'm glad you were willing to use your gun back there. Tell me, what did you think of your first encounter with the Germans?"

I didn't answer but kept on pedaling as fast as I could.

We both rode the bicycles hard. I couldn't keep up with Niko, so he slowed down. We didn't want to run into a patrol coming from the opposite direction and go through the same thing. At last, we came to our turnoff and headed southwest toward Hoornsterzwaag. Ten minutes later we slowed considerably and turned onto a narrow lane toward a canal.

Sitting on the bank were George and Jim, eating bread and cheese. When they saw us, they stopped eating and ran to us, grinning from ear to ear. George started talking excitedly.

Jim said, "We thought for sure you'd be in jail by now. We saw the Germans pick you up back there!"

"Where were you?" I asked.

"No more than fifty yards from you," Jim said. "We were in a ditch in water up to our ass. We rode past the road leading into Wijnejewoude and saw the patrol coming. We went around a bend in the road till we saw the ditch. We jumped in and hid just as you and Niko came along with the patrol right behind you. You all stopped right in front of us. George had his gun ready, so if you made a move against the patrol he was ready to help. When we heard the sergeant say Oosterwolde, he knew where you were going. George says they have many friends there and you wouldn't spend one night in jail — you'd be out by dawn."

It seemed George and Niko had planned to meet at this rendezvous before we started. After our encounter with the patrol, George was going back to Oosterwolde for help. He was about ready to leave when we came riding up. He had given Jim directions to Hoornsterzwaag and where to go after he got there.

I told Jim what had happened and how cool Niko was.

"I'll bet you're glad your Luger was in your suitcase and not in your belt," he said.

I pulled up my sweater, exposing the weapon. "What the hell are you talking about? We were both armed! We didn't plan on going much further before we made a move! We were ready!"

"Jesus Christ!" Jim yelled. "Suppose they searched you?"

"Then there would have been three dead Krauts back on the road or we'd have been lying there, or a combination of both. By the way,

Jim, where is your gun and where was it when you were watching Niko and I get captured?" I asked angrily.

"You know damned well it's in my suitcase!"

"What you doin' with it? Keeping it for a souvenir?"

"If I need it, I can get it," he replied, perturbed.

"Could you get it when you were ass deep in water?"

"All I had to do was take the suitcase off my bicycle."

"By that time it would be all over, Jim. In my opinion you should be ready! I mean *ready* to help!"

"Well, you do it your way. I'll do it mine," he said.

I walked over to George and Niko, leaving Jim alone with his thoughts. George got to his feet and shook my hand. He had a big smile, so I knew he was happy about the way we had solved our problem.

"I told George you were a good actor," Niko said. "We are pleased with the way you handled yourself."

Thanking him, I headed down to the canal. I took off my shoes and socks, sat down on a rock, and put my feet in the water. It was cold and invigorating. I ate some bread and cheese and was rolling a cigarette when Niko approached.

"Put on your shoes and let's start, for daylight will soon be gone. We still have twenty kilometers to go, but even in the dark it's good riding."

We rode as we had before, with Jim and George in the lead and us following five minutes behind.

Just before midnight, we got to the village of Hoornsterzwaag. We rode past the village until we came to a huge farmhouse with a barn in back and a stone outhouse between them. We leaned our bicycles against the outhouse. Through the darkness, I could make out the lay of the tremendous farm. At one time it must have been a big producer.

As we approached, a woman opened the back door. She was a middle-aged woman with the lines of hard work etched in her face. Short and buxom, she wore a long skirt and wool stockings instead of shoes. She looked at us unsmiling and said, *"Dag."*

The date was about November 4. It had been sixty-six days since I had been inside a house, not since Temmingh's in Diever.

We walked through an alcove into the kitchen. There was a huge round table in the middle of the room which would seat twenty people

131

easily. Thirteen men were sitting at the table. They were dirty, disheveled, and exhausted.

When we entered, the men got to their feet and greeted us warmly. We shook hands with each of them. We were introduced as the American pilots, but no names were exchanged. There were guns everywhere. Each man had a handgun in his belt. Stens and Enfield rifles were propped against the wall. As soon as we were introduced, George and Niko joined in their discussion. The talk was serious. It seemed the men had gone to receive weapons parachuted by bombers and something had gone wrong.

I felt uncomfortable. Whatever had gone awry left them in a dilemma. The woman, with a candle in her hand, motioned for Jim and me to follow. We went into a formal dining room that held a huge glistening table. The chairs were overstuffed in blue velvet. Though antique, they looked new. Genuine oil paintings adorned the walls with gold ropes and tassels, probably a likeness of her ancestors. She served us steaming hot food, boiled potatoes and cabbage, a small piece of pork sausage, green beans, milk, bread and real butter. It was by far the best meal I had had since I was shot down. I ate slowly, savoring each bite.

During the meal, I heard groaning coming from the front of the house. I ignored it until a man screamed. I looked at the woman. She shrugged her shoulders and went back to the kitchen. Finally, George and Niko joined us and she served them.

The moans kept getting worse, so I asked Niko about it.

"These men went to a field ten kilometers away to receive weapons from British bombers. It was a big drop but there were German soldiers hiding and waiting. Somebody told them. The Nazis shot our people as they were gathering in the canisters. Seven of our group are dead. One man was wounded, shot in the lower leg. It was blown wide open and the bone is sticking out. He is in the front room. It is difficult for him not to scream. There are still seven missing and ten were captured that we know of. We cannot look for the seven men till daylight. It is possible they are dead. The Germans are probably watching their homes, so we don't dare go there until it's safe."

"Did they kill any of the Germans?" I asked.

"They fired all the ammunition they had . . . they hope so."

"What about the ten who were captured? Is there any chance they'll let any of them go after they question them?"

Niko gave me a sarcastic smile. "Harry, my American friend,

they will all be dead within two days after they have told the Germans everything they want to know. Fortunately, the ten were from other groups and don't know about this farm. These men will have to go underground now until the war is over."

I thanked Niko for telling me about it. It was difficult for him since many of the people were his friends. Now I could understand the forlorn looks on the faces when we arrived.

The woman filled our teacups and brought more bread. I drank five or six cups. Niko said that George would go with the others in the morning to look for the missing seven men. We sat and smoked, not saying much. I thought of the missing men and their terrified families.

"I'd sure hate to be the informer when they catch him. I bet they'll cut his balls off," Jim remarked.

Niko spoke to the woman in Dutch. He told us to follow her and she would show us where to sleep.

We followed her upstairs to a room with no visible beds. She opened two of the four cupboards in the wall and inside was a bed, made up and ready to sleep in. The mattresses and covers were featherticks. The pillows were soft down. There was a wash basin in the corner of the room. Again, we hadn't been able to wash ourselves since we left the Wig-Wam. I scrubbed my body with cold water, brushed my teeth, and shaved in cold water with a dull blade, which was quite an accomplishment. I crawled into the bed stark naked and slept a solid twelve hours.

I might have slept fourteen if it hadn't been for the bomb. The explosion shook the house and rattled the windows. I heard the whine of an airplane engine and jumped out of bed to the window. A British dive bomber was attacking a small stone bridge crossing a canal a quarter of a mile away. His second bomb was a direct hit. The bridge came apart in the middle and fell into the canal. Smoke rose from a crater fifty feet away, where the first bomb had missed. I thought there might be some big Allied activity in the offing, perhaps even a second invasion.

The plane flew away in a westerly direction and never returned. No further air activity was observed all day. It seemed to be a small target to waste bombs on.

I put on clean clothes. I needed a haircut badly. My hair was as long as a woman's. Downstairs, Niko and Jim were sitting at the huge table in the kitchen. The men were gone, but the smell of stale tobacco smoke still clung to the air. Only the woman was there, dressed in a fresh dress. She seemed to have more color in her cheeks.

"Ah, good morning, sleepy head. Did it take a bomb to blow you out from between the covers?" Niko asked, laughing at me.

"I sure did sleep. Did you see the British plane?"

"Yeah, did a good job on that bridge too, huh?" Jim said.

"Yes," Niko answered, "it ruined a perfectly good five-hundred-year-old bridge for no good reason at all!" He looked disgusted. There was a tone of resentment in his words.

"Five hundred years?" I asked.

"Yes, that is just about the age of all the old permanent bridges in Holland and particularly in Friesland. They were erected over our canals in the fifteenth century or so. We hate to see them destroyed or any of our land destroyed for that matter. The atrocities of the Germans in Rotterdam, for instance, will never heal. God only knows how much of our real art was burned or blown up. We Dutch weep for our lost art treasures or a blown-up bridge as quickly as for a lost comrade."

"Have you seen the wounded man?" I asked.

"You can visit him if you like, but don't bother him if he is sleeping. He speaks no English. The doctor is due back soon to check his wound. He is in very bad shape and will lose his leg."

"War is the shits," I said.

"It is that, Harry," Niko replied. "It is safe to go outside and have a look around if you like. The German patrols come through the village, but everybody knows you are here so we will know when a patrol is within five kilometers."

Somehow they communicated over long distances. I never knew how. As far as I knew, all the telephones were dead. I never saw George or Niko or even Peter or Mimi, for that matter, use one.

"Thanks," I said. Jim and I put on our coats and went outside. The November air was brisk but not too cold.

"Let's walk to the bridge," I suggested. "I want to see how much damage the bomb did."

"How's it going, Jim?" I asked.

"Okay, I guess. I keep thinking about what you said. You know, about the gun and all. I hate the damned things! Flying was different; the fifty-caliber machine guns were for defense. But to carry a gun to just kill with just doesn't seem right."

"I guess I can understand that," I answered.

"It's hard to tell you how I feel. I'm not going to kill anybody in

134

cold blood. Like yesterday, if you had to shoot the three Germans, you probably would have had no trouble killing them. They had no idea you had a gun. That's killing in cold blood. Were they married? How many children would you have orphaned? I guess if we got in a gunfight with some Krauts, I'd shoot, but I'm not even sure about that! I'd probably hope that just by shooting at them we would scare them off!"

It was taking all the strength of character he had to talk to me. He was baring his guts to me and I felt sorry for him. He was no coward; anybody who had flown missions over Germany proved his bravery. Jim's problem was, I believed, that he had stateside morals in a wartime situation.

"I understand you, Jim. You know you don't have to talk to me, but if it helps to unload on somebody, that's fine. I understand your feelings. I think it's best you don't talk to anybody else about it but try to cope with the situation as best you can. I'm glad you confided in me and I thank you for it. Okay?"

He looked at me and smiled. "Yeah, okay, buddy."

We walked to the bridge. The bomb had done its job. It hit dead center and was probably a 500-pounder from the looks of the destruction. I looked at some of the fragments of the bridge and could tell more about the age of the structure from the mortar. It wasn't a form of cement in the modern sense, but the bonding agent was black and glazed. It looked like fresh mined coal or shiny silicone. That was very interesting. In the distance, we could see people coming to look at the bridge, so we made a hasty retreat.

We walked silently. The day was warming somewhat. Leaves were falling from the trees in the breeze. The dew on the pine trees glistened in the morning sun. Water gurgled in the streams, making pleasant sounds. Even the birds were chirping to tell us that we were disturbing their tranquility.

It was a great day. I stretched out my arms to gather it in. God, it felt good! The sky was the bluest I could ever remember, and the billowing softness of fleecy white clouds created ever changing shapes that never lost any of their beauty or purity. The breeze coming from the north held the promise of winter in its coldness. Cold weather? I hoped not. I remembered what Pete told me about the big cities. I was happy and felt a new friendship with Jim.

As we neared the farmhouse we saw two people on a motorcycle coming in our direction. Before we could hide, we saw they were women. They turned in at our farm.

"Well, something new has been added," said Jim.

"Probably nurses for the wounded man," I suggested.

When we got to the house, Niko was helping the girls put the motorcycle into the small outhouse. Inside, he introduced them.

"Harry, Jim, these are two Frisian friends of mine who have come to visit."

The shorter of the two, a blond girl, had a round face and the prettiest teeth I have ever seen. Niko introduced her. "This is Sjoukje van der Hoop, and this is Tini Mulder," he said, pointing to her friend. She was very pretty and about the same age.

The farmer's wife poured tea. We sat at the table and they spoke in Frisian. I excused myself when the doctor arrived and accompanied him to see the wounded man. The man was in his early twenties, had a stubble of a beard, and looked like he was used to hard work. He was muscular with large, hard hands. Typical of most Dutchmen, he had blond-brownish hair and blue eyes. Through his extreme pain, he managed a faint smile and greeted the physician. He nodded his head at me.

The wound was in the upper shin area of his right leg. A bandage, very lightly wrapped, had been placed over the wound with some sort of a wet medication. The doctor removed it and exposed a huge hole in the man's leg. It would never mend for it was almost shot off. No wonder the man was in so much pain.

He took some sterile gauze from his bag and dabbed away some of the mess inside the open wound as the man grimaced with pain. The medic produced some white envelopes, tore them open, and sprinkled white powder into the wound. He covered it again. I picked up the envelopes which had contained the white powder. The words on the package were "POWDER, SULFA, U.S. MEDICAL CORPS."

When I returned to the kitchen, the two girls were gone. Jim said they had ridden away on bicycles, heading north.

Later in the day, George came back. The seven men were accounted for. Two were wounded and found hiding in a ditch. Now they were with their families. Two others were dead and the other three were hiding with friends. They were all farmers and neighbors from north of the Hoornsterzwaag area. After the Germans got the information they wanted from those they captured, there would be a *razzia* to look for other patriots and weapons. Not only had the Germans been waiting in the field but there were also Landwatchers, NSB, SS, and SD men. Three of the enemy were killed and eleven wounded. The Nazis were sure to take hostages.

After lunch, George and Niko went outside and held an hour-long powwow. When they came in, we sat down in the dining room.

"Tomorrow morning at dawn we leave for Holwerd," Niko said. "We will not overstay our visit for these are good people and we don't want to cause problems. The man must now go further underground and the wounded man moved. The woman will have to face Germans alone, but she has done that before."

He put his hand on my shoulder. "I am afraid you and I will have to ride bicycles. Jim is dark-complexioned and he would be controlled by every patrol between here and the North Sea. So, he and George will ride on the motorcycle the girls brought and George will wear a policeman's uniform. But you and I, my friend, we will have to work our legs to give our ass a ride."

"How far is Holwerd?" I asked.

"About sixty-five kilometers, but the way we go, which is the safe way, is more like eighty-five. We'll go through Drachten, which is only about fifteen kilometers from here, and take a rest. There are many places we can stop along the way."

"How long will it take us?" I asked.

"Nine or ten hours of solid riding."

"I don't know if I can travel that far on a bicycle in one day, Niko. My legs hurt from the short ride we took yesterday."

"You will make it, Harry. Don't worry, I will help you. We will rest when you get tired. Leave it to me."

I opened my escape map to see where Holwerd was. Drachten, as Niko had said, was just a short distance from Hoornsterzwaag. But Holwerd was all the way up to the North Sea!

Niko awakened me at dawn. Jim was snoring loudly.

"Don't bring your suitcase, George will bring it," he said.

The farmer's wife prepared a hearty breakfast. I said goodbye to the woman and the wounded man, shaking hands with him, then Niko and I walked the bicycles down the driveway to the road and headed northwest, our eyes searching for trouble.

The first village we came to was Olterterp. We continued north and watched the road ahead. As Niko had predicted, it took two hours to reach Drachten. There was much activity in this large town, which was much larger than Meppel. We rode slowly down the main street until Niko suddenly turned onto a side street and stopped, pondering our situation.

"There are a lot of Germans in town. I don't like it. There are too many patrols. Maybe we should have come in from another direction, but it's too late now and we only have four blocks to go. Follow me about a hundred meters behind and if I give you a signal, drop the bicycle and hide, understand?"

He started out on his bicycle and I followed until he turned into an alley and rode four blocks, watching the cross streets carefully before he passed them. At the fifth street, he turned left and disappeared. I was there in less than a minute but Niko had vanished. I looked up and down the street, and when I didn't see him I decided to go back to the alley. Then, in the distance, I saw Niko on foot, waving to me.

"Whew!" I sighed, and jumped on the bicycle. When I reached him, he took the bicycle from me, walked between two houses, and rested it against the wall in back. As we neared the back door, it opened almost automatically. A young man darted by me quickly and walked between the two houses, pushing a bicycle. I wouldn't recognize him again if I saw him. We took off our coats and put them on a chair in the corner. The house was almost bare. It had a table, chairs, beds, an old sofa, and some assorted tables with knickknacks on them.

"This is my home," he said. "Nobody knows where I live so consider yourself very special that I have brought you here. The fellow who left in such a hurry is one of the most wanted men in Holland. He did not want you to see his face. All the people who live here, or those who just come and go, fight very hard for the underground. That man has probably killed twenty-five Nazis. He likes to kill them slowly, the way the Germans kill us."

Niko went upstairs and looked around. He checked the front bedroom. "Well, we are alone. We will leave before sunrise." He made lunch and after we ate, I lay down on the couch and took a nap. When I woke up, he was gone. I looked out the rear window and saw his bicycle was gone. I went into the front room and found some magazines, and sat down at the table while I looked at them. A couple of hours later I felt sleepy again.

Niko was a little wobbly and in an extremely happy frame of mind when he returned. "My friend you should have come with me," he said happily. "I had a couple of glasses of beer in the company of a very nice Jewish lady. Don't you think I look better?"

I laughed at him. "I think you had more than a couple of beers, my friend. You look like you just lost your virginity!"

"Well, not exactly," he answered, laughing, "but if I were a virgin, I wouldn't be anymore!" He laughed loudly. "Yeah, my little American friend, I should have taken you with me. There was more than enough to go around!"

He leaned back on the couch with a satisfied smile on his face. In seconds he was asleep without a care in the world.

We didn't ride our bicycles out of Drachten but pushed them through back streets until we emerged on the other side of town. Then we got on them and started riding. We came to a main artery which headed northwest toward Leeuwarden. On the other side we saw a German patrol on the road and just missed them. Quickly, we headed north on a narrow brick road to the village of Rottevalle and the town of Oostermeer a little farther on. The sun was up. It was beautiful as it reflected off a nearby lake.

For the first time, people on bicycles and on foot traveled the road, going from one village to the next. We seldom saw men but there were several youngsters and old folks. There was no indication of German patrols or troops. The Dutchmen were dressed for the morning chill, wearing woolen stockings and scarves. Riding was uneventful. A sign said the next town was Suameer.

"We will stop in Suameer for breakfast if you promise me you will not fall in love," Niko said.

"What do you mean?" I asked.

"We all fall in love with Greta . . . she's a beautiful girl."

There was a church spire and the largest windmill I had ever seen just as we entered the village. Though its vanes were tied down, it was in perfect shape and looked like a picture postcard.

We got off our bicycles and pushed them for two blocks. There were many women and old men walking. Women were busy washing windows and scrubbing sidewalks.

"This was a very religious town. The Germans don't bother its citizens for they are fearful of the wrath of these women."

We turned up a side street and walked for half a block to a small cottage. Leaning our bicycles against the back of the house, we went to the door.

"We eat!" Niko smiled. He knocked at the door loudly.

A young woman, perhaps twenty years old, opened the door.

"Ah, Niko!" she said, holding the door for us. We went through an anteway into the kitchen. Politely we took off our shoes as the girl invited us to sit at the table.

Niko introduced us in English. "This is Greta Rusk," he said. "Greta is the courier for our group, the go-between for some of the different groups in Friesland. Be careful what you say to her for her English is better than ours." He sighed. "If she likes you, you will know it. If she doesn't, you will know it quicker. Greta, this is my American pilot friend, Jan Veen."

"Niko, you can shut your big mouth anytime. Jan, pay him no attention. I'm very happy to meet you. You are welcome here."

My God, she was beautiful! Niko was right about that. She wore no makeup. She had smooth, olive skin, blue eyes, and light brown hair. Her teeth were perfect and white as snow. Her shoulder-length hair was combed back off her face. She was about 5'4 and weighed probably 115. Her figure was perfect, her breasts being her greatest asset. Every time she bent over, she exposed her cleavage — not on purpose, but normally as she went about the job of setting the table for us. Her legs were long and well formed. She wore no stockings. Her dress was solid pale blue with a white V-neck collar. She wore woolen knee-length socks.

After our initial greeting, she paid no attention to either one of us. I couldn't keep my eyes off her. Her graceful movements were quick and sure. She caught me staring at her and she smiled appreciatively, returning my stare questioningly.

She served us boiled potatoes, turnips, bread, cheese, and milk. I sat at one end of the table and Niko at the other. She seated herself between us and kept the conversation in English.

"We are headed for the North Sea," Niko said, "where George and I are trying to make some arrangements to get Jim, another American pilot, and Jan back to England."

She was very interested and asked if we needed a place to stay for the night or if there was anything else she could do.

Niko replied, with a nasty leer on his face, "Well, if you can find a lover for Jan, we would accept that invitation!"

His remark embarrassed me. It must have shown.

"When I get to the point of needing a man, Niko, you will be well down the road, my friend," she replied sarcastically. "You have finished your meal and it's a long road to the North Sea. The toilet is out back if you want to use it."

Niko smiled, got up from the table, and went outside.

She looked at me and I held out my hands in despair. I wouldn't have offended her for the world.

"You keep watching me . . . you like me, huh?" she asked.

I hesitated, searching for a reply. I was unable to believe my ears. Finally, I said, "I like you, uh-huh."

"I know you are going to Dominee de Boer's church in Holwerd and I go there as a courier during my travels through Friesland. If you like, I'll visit you."

"We move around a lot — " I started to say.

"Don't worry, I'll find you if you want me to. Shall I?"

"Please do!" I said. I was as happy as if I had good sense.

I damned near kissed her goodbye. I wanted to. Instead, I gently put my arm around her waist and squeezed it. When I went out the back door Niko had reappeared.

As we pushed the bicycles around to the front and I looked back at her, she threw me a kiss. We walked the bicycles back to the main road and went north.

"Damn, Niko," I said. "I'm not so sure I want to leave here right now. We had an invitation to stay all night."

He laughed. "She is a lot of woman. No one man can handle that one. She is fun to be around, but nobody makes it with her. She will come north in a week or so. If she decides she wants to see you, she knows where to find you. Remember my words!" He laughed again. "I'll stick with my Jewish lady in Drachten."

"Damn," I said aloud.

We had bicycled about 500 yards when we met a three-man German patrol that came out of nowhere.

"Take it easy," Niko said, all at once serious.

The Germans were on the other side of the road, walking, pushing their bicycles. We kept pedaling and Niko nodded to them as we passed by. The leader of the patrol waved at us, but other than that, they paid no attention to us. We went another hundred yards before I looked back. The patrol kept going. I exhaled the gulp of air I had held since we first saw them.

"I told you they were easier than the main road patrols," Niko said.

We rode through a good-sized town called Bergum. It was as big as Meppel but since we had just passed a patrol, Niko felt pretty secure going through the town. Other than Dutchmen and a few stray German soldiers in the southern end of the town, there was nothing to hinder our passage and we had no problems. I was still shaking from the patrol back in Suameer, but after we passed through Bergum my confidence was restored. Next we passed through Quatrebras and saw only good Dutchmen. The people were friendly, speaking to us as we rode by.

We kept riding northward. The riding was uneventful as we passed through an occasional village, speaking to some of the villagers and nodding to others. The fields, which should have been rich with fall harvest, were thick with weeds. The many windmills were idle, their huge vanes, or wings, tied at the bottom to keep them from turning. The roads were in disrepair; often entire stretches of pavement were chuckholed and others had bricks missing. It gave us a hell of a jolt when we'd hit an unseen chuckhole.

Riding through Veenwouden, Wasgwestemde, De Valom, Broeksterwoude, and Rinsumgeest, we passed two more patrols. Later in the day, my legs began to ache so we rode more slowly. My thighs and calves literally screamed out in protest because of the abuse. We stopped every thirty minutes and walked my cramps out. Finally, I had no more push in them.

We came to the village of Raard and pulled off the road, walking the bicycles to a house just off the main street. Niko knocked but there was no answer. We laid the bicycles against a fence and from under a flower pot, he found the key and opened the door. I hobbled to a chair and fell into it, unable to get the cramps out of my legs. He told me to get on the table and pull down my underwear. He found some cold cream and massaged my thighs and calves for fifteen minutes until they felt better. I pulled up my pants and fastened my belt. Niko went to replace the cold cream when the back door opened very suddenly. A very startled and frightened middle-aged couple stood there, their mouths agape, not knowing what to say. I just held out my hands and called out Niko's name.

The man was yelling at me as Niko returned to the kitchen.

"Mijnheer Wessum, mevrouw Wessum!" he said, holding out his hand. The man and woman in turn shook it. He explained to them how my legs had become sore from riding the bicycle and we had stopped at their house to find something to rub them with.

The woman left the room and returned holding a bottle with some brown liquid in it. "Drop your drawers," she said in Dutch. I understood her words and looked to Niko for help.

142

"Do what she says." He shrugged his shoulders, then sat down in a kitchen chair with a silly grin on his face.

I dropped my drawers. If my legs felt better after Niko finished massaging them, then this woman had fingers of magic! The medication she used was hot on my skin and went all the way to the bone. When she finished, my legs tingled from my ankles to my crotch.

Mevrouw Wessum made us a little snack, which we ate quickly. We said goodbye to them and I again thanked the woman and tried to make her understand how much I appreciated her work.

It was almost dark when we got to Bornwird, a kilometer beyond Raard. "Holwerd is only about eight kilometers," Niko said. "Are you going to make it all right?"

"I'm doing my best," I panted, for my cramps had returned.

Again, a German patrol appeared. They eyed us carefully but then passed us and waved. My legs hurt so much it was hard for me to pedal anymore. I looked back at the patrol. We were okay.

Niko rode his bicycle next to mine and put his hand in the middle of my back to push me. It made pedaling tolerable. We rode through Brantgum and Waxxens. It was after curfew, but we stayed on the main road to Holwerd.

At last, we could see Holwerd against the darkened sky. A pair of church steeples pointed skyward. We got off the bicycles and I fell down, unable to stand. The pain was unbelievable. Niko helped me to my feet and walked in front of me. I put one hand on his shoulders and pushed my bicycle with the other. I prayed we wouldn't run into a patrol.

We entered an alley and followed it to the main street, where we left our bicycles in back of a two-story brick building. We opened the solitary unlocked door. It was very dark inside, so I held on to Niko's coat. Carefully, he felt his way to the stairs and we climbed them, each step an agonizing effort for me. At the top, he knocked softly at the door. George opened it, revealing a single candle burning in a dish on the table. It reflected off Jim's smiling face.

"Hi, Harry," he said. "What's the matter? You're limping."

I had to laugh. I told him about the trip, about mevrouw Wessum and dropping my drawers.

As I was talking, George lit some more candles and placed them on the cupboard. He went into another room and returned with a woman. "Jan, this is my wife," he said in Dutch.

She smiled as I shook her cold, limp hand but didn't speak. By candlelight she appeared to be a small woman with a beautiful face. Her blond hair was neatly combed and she was well dressed. She seemed to be a delicate woman, not at all what I expected George's wife to be. After she checked the windows, making sure the light from the candle didn't filter outside, she felt the tea kettle and prepared warm tea.

She was an extremely shy person. She never held her head erect but kept it down as though she were ill. When she smiled it was only for George and it brightened her face. Never once did she look at Jim or me, even when she served tea. I felt that she disliked the position we had placed her in, but she tolerated it because she was entirely devoted to her husband.

As we drank our tea, Niko talked.

"We cannot stay here tonight. We will be staying in the church for a while. Most of the German troops are near Arnhem expecting another parachute invasion. I will go and awaken the minister of the church for his key. Rest until I get back." He added, "Jan, you should stand on your legs and try to exercise."

I did what he suggested, painfully.

A half hour later, he came back. "We are all ready!"

Quietly, we went down the back steps. Jim pushed my bicycle for me. The side door of the church was unlocked. We leaned the bicycles on the side of the building and went inside. A small stairway led to a hall where there were several rooms. A door opened to reveal a man holding a very dim flashlight.

"Niko, George, come up here," the man said quietly.

We went inside. Several big candles lit the room considerably. It was the kitchen, probably for use by the congregation in better days. A blackout curtain covered the lone window. There was a table and six chairs.

"This is Dominee de Boer," Niko said, introducing us. "These are the American pilots, Jim and Jan Veen."

We shook hands with him. He was short, probably about forty, with an unbuttoned overcoat doubling for a bathrobe. His face was pale, his bright blue eyes sparkled, and he had a wonderful smile. His thinning gray hair belied his years.

"Thank you for your help, Dominee," I said.

"Please sit down," he said in broken English. Painfully, I sat at the table along with the others. Niko told the preacher my legs were sore from the bicycle ride. He told about the massage mevrouw Wessum had given me. When he told him how she had ordered me to "drop my drawers," all of us laughed. "I understand she has told many men that," Niko continued, "but I don't think they all had sore legs, do you Dominee?" The minister didn't answer but got some blankets from a closet and apologized to us because we would have to sleep on the floor. When he left, he was chuckling to himself.

"Niko, I want to thank you for the help you gave me to get here. You must be tired after pushing me as far as you did. I hope I can repay you some day."

"No thanks needed. Anyway, we're here now and we are safe."

"Next time Jim rides the bicycle," I said. "By the way, Jim, how long did it take you and George to get here?"

"Oh, about an hour," he replied.

I could have killed them both.

We found places on the floor to lie down. I covered with a blanket. "Goodnight," I said, but there were no answers.

I lay there a long time. My legs ached as they never had before. The pain became so great that I got up and walked in the hall outside. It was a lousy night for sleeping.

As my eyes became accustomed to the dark, I went downstairs to the church. There were benches in a semicircle around the altar. I sat on a bench and my legs felt better. I thought about Greta Rusk, George's wife, the day's developments . . .

Temptation sometimes rears its ugly head. Occasionally I strayed. I guess it all started at the Music Box in Boise. I met a girl there by the name of Vesta. We were more than just good friends. Her husband, in the air force, had been shipped overseas, not flying but in a secure job as a squadron clerk. I introduced Johnny to her girlfriend and their apartment became our home away from home. She was a loving and considerate girl. I gave her a pair of earrings with intertwined hearts. Later, at Attlebridge, Bob Lehman took me to ground personnel's barracks and pointed to a picture on a shelf over one of the bunks. It was Vesta, wearing the earrings I had given her. Bob introduced me to her husband, a corporal, a handsome man and probably the biggest stud on the base who tried to bed down with every woman that wore a skirt. I was happy Vesta and I had our affair.

A lot of the guys got "Dear John" letters. Wives couldn't divorce them because military personnel were protected by the "Soldier's and

Sailor's Relief Act" which covered GIs in these situations. All military personnel had to sign a release before their wives could break the ties. The smart women had second thoughts: If the GI got killed, she wouldn't have to worry about it. It was "instant divorce." And there was the insurance to consider. Sometimes "Dear John" letters were a relief. I have known a lot of guys who got them overseas. Usually, the recipient would be heart-broken and he would mope around the barracks. He wouldn't eat, joke, or hang around with the guys. He would even talk of suicide. If he didn't smoke or drink he would acquire these vices. For all intents and purposes this kind of guy should have been grounded, but the crew felt a sense of loyalty to him and covered for him. After becoming a real pain in the ass, and just before he was about to sink over the edge, he would finally realize that she really didn't want him anymore. Once he got that in his head, he was practically cured. He would start sprucing up a bit, smile occasionally. Soon he was in the midst of a crowd at the pub, with his arm around some chick. The next day, back on base, he would tell what a great lay his chick was, and once again he was back in the fold.

There was a pub near our base called "The Five Ringers Pub" used by both men and women as a gathering place after a day of labor. The locals drank their pints of mild or bitter beer as well as gin, or scotch when they had it, and played darts. At first they resented the Yanks. They said, "You damned Yanks are overpaid, oversexed, and over here. Yer just too damned rowdy." They knew we flew B-24s out of Attlebridge. When the good folk began to miss some of their Yank acquaintances because they didn't come back to the pub, they learned those boys had "bought it" (been shot down). Their attitudes changed and they took the 466th under their wing. We became their boys.

The women had a separate section of the pub, while the men drank in the bar where the Americans were always the loudest. Anybody named Clark in Britain automatically had the nickname of "Knobby." So I became Knobby to everybody, even my crew. When Johnny and I walked in, the piano player played "Stardust" and we were greeted, "Hello, Johnny . . . Hi ya, Knobby."

I met a barmaid about my age who was very pretty. I kidded her and told her I'd sure like to get in her pants. She'd push me away jokingly and say, "Now, Knobby." One evening just before the pub closed, she told me if I'd wait for her I could walk her home. She lived just outside town, a short distance over some rural roads. A stone fence skirted the road about three to four feet high. As we walked along in the twilight, we came to a gate in the stone fence. She took my hand and steered me toward it.

"Come on, maybe I'll give you what you've been asking for."

I followed her through the fence, up a small rise to the field beyond. She sat down in the grass and I sat beside her. We started necking and one thing led to another. She slid out of her clothes and lay on her coat as naked as a jaybird. Needless to say, I soon had my clothes off and anxiously crawled on top of her but she pushed me away.

"Stop!" she said.

"Now what have I done?" I asked.

"You bloody Yanks are always in such a hurry to do everything. I'll show you how to give a lady some satisfaction. Easy now." She grabbed hold of me. "Easy, easy now," she ordered. "No, that will never do." She pushed me away once more.

"We'll just have to do it by the numbers. All right, Yank, easy. Ready now? By the numbers, one, two, three, four. Slowly, slowly . . . that's it. One, two, three, four . . . don't break the rhythm, one, two, three, four. Now you've got the hang of it . . . one, two, three . . . don't break the rhythm. Keep it up. Now you've got it . . . Oh God, Oh God, Oh God, Oh!" She let out several muffled screams. It's the only time in my life I ever laughed and still got the job done. She was embarrassed and mad as hell when I laughed. After I explained, being a pretty good sport, she laughed too.

We walked slowly to her house, talking of better days. The next night, after the pub closed, I took her home and we thoroughly enjoyed the evening — without benefit of any numbers.

Tommy Bell, Bob Lehman, Johnny, and I went to the Bell Hotel in Norwich one payday. We were loaded with money and were soon loaded on beer. Several "working ladies" lived at the hotel and soon we had four of the lovelies drinking at our table with us. Tommy's girl got mad because he was disrespectful. It was a problem. We apologized for Tommy and told her that Tommy was really a nice guy who had had a little too much to drink. However, she absolutely refused to reconsider anything.

Her speech is memorable. "I'm a professional prostitute!" was her drunken reply. "My health card is current and I can damned well choose whom I want for my clientele. I am not a 'fucking whore' as your friend has chosen to call me. I am good at my profession, which puts me far above that drunken sot. Take this 'pencil peckered lieutenant' back to your United States and tell his friends that he couldn't

147

even get in the pants of a 'fucking Limey whore' over in jolly olde England!"

With that, she turned on her heel and disappeared into a room.

Maybe it was the drinks, but I could say nothing in poor Tommy's defense after her speech. I laughed until I thought my guts would break. Tommy just stood there with his mouth open, unable to speak. We laughed so hard we got out of the mood for the ladies, so we really tied one on. Our topic of conversation was his "qualifications," which kept us in an uproar. He fell asleep with his head on the bar and we couldn't wake him up, so we carried him up to a room and put him to bed.

When I woke up in the morning, I was still laughing — hungover, but still laughing.

EIGHT

A wakening in the church, I cursed the day bicycles were invented. I went upstairs and found that George and Niko were gone. Jim, breathing deeply, was lying on his belly. I found the toilet, relieved myself, and washed. The small kitchen window wasn't boarded over, so I pulled the blackout curtain aside and saw the village in the daylight.

I went back down into the church. It was a beautiful structure built entirely of an unstained light wood covered with a coat of shellac to preserve its natural beauty. Some windmills were visible off to the south through the stained glass windows, none of them operational.

Niko, George, and the Dominee came in the side door. I was sitting in a pew, trying to decipher a Dutch song book.

"Is it too difficult to read?" the Dominee asked.

"Difficult? Yes," I replied, "but not someday . . . maybe."

We went up to the kitchen. Through the window I saw a little house about a hundred yards away. "My home," he said.

The cupboard held an assortment of food — tea, bread, cheese, and canned milk. Some cloth sacks contained flour and oatmeal. The sink had a cold water tap and wood was piled under it to fuel the stove. The Dominee built a fire in it, insisting on preparing our first meal. He heated some water, made oatmeal and tea, and after he blessed the food we ate heartily.

"God, what I wouldn't give for some ham and eggs," Jim said.

"Better not ask God for ham and eggs, Jim. Ask the Germans. You will have better luck, for they control everything," said the pastor. "Or wait for the Allies. Then you can have all the ham and eggs you want — sugar and coffee too for that matter."

"Jim, that kind of wishing and five hundred dollars couldn't buy a nickel cup of coffee right now," I said.

The Dominee continued speaking as he washed the dishes and Jim dried them. "Sometimes the Germans come here during their patrols around eight in the morning or six at night. They stay for about half an hour unless they take a nap where their superiors can't find them. Be sure the kitchen is clean and everything is put away. They always come to my house for the key. I usually go with them to pass the time of day. Sometimes I make them a sandwich. Good public relations, no? Come with me and I'll show you where to hide if they pay the church a visit."

On the wall in back of the pulpit was a trap door, clearly exposed to the congregation while church services were conducted, but it was so well concealed it was impossible to see. It was opened by a spring latch mechanism. We followed him up the steep steps into the dark rafters which were covered by boards forming a floor. The only light came from cracks under the eaves purposely left there for ventilation.

He put on his coat and went home, then Niko and George put on their coats. "We will be gone for a couple of days," said Niko. "The Dominee will check on you. We are going to try to make arrangements to get you back to England. Wish us luck!" They walked out the door saying goodbye in unison. We were surprised at their abrupt departure.

"Well, let's get out the cards!" Jim said. "I've got a lot of money to win back from you."

"Bullshit!" I said.

When we finally bedded down for the night, Jim owed me $192.

The following morning we had finished eating when the pastor came in the side door. He was upset because we hadn't locked the door from the inside. We apologized, explaining we didn't know we were supposed to.

"My wife has gone to Leeuwarden and I'm alone. I would like to invite you to my house later for dinner. We can get to know each other better. All right?"

At 2:00 we walked the hundred yards to his home, where he was waiting at the door. The house was beautifully decorated with lace curtains and a fireplace with painted Delft tiles adorning the surface. More Delft dishes decorated the walls and shelves. Antique lamps and two glowing antique clocks that chimed out the quarter hour hung on the walls. The furniture glistened.

We went into his study, a carbon copy of the living room but smaller. His huge desk was uncluttered. Oil paintings hung on the walls. He asked if we were armed and when I told him I was, he asked me to put my weapon in his desk until we left. I offered the Luger to him, but he opened the drawer and asked me to put it in.

He told us about himself. He was born in Rotterdam, where he had gone to the ministry, and became an assistant in Amsterdam. He and his wife, from Holwerd, had married after a brief courtship. His church was his first appointment. The attendance divided between the two houses of worship. Holwerd, he said, never had a *razzia* nor any serious problems with the Nazis. The citizens were polite and as a result they overlooked the young men they saw on the streets. The men who went to German work camps over the past years were never heard from again. In confidence he told about the tremendous amount of underground activity. He condoned it but didn't participate in it. "There are so many Jews in Holwerd a synagogue should be erected for them," he said.

He asked Jim about his life. Jim told him about Oregon and the small lumber town of Albany and how everyone depended upon each other for their livelihood. He was from a poor family but had no ambitions for wealth. All he wanted was to get home as soon as possible and marry the girl who was waiting for him. He told of the seven missions he had flown as the tail-gunner on a B-17 Flying Fortress. He told the Dominee he was a Catholic.

The Dominee listened with a great deal of interest and asked a lot of questions, many of them about his church and his priest. Though some of the questions were of a personal nature, I thought Jim answered them very well.

When he asked me, I gave the Dominee the story of my life in a nutshell. He was amazed that I had flown thirty-three missions.

"Tell me, Jan, how do you feel flying in the sky, dropping destruction and death on innocent, unsuspecting human beings?"

I told him about the V-1 in London. "Dominee de Boer," I said, "you didn't start this war and did even less to provoke it. Only Hitler and the ninety percent of German people who endorsed the National

Socialist concept of government are responsible. They are the ones who overran Europe with their blitzkriegs and Luftwaffe, bombing and strafing Rotterdam and London as well as Poland and Russia. Their bombs killed the innocent. It was the Nazis who were bent on bringing the world to its knees. Britain stood alone, taking all the Germans threw at them. The RAF shot down their bombers and the V-1 buzz-bombs. Finally, England's friends and allies came to her aid, at first with war materiel and then with the military, their own flesh and blood, much of it to be spilled in Europe.

"It galls me when I hear the statement you just made," I continued. "We don't aim at civilians. We aim at their war-making capability, or their men in uniform. Americans have a sense of 'fair play' bred in them, and we take that into account in our personal vendetta with the enemy. However, if enemy civilians get in the way of our bombing, so be it!"

The Dominee listened to every word. Then there was silence.

"Yes, of course, I have never talked to anybody in your position to explain how they felt." He paused and considered his next words. "Yes, I can understand it. When I was in Amsterdam, the streets ran red with blood! I can understand your feelings, Jan Veen. Many times I gave solace to the condemned about to face firing squads. Still, every man who faced the guns died with fear in his heart. I mourn for the innocent. Some day this war will end and I will have to answer to God for my human emotions. Here in Holwerd, all is peace and tranquility. Only the hardships of survival exist. If a change comes in Holwerd and my countrymen have no place to turn except to defend themselves, I think my choice would be a righteous one if I took off my collar, took up a gun, and joined in the fight against the Nazis. We will win in the end, Jan, there will be a victory! Afterward, I'll put the collar back on and pray to God for forgiveness." He bowed his head. "Will you please pray with me?"

I expected a lengthy prayer. Instead, he bowed his head, clasped his hands over his breast, closed his eyes, and the next fifteen minutes were spent in silent prayer. I felt a presence unlike nothing I ever experienced, the power of his prayer. I felt as if God were with us. I opened my eyes but he had not moved. When I closed them again I regained the feeling.

After supper, the Dominee motioned for Jim and me to come to the front window of his house. He held an arm up to prevent us from getting too close to the window. A three-man Grune Polizei patrol passed by, pushing their bicycles to the east. It was 6:00. They were alert, looking in all directions, taking mental notes. They wore their helmets and had Schmeissers across their chests suspended by highly polished leather straps. One of them, a giant of a man, had a huge silver and black German Shepherd tied to the handlebar of his bicycle. Little did I know what an important part that beautiful dog would play in my life.

As soon as the patrol passed through town, I went with the Dominee to his desk and got my Luger. We put on our coats and went for a walk. We walked about a kilometer out of town to a big windmill. Inside, I saw the massive wooden gears. The works were a masterpiece of precision. Each individual piece was fitted together without benefit of nails or screws.

"This is a grist mill," the Dominee explained. "If for any reason you should have to leave the church, come to this mill, go to the top, and hide. Someone will come for you."

We walked back beside a narrow rill in the fading daylight. The water was flowing slowly. It was so beautiful I hated to go back into the confines of the church, but we bade the pastor goodnight, went inside, and immediately locked the door after us.

We played solitaire by candlelight until after midnight. When we called it quits, Jim owed me $210.

George and Niko didn't come back for five days. Dominee de Boer received word they were making progress but wouldn't be back as soon as they anticipated. We spent our days playing the marathon game of solitaire and having an occasional talk with the Dominee. Twice he invited us to his home. He was always gracious and loved to talk about the United States.

One evening we went for a walk in the village. There were many people on the streets, including many men between the ages of sixteen and sixty-five. The town had a maze of back streets and alleys. I learned the layout of Holwerd quickly. We kept to ourselves and stayed away from the people we encountered.

Sunday morning we got up early and ate breakfast. After we cleaned the kitchen we went to the hiding place and made ourselves comfortable. The Dominee's voice was clear and moving as he presented his sermon, most of which I understood. The people sang many inspiring hymns. We stayed put until he called for us.

We played solitaire all day. When night settled in, Jim was in debt $410.

Niko and George came back that night. When they knocked at the door we let them in and sat at the table. They told of their plans.

"We did it! It was a very difficult thing to do, putting a workable plan together and getting permission from London to do it. It took a lot longer than we thought, but after the arrangements were made, things went well. We will leave here day after tomorrow. We are going to a small fishing village up the coast and wait for a message to be broadcast over BBC. When it is, we will go to a small island in the North Sea and be picked up by a submarine or an air-sea rescue boat. You will join your countrymen and we will join the Dutch forces."

"Thank you!" I said, shaking hands with them both.

"A week from today," Niko said, "you will be flying your bombers again!" George smiled, watching us enjoy our moment of happiness.

"Just think," Jim said, "we'll be back in England and be home in the good old U.S.A. another week after that! I won't have to fly the rest of my missions, just go home to Oregon."

I must confess, I did some mental celebrating of my own. I'd had too many disappointments in my life to set stock in a quick liberation. We hit the sack and I fell asleep immediately.

When I woke up in the morning, for the first time in a week my legs didn't ache. But the next two days were my longest. I was so excited and expectant because there was a good chance the plan would work. We just might make it back. However, in the back of my mind there was still a strong measure of pessimism. I was afraid something might go wrong. It all depended on getting picked up from the island, and getting out to it. With the invasion in full swing, surely the Allies would be in Holland before too long. We weren't important people, so why would they risk a rescue? That was "stinkin' thinkin'." Of course they would come. They had given the okay for the mission. When I thought positively, I could hardly contain myself. And I prayed.

There was an incident I cannot explain. On the day we were to leave, Jim, Niko, George, and I had finished breakfast and were sitting at the kitchen table cleaning our guns. George managed to get some gun oil and rags. I finished mine and stuck it in my belt. George proceeded to put the ammo clip back in his Colt .45 and laid it on the table in front of him. For no apparent reason, he picked up the .45 and fired two shots through the floor of the kitchen, missing my left foot by no more than a dozen inches! Niko screamed, cursing violently.

I jumped back, grabbed my Luger, and faced George. I didn't

154

point it at him, but I was trembling badly. He grinned and told Niko, "The gun works well!" Then he stuck it in his belt and went about picking up his rags and gun oil. We were so alarmed by his foolhardy stunt that we left the room and went into the hiding place, taking George with us. That's where the Dominee found us when he came out to investigate the shots. They were heard all over Holwerd, he said. An hour later we came back down and the smell of cordite was still in the air. The Dominee opened the kitchen window to let the smell out, but instead, the wind blew the odor into the church proper. The cold breeze cooled the temperature inside too.

The evening patrol went through Holwerd right on schedule. They headed east, the same direction we were going, and soon they were out of sight. Thank God they didn't decide to stop in the church for a rest, or the smell of cordite would have gotten the Dominee in trouble. Later, the Dominee told me it took a couple of days for the smell to dissipate.

We gathered our belongings in preparation for leaving. The pastor came back to the church to say goodbye. We stood inside the door talking. Finally, he said, "Let's pray." He prayed aloud in Dutch and finished in English with these words, "Protect these young men alone in a foreign land. See them home to their loved ones. Give them power and strength to face the tests that lie ahead. Bless them, Oh Father, Amen."

Our bicycles were leaning against the back wall of the church, put there by unseen hands. We tied our bags on them and walked them around to the side. Again, we all shook hands with Dominee de Boer.

"I wish you well till we are at peace again," I said.

He looked at me and smiled. "We'll meet again," he said.

We pedaled off. Niko and I led the way, with George and Jim about 500 feet behind us. A short time after we left town, we rode beside a very high dike on our left.

"The North Sea is on the other side of the dike," he said.

We went through a very small village called Visburt. Almost at once we came to a slightly larger village called Ternaard.

"The commanding officer of the underground for this area lives in this town," Niko said without elaborating further.

At dusk we went through Nes. It looked absolutely deserted. Darkness set in rapidly and it had been dark for some time when our destination, the fishing village of Paesens, came into view. The road went up to the top of the dike. I looked out over the North Sea for the first time from ground level. I had seen it so many times from the air. Though it was dark, there was moonlight filtering through the clouds and reflecting off the ripples in the water. It had a calming effect on me.

Riding the bike was something else, however, almost as hazardous as flying a combat mission. Huge chuckholes and ruts had been washed out by rains and use. Lack of repairs made it downright dangerous. We rode carefully and slowly, happy to reach our destination intact.

There were seven or eight men to welcome us when we pulled into a house on the intersection of the road we were traveling and one in the middle of the village. The men helped us with our bicycles and took our suitcases into the house. I understood much of what they said, essentially "Welcome to Paesens!"

There were many varieties of cheese on the table, as well as real butter, milk, and a lighter bread. A woman served potatoes with a tomato paste, cabbage, and turnips. She kept the teacups full. Everybody talked and laughed at the same time. It was a happy group. After shifting for ourselves for a week, we had a feast!

"The welcome seems like a circus," Jim said. "They're all so happy, gesturing with their hands and trying to speak English."

I was impressed by their honest display of friendship. I was also grateful when I was shown to an upstairs bedroom and steered by one of the Dutchmen to another closet bed.

When I settled in bed, I was amazed my legs didn't ache. I spent a rare restful night, without any nightmares.

In the morning I got out of bed, woke Jim, and we dressed.

"I know what you mean about sore legs," he said. "Mine ache just from the ride last night."

I couldn't feel sorry for him. Downstairs, the men and hilarity from the night before had vanished. The house seemed deserted until I heard a noise in the kitchen. I was met by the woman of the house. "*Dag,*" I said.

"Good morning," she said, "did you sleep well?"

"Yes, thank you. My name is Jan Veen."

"Yes, I know," she said, smiling. "I am mevrouw Visser."

She poured two cups of tea as Jim joined me. This was followed by oatmeal, bread, cheese, and milk. Mevrouw Visser bustled around the kitchen. She had an air of authority over her domain as she worked.

156

There was no wasted motion; each movement was the epitome of efficiency.

About midmorning, the men returned. They looked like the fishermen they were. They had been in the sea working in the tides. They didn't use boats. The catch was placed in a communal shed. After the Germans took what they wanted for shipment to Germany, the few fish left over were shared by the Dutchmen. A Landwatcher monitored their activities carefully. They were excused from working in the defenses by the Nazis.

The men went out in the back yard and washed. They changed clothes and when they came in, mevrouw Visser had their food on the table. Each of them ate like they were hungry, gulping food in big mouthfuls.

Teun de Jong, harbormaster for the island of Schiermonnikoog, took me by the arm and steered me into the front room. He had a checkerboard and a box of checkers under his arm. He sat the board on a small table between two chairs and motioned for me to sit down. We played checkers all day long. This fine Dutchman was so friendly and congenial and had to be the world's champion. He pointed out my mistakes but showed me no mercy, taking advantage of each one. The English he spoke was broken and difficult to understand. In desperation, so we could understand each other, we started speaking half in English and half in Dutch. We understood each other perfectly after that.

He had many stories to tell and related them humorously. He loved the sea and his island home. Three hundred Germans lived on Schiermonnikoog and manned the .88mm antiaircraft guns scattered among the sand dunes. They shot at Allied bombers and fighter planes. Among the Nazis stationed there were several SS, SD, and Landwatchers. Boats, he said, could only go to the island at high tide unless the driver knew the tides and the channels — and he did.

Teun de Jong had a face that one could never forget. It was well defined with many deep lines etched to form a permanent smile. He was only slightly older than I, about 5'10 or so, and muscular under his sweater. He worked hard and wore a skipper's cap that I'd have given anything to own. He was my favorite.

That night, Niko took Jim and me to the attic. The illegal radio was tuned to the BBC and the Germans' attempts to jam the broadcast were only partly successful. Messages to the underground groups came through loud and clear. The messages, in the tongue of the country for which they were intended, were in prearranged codes. When the messages came through in Dutch, all ears were listening. Probably fifteen messages were broadcast, each of them repeated a second time. When it was over, mijnheer Visser replaced the radio under a panel in the floor.

"What message are we waiting for, Niko?" I asked, noticing his disappointment.

"De vloed komt op, ik herhalen, de vloed komt op," he said.

"What does it mean?"

"The tide comes up, I repeat, the tide comes up. When we hear that message we have to hurry out to our little island and wait for the boat on the following night."

"What island are we going to?"

"Engelsmanplaat," he replied.

"Englishman's Plaat," I repeated, "where in hell is that?"

"Engelsmanplaat," he corrected, "is a very large sandbank between the islands of Schiermonnikoog and Ameland in the North Sea. They are islands in the Frisian island chain."

"Wait a minute," I said. I went and got my escape map and spread it out on the table. Niko pointed to Schiermonnikoog and Ameland. A small island between them was called Engelsmanplaat. It was just off the coast from Paesens. Now I knew why we were staying in this house.

"Where did Engelsmanplaat get its name?" Jim asked.

"I'll answer that," Teun de Jong interrupted with a twinkle in his eye. "Since time began, or since we have been keeping records at least, it was discovered that the worst sailors in the world, or the most foolhardy, or the bravest, take your pick, are the British. Almost all the ships which have perished on the sandbank called Engelsmanplaat, generally during big storms on the North Sea, have been British. How could it possibly have any other name?" He laughed. "Right now, there's a midget submarine laying on it and we don't know who it belongs to or even if there are any men in it. The Boche check it periodically but have deserted it to the gods."

"How about Britisherplaat?" I asked.

Teun laughed. "Oh, you are searching, aren't you?"

"Where do we get the boat to go out there?" I asked.

Teun looked at Visser. "No boat," he said.

"No boat?" I asked, sure that I had misunderstood him.

"Nope, no boat," said Teun.

158

Mijnheer Visser broke in. "We go out at low tide or else the water is too deep to walk in. We hurry when the tide is at its lowest ebb. We will wade through four kilometers of water, then across another four kilometers of sandy shoal to a life-house."

"Life-house? You mean lighthouse, don't you?" I asked.

"No, I mean life-house. There is a house constructed on the windward side of the *plaat* on stilts. It was built for those unfortunates who get shipwrecked. There was always a life-house on Engelsmanplaat for that reason."

"How safe is it?" Jim asked. "Don't the Germans check it?"

"We have had it under observation for six months now and have not seen a single German. They have ignored it completely. However, the life-house can be seen clearly from the island of Schiermonnikoog. There are two very tall lighthouses on the island and the Germans use these for observation posts. By the same token, Schiermonnikoog can be seen from the life-house too!"

"How deep will the water be while we're wading out there?" I asked.

"Most of the time it will be knee-deep or less. There are two small, waist-deep channels to cross. Maybe a little deeper."

"Christ, can't you get us a boat?" Jim asked.

I interrupted. "Who will lead us to the place?"

Teun put his hand on my shoulder. "Minjheer Visser and myself. We are familiar with the tides. We'll stay with you until the next low tide and come back to Paesens. Sorry, Jim, no boat!"

Niko spoke to me. "You and Jim will be the first! After you, we hope many Allied airmen will follow in your footsteps."

"Yeah," I said, "we're a bunch of goddamned pioneers." Then I had to explain what a goddamned pioneer was.

I again played checkers with the harbormaster, who talked with me during our game. He convinced me there was no danger in walking out there. Close to bedtime, he let me win a game. Although he said I beat him fair and square, he had a glint in his eye.

Later, lying in bed, I thought it had been well planned. All that remained was for the radio to set up a rendezvous and we would be off for the sandbank. There were still many things I wanted to know and I wanted to digest what I had already learned.

Except for mevrouw Visser and Jim, the house was deserted when I got up in the morning. I drank a cup of tea, which was all I wanted. Jim was in the front room reading *Vanity Fair,* a book written in English. The fisherman's wife had found it. I went outside to the back yard. A picket fence surrounded the house. It was white at one time but was badly in need of paint, as was the weather-beaten house.

On the road south of town, I saw two women riding bicycles headed in my direction. When they were about a city block away, I turned my back and leaned against the fence as they rode by. They turned in the direction of Holwerd. Five minutes later, one of them returned, rounding the corner rapidly as she rode up to me.

Greta Rusk! She stopped her bicycle and said, "Hello, Jan Veen, American."

"Hello, Greta Rusk, Frieslander," I answered.

"Aren't you going to invite me in? I'm through work now."

"Oh, of course . . . Please come in," I stammered.

I opened the gate and she wheeled her bicycle into the yard. I took it and leaned it against the house. We went up the steps. Mevrouw Visser was sitting at the kitchen table darning socks. I introduced them but found out they were friends. Mevrouw Visser poured tea as I helped Greta off with her coat. Jim came in the kitchen and I introduced them. He took a cup of tea and went back into the front room. As he left, he looked back, winked, and gave me the "okay" sign. He approved.

"So, where are George and Niko?" she asked.

"I don't know. They were gone when I got up this morning."

"How long have you been here?"

"This is our third day."

"Did you enjoy your stay with Dominee de Boer?"

"Yes, he is a fine man," I replied.

"Did you know I was there twice?"

"No," I answered, somewhat surprised. "Why wasn't I told?"

"Because it wouldn't have been good for me to see you then. I had too many things to do to help arrange for your escape. I am keeping an eye on you, you know."

Her voice had a calming effect. My God, she was a beautiful girl. If, as Niko had said, she was too much woman for one man to handle, it was a crime. Her blue eyes were crystal clear. She didn't need any makeup. I could count the hairs in her eyebrows and see the tiny pores in her skin, she was so close. She took my hand and held it in her lap and looked at me, staring into my eyes. She didn't say a word.

I didn't want to break the spell, but I said, "I couldn't keep my

160

eyes off you in Suameer and now I have the same problem. I hope I don't embarrass you."

"No," she said, "you don't embarrass me. I noticed you were attracted to me. It's been a long time since I have been interested in a man looking at me, let alone looking back. Wasn't it obvious I am interested?"

"And why should that be? Because I am an American flyer?"

"No, that doesn't interest me." She thought a minute. "Perhaps for the same reason I interest you. Isn't that possible?"

I could almost feel horns protruding from my head as the devil came out in me. "And why do you think you interest me?"

I caught a slight devilish glimpse in her eyes too. She raised her right eyebrow. "All right, you want me to say it. Because you are a young man and I am a young woman. Because whether I like it or not, there is a strong attraction between us. Whether it is physical or emotional, I don't know. I'm curious to find out its meaning as much as you are." She was dead serious but kept a faint smile on her lips. She looked at me for several moments. "Well?" she asked.

"Is that why you turned around and came back here just now?"

"It's the only reason I came back!" she replied, smiling.

I gave her hand a squeeze and she returned it. We sat there like two bumps on a log. I wanted to be alone, to kiss her. I wanted to have some privacy and talk to her. *How do you handle this situation in a strange house, in a strange country?* I asked myself. My answer arrived when George and Niko came through the door, both of them grinning broadly at the sight of Greta.

"*Dag,* Greta," Niko said. "How are you?"

"Good, now that I've got my work done. How are you, George?"

George nodded and sat down at the table. They spoke to Greta in Frisian and mevrouw Visser joined their conversation. The word "Engelsmanplaat" came up several times. I could understand a little of what they said. Finally, they fell silent. I drank my tea and joined them in their silence.

"Greta, why don't you take a bicycle ride with Jan?" Niko suggested. "The Germans have headed back to Leeuwarden. The town will be safe for a while and it will be good for Jan to see the countryside."

"Okay by you?" I asked. She nodded her assent.

I helped her with her coat, got into my own, and we went out the back door. I got my bicycle from under the porch as she retrieved hers.

161

Silently, we rode south, away from the main road for half a kilometer, then turned off on a side road. A kilometer later, we turned on another road, heading south again. We passed several houses before we came to the one she was looking for. We pushed our bicycles around to the back of the house and put them in a shed. She took a key from under the flowerpot and opened the door. Once inside, I closed the door and Greta locked it again.

She turned to face me. "There, Jan Veen. We are alone and can speak without anybody overhearing us."

I hung her coat on a hook in the anteroom along with my own. We walked into the kitchen. She put a couple of pieces of wood on the dying embers in the stove.

"I'm cold," she said, so I put my arms around her and held her close to me. "Better?" I asked.

She turned around within my arms and looked at me. Again, she stared into my eyes as she had done in Paesens. She gave me a gentle kiss on the lips and released herself from my grasp, walking back to the stove.

"The wood is burning . . . soon it will be warm," she said, sitting down at the kitchen table. She looked very sad and unsure of the position in which she had put herself.

It turned into a difficult situation. A wall had come up. "What's the matter? Have you changed your mind? Have you satisfied your curiosity?" I asked. "Or am I too forward with you?"

"Too forward? No, Jan Veen, I am afraid, I guess."

"Well, we're alone now, so you can say anything you want to me." She didn't reply. "There seems to be a wall between us instead of the kitchen table." Again I waited. "Have I offended you? Perhaps I am presuming too much, taking too much for granted." I spoke softly, not wanting to force myself on her.

She didn't reply but looked so defenseless and sad, as she sat with her hands in her lap, her head bowed deep in thought for a long time. Finally, she got up and put some water on the stove to boil. She started to come over to me, then stopped, stood beside the stove, and looked at me for a long time. She sat back down at the table once more. So we sat staring at each other.

I made up my mind not to push it. She had a right to change her mind. Five minutes passed. She was so very beautiful in her moment of indecision.

"So, let's be friends," I said, deciding on some small talk. "Is this weather normal for this time of the year?" She looked at me questioningly. "When do you start to get snow?" She stared at me without answering. "Do you ice skate? I heard all Hollanders do." She smiled a little, finally understanding my small talk. "Well, did you ever fall through the ice?"

She laughed. "Yes, and you finally broke it!"

She came over to me and sat on my lap, pushing her body next to mine. She put her arms around my neck.

"When I was a very small girl, five years old I think, I fell through the ice on the canal. I almost drowned, but my brother pulled me out. Before he could get me home, I almost froze to death."

We both laughed. She looked at me and parted her lips. We kissed long and hard. She returned my kiss as I have never been kissed before. She broke away and went back to the stove.

"Whew!" she said as she poured us some tea. "Let's sit down and cool off with a cup of hot tea."

We were on our second cup. I made no further advances toward her. We held hands and talked of many things. She talked of faith and trust in her fellow man. It disgusted her when her friends and other people had been betrayed. She became very serious about the subject. She filled my cup with tea again and kissed me lightly on the cheek.

"Excuse me a minute?" she asked quietly and went into the front part of the house.

I sipped my tea and thought about her words. I filled my cup again and was almost through with it before she returned to the kitchen.

"Jan," she said from behind me.

I turned around in my chair. She was standing in the doorway to the front room, wearing a filmy nightgown. All the details of her lovely body were clearly visible through the thin material as the light from behind filtered through it. She came over to me and put her trembling hand in mine.

"Come with me," she said.

Off of the living room was a bedroom. The shades were drawn and the room, though not completely dark, was dimly shadowed. Her clothes were draped over a chair in the corner of the room. The bed was against the far wall with the covers turned back. She sat down on it. I stood in the doorway like someone in a trance, surveying the beautiful, unbelievable scene before me.

"Come here," she said.

I walked, no, more like floated over to her. She put her arms around my neck and pulled me down to her and kissed me on the lips. Not hard, not demanding, but very tenderly. She broke away and looked at me.

"I hope this is right for us," she said softly. "Get your clothes off and get into bed. I'm getting cold."

Quickly, I undressed and got in beside her. We slid her nightie over her head and threw it on top of the covers. Then we wrapped ourselves in each other's arms. We lay there for half an hour, teasing, playing with each other, and exploring each other's body until the tender delights, the caresses, the long passionate kisses crescendoed into such a pitch we were unable to suppress our growing passions. At exactly the right moment, we made love. We made love slowly and tenderly, both of us wanting all the joy and fulfillment the moment could bring. And getting it.

Later, as we lay there, holding each other close, we finally came back to earth. Then we did the whole thing all over again, only this time it was twice as long and twice as wonderful. Afterward, we just lay there and talked.

"Jan," she said, "there is something I want to tell you and I don't know how to do it. Promise me you will take it the right way or I won't even try to explain it. Promise?"

"Of course," I said, expecting her to tell me she couldn't be serious about me or some such story.

"It's about George and Niko," she said. "They are a careless pair. They do all the dirty jobs the groups can't find anyone else to do. They are very brave but they are also very foolhardy and careless. George has lived in Friesland all his life. Before the war he worked for the railroad. But Niko just popped up from nowhere. Nobody knows him or anything about him. Somebody said they heard he had been accused of being an informant for the Germans. He is suspected of being an NSB'er or an SD man who has infiltrated the underground. We know George and we know he is to be trusted, but Niko we are not sure about. I'm telling you so you'll be careful, very careful."

She was trembling again. I pulled her close to me.

"One thing more," she said, almost sobbing. "I am a trusted courier with my group in the underground. I should never talk to anybody about our group's suspicions. You could cause me a great deal of trouble if they found out I told you."

"If that's the case, why did you?" I asked.

"My God," she said loudly, "don't you know? I'm lying here in bed beside you naked. I have given you all a woman has to offer! I have fallen in love with you." There were tears in her eyes. "I don't want anything to happen to you. I want you to forget this Engelsmanplaat business. There are many safe houses where you can stay. You can stay with me. There's a good hiding place in my attic." She was crying.

"Greta, I'll never talk to anybody about us or what we've said to each other. You have become the most important person in my life. I want you to know I never felt this way about anyone. If there is such a thing as true love, then I have that feeling."

"Jan," she said almost hesitantly, "there is one thing more I want to tell you. I have had one man before in my life and I was with him twice. We went together for two years and became betrothed. Finally, the Germans took him away to a work camp and killed him. An escapee from the camp brought some of his belongings to me, so I know he is dead. The escapee tried to rape me in my moment of grief, but I kicked him so hard in his privates I don't think he has straightened up yet." She laughed. "I want only one man in my life and I have chosen you without even knowing you. But I trust my intuition. I feel your needs are the same as mine, both emotionally and sexually. We will be good for each other. I know I have done the right thing. Harry, Jan, please don't ever hurt me. I have been hurt so many times since the war. I never dreamed it could be like this. We're so good together. I'm glad I'm with you, so please, please love me."

I kissed her sweet face and said all the things she wanted to hear, sincerely and bearing my soul to her. Then we made love again, slowly, deliberately, and passionately.

Later, I told her about my life and the disappointments I had in my marriage. She understood there would be a permanent separation as soon as I went home. I told her my future was up in the air after the war and how I felt about responsibilities.

"I do know one thing, Greta, from now on, any plans I make will include you, if you want me to."

"I do, oh yes, I do," she said happily. "But that's for when the war is over. While you are in Holland, we'll be together. We'll worry about tomorrow, tomorrow! No man wants responsibilities until he has them, then it's amazing how much strength he gains. You're no different from anybody else."

It was dark when we finally got out of bed. The house was freezing. We dressed and sat in the kitchen with our coats on, wrapped in

165

each other's arms to keep warm. Since we were leaving there was no reason to light a fire in the stove.

"I'm going to Holwerd tonight and Leeuwarden tomorrow. There are some things I have to pick up in Holwerd and some messages I have to take to the radio. I'll be back the day after tomorrow and we'll come back here. I forgot to tell you, this is my sister's house. I was with her this morning."

"Do you mean you're going all the way to Holwerd tonight? It's after curfew. You'll be caught!"

"No, of course not. I'll stay in a safe house so that I'll arrive when I'm expected. Anyway, I have a pass from the Germans so I can travel after curfew. We have a portable radio transmitter we move from one location to another. We send and receive transmissions to London. Didn't you know that?"

"No," I answered honestly. "I knew there was a communications network with England, but I didn't think any more about it."

"Only the radio operator knows its exact location. I rendezvous with him at a given time and place. I get the messages he has for me and give him the ones he is to send. That way, its location is always kept secret. We haven't lost a transmitter or an operator yet!" She was proud of that.

Reluctantly, we stood up to leave. She put her arms around my neck and kissed me warmly. We rode the bicycles close to each other, not speaking. When our eyes met, they locked lovingly on each other. It wasn't dark. The moon was high in the sky and the ride to the Vissers ended all too soon. I got off the bicycle at the gate and leaned it against the fence. Greta was standing beside hers when I took her in my arms and kissed her.

"It's good to belong," she said. "And I am yours — my body, my heart, and my very soul, Jan Veen. Don't you ever forget it."

"I love you, Greta," I said.

"And I love you too," she said. "Isn't it wonderful?"

"See you day after tomorrow. Goodnight."

"Goodnight," she said and rode off in the direction of Holwerd, waving to me in the moonlight.

I stood there until she disappeared down the main road. After replacing my bicycle under the porch, I went up the steps to the house. Jim and Niko were sitting on the porch in the darkness. I hadn't seen them and it startled me.

"Hi, Harry, how'd it go?" Jim asked.

"Okay," I answered, not wanting to sound enthusiastic. "Did the message come over the radio tonight?"

"No, Niko replied, "there was one something like it."

"Well, tomorrow is another day," I said.

I went in the house. I didn't want to be given the third degree by either Niko or Jim. This was a pretty special day in my life. Mevrouw Visser was in the kitchen finishing her daily chores. She asked me if I was hungry. I didn't have the guts to tell her I hadn't eaten all day except a few cups of tea, so I told her I had already eaten. She poured a cup of tea for me anyway and went on about her endless kitchen chores.

I pretended to be asleep when Jim came into the bedroom. He called out my name a couple of times and when I didn't answer he left me alone and went to bed.

The next day I was sitting in the front room, looking out the windows at the dike. Jim's book was on the table so I thumbed through it. Even though it was a literary classic, I couldn't get interested. My newfound relationship with Greta was foremost in my mind, and I was pondering what Greta said about the organization's suspicions of Niko. I recalled my personal relationship with him. He had been a particularly good friend, had given me a gun, a bicycle, a lot of information about the organization, and he loved his country. He had been a close companion and mentor and had introduced me to his friends, including Greta. He had pushed me at least twenty kilometers when my legs had given out. He was most considerate and it hurt him when the bridge was destroyed in Hoornsterzwaag. I had been in his home, and that in itself was a privilege.

I wanted to talk to Niko to see if there was any truth to the allegations. I couldn't question him, but a conversation slanted in the right direction would provoke him into expressing his true allegiance. It might be a way to see if he was sympathetic to the Nazis.

Another thing going through my mind was the decision I would have to make before the trip to the sandbank. I'd love to stay with Greta in Suameer. But was this even my decision to make? After all, there were others involved. My military duty was to try to get back to England, but it sure would be nice to sit out the rest of the war with Greta. Probably we'd wind up hating each other before we were liberated. My conscience would bother me for what I had done to my comrades.

Jim interrupted my thoughts when he came into the room.

"Are you reading my book?" he asked. I handed it to him.

"Jim," I said, interrupting him, "we've never talked about it, but what are your thoughts about wading through the North Sea and waiting to be picked up by a boat?"

"Great," he said, "except for the wet ass we'll get on the way out. We'll be back in England in just a few days, you know."

"Does it bother you to go out there with George and Niko? Suppose our boat doesn't come? How in hell will we get back to land again? Did you ever think about that?"

"No, and I'm not going to start now, for we're committed. The boat will be there. We'll get on it and it'll take us to Britain. I'm not worried about the 'what ifs,' for I have faith in George and Niko. They know what they're doing." He thought a moment, then added, "We're on our way home, Harry, believe me."

He turned back to his book and dropped the subject.

I wanted to tell him about the organization's suspicions regarding Niko, but I knew if I did, he'd let it slip. Probably he would blame it on Greta, calling it woman's intuition.

The more I thought about it, the more concerned I was about going. Would either one or both of them make an attempt on our lives? The future had never been so uncertain, even back in the Wig-Wam. One thing was for sure: I could never turn my back on Niko again. It was strange. I had always thought of him as a good friend. If Greta hadn't warned me about him, I would have considered him the best friend I had in Holland since Pete and Mimi or Oom Joop. I decided this wasn't "stinkin' thinkin'."

After lunch, George and Niko came into the house. They had been trying their luck at fishing. It was one of the rare mornings when there was no Landwatcher. They had a good time, but neither of them caught anything. They were both extraordinarily happy. They could see Engelsmanplaat clearly. It was not very far, only a few kilometers.

Later in the afternoon, Niko joined us in the front room.

"I have something to tell you. We have made a decision. We are going out to Engelsmanplaat tonight. The weather is good and there will be an extra low tide. Many of the people who live in Paesens are afraid the German patrols will hear about you and search for you, and of course that would mean a *razzia*. Many of them are Nazi sympathizers and are friendly with the patrols."

"What about the message?" I asked.

"On the night it is broadcast, mijnheer Visser will climb the church steeple and flash a light to us at exactly eleven thirty. When we

168

see this light, we can expect our signal light on the water. The British will flash a morse code letter 'A' to us, a short and a long light. We have a powerful flashlight with new batteries and will answer with the same flash. That's their signal to pick us up. It's as simple as that. Tonight we will leave for the *plaat* at exactly ten-thirty."

So, the decision had been made. Now it was time for me to make my decision. Was I going or was I going to forget it and stay in Holland with Greta? I went upstairs and lay down on the bed. I wanted to get some sleep but it wouldn't come. So many thoughts were racing through my mind. I dreaded the walk through the North Sea. And the life-house was so unprotected and vulnerable. After all I had been through since being shot down, I didn't want to do anything foolhardy and screw up the rest of my life, or end it right here. I was going to see Greta the next day. What would she say when she found out we had gone? I wanted to write her a note but decided against it. My mind was made up when I decided there was a good chance we'd be back in England in just a few days. When the shooting stopped, I'd come back to Holland. Then Greta and I could make a decision about our lives together. I got up, packed my bag, and took it downstairs. Jim had gone down an hour earlier, eagerly waiting for the walk. Much later, mevrouw Visser was alone in the kitchen. I went to her as she stood next to her stove. I spoke very quietly.

"Please tell Greta for me that I'm sorry, but I had to go. Tell her that when the shooting stops, I'll be back before I go home to America. Tell her . . ."

"I'll take care of it, Jan. I'll take care of it. I know what's going on in your mind and I'll take care of it." She kissed me on the cheek and kept patting me on the back.

169

NINE

"**I** will fix some hot food, for in November the water in the North Sea will chill you to your bones," mevrouw Visser said. She served us steaming hot tea, boiled potatoes, cabbage, and marmalade on fresh bread. Then she stood looking at us.

I smiled. "We can take care of ourselves, don't worry."

"Niko is . . ." She started to say something, then shook her head and, holding her apron to her face, left the kitchen.

"Now what was that all about?" Jim asked.

"I don't know," I replied, shrugging my shoulders.

Later, we listened to BBC but our message was not broadcast.

November 15, 1944, at exactly 10:30 P.M., mijnheer Teun de Jong, mijnheer Visser, Niko, George, Jim, and I stood in the kitchen of the Vissers' house in Paesens. There were two men whom I didn't know. One of them, who had just come in the door, spoke excitedly in Frisian to mijnheer Visser.

"The way is clear for us to go!" Niko announced. "There are no Germans or Landwatchers in the vicinity."

Mevrouw Visser was nowhere to be seen. Jim and I carried our suitcases and I noticed that George and Niko each had one too. We were all armed; Niko, Teun, and Visser carried Sten guns while George and I carried our pistols. Jim's weapon was in his suitcase. The fisherman's wife prepared some sandwiches and put some extra bread and cheese in a waterproof bag. She included three bottles of steaming hot tea.

Thus provisioned and armed we went out the back door and on down the steps, following the two strangers. We climbed twenty-five feet to the top of the dike. The sky was partly overcast. The moon shone down between the fleecy clouds. There was no wind, almost a dead calm. We reached the top of the dike and looked out beyond. In front of us was the North Sea. Moonlight reflected off the water. The visibility was good, but it was cold — probably near freezing, but tolerable.

Without hesitation we went down the other side of the dike and headed straight for the water's edge. The two strangers, our lookouts, were far down the beach, one to the right and the other to the left of us. Shortly, they were out of sight. The beach extended about 500 feet to the water's edge because of the extremely low tide. With no hesitation, we walked straight into the icy water and headed out to sea. The cold water shocked my system. Would I be able to stand the long walk through this?

After fifty yards I saw the markers. They were small tree limbs, not more than one and a half to two inches in diameter, imbedded deeply in the sandy bottom, sticking in the air perhaps eight to ten feet, and probably fifty feet apart. They blazed a trail for us to follow through the treacherous current. Walking was easy, but a numbness set in from my knees down. At one time the water went up to my thighs, but usually it was knee-deep or less. The more we walked the more feeling I lost in my lower limbs. There were no rocks or pebbles. It was a smooth and even surface. Visser stopped and waited for me.

"Teun, walk with Jim," he said. "We are going to cross the small channel." He said to me, "This will be the deepest part, so stay close to me. I can help you if the water is too deep."

George and Niko, bringing up the rear, heard his remarks.

Again we started walking. I put my suitcase on top of my head and balanced it with one hand. About fifty feet from where we stopped, there was a sudden dropoff and I went completely under water. I struggled to regain my balance. Finally, I got my feet back on the bottom and was in water up to my neck. It was a tremendous shock to my system and for a moment I couldn't catch my breath. I thought of the Luger in my belt but was in too much shock and agony to move it. My suitcase floated on the water. When I regained my balance, I

171

retrieved it and put it back on my head, the cold water dripping in my face.

In the channel we made slow headway. There was a tremendous current, and Visser held on to my arm until we were across. At last my body became accustomed to the frigid water and the going was less miserable. However, I lost all feeling in my lower extremities. Then, just as quickly as we dropped off into the channel, we came out again and the water was thigh deep. My face was freezing.

"There is still one more channel just before we get to Engelsman-plaat, but it's not as bad as this one," Teun said encouragingly. "Just be patient, we'll make it."

It seemed like we walked most of the night and I was trembling badly. There was nothing but water ahead and it changed depths, sometimes knee-deep, sometimes thigh-deep. Sensation started to come back to my upper body, but I was miserable with the freezing cold.

After what seemed like the entire night had passed, I could barely make out what looked like a shore line in the distance. There were no ripples to be seen for the first time.

"Is that Engelsmanplaat?" I asked mijnheer Visser.

He looked ahead. "Yes, that is it. And we are almost to the other channel, so be ready for it. It is not as wide but it will be almost as deep."

This time I was prepared for the dropoff. When it came, I went down slowly and the bottom leveled off when I was in water up to my neck. The icy water felt warm on my body. We fought the current again and in a few minutes started out of the deep water on the other side of the channel. It was only about a foot deep. A few minutes later we were out of water and on wet sand. We had walked four kilometers out to Engelsmanplaat, through the North Sea, in freezing weather.

I looked back the way we had come. Teun and Jim were coming out of the water. Niko and George had about twenty-five feet to go. Because of the darkness, I couldn't see the shore or the dike. I looked out over the sandbank but saw nothing. We walked to some slightly higher ground and changed our clothes. None of us had a second pair of shoes, so I poured the water out of mine and wiped them with dry socks. My feet still had no feeling in them. I got dry clothes from my suitcase and changed from my wet ones. Then I rolled a cigarette from the dry tobacco in my suitcase and lit it with dry matches. I prayed the boat would come so I wouldn't have to go through that coldness again.

172

We shared one of the bottles of tea then got to our feet and started walking.

The dry sand of Engelsmanplaat was more difficult to walk on than the bottom of the sea. The sand was deep and dry and didn't provide good traction. As a result, with every step I took, my foot slid back just a little, causing me to lose ground. In spite of it, we made good headway and soon were out of sight of the water. The sand kept getting in our low-cut shoes and occasionally we had to stop and empty them.

A half hour later, we saw an object on the dune. Even in the darkness, I saw it was an FW-190 which had probably belly landed for it was not burned or badly damaged. It was a total loss, however, and had been stripped.

"The plane has been here about two years," Teun said.

A little further on, we discovered a German magnetic mine. Measuring between three and four feet in diameter, it had some protruding fuses sticking out on about eight-inch pipes all over it. There was a fifty-foot chain with huge links attached. It was a menacing-looking weapon encrusted with barnacles and rust.

"This has been here a long time too," Teun said.

We gave the mine a wide berth and continued toward the other end of the *plaat.* More than an hour later, walking steadily toward the windward side of the sandbank, a small square object came into view. It appeared to be a box or packing crate resting in the sand. As we got closer, the legs appeared and we could see it was the life-house. The closer we got, the more detail we could make out. A half hour later, we were underneath it about 500 feet from the windward shore.

It was twelve by fifteen feet in size. The floor was about fifteen feet off the sandbank, supported by six mammoth pilings twenty to twenty-four inches in diameter and imbedded in the sand to a great depth. To strengthen the pilings, huge four-by-eighteen-inch beams were bolted with one-and-a-half-inch bolts to the legs, forming an "X" support on all sides. It had been built to last. The house itself was painted white, had a gabled roof, and a three-by-four-foot porch with no railings. The entry door was at the top of a vertical fifteen-foot ladder.

Inside the place, there was a small window on the far end with larger windows on both the windward and leeward sides. The door had an eighteen-inch window. There was good visibility from all four sides. In the corner beside the door was the larder to keep foodstuffs.

Strangely, it was clean. There were twelve full cans of condensed milk with sugar added. Also in the larder was a water reservoir that would hold about ten gallons of water. It was made of galvanized tin with a faucet soldered into it. The water reservoir held about two gallons of stinking, rancid water. Opposite the larder, a small pot-bellied stove sat on the floor with its stovepipe through the wall on the leeward side, then upward through the eave until it was two feet above the roof. It was topped with a cone-shaped chimney cap and heavy wires held it in place.

There was no fuel for the stove. Upon further inspection, I discovered the stove was old, but it was also brand new, having never been used. The building was secure from the weather.

Mijnheer Visser and Teun went down on the *plaat* and were soon back, their arms loaded with driftwood.

"Plenty of firewood around," Teun declared. He started a fire in the little stove. The life-house, with its thick, well-insulated walls, warmed quickly even with the small fire.

Teun sat down and talked. "The Germans can see this place easily from Schiermonnikoog, since it is only four or five kilometers from here. During daylight, the island will be a constant companion. Its twin lighthouses observe the *plaat* constantly. Should they see smoke coming out of the chimney, chances are you would have an unexpected visit. Also, if they saw you walking you would get even a faster visit. Be careful after you build a fire at night. Every time you open the door to the stove it will let out flashes of light from the fire and that can be seen over great distances especially on a clear, dark night. I am only suggesting these things to you. If it gets foggy, you are as safe as can be. Night time is the safe time to wander around. Don't make any visible changes to the life-house or the Boche will investigate. Remember, footprints cannot be seen from Schiermonnikoog, but if they snoop around, they will see them. Frequently at this time of year we have flood tides. These wash away all the footprints and everything else. It will replace your firewood with a new batch and you will probably find other strange objects too. Water can rise as close as five feet from the floor during a bad storm. That is about all I have to say."

We were all tired. I lay down on the bench with Teun's words echoing in my ears and woke up at noon. The stove had gone out but it was a sunny day. The wet clothes we had draped around the place the night before were dry, so I folded mine and put them in the suitcase. I field-stripped my Luger and ran a rag through the barrel to get the salt and moisture out, then spent a long time wiping the weapon to get it clean. I put it back together, put the clip of ammo in it, and stuck it in my belt.

Schiermonnikoog was plainly visible to the northeast. There were two very tall lighthouses, each of them well over a hundred feet high. There must have been a lot of Dutch habitation on the island because there were two church steeples adding to the skyline. Though I couldn't be sure, I strained my eyes and thought I saw various colored roofs on the houses.

If there had been fog or if the visibility had been poor, our two Dutch guides would have gone back to Paesens that morning. Since it was a bright sunny day, they decided to wait until darkness. We ate lightly. I had a single piece of cheese on a slice of bread and a cup of tea. Later in the afternoon, the four of us stretched out to get some sleep so we could stay awake through the night and watch for the signal. Teun and mijnheer Visser stayed awake. Later, Teun told me that the only things stirring on the *plaat* all afternoon were the birds, for Engelsmanplaat was a bird sanctuary.

At exactly 8:00 we shook hands with the two Dutchmen and they went down the ladder and disappeared into the night.

Now we were on our own. As previously agreed, if the message came over the radio on the first night, Teun would signal us twice as soon as they got back to Paesens, probably about 1:00 in the morning, the earliest they could get back. We all decided, however, we would watch out to sea for the light, taking two-hour watches and rotating during the hours of darkness. With the flashlight in hand, I took the first watch from 10:00 to midnight. I saw no signal from the sea during my watch.

I built a small fire in the stove, heated some water, and made warm tea. Then three of us went out on the sandbank and gathered in a nice supply of firewood for the stove. We lined it up under the bench and filled an entire wall with it.

If we weren't picked up in three days, we would be in deep trouble as far as food was concerned. We decided that when it rained, we should have something to gather water in, so the next night we went out on the *plaat* looking for cans, bottles, or anything that would hold water. Jim and I hit the jackpot. We discovered two big oxygen containers from American airplanes. They were intact and painted yellow. The glass on the gauges was broken, but the needles pointed to zero. If they had oxygen left in them, we could be badly injured as soon as we punctured them. Mustering all my courage, with the others standing a distance away, I took a piece of driftwood with a very large rusty spike in it and gave one of the canisters a hefty blow. The spike pierced it without a whisper of oxygen escaping. More confident now, I hit the other with the same result. Then, using two different pocket knives, and cutting at the canisters for two days, we finally severed them in two. Each half would hold three or four gallons of water. We drained the tainted water from the reservoir and threw the brackish stuff away. I took my clean underwear and wiped the inside of the tank until it was clean, then left the top off for it to air out. We had found some pieces of aluminum that looked like they came off an airplane, and although they had bullet holes in them we fashioned some down spouts and gutters. Everything was made to hold water. Now all we needed was some rain.

Our first full day alone on the *plaat* was spent watching the hundreds of species of birds. They were everywhere, flying, dipping, soaring, and nesting. We watched the water but always had an eye on Schiermonnikoog. We also watched in the direction of Paesens. If any Germans came out to the sandbank, that would be the direction from which they would come. I cleaned my Luger again and found the salt water hadn't been on it long enough to do any real damage. I kept it in my belt day and night.

When it got dark, we built a small fire in the stove and made some hot tea with the last of the water. We were cold from the weather, but extra clothing kept us fairly comfortable. The fire felt good. I took off my coat and backed my rear end up to the stove. The heat soaked in and soon the place was warm and cozy in spite of the freezing weather outside.

Somebody was always at the windward window watching for our signal light.

By 10:00 the *plaat* was drenched in fog. We couldn't see the ground at the bottom of the ladder with the door open. The fog didn't break all night long. Even though each of us stood watch, we couldn't possibly have seen a signal light from the sea. The following day was cold and miserable, foggy all day long, with no more than twenty or thirty feet of visibility. We kept a fire in the stove and wandered about on the *plaat* exploring as far as a mile away from the place. We found many things of interest, such as sea shells and bird's eggs, which we left undisturbed. We found rusty tin cans of European origin, bits and pieces of metal which looked like structural pieces of airplanes, and, strangest of all, an empty package of Camel cigarettes. Since we used our tobacco sparingly, I had just been thinking: *The first thing I'll do when I get back to England is buy a carton of Camels, and I'll sit back and chain smoke them till I finish the whole damned carton.*

The fog stayed with us until November 20. About 10:00 in the morning the sky began to brighten and shortly afterward, it lifted. Though we could see the twin lighthouses on the island, it was hazy. We let the fire in the stove go out by itself. We didn't see any smoke from the chimney, so we felt reasonably safe in that respect. Our footprints were more distinguishable from our lofty perch than from the ground.

We spent the day doing nothing. We were out of food, tobacco, and water, so we divided the twelve cans of sweetened evaporated milk, not knowing whether or not they were spoiled. They weren't. I ran out of things to talk to Jim about and he was no fountain of information himself. Niko had said nothing to make me suspicious of him. If he was a bad one, perhaps he had atoned for his sins and planned to do better things in the future. None of us were in particularly bad shape as far as hunger was concerned. The canned milk was thick as syrup and very sweet. Just a little bit of the stuff satisfied our hunger pangs. As we slowly emptied the cans over the next few days, we kept them to drink out of.

Since we were completely out of food and water, tempers began to run a little short. I had to be careful what I said to everybody. On the sixth night, I watched in the direction of Paesens and didn't see a signal light. It was my shift to watch the sea from midnight until 2:00 A.M. I waited until almost 2:30 before I awakened Niko to take his shift. I gave him the flashlight and lay down on the bench. George was restless so he got up and joined Niko. The two of them sat watching out the window together and talking.

Ten minutes later, George suddenly started yelling excitedly in Frisian. He reached for the flashlight in Niko's hand and Niko yelled at him loudly, *"Neen! Neen!"*

Niko wrestled the light from George's grip before he had a chance to signal. The two of them struggled for possession of it. Finally, in desperation, Niko smashed the light against the bench, shattering the lens and bulb, rendering it useless forever. He didn't break it accidentally. He deliberately broke it so George couldn't use it. But why?

Jim and I jumped to our feet and over to the window. Our eyes pierced the darkness but we saw nothing as we looked out over the

177

water for several minutes. All the time, George and Niko were arguing and cursing each other, getting uglier by the minute. Then the realization of what Niko had done struck him and George attacked him, flailing away with both fists. At first Niko tried to block the blows and talk to George, but after being hit several times in the face with some pretty hard punches, he hit back to defend himself. This enraged George even more. The two of them went to the floor with a resounding crash. They were in an all-out battle then, hurting each other with heavy blows and doing their level best to inflict permanent damage. They rolled near the stove and kicked it over with their feet, scattering hot embers all over the floor. Fortunately, they rolled away and Jim and I were able to right the stove, burning our hands in the process. We opened the door and kicked the hot coals out onto the sand below.

Then Jim and I started yelling at them. In the process of separating them, we both took a couple of pretty good blows ourselves. Niko hit me and the side of my face hurt like the devil. Jim got hit too but he didn't know by whom. After we got them apart, we forced each one to sit on opposite ends of the life-house and stood guard to make sure they didn't get into it again. They yelled obscenities at each other and settled down to lick their wounds. Both of them were furious.

Later, after it had been quiet for a while, I turned to Niko and asked what had happened.

"George said he saw the light on the water. I was watching too. It was a light but it wasn't ours. It was just a beam of light from a search light skirting over the water back and forth from far away. It wasn't the morse code 'A.' The light was on all the time and may have been from a German's patrol boat who was searching on the water. Or maybe they intercepted our message and wanted to see if anyone was out here. I don't know. It could have been anything, but it wasn't a short and a long light."

"Is it possible you just didn't see the short light first?"

"*Neen! Neen!*" he said loudly, getting angry with me now. "It was just a search light going back and forth, like I said!"

"How long did it stay on?" I asked.

"At least ten seconds, maybe longer."

I didn't question him anymore. I just thanked God the two of them hadn't used their weapons or we might all be dead.

Niko promised he would not start fighting with George again. I went back to the window to look out on the North Sea but I saw no lights. I thought if it was our rescuers, they might come to shore in a rubber boat to take a look anyway.

"Do you think you can handle these two?" I asked Jim. "I think I'll go down to the water's edge just in case there's anybody out there looking for us. Maybe I'll stay out there a while and watch, what do you think?"

"I think it's a good idea. If these two insist on busting each other up, to hell with them, let 'em have at it."

I checked my Luger, put on my coat and hat, then went down the ladder to the *plaat*. It was frigid and I had goose bumps from one end to the other. I walked the 500 or so feet to the water's edge and peered out into the black void. I saw nothing but stayed there for two hours. I would have stayed longer but got so cold I could no longer tolerate it. When I returned to the life-house, everybody was asleep.

In the morning, Niko must have looked at George wrong or vice versa because they got into it again. George was enraged. The fists flew and landed telling blows. There was a lot of name-calling and hair-pulling before Jim and I could get them apart again, this time without too much damage to ourselves. I was so afraid they would take a gun to each other, yet I was afraid to ask them for their weapons lest I reminded them they had them. I kept my mouth shut and hoped for the best.

Both of them slept through the day while Jim and I stayed awake watching them. We also watched Engelsmanplaat and all around the place for intruders. There were no more fights and all conversation ceased between George and Niko. Like a pair of young boys, they sat at opposite ends of the life-house and glared at each other. Because George didn't speak English, he was in a little world of his own. I felt sorry for him and tried to talk to him in Dutch but he wouldn't even acknowledge my existence. I decided to forget it. When Niko talked, it was only about the fight. He truly felt we would all be dead right now if George had answered the flash on the water. It was Jim who broke the barrier with George and talked to him in his limited Dutch. Whenever George talked, he was loud and had only one thing to say: what a son of a bitch Niko was. Of course Niko had regained control of himself and chose to ignore his remarks.

That night we kept a closer watch than ever on the sea. There were no more lights nor did any lights come from the land at 10:30. Our situation was starting to get serious. The food and water situation was desperate. I gathered up some of the cigarette butts on the floor, removed the tobacco, and made a cigarette out of them. I took a few drags off it and passed it around. We had conserved pretty well, I thought. But there were four of us eating, drinking, and smoking. When we were sharing everything, supplies went fast. We had only brought food for two days and we had stretched that out to seven. It was all gone and the cupboard was bare. My pants were beginning to get loose. We were all in the same boat.

In Havelte, a patrol was stopping people on the streets and checking identity cards. One of the men they stopped was carrying a Sten gun and was immediately arrested and taken to Steenwijk for interrogation. It was not necessary to torture the man; he was so frightened that he spoke freely, telling of his connection with the underground and giving the identities of all those he knew. He was threatened with death and told them he knew of a "hole in the ground" where Jews were hiding along with American pilots. He took them there in exchange for his life.

The Wig-Wam was quiet on the night of November 21. Oom Joop had gone home to spend the night with his wife and daughters and to take care of personal business. He left the place at 5:00. Franz, along with the seven others in the Wig-Wam, had gone to bed about 10:00 and were sleeping when a troop of German soldiers, led by the traitor, arrived just before dawn. The Germans encircled the place and captured all the men inside. The Wig-Wam was destroyed.

The soldiers took them to Amersfoort, where the SS and SD interrogators questioned them unmercifully and applied such tortures as were necessary to get the information they wanted. Some of them didn't survive the punishment. Franz and those who did survive were sent to Bergen-Belsen concentration camp, where they were murdered. Seven of my former comrades and a man I didn't know were annihilated by the Germans.

The Dutch traitor must have told the Germans about Temmingh, for he was arrested on the job in Meppel and sent to Amersfoort and then to Bergen-Belsen, where he was condemned to death. However, after Germany surrendered to the Allies, he survived, by some stroke of luck, and walked home. Fenna, his wife, had long given him up for dead. So goes the fortunes of war. Oom Joop never recovered Franz's body nor was he able to find out more about his fate.

The Germans kept their pact with the traitorous Dutchman. The

180

informer lost his mind because of what he had done.

On the eighth night, the rain came down in torrents. The tide brought the water level halfway up the pilings. Wind-driven waves hit the bottom of the life-house and crashed against the windward side of the building with powerful blows. It was a frightening and terrifying experience, especially when the building shuddered from the mighty waves. In spite of the wind, waves, and torrential rain, we braved opening the door to retrieve the water-filled oxygen tanks. We tasted the water and it was fresh, so we filled the reservoir. When the sun rose and the wind subsided, not only was the tank full but all our other containers were full of water and safely stored inside out of the weather. George and Niko as well as Jim and I worked as teams, for it was a matter of survival. We were wet but we weren't thirsty, nor would we be for a long time. Somewhere I read that Mahatma Gandhi, the ruler of India, had survived fasting for over thirty days, just drinking water. These thoughts were encouraging.

When daylight came and we looked out on the sandbank, the entire terrain had changed. The sand was smooth; there was no sign of a footprint, and the familiar things that were lying around were gone. We were in a whole new environment. It was foggy in the morning and hazy when it lifted.

We kept the fire going. It was great to drink all the water we wanted without having to worry. We had a lot more faith in the construction of the life-house. It had taken a beating but looked just the same as it had before. Not only that, but it didn't leak a drop.

In the afternoon, Jim and I took a short walk. When we returned, I climbed the steps with some difficulty. I discovered I was getting weak. I felt washed out and dizzy when I put forth any exertion. Although I made it, when I looked back at Jim I wasn't too sure he would. Niko and I both helped him up the last two rungs of the ladder. I told Niko how weak I felt and Jim complained too. The waist of my pants was at least four inches too big for me and my underwear constantly kept falling down inside my pants. I tied my belt instead of buckling it.

I thought of Greta almost constantly. Though younger in years, she was far more mature. She was so trusting. Was I man enough to return that kind of faith and honesty? For the first time in my life, in my total weakness, I felt a kind of strength.

181

What was she doing now, right this minute? I started to wonder if I would ever see her or anybody else again. The ordeal we were going through didn't look too promising and survival was more than just waiting to be rescued. We might have to go back alone, and I honestly didn't think I could walk through the sea again. What was her reaction when mevrouw Visser told her we had gone to Engelsmanplaat?

"Oh God, I don't wish anybody the problems we've got right now!" I said aloud, but nobody paid any attention. They were the first words to break the silence in over an hour. Strange.

The routine of everyday existence became just that — existing, nothing more. We kept getting weaker with each passing day. We knew it. We needed some nourishment but none was to be had. We thought of shooting a sea gull but were afraid the noise would carry to Schiermonnikoog. It rained again a couple of days later and we refilled the canisters and cans with water. We had no more high tides but at one time we got six inches of water under the building. Since none of us went down to the *plaat* anymore, we didn't worry about footprints. We did see new souvenirs each time the water rose. Our vigil was maintained both seaward and landward but to no avail. We took a leak off the porch but since we ate no food, we had no bowel movements. The driftwood lasted nicely, with about a month's supply stacked up inside.

On November 28 a miracle happened. George walked over to Niko and sat down, kissed him on both cheeks, with a childish grin on his face, and started talking. They spoke in Frisian so I couldn't understand. Jim and I smiled at each other, feeling a load had been lifted off our shoulders. They had so much to say that sometimes they talked at the same time.

Physically, we were in very bad shape. Not only because our clothes no longer fit, but our faces were gaunt and black circles encompassed our eyes. We tried to keep clean but I had only bathed my body a few times since we had arrived there. It had been days since I had really washed. *Now,* I thought, *I know how old people feel, having trouble moving around.* As far as I could tell, we all felt the same way. I never heard anybody say they wished they had a cigarette or something to eat.

Niko and George's marathon conversation lasted well over two hours. They were glad to be friends again. As far as I could tell, no mention was ever made of the light from the water.

Later, Niko came over to the bench we were sitting on.

"George is going back to Paesens. We are in such a weakened condition, he thinks he has more strength than any of us. He is going to follow the markers back to land and bring some help. You know if we don't get help soon we will all be too weak to do anything about it and we will probably die. We agree that in our condition it would be foolhardy for all four of us to try and go together. It is his decision to bring help to us."

We had to make sure of the tides. The only easy and sure way was to watch the water. At 10:00 in the morning, the water was the farthest from shore. About 4:00 in the afternoon it came within 200 feet of the life-house before it went out again. By the light of the moon we saw it again at 10:00 P.M. at the farthest distance. That wasn't too hard, we decided. There was a high and low tide every twelve hours and, as George said, when he got to the other side of the *plaat,* the fishermen would see him and help him across. It made sense.

On the morning of November 29, George made his way down the ladder to the sandbank. He seemed strong and had no trouble descending the ladder. He walked strongly once he was on the sand. The visibility on the *plaat* was good, but we couldn't see the island of Schiermonnikoog. The three of us, with our noses pressed against the glass, watched as George made his way across the sand. About 200 yards away, he turned around and waved at us with a clenched fist. Then he walked steadily to the south, never looking back again. We watched him until he was swallowed up by the morning mist in the distance.

Because of good local visibility, we felt confident he would be able to find the markers and the right place to enter the water.

"How long do you think it will take before we get some help out here?" Jim asked Niko.

Niko pondered the question. "Well, with lots of luck, help might come tonight with the ten o'clock tide. However, I doubt it. I don't look for anybody before tomorrow." He thought for a moment. "I don't think George will be able to come back, for he is weak from not eating."

We sat the rest of the day, waiting expectantly. In late afternoon the mist dissipated and we could see Schiermonnikoog again. Low tide would be at 10:00 P.M. Allowing another two hours to wade out, and two hours to walk to the life-house, help should come between 2:00 and 3:00 in the morning.

By 3:00 A.M. Jim and I were devastated. Niko, expressionless, didn't say a word but sat relaxed, looking out the window into the darkness. At 5:00 in the morning, completely exhausted, I gave up on any rescue for the day and fell asleep. I woke up at 2:00 in the afternoon and drank some water. Then I sat down at the window and watched in the direction of Paesens. By nightfall I hadn't seen a soul.

"What in the hell is the matter?" I asked Jim and Niko. "Why hasn't George sent somebody out here to get us?"

Our conversation took on an air of being ridiculous. There was neither sense nor sanity in the way we spoke to each other. I got dizzy spells when I moved around too much and damned near fell off the porch when I went out to relieve myself. Whenever I bent over, my head spun and I had spots before my eyes. Once, I fell on the floor on my face. Niko helped me to my feet. It was an effort to get back on the bench again.

Later, I said to Jim, "Do you know Thanksgiving came and went without us getting a drumstick? I sure as hell hope we don't have to wait here for Santa Claus. We'll never make it!"

"Hey, that's right. When was Thanksgiving?" he asked.

"Damned if I know. It's on a Thursday but they keep moving it around all the time. I guess it was either last Thursday or the one before. It doesn't make any difference . . . we missed it!"

The night of November 30 we all sat with our eyes glued to the window. It had been snowing and the *plaat* was white. We had a warm fire and though we were weak, we were lucid. For some reason, our minds kept playing tricks on us.

We played a game and even Niko joined in. We knew for sure we would be saved on this night. We moved our rescuers like pawns on a chessboard:

10:00. They left the house in Paesens.

10:30. They're in the water, following the markers.

12:30. They're putting on dry clothes.

1:00. They're passing the airplane.

1:30. They're passing the magnetic mine.

2:00. Our faces were pressed against the windows so hard the cold hurt our faces. We wanted something — anything — to move out there besides the occasional swirl of snowflakes.

Move . . . *anything!* Just *move,* damn it!

What a rotten disappointment. The game had been so realistic that we actually lived it, believed it. We knew it was more than a game: it was our life!

At the first sign of sunrise, Niko made an announcement. "I still

184

feel pretty good. I think if I got out and moved around a little, I would feel better. If no help comes today, tomorrow morning I will go for help myself."

"Not without me, you're not," I said. "I'm not staying out here in this death trap a day longer than I have to."

Jim agreed. "If we stay, it's an invitation to die."

"Something has happened here," Niko said. "I know George could make it to shore. Perhaps he was captured or even shot by the Germans while going ashore. Maybe, by some twist of fate, he drowned. Maybe there is a problem with mijnheer Visser's group or with the man himself for that matter." He hesitated, staring at the floor. "Well, the fact remains we can't stay out here any longer because if we do, we'll just starve to death. Better a German bullet in my brain in battle than that kind of death. I don't think either of you should try to make it. You are both in bad shape and very weak. You do what you want, of course, but I think it's better for you to wait for a rescue."

"Bullshit! We're going ashore with you!" we said together.

And so it was decided. We would watch through the day and wait through the hours of darkness. If rescue didn't come, we'd leave everything we had brought out with us. Each man would fend for himself. We would stay together, but each of us would have to sink or swim on his own. We were glad the decision had been made and we were sorry we hadn't gone with George three days before when we were stronger. I couldn't tighten my belt enough to hold the Luger, so I put my most prized possession in my suitcase and slid it under the bench. I wouldn't be needing it anymore.

At daylight I looked out the window. It was December 1, 1944, Christmas month. Merry Christmas! Better to say it now because the chances were mighty slim I'd be alive to say it on Christmas day. We had been on Engelsmanplaat sixteen days. We hadn't eaten for eleven days, and then it was only a morsel.

There was hardly any wind blowing outside and huge snowflakes were coming straight down. They melted almost as fast as they hit the wet sand. It was mesmerizing to watch them fall, almost hypnotic. It felt good to be mesmerized.

I let myself float off into the trance. I don't know how long I sat there in that state of mind. It seemed to me that between the snowflakes, somewhere in the distance, I thought I saw some movement. I snapped out of my dream and looked harder in the direction I had seen it. Nothing. My God, now my eyes were playing tricks on me! I kept

185

my eyes focused on the general area anyway.

Then I saw it again! A bit of color, black and tan, against white snow. And again! By God, there *was* movement, a man walking toward the life-house, just a short distance away!

"Jim! Niko!" I cried. "Somebody's coming! Somebody's here!"

They both pressed their faces against the window. At first, like me, they couldn't see him, but finally through the mountain of snowflakes they made out his form, walking steadily.

"It's George!" Jim yelled excitedly.

"No," said Niko, "I know his walk. It's a German soldier!"

We got our weapons and went back to the window. Again the figure disappeared. It was several moments before we saw him again in the falling snow. I put a round of ammunition in the chamber of my Luger. Niko loaded the Sten. Jim just sat there.

As the figure got closer, we could finally see who it was. It wasn't a German — it was mijnheer Visser.

I ran out the door of the life-house onto the porch. If Niko hadn't grabbed me I would have fallen off.

"Mijnheer Visser!" we all shouted.

He looked up and seemed surprised to see us. He climbed the ladder effortlessly, came in, and looked at us in disbelief. "My God!" he said in Dutch, "You are all so thin!" He looked around. "Where is George?"

"He left for Paesens to get help three days ago."

"George never came to Paesens."

Well, where is George? I thought, *He has gone someplace else, drowned, or he's been picked up by the Germans.* I dismissed the idea, for we had figured the tides too closely.

"When did he leave here?" Mijnheer Visser asked.

"He left here at exactly seven-thirty in the morning of the twenty-ninth," I said.

Visser thought for a moment. "That would be too late. The tide was well on its way coming in at seven-thirty. By ten o'clock, when he got to the other end of the island, the water was far too deep for him to cross."

"Oh, my God!" I said aloud.

The facts about what might have happened to our comrade were sinking in. *But no,* I thought, *not George. He's too smart to try crossing when the water was rising. No, he had to be okay.*

"You have lost a lot of weight since I brought you out. In Pae-

186

sens, everybody thinks you have gone to England. But mevrouw Visser insisted I check to make sure and bring some food with me in case you were still here."

He opened the sack he carried and put some bread and cheese on the bench. While we wolfed the food down, he made some hot tea. Not until then did he remove his wet clothing and sit down on the bench in his drawers while they dried by the stove. Niko had some clothes which fit so he put them on. I never ate anything that tasted so good in all my life. We ate most of it then bloated ourselves with the hot tea. Soon Visser was dozing off by the fire, tired from his long trek to the life-house.

I sat back and relaxed. With food in my belly, I felt life wasn't so bad. I was so stuffed that it hurt, but I could feel the nourishment spreading through my body and some of my strength returning. I no longer felt dizzy and giddy.

After Visser woke up and put on his dry clothes, he talked at length to Niko in Frisian. Again, I couldn't understand, but George's name came up frequently.

Later, Visser talked to Jim and me and Niko translated. "I will take you back to Paesens this evening if you think you have enough strength to make it. Otherwise I will go back alone and bring some help to take you back tomorrow."

"I have enough strength," I said. "I don't want to stay on this sandbank a day longer than I have to. I think I'd rather drown trying to get back than spend another day here."

Jim agreed. The decision was made. We would all walk back at low tide in the early morning hours.

Mijnheer Visser said, "After you left Paesens, the Germans started nosing around the village. They didn't have a *razzia* but there were three or four extra patrols each day. They paid particular attention to my house. One day a patrol came and asked for some tea. My wife invited the soldiers in and gave them the run of the house. They searched it very carefully. Once they were satisfied nothing was amiss, it was the end of it. After that, the patrols returned to normal. The message never came over the radio. Teun de Jong has spent many hours at night in the church steeple looking at the life-house through his high-powered spyglass. He never saw any activity, so he was certain you had been rescued. Then my wife insisted I come out to see."

In answer to my question, he said, "Greta has come to the house several times and talked to my wife. She's very worried."

Later, after dark, Visser went to the door and opened it. Snow was falling heavily. He closed the door and suggested we all get some sleep. "You will need all your strength," he said.

I slept four hours before he woke us up at 11:00.

"It's time to get ready to go to Paesens," he said. "We will leave about midnight or a little later."

He had prepared some hot tea while we were still asleep. He laid out the rest of the food and we ate. Much later, I put on my hat and overcoat, picked up my suitcase, and was the first to go down the ladder. After I started down I knew I was in trouble and dropped my suitcase for my hands were not strong enough to grip the rungs. I fell the last four or five of them, landing on my butt, unhurt. Jim had to be helped by both Niko and Visser.

We started walking away from our prison. Niko and mijnheer Visser led the way and talked constantly.

Jim spoke to me. "I'm still pretty weak."

"Yeah Jim, we all are, but we'll make it. Don't sweat it."

I turned and looked at the life-house looming up on the sandbank ominously. I don't know why I did it, maybe it was in retaliation, but I stuck up the middle finger of my right hand and waved at it. It made me feel better because it didn't get the best of us after all.

We walked slowly. The snow fell heavily in big flakes and wet our faces. It took us the better part of two and a half hours to reach the south end of the *plaat,* even though the walking was easier because of the wet sand. We rested several times on the way. Visser was very understanding.

When we came to the water's edge, I had many misgivings. We stopped before entering the water. I tied my shoes tightly and put my overcoat inside my suitcase, stuffing the thing in. My pistol was lying between my dirty clothes. All the time, I couldn't take my eyes off the murky water. *Jesus,* I thought, *I wonder if I can stand the first shock of the cold water?*

"Niko, stay with Jim. Jan, you stay with me. The water will be a little deeper than it was when we came out. The currents will be about the same and there are a few small waves. We will make it all right. Don't panic! Let's go . . . the sooner we get started, the sooner we will enjoy a warm fire in Paesens."

I put my foot in the water. "Dear God, it will be a miracle if we make it. I don't think I can." My thoughts were broken as we immediately started down into the deeper water of the first channel. Thank

188

God I knew what to expect. I balanced the suitcase on my head and promptly lost it when my head went completely under water. It was at least a foot deeper than when we crossed before. Mijnheer Visser, himself in water up to his chin, took hold of the back of my clothes and bodily lifted me until my head was out of the water. With his other hand, he retrieved my suitcase. Slowly we crossed the channel and a few minutes later we climbed out of it until it was waist-deep, then down to my thighs. My rescuer handed my suitcase back to me. The snowflakes felt warm on my cheeks.

Dear God . . .

The next hour was like a dream. The feeling was gone from my body. I felt my head was the only part of me still alive. A leg could have been severed and I never would have felt it. I couldn't understand how my legs kept moving, one in front of the other in unison, when I had no control over them. Mijnheer Visser helped me many times. Even if he had not been there and I had made it over the first channel alone, I would have perished within the first five minutes. In my mental agony, I would not have cared. He never took his hand off my back and when I stumbled or fell, he picked me up and made we walk. When I started to sag and go under, he would give me words of encouragement. He kept me moving. The tree branches, our lifeline, were some fifty feet apart and like milestones to me. It was a real achievement when we passed one. The hand on my back kept me going and sooner or later, we would pass another marker. We came to a very shallow marker where the water was only up to my knees. We stopped momentarily. Common sense told me I was becoming delirious, but there wasn't a thing I could do about it.

"We've about made it, haven't we?" I asked, dreaming.

"No, Jan, not quite," Visser said, trying to catch his breath. "We have come to the wide channel now." He looked at Niko. "Hold Jim and help him across."

I looked back at Niko. Jim looked like a wet noodle. I must have been in the same condition, for the man holding on to me was my only salvation. Without giving me time to think about it, Visser grabbed hold of my belt in the back. He took the suitcase from me and we started walking ahead very slowly. We went deeper and deeper into the water. Finally, my feet were no longer on the bottom and I held my head up to keep it from going under. Thank God my mentor was eight inches taller than I or we both would have drowned.

"You are doing just fine, Jan, just fine," he said over and over.

189

"Just put one foot in front of the other."

Keep on going now, I told myself. *One foot in front of the other . . . that's it, one foot then the other. Keep going, by the numbers now. Come on, Yank, one, two, three, four. Keep it up . . . one, two, three, four. Don't break the rhythm. That's it . . . one, two, three, four. Now you've got the hang of it. That's it.* I felt my face fall in the water and I really didn't care. That's what it wanted to do anyway. I felt Visser pull my head up and I coughed through my nose and mouth. It stung my nose sharply. *Christ,* I thought, *when did my head go under?*

Visser's voice came through my mental fog. "You're doing just fine, Jan, just fine. Only just a little bit further."

Then the water started to get shallow again. I was absolutely paralyzed from my eyes to my toes. How my legs and the rest of my body kept functioning, I'll never know. But there they were, one of my feet going in front of the other, sloshing through the shallow water, doing just what they were supposed to be doing. Walking, walking, walking.

"My God!" I said aloud. I was in water only a foot deep and I could see the shoreline not fifty feet in front of us. No, I must be dreaming. *I'm gonna die in this damned water!* I thought.

But mijnheer Visser's hand was firmly locked on my belt in back of me, pushing me forward, assuring me I was not dreaming.

We were out of the water. We were on dry land. We had accomplished the impossible.

"We've made it! We're in Paesens, Jan!" mijnheer Visser said.

TEN

M ijnheer Hans van den Horn, the local schoolteacher, was awakened by knocking on his front door. His wife Mientje, startled from her sleep, said, *"Duitsers!"* She sat up in bed. But Hans was expecting callers. Gently, he patted his wife and told her it was not the Germans. He hurried to the door.

His snow-covered neighbor, mijnheer Visser, stood in his doorway, seemingly more dead than alive. He was wringing wet in the subzero weather, a puddle of water forming at his feet. A younger bearded man hung limply at his side, unconscious and trembling. Two other strangers stood in back of his neighbor in much the same condition.

If he hadn't known Visser, the sight of these people would have frightened him to death. All the strangers had a month-long growth of beard, were sand-covered, completely sapped of their strength, and if they didn't get out of the driving snow, they would perish from exposure to the severe weather. Hans went out on the porch and relieved his neighbor of the burden he was struggling with. He picked the man up and carried him to the spare bedroom. The poor fellow was as light as a feather. Hans returned to the door and pulled mijnheer Visser into the house then relieved the second man and carried the dark one into the bedroom. He returned to help the last man, who had collapsed on the porch.

Hans's wife came out of the bedroom. "These are the men from

Engelsmanplaat?" Her question was more of a statement. "Everybody was sure they had been picked up by a submarine."

Mientje took charge immediately. She covered her neighbor, who had slumped to the floor, and Niko, who was lying beside him with wool blankets. She pulled down the covers from the bed and instructed her husband to remove Jim's clothes while she removed those of the other man. Her husband lifted both men gently into the bed and covered them with a huge comforter.

Long afterward, I regained consciousness. I was amazed to discover I was in a bed. I recalled walking through the freezing water and I vaguely remembered getting back to dry land. After that, my mind was a blank. I could feel Jim shivering beside me. I hadn't regained feeling in most of my body and I was shivering too. Maybe I was dying or, worse yet, maybe my limbs were paralyzed and would have to be amputated. I passed out again.

Much later, it was dark. A woman awakened me, holding a cup of hot tea in one hand and a candle in the other. The man with her held my head as she spoonfed the entire cup to me. They did the same thing for Jim. A few minutes later, they brought a cup of broth and fed that to us. I went back to sleep wondering who these people were.

The next time I woke up it was daylight. Warmth had come back to my body and there was no more numbness, but the moment I moved I started burning and prickling. When I lay still, it wasn't bad. Finally, my body burned so badly I could hardly stand it. I threw the covers off me and it was an hour before it subsided. Then I got chills and trembled until I thought I would shake apart. Then I got hot again, and on and on. Jim was sleeping soundly and breathing heavily.

The next time I woke up it was still daylight, and I felt like I had a fever. I had to take a leak so much I could hardly stand it. There was a door in the corner which I presumed was a toilet. I pulled the covers off and very painfully sat up on the edge of the bed. The room was spinning, but I waited for things to come back into focus. My suitcase was on the floor so I reached for it and fell flat on my face with a thud. At once the woman was beside me, covering me with a blanket. I struggled with the thought of being naked. "Now where in hell is my underwear?" I said aloud.

"I have washed all your clothes," the woman said in Dutch. "I will bring them." When she returned she laid a pile of washed and ironed clothes on the chair.

"Where is the toilet?" I asked, somewhat embarrassed.

"Off the kitchen," she replied. "If you feel up to it, I have some warm water so you can wash yourself."

I stood up and she put my arm around her shoulder. We walked to the bathroom and she closed the door after me. I relieved myself in the receptacle and looked in the mirror.

A complete stranger peered back at me, red-bearded, with long, snarled hair, yellow teeth, and bones clearly visible under the skin. *This can't be me,* I thought.

"Do you want to wash up?" the woman asked from the kitchen.

"Yes, please."

Five minutes later a washtub half full of warm water sat in the middle of the kitchen floor and I washed myself, having no trouble sitting in the small area the tub provided. When I was through, the water was filthy despite my long trek in the North Sea. I put on clean underwear and a pair of pants. They were fully eight inches too big around the waist. I put the belt in the loops and tied it to hold them up.

I called for the woman and she came into the kitchen accompanied by the man. "How are you feeling now?" he asked with an Oxford English accent.

"Terrible," I answered honestly. "How is Niko?"

"He has been gone for some time but will be back shortly."

"Gone? I can't believe it. Is there any word on George?"

"No, nobody has seen or heard about him. He's either drowned or met with foul play. Niko, like everybody else, is out searching for him. Mijnheer Visser has seen the doctor and has taken nourishment. He's in bed, completely exhausted."

"I owe him my life many times over," I said, deciding I'd live after all.

"Yes, I know you do. Getting the three of you back to Paesens in a rising tide was truly a test of human endurance."

I tried to stand up again. Though my legs were weak and rubbery, I stayed on my feet, getting only slightly dizzy, and tried to get back into the bathroom.

"You are very wobbly," he said, laughing. "Sit down and have a cup of tea, then I'll help you with those whiskers."

I drank the tea and ate a bowl of oatmeal.

"My name is Hans van den Horn and this is Mientje, my wife. I am a school master and my wife raises our three children."

He was a huge six-footer, about thirty years old. He wore heavy horn-rimmed spectacles. In spite of his weight, he was agile and moved about quickly. He was almost bald and wore an ascot. He was sincere and smiled frequently.

His wife was a petite woman, no more than five feet tall. She was saucy and had a lot of gumption. I liked her. Their children were staying at a friend's house for their own safety. I thanked her for the oatmeal as Hans took me into the bathroom, where he trimmed my whiskers with a pair of sharp scissors as close to the skin as he could. His wife brought hot water and he got my razor. He gave me a water tumbler with straight sides and I honed the blade by holding it on my finger and running it around the inside of the glass. It took thirty painstaking minutes to shave. I pulled my whiskers from the skin more than I shaved them and afterwards my face burned and smarted. I nicked myself several times. I looked at the improvement in the mirror. Still, I was skinny and my face looked drawn.

I got dressed and went back into the front room. "If you are wondering where your Luger is, I have cleaned it and put it away," Hans said. "I will return it when you leave."

When I sat down on the davenport, Niko returned. He was surprised to see me out of bed. "Hello, Jan, how do you feel?"

"A lot better, but Jim's still sleeping."

"Come into the bedroom for a minute, will you?" he asked.

He closed the door and said, "I have to leave for a while on some errands. There is close timing involved and I have no timepiece. Can I borrow your watch? It will only be for a few days."

"Of course, Niko," I said, taking it off my wrist. "Is there any word about George yet?"

"No, I'm really worried. The people here suspect foul play. Some think I might have been involved, but you know better. I'm going to Holwerd to see if his wife has any word from him."

He picked up his bag from the corner of the room and we returned to the front room, where he thanked the teacher. "Goodbye, Jan Veen," he said. "You are one of my best friends. I like you a lot. Say goodbye to Jim and I'll see you in a few days."

He walked out the back door, got on his bicycle, and rode past the front of the house, heading for the road to Holwerd.

I never saw Niko again.

The doctor came about an hour later. He was a heavy, short man who carried a black bag. Hans let him in the front door and took his hat. The medic brushed the snow off his coat. He examined me first, then went into the bedroom and awakened Jim, who sat up and stretched. He looked ferocious with wiry, black whiskers covering his face.

"I've got to go to the toilet before anybody can look at me," he said, getting out of bed, still naked and staggering. I put a blanket around his shoulders and led him to the toilet. Afterwards, I took him back and he looked in the mirror.

"Jesus Christ! Look at that! Who is he?" He looked at me. "When did you shave and clean up?" Not waiting for an answer, he sat down on the bed, and said, "Wow, I'm beat!"

The doctor took a stethoscope out of his bag and listened to Jim's heart and lungs. "Under the circumstances you gentlemen are in good shape. No sign of pneumonia." He recommended two days of rest with lots of hot liquids. We thanked him and he left.

Jim was so skinny, I could almost put my two hands around his waist. The teacher said mine was even smaller. I suggested Jim take a bath and shave. As we went through the living room, the teacher's wife looked at Jim with fear in her eyes. He did look menacing. I introduced him to her formally and as soon as he smiled at her, the look of fear left her face. If I thought I had trouble shaving, the hour-long ordeal Jim went through was sheer torture. I helped him all I could, using the same scissors and cutting his beard as close to the skin as I could. But when he started to shave, he pulled most of his whiskers out rather than shaving them off, as I had done. "Where can we get a haircut?" he asked.

"I'll call the corner barber shop for an appointment."

"You're a smartass since you found out you're alive."

After the shave, Jim washed the grime from his body. Once he was dressed in clean clothes, he looked pretty good. He staggered into the front room. The schoolteacher smiled at us.

"Well, I must say you certainly look a lot different than you did when I opened the door for you the first time. What do you say we get some hot potato soup in you?"

We went to the kitchen and gorged ourselves. Jim ate for the first time since we left Engelsmanplaat. Even though I had oatmeal earlier, I kept up with him. After eating, we were so pooped we went back to a bed with clean sheets and slept until sunrise. In fact, we woke up at the same time.

On the afternoon of December 6, mijnheer Visser came to see us. He looked a lot better than he did the last time we saw him. He took off his coat and the three of us sat down.

"There has been no word from George," he said. "He is not in any of the safe houses we know of and we fear he probably drowned in the sea. Niko has visited some places of which we knew nothing about, with the same result. Niko has now gone to the south of Friesland."

"I know, I loaned him my watch," I said.

Mijnheer Visser smiled at me, then continued. "I have only one question to ask both of you and I want an honest answer."

"Of course," we answered in unison.

"Did Niko leave the life-house after George came to shore?"

"No, he stayed in the life-house until you came," I said.

Visser looked at Jim.

"That's right, mijnheer Visser, just like Jan said."

"Then George was alive the last time any of you saw him?"

"George went down the ladder, walked a couple of hundred yards, and then waved his arm, making a fist with this hand. We watched him till he disappeared from view," I said.

"There's no way Niko could have killed George?" he asked.

"Mijnheer Visser, let me tell you this. If Niko had left the life-house even for a second, one of us would have known it. We were on edge, waiting for somebody to come out and rescue us. Unless Niko found George after we came off Engelsmanplaat, there is no way he could have killed him. And, if that's the case, where in hell was George for three days before we got back? He was not shot or taken prisoner by the Germans."

"Mijnheer Visser," Jim said, "it's just like Harry, 'er, Jan said. Niko didn't have an opportunity to kill George at all!"

"Thank you very much for the information. It will help to clear things up in the future. There have been a lot of Germans and Land-watchers in Paesens looking for American pilots lately. Last week an SD man was here and questioned several of the townspeople who are sympathetic to the Germans. It's not safe here."

"I'm sorry . . ." I began.

"Jan," said the schoolteacher, "don't worry about it."

"So," continued Visser, "tomorrow you and Jim will be moved to a new place. You will leave separately. It is only eight kilometers and you will ride with a courier as soon as the patrol has gone through town in the morning. Jan, you will leave with her and will dress as a lady. Jim, you will leave about ten in the morning, and Jan, you will leave shortly after." He stood up and shook hands with us. We walked him into the front room.

"I probably will not see either one of you again. May God bless you both. Get a good night's sleep so you will be strong enough to ride the bicycles tomorrow."

He turned to go out the door. I took his hand and shook it.

"You saved my life and Jim's too. I want to thank you for all the things you and your wife did for us. You risked your life to save ours. We went through a hell of an ordeal and without your help, I would have perished. I am in your debt forever, my friend. I'll never be able to repay you. I hope God keeps you and mevrouw Visser safe through the war." I spoke in Dutch.

There were tears of gratitude in my eyes for this heroic man. "Please thank Teun for helping us, if you will," I said.

Mevrouw van den Horn helped him with his coat. He shook hands with us again and left.

The following morning the teacher gave us back our guns. They had been cleaned and oiled. As usual, Jim put his in his suitcase. I put mine in my belt. The holster and clips went in my suitcase. "Who cleaned our guns?" I asked.

"I had nothing better to do so I thought I would get the salt water off them. They're beautiful weapons, by the way," Hans said.

Promptly at 8:00 Sjoukje van der Hoop came.

"*Dag*, Jan, Jim, how are you?" she asked.

We were surprised she was the one who was going to move us.

"How come you left Hoornsterzwaag so soon?" I asked. "We didn't get a chance to say goodbye to you and Tini Mulder."

"We had a long ride to make before dark and had to get started early. We told Niko to tell you goodbye. I heard about George," she said. "Too bad."

Jim put on his coat, took his suitcase, and said, "See ya."

They strapped Jim's suitcase on a bicycle and left.

I had another cup of tea. Mijnheer van den Horn came into the kitchen. "I must leave for school now. I'm glad to have made your acquaintance and I hope we meet again someday." He shook my hand, kissed his wife on the cheek, and left.

"Well, we have to dress you in women's clothes," Mientje interjected.

"What?" I asked. "I thought Visser was joking about that."

"No, no joke. You are going to ride a ladies' bicycle."

197

"A girl?"

She went to the back porch and brought in some clothes. "I think these might fit," she said.

It was not a bad idea, really. We had a great time. I went into the bedroom and took off my clothes except my underwear, then put on a woman's full slip and a dress. I came back in the living room and we both had a good laugh. We decided on a particular blue one with lace on the sleeves and collar. "This dress is really you," Mientje said, and broke up laughing. The blue one had more room in the skirt for me to move my legs around. She located a pair of ladies' shoes, big ones with small heels, which fit pretty well, and a pair of black stockings which would be held up by some large rubber bands just above my knees. She combed my hair and put a scarf over my head. We topped this off with a full-length black coat with a big collar. I dressed in my own clothes and lay the female attire on the bed.

About 11:00 I saw a figure go by the window into the back yard. Knowing mevrouw van den Horn wasn't expecting anybody, I went into the bedroom and closed the door. There was a loud knock at the door and in a few minutes I could hear two women speaking softly in the kitchen. Then there was silence.

Minutes later the teacher's wife called to me. "It's all right now, Jan. Come on out."

I opened the door and stepped into the living room. Greta was framed in the doorway, her legs crossed and her forefinger stuck in one corner of her mouth with a smile on her face. We met halfway across the room as she came into my arms.

She pulled away from me and said, "My God, you are so thin!"

"Yeah, I lost a pound or two."

I held her at arms length. "My beautiful Greta, more beautiful than I remembered," I said, now holding her close.

We sat next to each other on the davenport. She brushed my hair back from my face and stroked my cheeks.

Mientje excused herself and went into the kitchen.

"Was it bad out there?" Greta asked. "Tell me about it."

"No, not at first. It was bad walking through the water to Engelsmanplaat, but after we got to the life-house it wasn't so bad. I worried about getting food and water until it finally rained, but we were a long time without food."

I told her about the fight between Niko and George.

"We were cold and hungry after that. We began to doubt if we'd make it. Our minds played tricks on us and we couldn't rationalize clearly. Niko couldn't have killed George unless he did it after we came back. He never left us for three days. George was determined to come for help, and God knows we needed it. We couldn't have talked him out of it for his mind was made up, nor did we want to at that point. We were all so weak. The walk back from Engelsmanplaat was the worst thing that's ever happened to me. I'd be dead if it weren't for Visser. It was hell! Greta, how do you thank a man for saving your life?"

She listened with tears in her eyes and pulled me closer. "As far as I know, the radio message never came over BBC," she said. "It was a terrible mistake for you to go there before it was aired. The people in Paesens were troubled with you in the village. A Landwatcher heard about you and was searching for you."

Mevrouw van den Horn brought some tea and joined us. We drank the hot brew and talked more about my ordeal.

"I must be going," Greta said. "I'll be back to see you tomorrow. You are going to Ternaard. I have talked to the nurse you'll stay with and she thinks it would be wonderful if I come to see you. I can come as often as I like."

Greta got ready to leave. I walked her to the back door.

"Did you miss me while you were out there?" she asked.

"You're joking! Of course I missed you!" I kissed her neck.

"Mmm," she murmured. "I'm sorry I've got to leave, but this is underground business and I'm already late. I've got a lot of messages for the radio. See you tomorrow." I kissed her goodbye. "Keep that up and I'll see you tonight," she said, pressing herself to me. "I love you, Jan Veen," she said as she walked out the door.

"And I love you too!" I said after her.

I packed my suitcase and took it out to the anteroom. The teacher's wife prepared cheese sandwiches and tea.

"I heard there was a romance between Greta and you, but I had no idea it was so serious. I have known her since she was very small. She's one of the finest girls in Friesland."

At that moment Sjoukje knocked on the door. "Well, Jim is waiting for you. He is at a nurse's home. It's only eight kilometers and close to the dike. Is your bag packed?"

I nodded in the affirmative.

"Did Mientje tell you to dress like a woman?"

"Yes," I said, "and I make a beautiful girl."

"Do you feel strong enough to ride a bicycle?"

I told her I did, and went into the bedroom to dress in the women's attire. When I returned to the kitchen, they laughed. I joined them. I put my own clothes in the suitcase and strapped it on the bicycle, then went back to the house to shake mevrouw van den Horn's hand. She brushed it aside, put her arms around me, and kissed both my cheeks. "Godspeed," she said.

Sjoukje and I rode past mijnheer Visser's house, then turned onto the main road leading out of Paesens toward Holwerd. It was a clear day. When we rode to the top of the dike, I could see a long way into the North Sea, but I couldn't see my old nemesis, Engelsmanplaat. In fact, I didn't ever want to see the damned place again as long as I lived — peacetime, wartime, or anytime.

We rode on for a while until the road came down off the dike, then we traveled beside it to Ternaard. It took us an hour to get there and we passed only a few people riding on the road.

In Ternaard, we got off the bicycles and pushed them.

"I understand the head of the underground is going to have a meeting with you soon. But I am not supposed to tell you this."

"My lips are forever sealed!" I said dramatically, holding my hand over my head in a Shakespearean gesture.

"Huh?" she said, looking at me like I was an idiot. "You Americans."

I was laughing at her when we turned in beside a small, tan brick two-story house on a lane between the main road and the dike. It had a red tile roof with brown trim. The yard was a mess. In the back yard, we laid our bicycles against the house.

Sjoukje knocked at the door and Jim opened it. He roared with laughter when he saw me wearing women's clothes.

We entered the kitchen of the house, where a small, frail, slender lady stood in back of Jim. She smiled as we entered. After the formal introduction, the sister shook hands with me and continued to talk to Sjoukje in Frisian. I followed Jim upstairs to our sleeping area. After I changed clothes, I put my gun in my belt and pulled my sweater down. Jim shook his head. When we came back down, the old woman poured tea.

Sjoukje told us about the woman.

"The sister," she said, "is a nurse, and until recently she worked at a hospital in Leeuwarden, some forty kilometers west of here. Although she's still active, she no longer makes the long trip because of the lack of transport. Now she devotes her time to helping the local people. She is looked upon as a saint. She is a wonderful person whose bravery is unquestioned."

I asked Sjoukje the sister's name.

"Just call her Sister, that's all. Names do not count now."

After lunch, Sjoukje said she was glad to have seen Jim and me again and hoped we would be comfortable. I watched as she left, pushing her bicycle toward the main road.

We spent the rest of the day looking around our new surroundings and trying to talk to the sister in Dutch. She spoke Frisian and nothing else. It made communicating difficult. Her home was old and so was everything in it. Her furnishings were well kept and she was proud of them. She had a place for everything and everything was in its place. After supper, she retired early and we went upstairs.

About 10:00 the following morning, Greta came to the house. She was beaming. However, she didn't make a display of her affection when she came in.

"I just came from mijnheer Nauta's house. He has given me permission to take you to my sister's house as long as we use the back roads and you dress in your special outfit."

"Great," I said, "do you mind, Jim?"

"No. I might envy you, but I sure as hell don't mind."

I went upstairs and put the woman's clothes on over my own. Again I put the Luger in my belt and rolled up my pant legs.

When I came downstairs, I decided to swing my hips and act very feminine. They all laughed.

We walked the bicycles to the street then pedaled slowly to her sister's. We put the bicycles in the shed.

The kitchen stove had a fire in it.

"Is your sister here?" I asked.

"No, she is in Amsterdam, to try to find our family. We have enough food and firewood to keep warm, so she is looking for them to bring them here. Why did you ask?"

"Because there is a fire in the stove."

"I stopped and built it before I came for you." She smiled. "Jan, please get out of those silly clothes. I want a kiss, but not from another woman."

I went to the front bedroom and took off the clothes. I rolled down my pant legs and tucked in my shirttail. Returning to the kitchen, I kissed Greta for a long time.

"I went to my home in Suameer for the first time in three weeks yesterday. I have been staying here ever since you went out to Engelsmanplaat. Everybody in Paesens thought you were in England. When I discovered you had been brought back from the *plaat,* I heard they were not sure that you and Jim would survive the ordeal you had been through. They wouldn't let me come to see you. We were under orders to stay away from mijnheer van den Horn's house until it was certain the Germans didn't know you were there. I was angry when George and Niko took you out there in the first place. God, what stupidity!"

She took my hand in hers and looked at my face.

"When I left you in Paesens, I had a feeling something like this would happen. I was very upset when I came back from Leeuwarden and you were gone. I prayed for you, Jan, and I thank God you are all right. You look so thin and frail."

Then, with a mischievous look in her eyes, she said, "Do you think you are strong enough to . . .?" She whispered what she had in mind in my ear.

"Well," I replied, "there's only one way to find out."

As we undressed in the bedroom, the sight of her beautiful body aroused me. She glanced down at me. "There's certainly nothing wrong with that!" she said, pushing herself against me.

We stayed all night at her sister's house. It was early morning when we both went to sleep wrapped in each other's arms. She had held nothing back, and trusted me as completely as I did her. We talked about Niko. I told her he would be back in a few days with my watch. She was interested in the fact that, though he was so weak from our ordeal, and further weakened by the walk to the shore from Engelsmanplaat, he still had the strength to get out of bed after a few hours of rest and search for George. I didn't know where Niko had gone to look for him. She made mental notes of everything I said.

When we woke up, the sun was shining in the room from around the drawn curtain shades. Naturally, one of the tiny rays of sunlight was shining in my eyes. Greta had her leg thrown over me and her arm was around my neck. I awakened her, trying to untangle myself. It was so cold in the house, I could see the vapor of my breath in the frigid room.

"I'd better make a fire in the stove," I said.

"Let's both make it," she giggled and threw the covers off us. She jumped out of bed and pulled me after her. Both of us were naked and shivering, but we ran into the kitchen and quickly built a fire. Once it was going, we ran back to the bed and into each other's arms. We made love to keep from freezing.

Later, after she prepared some breakfast, we had more tea. Both of us hated to leave the comfort of the place. I had the feeling she was embarrassed by her relationship with me, so I asked her about it.

"Are you ashamed we care for each other where your Dutch friends are concerned?"

"No! Oh my God, no," she replied. "I'm not ashamed of it, but I did have reservations about falling in love with you. I don't feel that way now as much as I did when you went out to the sandbank and left me. You could have gone back to England, not knowing if I was pregnant, never worrying about your Dutch girl."

I interrupted. "Let me tell you one thing, Greta, if I had gone to England, as soon as I could, I would have been in Suameer sitting on your doorstep waiting for you."

"I believe it now, but I doubted it then. You see, I worried that if it was all one-sided and I was the only one in love, with all my friends in Friesland knowing about us, then I would have been a laughingstock. I couldn't bear that."

"They wouldn't have been very good friends if they had made fun of you, would they? But you don't have to worry about that! We'll be together as long as you'll have me, if we survive!"

She smiled. "We'll survive the war," she said. "Think of all the good years we'll have together then."

We were both glad the air was cleared and we had a definite understanding. She seemed like a new person and we were much closer afterwards. I was floating on a cloud.

Just before noon, I dressed in my women's clothes and we went back to Ternaard. We rode side by side on the back roads.

"What are you going to tell the sister when she asks why we didn't come back last night?" I asked.

"I'm going to tell her the truth, that we're in love!"

"Good! I hope we don't run into any German patrols."

"If we do, you will flirt with them and keep right on pedaling down the road. They don't dare to fool around with women when they are on duty, for they are punished severely if they do."

We rode into Ternaard without passing another soul either on foot or bicycle.

Jim came to the back door. "Where in hell have you guys been? When you didn't get back by curfew, half the Frisian underground were searching for you! Now that you're okay, I know where you've been, you lucky devil," he said, grinning. The sister took Greta's hand. They talked and finally the sister put her arms around Greta and hugged her.

I went upstairs and changed my clothes.

Later, I asked her, "Well, did she ask where you were?"

"No, but I told her, and I told her how we feel."

"What was her reaction?"

"You saw her when she put her arms around me. She invited me to stay here too. She said it will be nice to have a good friend living in America."

"Well, I'll be damned. What do you think?"

"I'll live wherever you want. If it's America, it's okay!"

"Well, there go our reputations," I said. I had to explain what reputation meant.

The sister seemed grateful to have someone to talk to. We had a joyful lunch, Greta translating our conversation.

There was a knock at the back door. Jim and I flew up the stairs and sat quietly on the bed. The sound of a man's voice filtered up the stairs. Greta called for us to come down.

A balding, thin-faced man with blue eyes and milky white skin stood in the middle of the kitchen. He was well dressed, wearing a tailored business suit and a silk tie. My first impression was that he could be the original "Howard Milktoast." But his voice belied that impression. It was deep, concise, and commanding.

"Mijnheer Nauta does not speak English," Greta said.

We both shook hands with the visitor. Looking closer at the man, he appeared to be ill. But regardless, his clear blue eyes pierced my hide when he looked at me.

Greta translated.

"My name is Albertus Nauta. It is my real name, not an alias. I lead the organization in this area. Jan, you and Greta gave us quite a fright last night when you didn't return, but we found your bicycles in the shed in back of Greta's sister's house and knew you were safe. After that we really didn't expect you back before today since Greta had previously expressed your fondness for one another. So long as your relationship doesn't interfere with organization business, we certainly have no objections to your personal lives. I will say this, however: Greta is one of our favorite daughters. Don't trifle with her affections. Do you understand what I'm saying to you?"

Greta was red-faced as she finished translating. I touched her blushing cheeks and told her to tell him it was no trifling matter.

He nodded after she translated. "Now down to business. We have a lot of activity in this area of Holland. I will not, for now, burden you with details, but since you are now my responsibility, I will radio London and let them know you are with us. At least then they will know you are alive. Do you understand?"

We nodded in the affirmative and he continued. "A man, whose identity I am not at liberty to disclose, will probably ask both of you, since you are no doubt weapons experts, to work with the organization and participate in some of our activities. To start by instructing Dutchmen how to use guns and other weapons. If we ask you to participate, what will you do? Jim, how about it?"

Jim had his answer ready. "First of all, I want you to know I don't want to participate in anything." It was an honest reply. "All I want to do is get home in one piece. I want to go someplace where I can live until I am liberated. I want you to know I appreciate all you folks have done for me, but I've been close to death so many times I just want out." He was trembling. "I just want to go home."

Greta carefully translated Jim's words. When she finished, she gently placed a hand on his shoulder.

"Jim," Nauta said, "I have just the place for you. I will make arrangements and we will move you where you will be safe until the end of the war." He patted him on the shoulder then looked at me. "How about you, Jan? There is room for two."

I didn't reply immediately. I mulled the question over in my mind for several moments. I knew what my answer would be, but it was difficult to answer the man.

Finally I said, "Now that would be nice! But I'd be bored to death. I will assist you any way you think I can. I know weapons pretty well, and I don't mind being moved from one place to another. I only pray I'm not found in somebody's house by the Germans. I don't want people murdered for harboring me. I'm not a brave man. In fact, sometimes I'm so scared I wake up at night with the shakes. I can understand what Jim is saying and it's the right decision for him."

When Greta was through translating he looked at us. "Then I will proceed with plans for both of you. In the meantime, you will be safe here with the sister. We are watching the house for her safety as well as yours. You will hear from me."

He made some remarks in Frisian to the women, smiled, and held up his hand in the gesture of a salute as he went out the back door, closing it gently behind him.

Later, Greta and I were alone in the front room, talking. "I want to tell you about my fiancé, for Jim's attitude reminds me of him so much," she said. "His name was Jan too. He felt what the underground did was wrong. He was approached many times but would never help. Jim reminds me of him. He would say, 'Let the other man do it! Let the other fellow get his head blown off. Not me!' My father and mother died working for the cause of freedom from Nazi brutality. I have been involved since I was sixteen. I can't understand how anybody can refuse to help their country. Jim isn't a Dutchman, so why should he help us? I loved my fiancé but detested him politically. On the other side of the coin, I have seen young men, school mates, whom I thought were truly patriotic, turn on their fellow man, join the NSB and become members of the SD or the SS. Traitors all!"

She cuddled in my arms.

"I'll tell you something I have never told anybody else in my life." She looked straight into my eyes. "I have killed a man. May God forgive me, but I'd do it again if I had to."

"I've killed too," I said, telling her about the two German soldiers I killed the day I was shot down. Somehow, I had never thought about it.

"There is one more thing, Jan Veen. I am so proud that you think enough of my people to help. I'm so proud!" She snuggled further into my arms and held me. Then she didn't say another word.

The following day was Sunday. The sister and Greta went to church in Holwerd, riding their bicycles. When they returned, Bertus Nauta and his wife were with them. Jim let them in the kitchen door. Greta introduced Bertus's wife as Tini. She was twenty-eight years old, plump, charming, and very well dressed, and she spoke a little English.

I helped the women with their coats and hung them in the closet. The sister went to the kitchen to prepare dinner.

"I have some news for both of you," Bertus said. "We will meet tomorrow night at my house. Jan, Greta will escort you after supper. Jim, we have made arrangements for you to go to Dokkum on Wednesday. You will stay with a Dominee until we are liberated. It's not too late to change your mind."

Jim looked at me. "You know how much I want to be in a safe place, Harry. You're my best friend. But I like living too." He looked at Bertus Nauta. "No, that's what I want," he said.

As Greta translated his reply, Bertus nodded. Bertus and I went into the front room with Greta to translate. He helped me understand some of the ways they would use me, considering the language barrier. They desperately needed somebody to instruct on the use of weapons. He confided in me that some of their activities were risky. So far his group got the job done without the loss of a single man. He was proud of their record and prayed, he said, it would stay that way.

Everybody decided George had drowned at sea while trying to wade ashore. Niko, on the other hand, had vanished. He had been part of Bertus's group, and was last seen in Drachten. Greta told Bertus about my wristwatch.

The following night, after the patrol went through Ternaard, Greta and I walked to Bertus's home. Dressed in my women's garb, Jim playfully patted me, then pinched my rear end as we left. Tini greeted us at her back door. We removed our shoes and she led us into the front room. Bertus and two strangers stood when we entered. There were broad smiles on their faces when they saw my attire. I sat down in a chair and slipped out of the dress. As I rolled down my pant legs, Greta took my dress out to the kitchen. Bertus closed the door after her.

The older of the two strangers walked over to me. I stood up and shook hands with him.

"I am Harry Wessels." He had an Oxford English accent. "Now we have two Harrys in the room," he said, smiling, as he returned to his chair.

I smiled. "You speak better English than I do."

"I had better. I am an English professor at the college in Groningen. My real name is Harry Wessels and my job is to officiate over our operation in Friesland. I'll not mince words with you, but we will have some straight conversation. First of all, I have a message for you."

He handed me a small folded piece of paper. Unfolded, it was about three inches wide and some eight inches long. There was a typewritten message on it.

"Go on, read it and give me your answer," Wessels said.

T/SGT HARRY A. CLARK 19000426

WILL YOU VOLUNTEER TO ASSIST UNDERGROUND MOVEMENT IN HOLLAND AND GIVE ALL ASSISTANCE POSSIBLE STOP PRIORITY ANSWER STOP.

TINKER, SHAEF HQ, LONDON

I read it twice. I really didn't believe it was genuine. But it had my correct serial number. Only Pete back in Meppel knew it. I had written it on his questionnaire. Strange, I had already agreed to help. I returned the paper. "I have already told Bertus I would help in any way I can."

"Good," he replied, "I like to hear these things first-hand. I will relay your reply to London tomorrow." He thought for a moment. "I want to thank you."

"What do you want me to do?" I asked, even though I was certain I knew he wanted assistance teaching armament.

"Primarily, we want you to instruct our people to use the weapons we receive in air drops. Most of them come packed in heavy grease and the instructions are in English. What sort of weapons do you know well?"

I thought for a moment. "I am familiar with .50- and .30-caliber machine guns. I know .20 and .35mm aircraft cannons, .45-caliber Colt pistols, American sidearms, Thompson submachine guns, .38 Smith and Wesson revolvers, British Sten submachine guns, Enfield rifles, Gerand rifles, .30-caliber carbines, 12-gauge shotguns, and I know a little bit about bazookas, mortars, and plastic explosives. That's about it."

Wessels nodded to the stranger, who removed a .45 Colt Automatic from his waistband. He brought it to me.

"Please field strip the weapon," Wessels said.

The Colt was loaded with a shell in its chamber. The hammer was pulled back and only the safety prevented it from being ready to fire. "This is bad," I said, shaking my head. "Never carry a weapon with a shell in the chamber and cocked like this." Wessels translated my words to his friend in Dutch.

I removed the ammunition clip, slid the bolt back, and took the shell from the chamber. I pulled the bolt back several times to clear it. Field stripping the weapon in a matter of seconds, I laid the pieces on the floor in front of me. The barrel was filthy. The area around the firing pin had dirt and grit on it. I told him he had a dirty gun and it might misfire unless it was cleaned. I put the weapon back together and put the shell that had been in the chamber in the clip before I shoved it back in the butt of the gun. This time I put it on half cock and set the safety.

"Very impressive," said mijnheer Wessels.

"Let me show you a couple of things about this weapon." I emptied the gun of ammunition and cocked the hammer. "If someone points this weapon at you and the opportunity arises, try to hit the end of the barrel with the butt of your hand. When he pulls the trigger at the same time, the gun will not fire." I demonstrated several times, then the others tried it.

"This might give that split second somebody needs to disarm the aggressor and immobilize him."

Wessels was impressed by my knowledge of the weapon and said so. "You certainly know this weapon," he said. "Tell me, Jan, would you be willing to work with our people in some of the dirty business we sometimes get into?"

"It all depends. Such as?"

"Oh, getting weapons from the air when they are dropped from the Lancasters, cleaning them, making inventories of those we receive and another record of their distribution. We have a lot of explosives which look like putty. We have just stockpiled the stuff because we're unfamiliar with it. We do have instructions in English, but I am not a weapons man. Could you teach our men to use the stuff?"

"Yes, I could."

"As the time grows shorter for the Allies to start their big campaign against the Hun, we will probably really get into sabotage and dirty work against them. Will you be willing to fight?" He smiled. "You may have to kill, are you capable of that?"

"Mijnheer Wessels, I know what you have in mind for me to do. Don't worry. When the time comes, I'll be there."

That seemed to conclude our conversation, for Harry Wessels then spoke to Bertus Nauta and the stranger who, when he retrieved the gun from me, replaced the shell, cocked the hammer, and stuck it in his belt. If it fired, he'd chirp like a canary the rest of his life! I didn't know if he put it on safety.

Bertus opened the door to the kitchen and spoke to Tini. She and Greta came in with a tray with tea, bread, cheese, and marmalade. Greta sat on the floor next to my chair and held my hand. When Wessels saw this, a smile came across his face and he spoke to her in Frisian. Greta's face turned red.

There was a lot of conversation. None of it was in English. I picked up a word or two. Greta told me they were speaking pure Frisian, which was similar to but different from Dutch.

"It's very difficult to understand," she said.

"Do you understand all of it?" I queried.

209

"Of course. I'm from Friesland, remember?"

We finished our tea and Greta took the dishes to the kitchen as the three men got to their feet.

"Well, Jan," said Wessels, "officially I want to thank you in advance for your assistance. Your knowledge of weapons will be invaluable to us. Also, I'm happy you and Greta are getting on so well." He smiled. "You seem to be a decent chap and all that, and we do think very highly of her." He spoke to her in Frisian.

She smiled at her leader and said to me, "Well, let's get you back into your bloomers and bra. It's time to go home."

After I pulled the dress on, I shook hands with the three men. As I turned to leave, Wessels put his hand on my arm.

"Oh yes, we are moving you from the sister's house. It's too difficult for you to move around freely from there."

On Wednesday, a man I had never seen before came to the sister's house. It was snowing and he had snow packed on the front of his coat from riding against it on his bicycle. The sister gave him some hot tea as he sat down at the kitchen table. He had come for Jim.

Greta, who was acquainted with the man, translated.

"The Germans don't like to ride their patrols in the snow so today will be a good day for us to ride," he said. "We take the back roads where we can stop at safe houses to get warm."

Jim had packed his clothes the night before. The sister had washed and ironed them and even packed his suitcase.

He asked me to go upstairs. When we were alone, he said, "You're a good buddy, Harry. You haven't bitched about my shortcomings and you haven't preached to me either. I appreciate it. When the war is over, if we both make it, I hope we can continue our friendship. I really don't make friends too easy, but I guess you have already guessed that. We know an awful lot about each other, almost like brothers." He paused. "Hell, I can even tell the next time you're gonna take a leak!" He had tears in his eyes and I put my arms around him.

"You're a hell of a bawl baby, Jim," I said, "cut that shit out or we'll both be doing it." He backed away from me. "Thanks for your friendship, buddy. But, we'll see each other. I owe you five hundred and twenty bucks! Let's make sure you stay alive to collect it! Okay?"

"I will. Greta will let me know where you are and I'll get word to you through her. Take care of yourself."

We shook hands and went downstairs. Jim put on his coat and hat. He shook hands with the sister and Greta and said *"Dag"* to the sister. She smiled and said something in Frisian.

"Take care of him, he's a hell of a guy," he said to Greta.

She smiled and kissed him on the cheek.

He and the Dutchman began pedaling south. It would be the last time I saw Jim for a long time.

Greta and I had not made love since she started staying at the house. She slept in a room downstairs next to the sister's bedroom. It was difficult not to be able to hold her.

"What goes on between us is special and private," she said. "It would be wrong, and for now I want to continue that way. Soon we'll have plenty of time together to do just as we like."

Greta ran messages for the underground on Wednesday and didn't come home until about 9:00 that night. She was cold and hungry and had fallen with her bicycle on the slippery road. She had a bruised knee which was skinned badly. We sat on the davenport and I held her shivering body close as the sister put a dressing on her knee. I held a cup of hot tea for her to drink. A little later, after Greta was warm, the sister put some food on the kitchen table and retired for the night. Greta ate, then we went back into the living room, blew out the candles, and sat in the dark.

"I went to the radio today. There is a message for you but it's to be delivered by Bertus Nauta. Would you like to see it?"

"Thanks, Greta," I said, "but I think you had better go by the book. I don't want you to get in trouble on my account."

She snuggled a little closer to me and said, "I want you so badly right now I can hardly stand it."

"Me too," I replied, kissing her passionately.

We slid down onto the floor in front of the davenport and made love quietly. Later we went our separate ways to bed.

On Friday, Greta's knee was better and she removed the bandage. It was the same day I was to be moved from the sister's house. Greta confided to me that when we moved we would be together. She knew where we were going but preferred to tease me about it. I washed, shaved, and cleaned myself as well as I could in cold water, then put on some fresh underwear and a clean shirt before I went downstairs.

211

The sister was alone in the kitchen. I sat at the table.

"Greta?" I asked.

She put her hands together and put them beside her head then pointed to the bedroom, indicating Greta was still asleep.

I went to the bedroom and peeked in. She was in bed, breathing deeply. I walked to the edge of the bed and stroked her hair gently. She opened her eyes and smiled at me.

"Good morning," she said happily. "I love you, Jan Veen!"

"I love you too, sleepy head!" I answered. Then I had to explain what a sleepy head was. Finally, I threw the covers off her. "Come on, lazy bones!" Then I had to explain lazy bones.

After breakfast, we spent the morning talking and joking. The sister joked with us and Greta got a kick out of translating to her. We made a good time of it.

"I wonder when I'm going to be moved," I said after lunch.

"We can go any time you want. It's lonesome here for the sister when she's alone, so I thought we'd wait until after supper. Is that all right with you?"

"Yes, that's very thoughtful of you."

We included the sister in all our conversations for the rest of the day. After supper I packed my suitcase. Greta helped in the kitchen while I put on my dress. At dusk we tied the suitcases to the bicycles, said goodbye to the sister, and pushed our bikes to Bertus's house. Tini had been watching for us and showed us where to put the bicycles in a shed.

Again we left our shoes by the back door and Tini showed us the bedroom we were to share upstairs. We took our suitcases up and I shed my dress before we went back down. At the kitchen table, Tini poured tea and spoke to Greta in Dutch, which I understood. Bertus was out of town and wouldn't return for a couple of days. She said Greta was to take me to Paul's, a farmhouse about ten kilometers away.

"Do you know where the farmhouse is?" I asked.

"Of course. I've been there many times. I don't know if I'm supposed to tell you this, but that's where they store the weapons they receive from airplanes. Wait till you see how well they are hidden. The farm is well guarded."

"Please don't tell me things I'm not supposed to know. If I accidentally mentioned it, they'd know it came from you. I appreciate your trust in me and I appreciate their trust in me."

She looked at me and smiled. "I don't think you could ever drop something in conversation that could hurt me. You are now a part of us and we all trust each other. Don't worry about what I tell you, it's all right."

Tini and Bertus slept downstairs. There was a hiding place in the floor of our room upstairs. A special board could be lifted next to the baseboard and a door was exposed. Once this was lifted from the floor, there was enough space for four people to lay down comfortably. While inside, a rope on the inside was pulled and the baseboard slid down and locked in place. The room had closet beds and they were wide enough for two people to sleep side by side comfortably. Greta and I each had a bed. Tini had showed us our sleeping quarters with a sly twinkle in her eye. We always made sure both beds were messed up each morning. I don't know who we thought we were kidding.

The first evening we were there, Tini tried her limited English on me. Some words she knew better than others. I tried my Dutch on her and I guess my Dutch was just as bad as her English. Greta laughed at us both.

I liked Tini. She was a very heavy-set woman, quite a bit younger than Bertus. She wore horn-rimmed glasses, had clear white skin, and never wore any makeup. She was not particularly obese but was large all over. She was very graceful. She took my Luger from me and pushed a spring-fed board on the kitchen wall which opened to reveal a cache of several pistols hidden inside.

"You can have your gun whenever you want it. Just help yourself," she said, putting my gun with the others. She showed me how the mechanism worked. Later, I put the holster and the spare clips of ammunition in the cache too.

"Tomorrow will start a new life for you, Jan," Greta said. "I think it's time you got a good night's sleep," she added with a sly grin on her face. "Let's go to bed."

ELEVEN

S unday morning Greta and I watched the German patrol go
through Ternaard. They looked frozen and miserable as they mushed
their bicycles through the freshly fallen snow.

Greta washed and ironed our clothes, then we started for Paul's. I
wore my own clothes and the woman's coat, with a bandanna over my
hair. The Luger was secure in my belt.

We headed south out of town and turned east at the village of
Hantum, four kilometers from Ternaard. Four or five kilometers further on, we turned south on a dirt road, then turned on several small
roads until we came to a farmhouse with a huge barn. We turned in the
long driveway and walked to the back door. A balding man wearing
farmer's coveralls opened the door.

"Ah, Greta," he said, smiling, "this must be Jan Veen." He held
out his hand and I shook it. "Come in, come in. I'm Paul."

He spoke Dutch rather than Frisian, so I understood him. We entered one of the biggest kitchens I have ever seen. A table capable of
seating thirty people stretched across the wall. There were two benches
on the side and chairs on the ends. Greta laid her coat over the back of
one of the chairs and poured tea.

"I'm glad we have someone to teach the weapons," Paul said.

"I'll do all I can to help," I replied in Dutch.

"We'll have our tea then I'll show you the barn."

We finished our tea and I followed Paul out the back door. We slid into some wooden shoes and walked to the barn. It was an immense structure with a thatched roof and thick brick walls. Many stalls ran along the inside walls where animals, cows I supposed, had been. Farm machinery replaced the cattle in order to keep it out of the weather. Running the full length of the barn, down the center, was a haystack measuring a hundred feet long by twenty feet wide. We circled the machinery and went to the far end. He rolled a small wagon away from the haystack and with a pitchfork pulled some hay away from the end, exposing a concealed door. The haystack was hollow. Overhead he found the light switch and illuminated the interior brightly with light.

On the far end was a '38 Chevrolet four-door sedan. Several canisters were piled along the walls. Work tables lined part of it. Neatly stacked in the middle was an arsenal of rifles, Sten and Bren guns, bazookas, ammunition, and untold boxes of weapons. It was an awesome display! I walked from one end to the other. I was familiar with all the weapons except the bazookas. Paul switched off the light and closed the secret door, checking carefully to make sure he had covered the entrance with hay. Satisfied, he rolled the wagon in front of the door again.

In the house, Greta asked, "Well, what do you think of it?"

"Have you ever been in the barn before?" I asked.

"Harry, it seems like I spend half my life unpacking and cleaning guns from the containers. Yes, I have been here many times. There are many places like this in Holland."

"How does Paul get electricity for the lights?" I asked.

He smiled. "Grand larceny! It has gone undetected since they cut the power to our houses." We went to the back window and he pointed to a power line in back of his barn.

"We made a special hollow pole with wires running down the center from one end to the other. We buried heavy wires from the barn to the base of the old telephone pole. One night when we were ready, we removed the old pole, disconnected the wires from the cross arms, and let them hang. We took the cross arms off and replaced them on our pole. Then we put our pole in the ground in the place of the old one, reconnected the wires to the cross arms, and connected our wires from the barn to theirs. It took ten of us all night to get the job done. The power line goes to the islands of Ameland and Schiermonnikoog. There is always power from the big generators in Leeuwarden feeding it." He laughed. "A first-class job, don't you think?"

I certainly had to agree with him.

We decided I would start on Monday morning. I left him a list of things I would need, including a ledger to write in and a lot of rags. He said he would have twelve or fifteen men there by 9:00. Greta and I declined lunch and rode back to Ternaard in heavily falling snow.

She spent Sunday morning delivering messages and came home shortly after noon. Bertus walked in a little later.

I was sitting at the kitchen table working on an old clock, an antique of Tini's, that had quit running. I took it apart and had gears and pieces lying all over the table.

"You can repair clocks?" Greta asked, sitting down.

"This is my first try at it."

I found it had a broken main spring. I removed the broken end, heated it to take the temper out, and wrapped it around the anchor pin. I spent most of the day cleaning the gears and getting rid of years of accumulated dust.

Bertus shook hands with me and laughed at all the parts on the table. Greta translated.

"Paul told me you stopped by. What did you think?"

"I couldn't believe my eyes," I replied.

"You are starting tomorrow, then. We want to get started."

"I'll be there before nine o'clock."

"The rifles are the most important, I think. We have a lot of them. We want everybody to be able to shoot them accurately. We have about a hundred rounds of ammunition for each gun. After you have trained the men, give them the guns and ammunition. They are their responsibility after that. We have to empty the barn to make room for weapons still hidden in containers elsewhere."

Greta gave him a piece of paper and he handed it to me. To the best of my recollection, it read:

TO: STAFF SERGEANT HARRY A CLARK 1900042

UNDERSTAND YOU VOLUNTEER TO ASSIST WITH FRIESLAND GROUP

STOP NEW CODE NAME IS VEEN STOP RADIO REFERENCE IS VEEN STOP

NEW ASSIGNMENT TDY OFFICE OF STRATEGIC SERVICES COMMA OSS STOP

TINKER SHAEF LONDON.

Real "Cloak and Dagger" stuff, I thought to myself after I read it. Greta threw it in the stove.

Bertus spoke to Greta in Frisian. She shook her head negatively and finally spoke to me with a hurt look on her face.

216

"He thinks I gave the note to you before."

"Let him think it," I said, "forget it. Come sit by me and help me put this clock back together." She pulled her chair next to mine. We wiped each gear and part a final time. The internal parts looked pretty good, but it took over an hour to get it back together again. I put the works back in the case, wound the spring tight, and set the pendulum in motion. It worked, chiming on the hour. As it did, Tini came in from the other room and was delighted to see it running for the first time in many years.

We went to bed early. Greta snuggled close to me after the house was quiet. We made love quietly for a long time.

The following morning we were up at the crack of dawn. We decided to beat the patrol, so at about 7:00 we rode to the farm. Paul opened the door as we came around the corner.

"*Morgen!*" he said cheerfully.

"*Morgen!*" we both answered and went into the kitchen.

A strikingly beautiful woman, in her thirties, with just a hint of a smile on her face greeted us. She stood about 5'8 and weighed about 140.

"This is my wife, Tinka," Paul said proudly.

"*Morgen,* Tinka," I said.

"Hello, Jan Veen," she said in Dutch. "It's good to see you, Greta. I heard you were in the vicinity. Staying in Ternaard, aren't you? Now we will get to see more of you, I hope."

The tone of her voice was not kindly but had a malevolent ring to it. I decided she was somebody I didn't like.

Later, she and Greta became absorbed in serious talk in Frisian. I was relieved when Paul called.

"Come on, Jan, we have people in the barn."

Greta walked over to me. "See you for lunch, okay?"

"Okay," I said.

She kissed me tenderly. "I love you, Harry."

"You know, that's the first time you ever called me Harry."

"Yes, I know. I'll see you later, I love you," she said.

She stood framed in the doorway, watching us go to the barn.

Strange, I thought. *She has never been so open with her affections before.* Inside the barn I dismissed it from my mind, for I had a serious job to do.

A Dutchman holding a Sten gun in his arms stood guard by the entrance to the haystack. As we neared, he opened the door.

217

Eight men were waiting. The youngest was sixteen and the oldest forty. The men wore wooden shoes and sat on the floor.

"This is Jan Veen. He is an American pilot who has been in Holland about five months. His job for the American government is to show us how to use the guns. He speaks Dutch badly but I think you can understand him." He laughed, then stood back.

I asked, "Does anybody speak English?"

I waited a few moments and, finding I had no takers, said in my best Dutch, "Okay, we'll do the best we can."

I took an Enfield rifle from a stack leaning against a work bench. I looked the weapon over carefully. The weapon had been wiped free of the protective coating of cosmoline and didn't look too bad. So, from the same stack, I issued each man a rifle. I asked them to do exactly as I did. I laid a large piece of cloth on the bench and pressed the release so I could remove the bolt from the rifle. Each of them did the same. I looked through the barrel of the rifle, holding it up to the light in the ceiling. As I suspected, the cosmoline had never been removed. I explained the barrel might explode if it was fired with cosmoline in it.

I explained to Paul what a cleaning rod looked like. A look of discovery came over the man's face. "Oh, them?" he said, "I know what you mean." He went into some boxes in a corner and brought one to the workbench. He removed some cleaning rods, gun oil, and oil-treated pads. "We were going to throw these away for we could find no use for them."

I issued a cleaning rod to each man. We cleaned the bore of the barrels until they looked chrome-plated. They were in remarkably good condition. Next, we removed the barrels and completely cleaned each part of the rifles. I took live ammunition and loaded the internal clip, shoving it down into the weapon. Then I unloaded it and showed them how it was done. I explained how the sight could be raised, lowered, moved right or left so it could be fired confidently at different distances with great accuracy. Showing them how to hold the weapon properly, I used the sling from both a prone position and standing or kneeling position. Finally, they learned how to carry the rifle with the sling. They asked many questions. It was amazing but I understood what they wanted to know and in my limited Dutch was able to establish a rapport with them. We talked the better part of the morning when Paul called a break for lunch.

"You are a good instructor, Jan Veen," he said as we walked back to the house. "You are going to have a very busy time in Friesland. The men understood you very well too."

We entered the house. Tinka put lunch on the table. Greta was nowhere to be seen. I asked where she was.

"Oh, she had to leave," the woman replied.

I sat down at the table and waited for her to continue with an explanation but none came. I asked, "Well, where did she go?"

"She went back to Ternaard."

"Will she be back by the time I'm ready to leave?"

"I doubt it. Stop worrying. Someone will take you back," she replied sarcastically.

I restrained myself. "Well, thank you." I put on my hat and coat, went out the back door, and sat down on the steps. I rolled a cigarette, touched a match to it, and inhaled the raw smoke.

Why in hell had this woman been so discourteous? I wondered. *Maybe she just doesn't like Allied airmen. Greta will explain it to me.*

Paul came out of the house. He didn't mention his wife's sarcasm or the fact that I hadn't eaten my lunch.

I was glad to start work and get the incident off my mind. There was a huge vise on the workbench. I took some pliers from the toolbox. After removing a single round of .30-caliber rifle ammunition, I placed the pointed end in the vise. With the pliers, I twisted the casing until the two separated. I unloaded fifty shells and put the black powder in the ammo box. After piling some rags on the floor, I fired each round into them. The priming caps were now rendered harmless. I replaced the bullets in the casings and had fifty rounds of dummy ammunition with which we could practice loading and unloading. The men had a good time doing it. They practiced aiming and I showed them how to use the sights.

Our last hour they practiced loading the rifles, aiming and firing them at bull's eyes we drew on paper and set up at the far end of the haystack. When they left in the afternoon, they knew as much about an Enfield rifle as I did.

I got a great deal of satisfaction from my first day's work. It was almost dark when we quit and the last of the men departed from the barn. Paul listed the serial number of the guns in the ledger and along beside the number the man's "alias." That way, if the Germans ever put their hands on the ledger, they couldn't identify the man to whom the weapon was issued.

Tini Nauta was waiting when I came in. Tinka disappeared into another part of the house. I donned my woman's clothes and we rode to Ternaard.

I asked Tini about Greta and all she knew was that Greta had to go to Zwolle to do some important work.

"Bertus will clear it up for you. Women don't ask questions in these matters," she said.

I cleaned up, then went to the kitchen and sat down to eat.

"*Dag,*" I said to Bertus. He nodded his head.

Bertus blessed the food, reading from the Bible. We put the food on our plates and ate silently. When we finished, he said in the easiest Dutch he could muster, "Greta has gone south on an important errand. She left word that she would be in touch with you as soon as possible and for you not to worry. She wanted to tell you herself, but we arranged some hurried transport to Zwolle so there was no time. She'll be in touch soon."

I told both Bertus and Tini how Tinka had acted toward me. I asked if they knew why she was so sarcastic. They didn't voice an opinion but later, after Bertus went to bed, I was sitting alone working on another clock a neighbor had brought in. Tini came to the kitchen and sat down opposite me.

"Tinka is a strange woman," she said. "Greta probably told of her feelings for you and Tinka didn't like it. You knew that Greta had once been engaged, didn't you?"

"Yes, she told me about him."

"Well, Tinka was her fiancé's cousin. That might have a lot to do with it." She patted me on the shoulder.

The following five days were duplicates of the day before. The only exception was that we started a little later in the day. The first six days I instructed a total of ninety-one men. Each of them took his weapon home along with a hundred rounds of live ammunition. They knew how to clean them, aim and fire them. By the end of the week, I was riding to Paul's alone.

Ernst Scheufele had been evading American fighter planes all day. Flying at a low altitude with his squadron, he was seeking targets of opportunity when he saw some flak guns and immediately dove to attack them. After his first pass, he turned sharply and gained altitude only to be shot down by the American guns. His leg was wounded severely. It proved to be the end of his military career. He had shot down a total of eighteen enemy planes including three four-engine bombers and two Mustangs, but most of them were P-39 Aircobras on the Eastern Front. He was kept in an American hospital in the POW area. For a year he remained a prisoner, and when released he had a bad limp.

On Sunday, after Bertus and Tini came home from church, Tini went to the kitchen to prepare dinner. It was the custom in Holland to use the living room only on Sundays and holidays. The balance of the time, it was closed. This was Christmas week, so Tini declared the living room would be open. Bertus tried to talk to me in Dutch, something about an Englishman and weapons, but I couldn't understand him. He was reluctant to tell Tini so she could help.

After we ate, we retired to the living room. I was looking at a magazine when a loud knock came at the back door. I closed the door between the kitchen and the living room quickly then stood beside the door so that if it opened, I'd be behind it.

It was a stranger's voice. Bertus got up from his chair and went to the kitchen to greet the stranger. They came in the living room together. Bertus said, "Englishman."

"How ya doin', matey?" He had an almost cockney accent.

"I'm fine," I replied. "Were you shot down too?"

"No, no matey, I'm a bloody agent. I've been going around teachin' these Dutch blokes how to use our guns and the like. I'll tell you this, matey, I'm damned glad to have you aboard. As a matter of fact, I'm jolly well going to send more of the group to you so I can head south where they don't know which end of a Sten is which. Where's your mate? Jim's his name, isn't it?"

I told him of Jim's decision. "How did you find me?"

"Oh, I have known about you Yanks since you were in Hoornsterzwaag. I followed your adventure out to Engelsmanplaat and back. You had a pretty tough go of that one, didn't you?"

I told him what had happened as Tini served us tea.

The Britisher's name, ironically enough, was Tommy. "I'm from Southampton, born and reared," he said.

He was one of the most interesting men I have ever talked to and filled me in on many things I had wondered about. The wounded man in Hoornsterzwaag had died from the infection in his leg. Nothing more had been heard from either George or Niko. It seemed they had disappeared from the face of the earth. There was a *razzia* in Paesens

221

three days after we left. Nothing was found and there was no punishment handed out.

Tommy spoke Dutch about as well as I. He traveled openly on the roads and had been controlled many times by German patrols, but his papers were in order and he never had problems. He had been in Holland for almost a year and had been in the British army for more than seven. If he lived through this one, he intended to make a career out of it. He received his training with British intelligence (MI9), as well as the OSS, before parachuting with a weapons drop by the Carpetbaggers into Holland in January 1944. He was in constant communication with London. Part of his job was checking on downed airmen. I told him of the messages I received, supposedly from SHAEF in London, and he told me that the names of Tinker and Tinsdale were bonafide. We discussed weapons training. He had never thoroughly trained ninety-one people in a week.

"Whatever you're doing, matey, don't change a bloody thing! You're doing a good job of it."

To train the Dutchmen, he went from place to place and stayed at prearranged safe houses. With a paper and pencil he drew the mechanics of a bazooka for me. Afterwards, I had a mental picture of how to operate the thing and felt I could instruct my people on its use. He told me how to handle plastic explosives, how to use the detonators and set the timers. I appreciated the information he gave me. He said if I ever wanted to get in touch, any courier would get word to him.

"The big thing about our jobs is this, matey. Stay armed always! Never be without a weapon within your grasp. Always fight the Germans rather than surrender. Nothing surprises them so much as when you point a gun at them and pull the bloody trigger. They go down with a look of amazement on their bloody faces. Don't be bashful to shoot 'em, for they'll sure as hell shoot you at the first opportunity, and don't forget it. All you're doin' is beatin' 'em, to the bloody punch! Make damned sure you kill the buggers, none of that arm or leg stuff."

I asked him to stay overnight to see how I worked with the groups the following day. He declined because he had to be with a group farther south. He stayed for supper and left at 10:00 that night. I really liked Tommy and told him I hoped I'd see him again. He put on his boots and laced them up at the back door.

"This is my favorite time to travel the roads. I can hide in the dark just as well as the bloody Jerrys," he said.

I walked outside with him. It was bitterly cold. He retrieved his bicycle and took a Sten gun off the handlebars, slung it around his neck, and got on.

"Oh yeah, Yank, one more thing I'll tell you. Another one of my jobs is to check on people like you to make sure you're who you say you are. You're a bloody Yank all right! See ya!"

He was off, headed west on the main road toward Holwerd.

Loel Bishop of Dumas, Texas, and Howard De Mally of Rochester, New York, were nice young men. Peter van den Hurk hated for them to be holed up in a barn for the Christmas holidays, so he brought them to mevrouw de Groot's house. The American flyers appreciated it and looked forward expectantly to a warm bed and a homemade meal.

But someone had told the Germans about Peter's involvement working with downed crewmen. Shortly after they arrived at the house on Veerdstraat, the Germans broke in and found the two Americans hiding behind the drapes in the living room. They were taken away and eventually were sent to a *stalag luft* in Germany. Mevrouw de Groot and her daughter managed to sneak out the back door to a neighbor's house down the street and were not captured.

For Peter and Mimi, however, it was a different matter. They were taken to the jail in Meppel, only because the building being prepared by the SS for such occasions was not completed. In the jail, they were both severely beaten and tortured by SS man Hugo Franz Muller and a Belgian SS man, Messerschmist Demesmacher. Peter gave them information which would do them no good, things they already knew. They were sentenced to be shot on Christmas morning.

On the afternoon of December 24, a group of approximately seventeen KPers (as the underground was known) stormed the jail and freed Pete and Mimi. The KPers killed several of the SS men and Germans as well as some of their own collaborators. They were taken to a farm about ten miles from Meppel. A few days later Pete felt uneasy, so they got on their bicycles and went to another farm a few kilometers away. On the way there, they passed by members of the SS who were en route to the farm where they had been staying. The farmer was taken away to a labor camp but survived the war.

Christmas day! I had the holiday spirit and wished I had something to give to all the people who helped me and those who gave me advice. I had received so much from them since August 15. I missed Greta and often I lay awake at night thinking about her and worrying for her safety. I inquired of Bertus every day if he had heard anything about her. The answer was always the same.

I knew she was loyal to the organization and if she was needed in the south of Holland, that's where she would be. The lack of communication puzzled me. I knew she would come back and I would wait for her until hell froze over. It would have been wonderful to spend Christmas with her.

Overwhelmed by the holiday spirit and with a lump in my throat, I told Tini and Bertus they were good friends and I loved them both. They wished I were in America with my family.

Tini cooked a feast on Christmas day. She made potatoes, cabbage with cheese melted on it, some other vegetables, and last but most important, a small piece of sausage. I couldn't believe my eyes. It was a patty about three inches in diameter and a half an inch thick. Bertus blessed the food and each of us saved that special piece of meat for last, savoring each mouthful. I'll never forget Christmas of 1944.

Sometimes I'd sit around the house looking for things to do. I think I had repaired all the broken clocks in Ternaard when Tini suggested, "Why don't you use my spinning wheel and spin some wool yarn? I have a friend who will knit a sweater for you from it. It will make a fine souvenir."

So, she taught me how to operate the spinning wheel. It was over a hundred years old but ran perfectly. Somehow, somewhere, she got freshly sheared wool. After she showed me how to use the device, I began. It was important to make the yarn the same density and thickness. I worked every evening and all day on Sunday spinning yarn. It took a month for me to spin enough to knit the sweater. Whenever I'd spin enough for a skein, Tini boiled and washed it to get the lanolin out. The dirty gray mass turned into snowy white virgin wool. We amassed several skeins before her friend started to knit. Occasionally, Tini would bring part of the incomplete sweater home and hold it up to me to see if it would fit. There were vertical chain stitches around the torso and sleeves. Three weeks later it was done. It was a little large.

"When you fatten up and gain your weight back, it will be just right for you. You're pretty skinny now, you know."

Later she found some more clocks for me to repair. Some of them

I could fix, some of them I couldn't. One of them had somehow come apart. None of the pieces were missing and I managed to put it together again. It helped pass the time.

I was busy in Paul's barn too. The group leaders were given English revolvers and American Colt .45s. They were easy to field strip and understand. The most difficult part for them was the sights. They all thought they were Gene Autry, drawing the weapon from its holster, pointing and shooting from the hip. As soon as they understood the sights were the same as a rifle, they started aiming. Up to this point we had not issued any Stens, bazookas, or plastic explosives.

Just before the new year, Bertus told me we were going to work that night. It was a particularly cold night when we left the house at 10:00. We rode south to Hantum, then east to the vicinity of Metslawier. We entered a farmhouse packed with about twenty men. The men, expecting us, knew who I was and greeted me as one of them. A couple of the men I had trained shook hands with me. Everyone was armed. I had my Luger and a Sten gun with two spare clips. Bertus told me we were going to receive weapons from a bomber drop but he didn't elaborate. I nodded off in a chair. When he awakened me at 1:00 A.M., I put on my hat and coat.

An almost new flatbed truck with stake racks waited outside the door. The engine started and it was whisper quiet. We loaded onto the back and went through the fields. We stayed off the roads until we were almost to our destination. The driver was skillful and knew the terrain without the use of headlights. It took twenty minutes to get to our destination.

We stopped at a gate leading into a huge, flat, treeless meadow. I was to be one of four lookouts. When the truck stopped at the gate, I got off, remembering all that Bertus told me. This was my post. If anybody came or if I even saw anybody, I was to run as fast as I could into the field and sound off. If they came too close before I saw them, I was to shoot two warning shots in the air with my Luger and escape any way I could.

After I got off the truck, one of the men opened the gate and the truck passed through. I closed the gate behind it and was left alone in the dark. I took the Luger from my belt, put a round into the chamber, and set the safety. The weapon was warm from being next to my body and felt good in my cold hands. Soon it too was icy cold, so I put it back in my belt again.

It was a cloudless night with no moon. I could see a few stars indicating there was a high, thin cloud cover. I paced back and forth, shivering, watching the road and the fields carefully. I couldn't see or hear anything, even though I knew that just a short distance from me preparations to receive the canisters were being made. I walked rapidly to keep up my circulation and shook my hands and arms to drive out the cold.

At exactly 2:00 I heard the distant drone of airplane engines to the west. It didn't get louder for several moments but when the sound did get louder, they suddenly hushed as the pilot pulled back on the throttles as he neared his drop zone. I saw the shape of the two Lancasters in formation a quarter of a mile away. They flew directly overhead and seconds later, the huge engines came to life as the pilots gave them full throttle. Beyond the gate, I saw the unmistakable shape of parachutes. The plane's engines were spewing blue flame from their exhaust stacks as they climbed out of the drop zone.

I looked at the meadow where the canisters were coming down. Many lights in a row, about 200 feet apart, had guided the Lancasters to their destination. Even as I watched, the lights went out. In no time, the parachutes came to earth, their containers landing with a thud. A lone parachute hung in a tree and was immediately cut down by several men who knew exactly what they were doing. In ten minutes, all was silent again.

I opened the gate for the truck, now filled with canisters. The driver had one man with him and they waved as they disappeared down the road and into a field. Bertus was the last to leave.

"Now, let's go home!" he said. After we retrieved our bicycles at the barn we headed back to Ternaard at a brisk clip.

Tini, who had waited for her husband many times before, knew when we should arrive and had hot tea waiting. We drank it quickly and went to bed. We were both pooped.

Greta had been gone for over a month and I was getting more and more frustrated because I couldn't get any information. I felt both Bertus and Tini knew what was going on. Whenever I approached Tini, she assured me Greta was all right, working on a very important job in the south. People were relying on her to make decisions. Tini promised she would have Bertus try again to get a message to her. I thanked her, but I knew something was wrong. If Greta changed her mind about us then I was entitled to know. I couldn't figure it out and I wasn't at liberty to find out for myself. The thought never occurred to me that she might be ill, arrested, or even dead.

During the ensuing weeks, I accompanied Bertus to receive weapons from the bombers. I always acted as a lookout and understood the language barrier kept me from doing anything else. One of us had to be the lookout anyway. I spent much time teaching the weapons and we distributed guns rapidly. I inspected each weapon before it left the barn. Paul kept an accurate ledger. The barn quickly emptied of all but a few bazookas and plastic explosives. The Sten guns were issued to the leaders of the groups or those they designated. I insisted the fuses and timers used to set off the plastic explosive be kept in a place away from the barn. When new canisters came, we trained new men.

One of the Dutchmen heard a German officer tell a group of the citizens that the Dutch Resistance had more weapons than the German Army of Occupation. The man who told me this was hiding in a church steeple where there were more than a hundred rifles hidden as he listened to the German officer's oration. The German was probably right. But the German Army of Occupation were veteran battle-trained troops. They had armored cars and tanks.

One day we got several canisters which had nothing but Sten guns in them. We had plenty of people waiting for them so I had twenty men in the barn. After we cleaned the weapons, I issued the ammo to them. One of the Dutchmen put a full clip in his weapon but the safety didn't work and he fired a single round. I was really irate and in my finest Dutch told him it wasn't a toy but a deadly weapon that could kill. I looked at the weapon and discovered the defective safety, so we destroyed the weapon. I wouldn't have been so angry over the incident except for the hole it made in the box on which I was sitting. The bullet missed my knee by barely six inches and my balls by less than one inch.

In the middle of February, Bertus brought a man home with him one night. His name was Joe. He was a Dutch saboteur who loved blowing up things. A demolitions expert, he had been a member of the Dutch army. Since the Allied drive northward was so imminent, the leaders of the Resistance believed they should start readying themselves to assist the Allies. Squads of men trained in the use of plastic explosives were formed.

Plastic explosives looked like common putty both in color and density. In fact, you couldn't tell them apart if you held both in your hands. Plastic explosive was more powerful than dynamite. It could be molded to fit into any crack or crevice and was so adherent it could be just pushed onto a flat surface of glass, steel, or wood and it would stay. It could be thrown, jumped on, or beat with a stick and it wouldn't explode. The detonator was a small, electrical, firecracker-sized device that exploded the stuff every time and could be stuck to, or shoved into, or taped to the plastic. Timers could be delayed from seconds to several minutes.

Joe stayed at Bertus's house. After breakfast the next morning, the three of us went to Paul's barn, where he examined our stores of plastic explosive. He was delighted with the quantity. It was simple to explain the mechanics to him. We had hand-held twist generators and I explained how they operated. There were several coils of wire on hand too. The generators sent an ample charge of electricity through the wires to fire the detonators. Afterwards, Joe left, not saying a word.

The next time I went to Paul's, the explosives were gone.

In the city of Leeuwarden, southwest of Ternaard, the prison or *"Gevangenis,"* as they call it in Dutch, was notorious. Its primary function was to torture or put to death captured Dutchmen suspected of being members of, or sympathetic to, the Dutch Resistance. The blood-curdling stories that leaked out told of the brutal treatment behind the walls. Every manner of torture, medieval, modern or other, was practiced there. The SD and the SS officiated from within the confines of its walls. The sound of gunfire was prevalent, for execution was the final answer after the interrogation was over. When the Nazis wanted information, the unfortunate Dutchman fell victim to unmerciful torture and in the end would beg the Nazis to allow him to tell what he knew.

They were particularly adept at medieval torture. Often, a day or two after his capture, the Dutchman (or woman) would not be recognizable to family or friends. The standard fare was broken bones, disjointing, toenails or fingernails pulled out, severe burns from being tied naked on a steam radiator, or rib cages badly crushed from continual abdominal pounding. A particular enjoyment was to attach wires from the coils of an automobile ignition system to a man's penis or scrotum, or both, and burn them unmercifully. Using clamps on a male prisoner's testicles usually brought unconsciousness long before it brought confessions. Women were not immune from their inhumanity. Often, they were tortured by shoving broom handles into their vagina until it broke through into their internal organs. Sometimes they used wire coat hangers instead. Hanging naked women prisoners by the heels and beating them with wet knotted turkish towels was especially effective.

These things really happened in Leeuwarden. The hell of it was, the place was full of prisoners all the time, usually hundreds of men and women undergoing the treatment. The Nazis, adept at their art, kept it up all day without letup. Nobody lived. I can't understand how any human being can treat another in that manner, wartime or not, for the sheer joy of it. Though the Nazis were an army of occupation in a neutral country, this outrageous desecration of life was totally inhuman. I prayed those Nazis would have to pay for their crimes.

Harry Wessels was captured by the Germans and taken to Leeuwarden. He had personal knowledge of all underground operations in Friesland and probably most of Holland too. He was an important prisoner. If the Germans discovered who he was, and he talked, the entire operation would be in jeopardy. Many heads would roll. As a result, the organization heads held a meeting. A plan was formulated by the group commanders. On the day he was captured, thirty members of the Leeuwarden group, dressed in German uniforms, carried out a daring plan.

From one of the hundreds of haystacks in Holland emerged a Chevrolet sedan camouflaged with German emblems. Thirty men from the Leeuwarden group converged on the prison at a prearranged hour and stormed it. They captured the guards, disarmed them, and placed them in the cells from which they released 120 prisoners who were able to walk. Several guards were killed as well as many SS and SD.

Harry Wessels was released unharmed. It was impossible to move the men and women who had suffered the tortures, so they left weapons with them to use on their captors or themselves if they saw fit to do so. The escapees were taken to safe houses in and around the city. Nobody outside the walls of the prison paid attention to the shooting, for it was a common occurrence anyway. Harry Wessels, who had not been interrogated, was hidden in a safe house and resumed his leadership of the organization. Nobody taking part was even so much as scratched.

The Germans were furious! The SS commander in Holland took reprisals and hundreds of innocent Dutchmen lost their lives in front of firing squads. *Razzias* were held throughout Friesland with more killings. Others were taken captive and sent to forced labor camps. Bergen-Belsen concentration camp had an influx of Dutch prisoners. Landwatchers and Dutch members of the SD, whom the Germans said should have known about the raid, were done in.

When they held a *razzia* in Ternaard, Bertus and I were captured. Under normal circumstances, we would have been forewarned. But this time, because it was a reprisal, we heard nothing. We'd just finished breakfast and I was getting ready to go to Paul's when we saw the German trucks stop outside. We started for the stairs to get into the hiding place, but the Germans caught us.

Neither of us was armed, our weapons hidden in the wall of the kitchen. We were shoved and pushed by the rifles of our captors and taken outside in freezing weather, where we joined other men on the road. Two of them were men I had instructed but they offered no sign of recognition. A pair of guards watched us while the balance of the Germans, about thirty of them, searched the little village. Bicycles, including ours, were loaded onto trucks. Parachute shroud line was found in a house. The occupants and two Jews found in another house were sent away in a truck.

During the search, a German officer ordered the guards to take us to the edge of town to a farmhouse. As we were marched along the road, we saw soldiers roughing up some women, taking special delight in body searching them. They threw away personal belongings in every direction. We were marched east of town to a small stone building beside a barn and lined up outside. We all thought we were going to be executed. Instead, they herded us inside to await our fate. We decided that if they meant to shoot us, they would have done so before putting us inside. We would be questioned and tortured, that was for sure.

The fact that I was an American pretty well sealed the fate for these men, but only Bertus and the two men I trained had knowledge of my identity. Occasionally, the door opened and another prisoner would be shoved inside. We watched through the small windows at the progress of the *razzia* down the road.

"Your wife is coming up the road," a man said to Bertus. "She's carrying a basket on her arm."

As she approached she called out to the guard and started arguing bitterly with him just outside the door. She was waving the basket in the air, proclaiming that all she wanted to do was give her poor husband some food to take to the German "work camp," but the guard yelled back saying, *"Nein, nein!"*

Tini put on a good act. She was screaming, crying real tears, and

230

sobbing loudly. Finally, she screamed, "All I want to do is give my poor husband some food."

The guard relented, examined the contents of the basket, and opened the door. "Nauta," he called.

Bertus stepped forward and Tini, who had forced her way in behind the guard, gave the basket of food to her husband, throwing her arms around his neck. When the German turned to separate them and push Tini outside, Bertus hit his helmeted head with a boulder, fully six inches in diameter, which he had dislodged from the wall of the building. There was a resounding "Clank!" as the helmet fell from his head. The guard went to his knees as Bertus hit him again on the back of the neck. The Kraut was out cold. We pulled him to a corner while the others disarmed him, taking his rifle and ammo belt. Somebody threw me a potato masher (German hand grenade) and I stuck it in my belt. Tini lifted her dress and took Bertus's pistol from her bloomers and gave it to him. The second guard had disappeared.

"We go one at a time," Bertus ordered the others. "Jan, stay close to me."

Tini, Bertus, and I left the building, walked fifty feet to the barn, skirted around in back of it, then down to a ditch that was about knee-deep in running water. We walked away from town for about 300 yards, got out of the ditch, and bent over as we walked through waist-high grass and reeds. There was very little snow on the ground and we didn't leave footprints to give away our trail. If we saw snow ahead, we went back into the ditch until the ground was clear of the white stuff again. We did this for at least a kilometer. In the distance we heard the sound of the German trucks. Bertus stood and saw them moving around the village in search of those of us who got away.

I had never seen an outward display of emotion between Tini and Bertus. But now, half freezing, they were in a loving embrace, kissing each other tenderly. They spoke quietly and said words I could never understand and did not want to hear.

Afterward, I thanked Tini, and told her I thought she was the bravest woman I ever knew. She smiled and kissed my cheek.

We walked another kilometer to a windmill, which we entered to see if we could warm our freezing feet. Mine were as numb as they had been on my walk out to Engelsmanplaat. We had been moving at a rapid pace, and though Bertus and I didn't have a coat, only my feet were cold. We found some old bags in the mill; some were burlap and others were white cotton. I removed my shoes and socks, wrapped my feet in the dry cotton, and felt some relief. I covered my shoulders with burlap sacks to give me some warmth. We went up in the loft. There were windows all around it. We put our shoes and socks in a ray of sunshine to help them get dry.

Later in the day, watching Ternaard as closely as we did, we saw no activity at all. We decided the Germans must have gone.

Bertus, his feet still cold, decided he would go back to the village and investigate. We wanted him to stay until morning but he was insistent. He donned his wet shoes and socks then wrapped his feet in two of the cotton sacks. He kissed Tini lightly on the cheek and left, headed back the way we had come.

Tini and I climbed the stairs to the top of the mill and took up positions on each side. We could see the landscape on all sides. We watched Bertus until he disappeared from view. We both thought it would be better if we didn't talk.

It is an amazing phenomenon how the eyes can adjust to the darkness. Well after dark we could see Bertus returning and we could recognize him at least a quarter of a mile away. When he came in, he gave me my coat and hat and some dry socks. He also gave me my holstered Luger and the two spare clips of ammunition. He was armed with a Sten gun. Producing some cheese and bread from one of the cotton bags, he divided them and we ate ravenously.

Only the four people had been captured by the Germans. Our comrades from the stone house had escaped too. The Germans made a second search but they were gone. There were no reprisals for the injuries inflicted on the German guard, but the name Nauta was on the lips of all the Germans. The *razzia* produced no weapons and no ammunition. All the bicycles had been confiscated except Tini's, which was in back of the shed and was overlooked. A few trinkets and souvenirs had been taken as well as some cameras. The big loss were the two Jews and the family. None of them were members of the underground, and where they got the shroud line was anybody's guess. Bertus knew the family the Jews were living with but they were not bothered. The men who had escaped were grateful for Tini's courage.

Bertus felt it wouldn't be safe to return that night. It would be safe for Tini unless the same soldier saw her, but that was unlikely. We went to the pile of bags and each of us took enough of them to make a bed. When I lay down, I was asleep before my head hit the makeshift pillow.

The only window in the mill with the sun shining through was in

232

my line of vision and awakened me early in the morning. I got out of my bed of bags. Tini and Bertus were still asleep. Outside, the beautiful February sunshine welcomed another day. There was nobody in sight so I went down the steps of the mill and walked into the field, making certain I didn't step in any snow. I shivered as I relieved myself in the crisp morning air.

When I went back in, I woke Bertus and Tini. They also took a walk in the morning sun.

We had slept in our wet shoes and covered our feet with several bags. As a result, our shoes were dry. I took them off and wiggled my toes around a little before putting them on with my dry socks. We decided the best way to go back to Ternaard was to walk back over the same route again. So, Bertus took the lead, followed by Tini and then me. We walked to Ternaard in half an hour.

Tini went in first to see if the coast was clear. Nothing was missing as far as she could tell. They hadn't discovered the hiding place for our weapons. The house was unlocked and the rear door was ajar, even though Bertus said he thought he closed it the night before. Tini started a wood fire in the kitchen stove and soon there was warmth in the house. She prepared something to eat.

We stayed all the rest of the day and all night. Bertus watched all night for unwanted visitors. He told me he would wake me up during the night to relieve him, but he never did. I slept restlessly until the crack of dawn. I dressed and went downstairs to find him asleep in a chair in the living room. Tini came down a little later and made some tea. We didn't disturb Bertus but he woke up on his own about an hour later. He drank a cup of tea, changed his clothes, and left, riding Tini's bicycle. He advised me to stay close to the hiding place.

I packed my suitcase and stayed upstairs, for I knew I'd be moved shortly. Several women came to see Tini, including the sister, who had no problems during the *razzia*. Tini called me downstairs around noon for lunch.

As I finished eating, Sjoukje van der Hoop came in the door unannounced. She told me I was going back to Holwerd.

"Am I going back to Dominee de Boer's?" I asked.

"No, I'm taking you to a safe house."

"When are we leaving?"

"As soon as mijnheer Nauta returns," she replied. "You had better dress as a lady in case we run into a patrol. They cover all roads the last few days. They're no longer on a schedule. I saw five patrols go through Holwerd today. There's usually one."

I told her I hadn't seen any patrols. Then I went into the front room, where I changed into my women's clothes.

Bertus returned an hour later. He came in the back door and was very pleased to see Sjoukje. They spoke in Frisian.

"Bertus wants to thank you for your help with the weapons," she said. "The men you have trained can teach each other now or until we get some weapons we are not familiar with. He says you will return here later, but for now, it's too dangerous."

"Will you please try to get word to Greta and tell her what has happened here and where I'll be?" I asked Bertus. "I know something's wrong. I think you know but you won't tell me. Maybe you think it's Greta's place to tell me. That's okay, but get word to her."

Tini looked at Bertus expectantly. All he did was extend his hand to me. I looked him in the eyes but they wouldn't meet mine. I shook his hand and said, "I want to hear from her soon."

Tini gave me a hug and kissed my cheek. I thanked her for everything she had done and returned her kiss.

"Come on, Jan," said Sjoukje.

I lifted my dress and took the Luger out of my belt to make sure the clip was full of ammunition. I put a round in the chamber and set it on safety. At least it was ready to shoot without cocking it if I needed it. I put it back in my belt.

Sjoukje told me to ride Tini's bicycle. I secured my bag on the back of it and we got on them and rode out to the street.

Half a block later, we turned west on the main road in the direction of Holwerd. As soon as we turned the corner, we saw the German patrol heading toward us.

Sjoukje slowed her bicycle until I caught up to her. We rode side by side past the German soldiers. Neither one of us looked at them, but out of the corner of my eye I saw them ogle us and smile. We never looked back but just kept on pedaling.

My heart was pounding in my chest.

"There. Now an American pilot has been flirted with by the German Green Police." She was laughing, and for the first time I saw that she too held a pistol in her hand, barely covered with the end of the scarf she wore around her neck. She put it in one of her coat pockets as if it was a daily occurrence.

Sjoukje was barely seventeen years old.

TWELVE

We rode a block past Dominee de Boer's house then turned
right to the edge of the village. There was a store on one corner, a tan
stucco house on the second, and open fields on the other two. We
turned right, past the store, and into a short gravel driveway beside it.
We put our bicycles in an open shed in back. I untied my bag and followed Sjoukje into the store. The shelves were empty.

A thin woman in her forties came through the door. Her faded
dress was clean and her graying hair was neatly done in a bun. She
spoke to Sjoukje in Frisian then picked up my suitcase. She smiled and
nodded her head in the direction of the door leading into the house.
We entered the dining area with the kitchen behind it. She motioned
for us to sit down at the table and left with my suitcase.

I felt uncomfortable. The lack of communication made it difficult. I couldn't think of a thing to say.

Five minutes later the woman returned, accompanied by her
daughter, three sons, and husband, who was the butcher for the village. She introduced the family in Dutch, speaking slowly. "My husband, Gerit Stielstra, my oldest son, Rolf, my next son, Pieter, and
my youngest son, Sjors. This is my daughter, Frieda. My name is mevrouw Stielstra."

My consternation vanished for it was plain to see this introduction had been rehearsed. Everyone was dressed in their best clothes.

235

They were courteous and waited expectantly.

In my best Dutch I said, "My name is Jan Veen in Holland. I was shot down six months ago in Drente. I am an American pilot. I live in Los Angeles, California. You may call me Jan."

The boys were about twenty-one, nineteen, and fourteen. The daughter was probably twenty-two and on the chubby side. She was not an attractive girl, but I discovered later that she had a terrific personality. I liked the whole family immediately.

The butcher was a big man in his fifties. He wore glasses and was the only one not dressed in his best clothes. As soon as introductions were complete, he excused himself and went outside.

We smiled at each other and the ice was broken. They broke up their little formation and joined us at the table. The woman poured hot tea into mugs the size of coffee cups. Finding that I was not learned in Frisian, they thoughtfully kept the conversation on a grammar-school level, saying they understood me. They were extremely polite.

"Would you like to change clothes?" the woman asked.

The youngest son had kept giggling and stared at me. With my long hair and female attire, there had to be some unanswered questions on his young mind.

"Thank you," I replied and took them off while I was still sitting at the table. I had my own clothes on under the dress.

"Camouflage!" said Sjors, the youngest son. "Right, yes?"

"Right, yes," I agreed.

"I will wash these for you," said mevrouw Stielstra as she took them from me. I was so interested in making their acquaintance I had forgotten how I was dressed.

Sjoukje announced she had to leave. "I'll stop and check on you soon," she said, getting up from the table. She kissed me on the cheek. "You are beautiful, you know, when you're dressed like a lady." She walked out the door, smiling.

So began my second stay in Holwerd. But this time it would not be a lonely existence. This time, I had a family.

But why, I asked myself again, *why would this man and his wife risk their family's lives by allowing me to live under their roof as one of their own?* They didn't belong to the underground. After what had happened in Leeuwarden, there was bound to be a *razzia* in Holwerd sooner or later. The three boys and their father were hiding from the Germans because of their age, and I felt guilty giving them added responsibility. But I stayed.

236

They put me in the room with Rolf, the oldest boy. As in the older homes, we slept in closet beds which were wider than most and had wonderful feather tick mattresses and covers. There were two windows in our room. One looked down on the main road to Ternaard. The other looked out toward Leeuwarden. I could see everybody coming and going. It was a particularly cozy spot, and I enjoyed just sitting there, watching people carry on their daily activities. I decided to rewrite my experiences using alias names and places.

The house didn't have a hiding place. If the Germans came, I'd be captured for sure. But it had a sort of basement where Rolf experimented with hydraulics. He could do extraordinary things with pipes and water under pressure. Because the Germans had cut the wires to every house, there was no electric power; all the homes in Friesland were dark. The only source of light was candles. The same electric poles carrying power to Paul's farm ran beside the window in Holwerd! Rolf, ever ingenious, removed lengths of fine wire from an old magneto. The uninsulated wire was no thicker than a strand of hair. At night he climbed the pole and, wearing rubber gloves, connected a length of the wire to the three wires on the pole and hooked the other ends to the house at the point where the wires had been cut by the Germans. On the ground, the wires were so fine they were invisible. They provided enough electricity to burn two light bulbs at the same time. A third light overloaded the circuit and the wires would burn through. Late at night, after everybody had retired, Rolf connected an electric heater turned to its lowest setting for his mother's comfort. We had electricity for the radio and listened to all BBC broadcasts. Occasionally, one of the wires overloaded and burned through. When this happened, Rolf would climb the utility pole and install a new wire after dark.

The only problem I had while staying at the butcher's house was the lack of secrecy. I'm sure all of Holwerd knew there was an American staying at the Stielstras. Thank God, word never got out to the wrong people. But it was an uncomfortable situation.

The patrols settled down to regular hours. It was routine to go out in the evening. After the last patrol went through the village, and almost before they were out of sight, the young men congregated in the streets. Sometimes I could look out the window and see the patrol on the road leading to Ternaard while in the other direction I could see the youngsters begin to gather.

One of the patrols that passed through daily was the Green Police. The largest of the three Germans was at least 6'4. This was the sergeant with the German Shepherd. The black and silver animal's tail formed a ring as it curled onto his back. He looked to his master for commands and obeyed them instantly. I was envious of him for owning such a beautiful beast. The patrols seldom stopped and then only for a drink of water. They were older than other patrols and more suited for patrol duty than war. The sergeant was not a German but an Austrian, and had been a forest ranger or boswachter in the Black Forest near Munich, Germany. A handsome man, he appeared to be biding his time, waiting for the war to end.

I started walking in the evenings with the Stielstra boys. Sjors spoke some English and helped me with Dutch as I helped him with English. We walked out in the countryside where there were some windmills. Some pumped water and others were grist mills.

A week after I had been at the Stielstras, Dominee de Boer visited me. We discussed the George and Niko mystery for neither had ever been heard from. He was interested in our adventures on Engelsman-plaat so I told him the whole story. I told of my activities while I was with Bertus. He laughed when I told of our capture, especially the act Tini had put on.

"Jim is staying with Dominee Visser in Dokkum, an old man whom the Germans leave alone. He is comfortable and safe."

"What about Greta? I have to know something, good or bad."

"I have not seen her," he replied. "I heard that she was in Deventer or Zwolle on a project. I will find out for you." He felt Holwerd would continue to be a safe village. There were never problems with the Germans and he cooperated with them completely. His wife was disappointed she hadn't met Jim and me.

"Please visit us soon so you can speak with her too."

"It'll be my pleasure. Just let me know when," I answered.

Several days later, Bertus Nauta rode his bicycle to Holwerd to visit. "There is a man named Jon staying with us. We are staying in our house but we watch closely for Germans and Landwatchers. Jon is a brave and daring fighter. I want you to meet him. I am sure he will still be with us when you return."

"Have you heard from Greta?" I asked.

"No, but I am suspicious about her disappearance since there has been no word at all," he said.

I was alarmed by his words.

"I have talked to Paul but he knows nothing. Harry Wessels is living quietly in Groningen and still directing our activities as usual. Tini sends her love. We have never seen the German guard I hit on the head."

We visited for over an hour. I hated to see him go, but I appreciated the fact that he took the time to visit me.

Frieda, the butcher's daughter, was engaged to marry a man by the name of Pieter Woudsma. He lived diagonally across from her in a tan house. He often visited and courted her in the parlor, most respectfully and chaperoned. They talked in the evenings and on Sundays. Occasionally, they held hands and spoke in low voices to each other. Pieter spoke good English and was well educated. His appearance was typical of most Dutchmen, with blond hair and blue eyes. He had a winsome smile. His brother was a feared fighter with the underground but had been captured by the SS and taken to the prison in Leeuwarden some months before. The family didn't recognize his body when the Germans released it.

They were from the town of Dokkum, but Pieter stayed in hiding with his aunt in the tan house. He loved to play chess and I sometimes played with him in the afternoon at her house. He was an excellent player; I never won or even tied. His aunt knew I was an American, and when unexpected guests came to call on them while I was visiting, I put on my *"doofstoom"* act. Pieter would tell them of my handicap and they would look at me with such pity that I was embarrassed — but safe!

One morning after the patrol had gone through town, Sjors asked me to go with him because he wanted me to meet somebody. We walked across town. I was upset because he had taken me so far from the house, but he assured me it was all right. We turned into the walk of a small white house and Sjors knocked.

"Sjors, how nice of you to come and visit. This must be your flying friend." The voice, in flawless English, came from an attractive blond.

She smiled and held out her hand. I took it and introduced myself. "I'm Jan Veen."

"Please sit down," she said, pointing to the kitchen table. "I've just made fresh tea. May I pour a cup for you?"

Before I could answer, a youngster about the same age as Sjors got up from the table and greeted us. "This is my friend, Jacob," Sjors said.

The boy nodded his head to me and, like the good friends they were, the boys fell into instant nonstop conversation, laughing and joking with each other. At last, they went upstairs to the privacy of Jacob's room.

"So you are the American pilot I have heard so much about," she said, sitting down opposite me.

"Yes, I am an American," I replied.

"My name is Katina," she said. "The boy is in my care. His family was killed in Rotterdam and he has been in my care for two years. Though we're not related, I'm beginning to look upon him as a younger brother or even a son."

"It's nice for Sjors to have a friend his own age to play with. They seem to like each other's company," I said.

She was a beautiful woman. Her dark brown eyes complemented her olive complexion. She was about my height. I noticed her long, straight legs as I followed her into the house. The tops of her ample breasts were exposed by the V-neck of her frock.

She ignored my comments about the boys.

"I am a Jew, you know. I am from Rotterdam and have been hiding in Holwerd for three years. The people here don't even look at me as an outsider anymore."

"You have blond hair. You're fortunate in that respect."

"I bleach it every week to keep it blond. The natural color of my hair is dark brown, almost black." She handed me a cup of tea. "What do you do to pass the time away? You have a language barrier to overcome and you are unfamiliar with our customs. It must be very difficult."

I'd never thought about it before because I thought I fit right in no matter where I was. I was probably odd to the Dutch, just as some of them were to me. I was more outgoing and usually I'd say what was on my mind, undoubtedly without thinking. Yet, I was accepted and people seemed to like me. Were they just being polite while they really objected to "that American"?

"People here look at me because I am a Jewess," she continued. "They stare no matter how many times they have seen me. I might just as well walk down the street with my breasts exposed. The looks I get would be the same. I know they say, 'There goes that Jew!' behind my back as their eyes look at me from head to toe to see how I am different. I am sure the same people in Holwerd would like to talk to you for you would be more acceptable to them. To fly an airplane, you must have special skills and knowledge stored in your brain. But they will wonder what kind of a man you are. Have you the same military demeanor as the Boche? Are you as cruel and heartless as they? Tell me, Jan, what kind of a man are you?" Her voice was getting louder as she continued her dissertation. She was almost angry and her sarcasm was bitter. I sat quietly for it was the first time I had ever been analyzed by a complete stranger.

We were scarcely three feet apart. Her brown eyes were penetrating mine. I stared back at her, then I spoke.

"In America," I said, staring back at her, "no matter what our religious beliefs are, unless somebody dislikes another, they are never rude to them. We take our friends for granted or at face value until they prove otherwise. I think you are being rude to me for no reason. Is it because I am an American? Is it because I am a man and you are a woman? I don't know what your problem is. We are what we are and we'll have to live with it."

She started to interrupt. "Let me finish," I demanded. "To answer your questions, I am not like the Boche. I can't harm an animal let alone another human being just for the sake of hurting them. I'll fight back when I am cornered and I'll fight to the death if need be, but I'll not put any man in a corner just for the sake of hurting him. The same to you, Katinka, why should I want to harm you? Because you are of another faith, another nation, another sex? I don't think you understand that a soldier can be human too, even with the enemy. And you are not the enemy, Katinka, not mine anyway."

Her face was red as a beet. "My name, sir, is Katina, not Katinka! If what you say is true, then why do you kill so many people with your bombs? I was in Rotterdam hiding in the basement of our house and we were bombed unmercifully at the beginning of the war. When I came out of the basement, my city, my beautiful Rotterdam was gone! Rubble! My mother and father and my betrothed and most of my friends were killed. Their bodies were never found! So don't sit there and tell me you are any kind of a human being when you can do that to your 'fellow man!' "

Tears flooded her eyes.

"Katina, we didn't do that. It was the Germans. We bomb the Germans' war-making potential, their factories, railroads, their submarine pens and materials the Germans use to make war. There are times when the bombs kill many people. This we can't help."

She seemed to calm down a little bit. I took my time and told her about the V-1s and V-2s used against England, how it completely

241

changed my mind about the Germans. I told her of the Nazi cruelty I had witnessed since I was shot down.

She was crying and not paying any attention to my words.

What the hell, I thought, *she's deaf to everything I say to her. I don't even know her . . . to hell with it!*

I got up from the table and put on my hat and coat. "Thank you for the tea," I said, but she didn't move.

I walked out the back door without saying goodbye. Now who was being rude?

The following week I played chess with Pieter Woudsma a few times. The Allies seemed to be stalemated and not advancing, so I couldn't get interested in anything. I thought many times how Katina had torn into me, taking out her hatred for the Germans on me, comparing me with them because I flew in a bomber. Too bad. She was a beautiful woman and her loss in Rotterdam had been a traumatic experience. We could have been good friends. I was afraid she might tell somebody there was an American at the Stielstras and I spoke to Gerit about it.

"Don't worry about it," he said. "Every time an Allied airplane flies over Holwerd, she goes into hysterics. She was probably so upset because you are a bomber pilot. She associates you to the death of her family and loved ones in Rotterdam. I will have somebody speak to her. Don't worry, it will be all right."

"I'm telling you we should find a place to make a hiding place!" Rolf said to the family during supper. "If there is a *razzia,* where will we go? Where will Dad go?"

Rolf and Sjors were really concerned. "The proper place to put one is in the basement," Sjors offered. "We could probably dig a good hole in the floor and cover it with heavy planks."

"No, that would never do," said Rolf. "We would have to carry the dirt out and dump it someplace. If the Germans ever saw that much dirt, they would know immediately. If they searched in the basement, as soon as they stepped on the planking even if it was covered with dirt, it would sag and they would know we had a place to hide there. No, a hole in the floor of the basement is not the answer. There has to be a better place."

Without mentioning any houses, I told them of the elaborate hiding places I had seen in Holland. I told how the stairs were raised to expose a good hiding place. We examined the stairs in the house but there would be no room to put anybody behind them. I suggested,

"When you do find a place, keep it simple — the simpler, the better."

"I know a good place for one," said Sjors.

"Where?" asked Rolf.

"In the shed, out back."

"Oh, Sjors, shut up. There is no place out there," said Rolf.

"Oh yes there is. In the morning I'll show you."

We continued to talk about a good hiding place. It had to be big enough to hold five and more if possible. Rolf mentioned there was an abandoned well across the road which might hold some possibilities. We decided that tomorrow we would find a place. It had to be close enough to get to in a moment's notice. It had to be completely undetectable and kept a family secret. Its location was not to be divulged to anyone, with the possible exception of Pieter Woudsma, who was almost family anyway. There must be no delay!

When we went to bed I tried to think of a possible site. We had combed the house, upstairs, downstairs, attic, and basement. There were several possibilities but no real one. Sjors came in at bed time.

"I know where to build it and I will show you tomorrow."

"Oh, Sjors, go to bed!" Rolf ordered.

After breakfast, Sjors was frothing at the bit to take us out to the shed and show us a good spot for the hiding place. We put on our hats and coats and followed him out the back door. To appease him, we'd have a look. He pointed at the shed.

"There!" he said, pointing his finger.

"Where?" asked Rolf.

"Right where we keep our bicycles!" the boy said.

The shed was approximately twenty-five feet long and fifteen feet in depth with an additional twelve feet forming a loft which went over the neighbors' back room at the rear of the shed. Off to the right side was a cubby-hole with the floor of the loft covering it. The area was five by twelve feet in size. It was full of paraphernalia, long unused and forgotten. If a matching brick wall were built across the five-foot opening, tight against the ceiling, it would be invisible. If a trap door were made to let us down inside the place, it would be a wonderful hiding place and would withstand the closest scrutiny. I visualized it after it was completed. If the job were done right, it would be impossible to detect. There was a ladder going up to the loft from the shed and several bales of long forgotten hay stored there. Three existing walls were already in place, including the neighbors' wall in the back. We needed only to build a five-foot brick wall and a trap door.

Sjors shrieked. "We can hide fifteen people in there!"

"We'll have to get a brick mason," Pieter said.

"No," I said, "If we hire a mason, that will be one more person who'll know. I've never laid a brick in my life, but if you get the matching brick and some grout, I'll build it!"

Rolf, seeing the possibilities, got excited. "Pieter can make a ladder to go down into the hiding place for we could never get out without one. He is a good carpenter and can figure out a secret door at the top. I know where I can get the bricks." He turned on his heel and walked out to the street.

That afternoon, brick started piling up inside the shed. I don't know where Rolf got them. Cement was no problem; sand was plentiful. Before nightfall, I had dug eight inches into the ground across the five-foot opening and poured cement in it along with the first three courses of brick. They matched perfectly and I kept the bricks in line with the existing bricks on both sides of the opening. I set the bricks two deep to give the wall added strength. We had no trowel so I used a kitchen spatula and a garden trowel to put the cement on the bricks. All in all, as work progressed, the bricks looked pretty much like the existing walls. I placed spikes in the grout between the bricks, six feet high and others seven feet high, to hang things on after the cement dried. The wall looked like the original when it was finished. I put in a peep hole about five feet up. The whole job took ten days.

The day after I finished, we painted the newly built wall and the surrounding walls with whitewash to match the rest of the place. While the paint was still wet, we threw dirt on it and rubbed it around slightly to match the old paint on the other walls. After it dried for two days, we went back in the shed and hung an old tire here, chains there, rags, bicycle chains, coils of rope, old coats, anything on the old nails and new ones I had put in the new wall. We brought down some boards that were piled in the loft and leaned them against the new wall. The walls were identical.

Pieter had done a masterful job with the trap door in the loft. It was impossible to see, even without the bales of hay which covered it. He made an internal lock so that it couldn't be opened from the outside. A ladder went down inside, and only the peep hole and a few cracks in the wall of the neighbor's shed let in any light at all. We could observe any activity from the back door of the neighbor's house. I saw the lady of the house come out into the shed and take some clothes off a clothesline. She went back in and left the door open. I didn't mention it to the others because they would find out soon enough for themselves.

We made a few dry runs to see how quickly we could get into the place. We could make it from any place in the house in under a minute.

Rolf and I went walking a couple of nights later, south of town in the direction of the windmill. We ran into Katina and a girlfriend on the path. They passed by us as if we didn't exist.

"*Dag,* Katina," I said as we passed. She didn't answer.

Later, I sat at the kitchen table, working on the Stielstras' clock. Sjors was sitting with me.

"I saw Dominee de Boer today. He wants you to come for supper tonight," he said.

I thanked him, went upstairs and shaved, changed my clothes, and walked the two blocks to the Dominee's house. The minister opened the door before I had a chance to knock.

"Come in, Jan, I would like for you to meet my wife."

A petite lady about forty years old entered the living room. She was tastefully dressed in a pink dress. Her hair, slightly gray, was combed back neatly in a bun. In my opinion, she looked exactly like a minister's wife should.

"Jan Veen," he said, "mevrouw de Boer."

"I'm happy to know you," I said in Dutch.

"I speak some English," she said, "and since we are alone, it would be better if we spoke so. I am very happy to make your acquaintance also."

She seated me in a comfortable chair then left the room. Dominee de Boer sat across from me. He kept the conversation light and wanted to know what I had been doing. Finally, he got down to the subject of Greta. "I have some news about Greta."

"Good! Is she all right?" I asked.

"Yes, she is fine and is in Suameer. She was in the south of Holland for a long time. I have talked with her and I know why she left in such a hurry. If you prefer for her to tell you, I will say no more." He looked at me, waiting. I nodded my head in the affirmative, confident of good news.

"Then I shall be the one to tell you," he said.

"Please do," I said, bracing myself for the worst.

"As I understand it, the first day you went to Paul's farm to instruct with the weapons, you met Tinka, Paul's wife. She lives in Groningen most of the time and leaves Paul to shift for himself. She does not like the farmer's life. Her cousin, Jan, was once engaged to Greta and was captured by the Germans. He was supposedly killed by them. The fact is that he was not killed but escaped from a work camp near Bergen-Belsen, where he was imprisoned. He was near death when the organization finally got their hands on him and put him in a safe house in Zwolle. Jan told the organization to get in touch with Tinka and she would know what to do. They got word to Tinka, telling her he was in bad shape and he was not expected to live. The day you went to Paul's, Tinka, who had found out that morning about Jan, told Greta that her place was with the dying man in Zwolle.

"Greta went to Bertus Nauta, saying she had to get to Zwolle at once. She didn't give him a reason but he arranged for transport to Deventer. Her friends there knew the whereabouts of Jan. He was alive but didn't recognize anybody, including her. She has been with him all the time, nursing him back to health. He was in terrible shape and is still in a weakened condition. He is at her home in Suameer. The Germans tortured him badly. It is a miracle he survived his escape."

He paused before he continued. "Greta will come to my house as soon as she can. She wants to explain a decision she has been forced to make. It hurts me to be the one to tell you this, but she feels she should take care of him as long as he is sick. When I told her I should tell you about this turn of events, she said no, she wanted to tell you herself. I insisted I tell you. So if you don't want to see her, tell me and she will never bother you again."

I sat silent for a long time, deeply hurt.

"Jan," he finally said.

"Yes, Dominee," I replied, still deep in my thoughts. Was it really hurt I felt? What a terrible experience for her to endure. Yes, it was hurt, but also sympathy and compassion. "Yes, of course I want to see Greta again. She has a tremendous responsibility to shoulder. My first impulse is to go to Suameer and help her. But I want to do what's best for both of us. She's loyal and I admire her for it."

The man, full of compassion himself, could only smile.

The minister's wife tried to make small talk at the supper table without much success. I was broken-hearted and showed it. I hated that the Dominee's wife and I had met for the first time under these conditions. The Dominee had forewarned her what he felt would transpire. She gave up any attempt to carry on a conversation. We ended supper with a prayer by the Dominee.

"I had better get back to the Stielstras before it gets too late," I said, refusing their invitation to stay longer. "Thanks for the delicious meal . . . I wish the circumstances were better."

"I understand," he said, "but there will be another time."

I crossed the road crying like a baby. When I got back to the Stielstras, I sat in the shed half the night, just thinking.

My problems evading the Germans were bad enough. Now I had to take on this added burden. I decided to put it behind me and concentrate on getting home alive. Greta did what she should have done according to their custom. If the situation were reversed, I believed she would have done the same for me. The old saying, "Out of sight, out of mind," held true to some extent, for it had been over three months since I had seen her. In retrospect, I thought of Lois Oakley in California. I wasn't nearly as filled with remorse as I had been when she died. And I was able to cope with that tragedy. A meeting with Greta would be tougher than hell on both of us. I decided to let the chips fall where they may. We would both live through it if the Germans would let us. But I shed many tears for many nights.

A few days later, sitting upstairs in the bedroom, I was looking down on the street. Two Germans stopped and leaned their bicycles against the fence. They adjusted their Schmeissers on their chests and went to the front door of a house across the street, knocking loudly. A man whose name was Peersma, I think, lived there. He took care of the distribution of ration books for Holwerd and the surrounding area. An elderly man of perhaps sixty-eight or seventy, he lived alone; his wife died before the war. His only son, a farmer, lived in Australia.

The two Germans knocked again, this time with the barrel of a Schmeisser. Mijnheer Peersma came to the door and a considerable verbal confrontation ensued. Angry, the old man went back into the house and closed the door. The irate German soldiers banged on the door again, almost hard enough to break it in, and the old man returned. One of the Germans waved his machine gun at him and told him to accompany them. Again, the man went into the house, presumably to get his hat and coat. He made the mistake of closing the door, and this time the Germans broke the latch open. They brought the old man out and literally threw him to the ground. He got to his feet and foolishly began to run up the street toward the center of town. The two Germans took aim with their machine guns and fired two short bursts. The old man fell dead on the street, blood spewing from many bullet holes.

After he fell, the patrol slung their Schmeissers over their shoulders and, without looking back, lit cigarettes, got on their bicycles, and rode in the direction of Leeuwarden. The life they took meant no more to either of them than stepping on a bug. It didn't take much more time than that either.

Mijnheer Peersma lay there for several minutes unattended. His body started its death throes, jerking and trembling. At last he lay still. Some women came out of houses, wrapped his frail body in sheets and blankets, then carried him to his house.

This wasn't an isolated case. The brave members of the Nazi Aryan race could do no wrong. What bravery they displayed with an old man. But their day was soon coming!

As long as I was in Holwerd, I was never able to find out Mijnheer Peersma's problem with the Germans. He was laid to rest next to his wife, with Dominee de Boer officiating. There was no family in the area anybody knew of, so no relatives came. None of the Stielstra men went to the services because they felt the Germans would be watching to see which men attended. From then on, Sjoukje van der Hoop distributed the ration books.

Just before noon the day after the funeral, mevrouw de Boer came to the Stielstras. I was alone in the kitchen when I saw her coming. I opened the door.

"How are you, mevrouw? May I have your coat?"

"No," she said, "I have come to tell you that Greta is at our house. She expects you any time you can get there."

"Thank you. If you'll wait a minute, I'll walk you home."

"No, I prefer not to be there when you come. But there is one thing I want to tell you. I have known Greta for many years. She has been through a great deal of pain and heartache in recent months. She is not the same girl you knew in Ternaard. Please be kind to her."

"Of course I will," I said.

The minister's wife left before I could say any more.

I ran up the stairs two at a time, combed my hair, and put on a clean shirt. Soon I knocked at the Dominee's rear door.

"Come in, Jan," he said, opening the door.

Greta was sitting at the kitchen table alone. She got to her feet when I came in. I raced across the room to take her in my arms. I didn't kiss her but she returned my embrace.

"How are you?" I whispered.

"All right. Oh, Harry . . ." She didn't finish her sentence. Her words choked in her throat and she couldn't get them out. She was

248

clutching me and we stood like that for a long time. As we separated I looked into her face. Her eyes were wet and red. She held both my hands in hers as we sat down next to each other.

The Dominee excused himself and left us alone.

She had lost a lot of weight. Her hair was disheveled and she had become careless about her personal appearance. There were dark circles under her eyes. Tears were streaming down her face. I tried to contain myself and put one arm around her waist and pulled her close. She came willingly and we didn't move for a long time. Each time she started to talk, she would get a catch in her voice. I talked to her, and it cleared the air somewhat.

"Did you know Bertus Nauta and I were captured in a *razzia?*"

She shook her head negatively. I told her the story. When I told her about Tini screaming to get into the little stone house and Bertus hitting the German on the head, she smiled then laughed a little. I told her where I was staying, how great the people were, and about building the hiding place.

She stopped crying but still couldn't talk.

"When do you start to get snow?" I asked.

She looked at me curiously.

"Do you ice skate?"

She smiled a little.

"Well, Greta, tell me, did you ever fall through the ice?"

"When I was five years old and my brother pulled me out." The tears streamed down her cheeks again. "I'll never forget that conversation, my darling," she said.

"Me either."

A few minutes later, she started to talk.

"I'm sorry for all I've put you through, Harry. I know you were worried about my welfare. Paul's wife Tinka should have explained about the news she had given me about Jan. Instead, she told nobody but me, not even Paul. You have worried too much. I would have told you myself. It was nothing to hide from you. I left early in the morning, scarcely ten minutes after you started your work, as soon as she told me." She looked into my eyes. "I know now that I have made the biggest mistake I'll ever make in my life after seeing you. Oh God, Harry, forgive me!"

Again, tears streamed down her cheeks. "I was in Deventer late that night after Bertus arranged a ride for me in a truck. When I got there, my friends bicycled with me to Zwolle. I hardly recognized Jan and he didn't know me. He was completely exhausted and had been beaten so badly, especially around the head. He was conscious only part of the time. He was as filthy as the dirty attic he was in. We'll never know how he escaped, but he managed to get to a man he knew in Zwolle. The man hadn't even tried to help or feed him. He was almost starved to death." She stopped talking for a moment and looked at me. "I know I am talking about another man but I must tell you the whole story to make you understand."

I didn't say anything so she continued. "My intentions were to nurse him back to health and when he was all right, tell him about us and wish him well. But, it didn't work out that way." She paused and sighed deeply. "I nursed him, fed him, bathed him, and cared for him until he was able to travel. First we took him to Deventer to my friend's house, where he gained some strength. It was the first time we were able to get a doctor for him. We discovered Jan is no more than a vegetable. He's not able to cope with anything, and has the mind of a six-year-old child. Two different doctors said he is brain-damaged and it has affected his motor functions and intelligence. He cannot remember who he is most of the time. The doctors both volunteered the information that as far as sex is concerned, he is not capable of it, for the Nazis destroyed him physically. They burned his penis and testicles off. He screams terribly when he sleeps.

"About two weeks ago we managed to have him transported to Suameer. That's where he is now. A friend of mine, who lost her husband to the Germans, has moved into my house and helps me with him. He doesn't know which one of us is which. He's getting the best care we can give him. The local doctor has been to see him several times. Physically, he has pretty well recovered, but mentally he will never be any better. He can do menial tasks such as dress himself and dig in the garden. But he can't add two and two or tie his own shoelaces."

She stopped talking and went to the sink for a glass of water. She came back to the table and took a long drink, thinking of what to say next. We sat very close and again she took both my hands in hers.

"I have no control over what has happened since I came back to Suameer. Before I tell you more, I want you to know I love you more than you'll ever know. There can never be another man in my life again for that is the way I have been raised and it is my belief. I have done what I think is the right thing according to my Frisian upbringing and you must understand that too. When I thought Jan was dead, the things you and I did together were wonderful and right. I would do them again without hesitation. Jan had a setback, and though it's true it was of his own doing, I must remember he was my betrothed. Too many people know about you and me. The old Frisians look down on what we were to each other. Those of the old school expect me to be a good Frisian woman, pray for forgiveness for loving you, and tend for my betrothed for the rest of my life. And Harry, that's the catch. We were betrothed! After counseling with my Dominee in Suameer, my solicitor, and my close friends, the Dominee from our town married Jan and me last Saturday. I'm a married woman."

She stopped talking and looked at me. I felt as though I was going to pass out. From the depths of my consciousness, I almost suspected something like this had happened. Greta started talking to me but I couldn't hear her words. I was dumbfounded.

I looked at the tears flowing down her face.

"My heart is broken," I said. "I'm more hurt than I've ever been. I love you so, but what more can I say? There's nothing I can do. I'm beat before I start. I'm sorry he's not the loser instead of me. But I'm proud of your loyalty."

She put her arms around my neck, facing me. We sat like that for a long time.

This would probably be the last time I'd see her for the rest of my life. I feasted my eyes on her and the tears flowed. I put my arms around her and pulled her close, never wanting to let her go.

I whispered in her ear. "If anything should ever happen, you know, promise me you'll get in touch with me and no matter where you are or what you're doing, I'll come for you."

"No, Harry, I'll come to you!" she said. "There is only one more thing I want to say and I want you to listen well for I will only say it once unless someday we are together again. I loved you honestly and unashamed. I'll remember our time together and I'll think about it every day of my life. I will cherish every minute of it. I will never deny our love to anyone, even Jan! I wish I had the courage to stay with you just one more night but I'm afraid I wouldn't have the courage to leave you in the morning or ever face my husband again. I'm going to leave now for if I stay here another minute, I'm afraid I'll weaken."

She kissed me on the lips tenderly then removed her arms from my neck. She got up from the table and called the Dominee's name. He came at once.

"I want to thank you for bringing Harry to me. We have had our talk and now I must go. It is a long ride back to Suameer and I want to get back as soon as possible." She shook his hand, then stood facing me. I took her coat from the chair and helped her on with it. The Dominee turned his back to us.

Aloud she said, "Harry A. Clark, American, Jan Veen, Dutchman, I love you now and I will love you after this life is over."

"And, I love you, Greta," I said. She kissed me again, even more tenderly than before. It was the last time.

She walked to the door and I followed her outside. She got on her bicycle, looked at me for a long moment, and waved as she pedaled off, heading south toward Suameer.

The Dominee put his arm around my shoulder. "I'm sorry for you, Jan," he said. He went inside his house, leaving me alone.

Slowly I walked back to the Stielstras. I walked past the German patrol on the way back and scarcely noticed them. I was so close to them the German Shepherd sniffed my hand. The Austrian soldier looked at me strangely but did nothing. He didn't stop nor did the rest of the patrol.

I did a lot of talking to myself to get through the next week. I stayed pretty much to myself and when I was alone, I talked aloud, trying to reason the situation. I told myself she had no alternative and I felt sorry for myself. But, by the same token, I was proud of her. I did everything I could to put her in the back of my mind. I walked a lot after the patrols went by at night. Life would be no bed of roses for her either, tending a mental invalid forever.

One night, after I had somewhat recovered, there was a knock on the door of the Stielstras' house. Sjors and I were sitting at the table doing his English. Before I had a chance to leave the room, the butcher's wife opened the door and Katina came in. After the women exchanged pleasantries, Sjors got up and helped her with her coat. I said hello, then sat back and did my best to ignore her. After a while she said, "Jan Veen, you can turn your head away but you can't ignore that I am here!" I looked at her. She was staring at me with a half smile on her face. She had spoken to me in English. I don't think Sjors understood what she was saying. Then she turned her back and continued talking with the butcher's wife.

"I think she is still mad at you," Sjors whispered.

"Shush, young one!" I said.

When mevrouw Stielstra had finished the supper dishes, the two of them sat at the table and talked over a cup of tea.

252

I was a little disappointed when she was ready to leave. I was at least hopeful we could talk long enough to straighten out our differences and become friends. I felt she was the kind of person I wanted for a friend instead of an enemy.

The two women concluded their conversation and Katina rose to her feet. Sjors got her coat and helped her with it politely. She thanked Sjors, then faced me.

"A gentleman would at least walk a lady home," she said.

"You want me to walk you home?" I blurted out, surprised.

"If you are a gentleman, I would appreciate it, yes."

Hurriedly, I put on my hat and coat. At the back door, I slid into my shoes. I smiled at mevrouw Stielstra and Sjors.

"I'll be right back," I said, holding the door for her.

Sjors winked at me as we left the house.

We walked to the road. I turned in the direction of her house but she took my arm and steered me in the opposite direction. "Where . . . ?" I started to say.

"I want to talk to you, so let's go the long way. It's a nice evening and I won't hurt you." She took my arm, laughing.

We walked along the side of the road so we wouldn't be recognizable to the eyes of other strollers. It was dark but there was a bright moon, and since there were others on the road we waited to talk. There was a feeling of spring in the air. We strolled down the road in an easterly direction, beyond the town itself. We came to a small stone bridge with heavy wooden railings. She stopped and placed her elbows on the railing, looking down at the ripples in the water reflected by the moonlight.

"Did you ever wonder where this water came from and where it will go? How old is it? Where will that tiny drop of water, the one dripping off the rock, be in five years? I'm stupid, wondering about that damned drop of water, huh?" She turned around and faced me, her back against the railing.

I stood beside her, still looking into the stream. "I guess water pretty much stays in its own environment for a long time. I know part of it dissipates and goes into the clouds, only to fall back on another part of the land. But once that happens it goes back into the streams. What do you think?" I asked.

"I never thought about it that way. I suppose you're right, but it really doesn't make any difference, does it?"

"I guess that's the first thing we've agreed on, isn't it?"

253

She looked at me. "No, I don't think so. I think there is something else we agree on too." Her eyes penetrated mine.

"And what's that?" I asked.

She took a step closer toward me and unbuttoned her coat. She stared at me. "Do I have to say it?" she asked.

I decided to play dumb so I stood still.

"Yes, Katina, I'm afraid you will. I don't know how to take you, for I want us to be friends. The last time I tried to talk to you, you hated me."

She opened her coat again and put both her arms around my waist. I kissed her lightly with a friendly kiss, but she pulled my head to her and kissed me hungrily. Gently, I pushed her back to the railing of the bridge and looked down into the water again. She glared at me menacingly. As quickly as it started, it stopped. She was panting and gasping for air, having lost control. Her aroused body trembled and then became absolutely rigid as she looked at me. Finally, she relaxed.

"Did I do something wrong?" she asked.

"No, you did nothing wrong. I just don't understand you."

She didn't answer but stood there a long time. It was a good feeling for someone to want me. Finally, without a word, she took my hand and started walking back toward the village. Our conversation did a 180-degree turnaround. She started talking about the war.

"Soon," she said, "it'll be over. It will be wonderful to take Jacob back to Rotterdam."

We walked past the Stielstras and onto the main road where she lived. As we came closer to her house, our pace slowed as though she didn't want it to end. Once we parted company, she would be alone for a long time. We walked around to the back of her house. It was very dark and quiet. She unlocked her door.

Her remarks were uncalled for. "I am not a whore," she began. "I have never made love unless I had a high regard and much love for my partner. Tonight I almost gave in to lust. Pure, selfish lust! It will be a sleepless night for me for I let my passions become aroused. For the last four years I kept control of myself and put my feelings aside. Now this . . . now I have allowed this to happen.

"Stupid, stupid, stupid!" she almost yelled. "When I met you last week, my tears were as much from being aroused by you as they were from talking to you about the war and the bombing. On the bridge back there I wanted you to make love to me then and there but now I have returned to my senses. It will be a long time before I am myself again." She turned her back on me again.

"You're no whore, Katina," I said. "You're pretty normal, I think. Thank you for the things you just said."

She kissed me lightly on the lips and said "Damn," as she pushed away from me.

"Goodnight, Jan Veen!" she said, whispering. She went into the house and locked the door behind her. She did it so fast I was taken by surprise.

Inside the house, Katina was looking at me. She did not light any candles and watched as I started walking down the path beside the house. She followed me, going from room to room until I got to the road where I turned and headed in the direction of the Stielstras. I didn't look back. She started crying and went to her bedroom, undressed, and got into bed. There was one thing she was right about. She didn't go to sleep until the sun had risen in the east. Neither did I!

I wanted to go back to her house the next day and apologize, but I thought I had better keep away from her for a while. She was a strange one. I liked her and felt sorry for her, but I didn't want a relationship with her. It was best to leave well enough alone. By my very nature I felt defeated.

The following morning, after the patrol had gone through town, I saw Pieter trying to repair an electric motor.

"That's hard to do without electricity to test it, isn't it?"

"It's only a brush, I think. I have to replace this one." He pointed to one of the brushes on the armature. "I'll test it tonight in the room after all the lights are out."

"I think I'll walk into town," I said.

"The patrol just went through, but be careful," he said.

I walked by the church. I saw Dominee de Boer leaving by the side door and we waved at each other. I proceeded up to the corner of Katina's street and decided I'd call on her. I went to the house, walked around to the back, and knocked at the door. There was no answer. I looked in the kitchen window but didn't see anybody so I knocked again, this time much louder, and I called her name. Still no answer. Returning to the front of the house, I tried the front door with the same results.

Probably visiting or shopping, I thought, and walked back to the Stielstras. I decided to try later in the day.

I went back in the middle of the afternoon. Still no answer. After the last patrol, there was still nobody home.

"I must be an ogre. My luck with the opposite sex is awful!" I said to myself. I couldn't figure out what happened to Katina, or where she had gone. I didn't think she was hiding from me.

Sjors was doing his studies at the kitchen table.

"Have you seen your friend Jacob lately?" I asked.

"No, he left with Katina for Dokkum day before yesterday. They went for some school books. Katina teaches Dutch to the kids in town, so they went to Dokkum to exchange books. They'll be back tomorrow if the books aren't too hard to find."

"Thank you, Sjors," I said, starting to walk away.

"Don't worry, Jan, Jacob says she likes you too!" he said, grinning from ear to ear.

THIRTEEN

The morning of March 25, 1944, Pieter Woudsma was picked up by an SS officer and a truck full of SS troops. His destination was the prison in Leeuwarden. Frieda Stielstra was hysterical. The family tried to reassure her, though we all knew the man was doomed. I was concerned for the Stielstra family. From the information I heard regarding the Germans' means of interrogation, he was sure to tell about me. I felt I should be moved from Holwerd and away from the family.

I went to Dominee de Boer. He was aware of Pieter's capture and agreed I must be moved. He would get word to Bertus at once.

After supper, I talked to the family. "The Germans will undoubtedly find out from Pieter that I'm staying here. If I'm caught, it will be your doom," I said.

They agreed. But mijnheer Stielstra had a solution. The house in back of theirs was vacant. They were tending it for the family who lived there. They were sympathetic to the Germans and had left a year before for the south of Holland. It was completely furnished and contained their personal effects. Gerit suggested I gather my belongings and move into the vacant house at once. I could continue to have meals with the family, but the rest of the time I would stay in the house. I moved immediately.

As I walked around town that evening, I saw Katina. She was riding her bicycle. I waved at her but she didn't wave back, so I told myself she didn't see me. A little later, I met Rolf.

"Hi, Rolf, where are you going?" I asked.

"To the blacksmith's. Come with me. He wants to meet you."

The smithy was on the outskirts of town. We entered the smoky shop and saw the huge forge, a giant steel anvil, and the many tools familiar to the trade. The blacksmith was just finishing a piece of metal. When we walked in, he stopped, dropped the metal into a vat of water, and approached us.

"Hello," he said, "how are you? So you are the American." He spoke slowly and I understood him. Two other men entered before I replied. They took a seat on a bench by the wall.

"They are friends," he said as we shook hands.

Rolf was talking to him about some work for the *winkelier,* when the door to the smithy opened again. The German Grune Polizei entered, his Schmeisser hung around his neck, his helmet on. He startled all of us as we froze in our tracks. I was probably the most frightened; inwardly I trembled. The man was outlined in the doorway of the shop, revealing his size. His leashed dog stood close to him, panting, with his tongue hanging out on the side of his jowls. He seemed to understand his master's purpose in our encounter. There was something ominous about the pair as they stood there silhouetted.

He walked into the shop and closed the door behind him. He stopped less than three feet from me. The dog was between us, wagging his tail. After sniffing my hand, he licked it as he sat down. I patted the animal on the head and scratched his ears.

The German towered over me. He was a handsome man and said something to me in German, using the word *hund* (dog). I think he was telling me his dog liked me.

He dropped the leash and walked around the forge, looking at the tools and equipment. He walked to the two men sitting on the bench, checking them visually for a moment, then stopped in front of the blacksmith and looked him in the eyes. All the time the dog sat beside me, watching his master's every move. He came back to us and laid his hand on Rolf's arm.

His Dutch was bad. "There will be a *razzia* in Holwerd at dawn." He looked at Rolf, then at me. "Get this American pilot out of town before then!" He motioned to me. Then, to all our surprise, he said to me in English, "Good luck, American."

He picked up the leash, turned around, and opened the door, departing without looking back. He closed the door quietly.

The smithy was the first to recover from the shock. "Spread the word," he said, "there's not a minute to lose."

Rolf and I left the place, each going our own way. I told him I'd stay in the hiding place for the night.

I went straight to Katina's. I knocked on the back door. This time I heard a voice from within. "Who's there?"

"It's Jan," I answered.

She opened the door. The house was dark inside.

"Not tonight, Jan," she said.

"No, you've got me wrong, I've come to warn you. There is going to be a *razzia* tomorrow morning at daybreak. If you have no place to stay, we have a good hiding place where we can hide you and the boy."

"Oh," she said nonchalantly, "how did you find out?"

When I told her what had happened she listened in disbelief. "I'm not lying to you, there will be a *razzia*!"

"Well, thank you," she said and started to close the door.

"Hey," I said, "wait a minute. You can't stay here in the house. Even if you're not caught, what about Jacob?"

"We will not be here at daybreak. Don't worry about us."

She closed the door and disappeared in the house.

"You're a rude bitch!" I said aloud.

I went to Dominee de Boer's and knocked at his door several times before he answered. He apologized, saying he and his wife had retired early and were both sound asleep. I told him about the German then I went back to the *winkelier's*. When I walked into the kitchen, the whole family was there.

Gerit spoke to me when I came in. "Jan, I'm glad you are here. We will all go to bed just as we have planned. You will sleep next door and I will watch through the night. At the first sign of a *razzia* I will awaken each of you and we'll get in the hiding place. Most of us snore. If we go into the hiding place now, the woman in back will hear us and realize there is a room in back of her. We can't risk that."

"Do I snore?" I asked, surprised.

"Yes, you do, Jan," the butcher's wife said, "and very loudly."

It was still dark when Gerit Stielstra awakened me. I went to bed with my clothes on, removing only my shoes. I heard him when he entered and jumped out of bed. The two of us made the bed and closed the doors to the closet. I put my Luger in my belt and quietly we went out the front door and around the butcher shop to the shed where Pieter and Rolf were waiting.

"Our breakfast!" Sjors proclaimed, carrying a bag.

I could hear the engines of the German trucks taking up positions around town, waiting for dawn to start the *razzia*.

The five of us climbed into the loft, followed by mevrouw Stielstra. We opened the trap door and descended into the darkness. Once inside, Rolf locked the trap door. We could hear mevrouw Stielstra as she shifted some of the bales of hay over the door and spread some loose hay around the floor. We heard her go down the ladder into the shed, then all was quiet.

Shortly after sunup we heard activity around the village. Each of us took turns at the peep hole. When it was my turn, I saw ten armed German soldiers walk up the street, past the driveway to our hiding place, without looking. Occasionally machine gun fire erupted and once there were shots from either a rifle or a handgun very close by. Several times trucks passed by but didn't stop. Each time they did, we were hopeful the Germans were leaving town, but they were only changing locations.

We heard a man's voice coming from the back room of the house next to us. I looked into the hole to see who it was. A German officer was looking at some documents the woman had given him. She was attired in a very revealing nightgown. The officer questioned her and obviously got the right answers, for she smiled as he patted her on the fanny. They went in the house and closed the door behind them.

It was four hours before things quieted down. We ate some sandwiches and continued to wait. Two more hours passed before mevrouw Stielstra climbed the ladder to the loft. She removed the bales of hay and looked down at us.

"The Germans have gone," she announced. "I have walked over most of the town and they have all left."

Gerit told us he would check for himself. An hour later, he returned and gave us the "all clear."

I had survived another *razzia*. Thanks to an enemy soldier and his dog, a caring and loving family, and our own foresight to build the hiding place, we had survived. When we came outside, we discovered the Germans had searched every house in Holwerd except that of the Stielstras.

Dominee de Boer told us why. He was among the German troops as the *razzia* was going on. As soon as the affair was over, he came to check on us. "I was considerably worried about you, Jan, but I didn't know you had built such a fine hiding place. The German Grune Polizei, the one with the dog, stayed in front of the butcher shop and several times I heard him tell soldiers the house had already been searched. Later, I heard him tell some officers he had already searched the house and mevrouw Stielstra cooperated completely. Lying to his superiors, he said they always gave preferential treatment to his patrols.

The Dominee told me I would be leaving Holwerd the next day.

The Germans had taken about a hundred bicycles as well as a lot of food and cheese. Approximately a hundred young men had been discovered in various hiding places and were taken away in trucks. For the most part, they were teenagers not yet sixteen. It was doubtful if they would receive any punishment. Because they were hiding, they might have to work in the defenses. Nobody was killed, although the Germans had shot at a man fleeing through the fields and missed. As *razzias* went, this one wasn't too bad for the citizens of Holwerd. They got off lucky. A cache of about a thousand weapons was hidden in the church and various other places around town and the Germans hadn't found them.

Later the same day of the *razzia*, Dominee de Boer brought word about Pieter Woudsma. He directed most of his remarks to Frieda, who was on the verge of fainting. Her white face and blue lips did not belie her hysterics. Pieter Woudsma was dead! He was only questioned about his brother's group. What else he told them, and what he told them about Holwerd in particular, no one will ever know. The bloody pulp of his broken body was picked up by his family in Dokkum for burial.

I was shocked and saddened by the news of Pieter. He would have been a good husband and father. The Germans had no right to torture and kill him, but this was typical of Nazi inhumanity. If he had told them about me, the Stielstras' shop would have been torn to shreds. I will always remember him and be grateful for his friendship.

And I would miss my friends in Holwerd. I had been in the village two months and considered the Stielstra family as my own. They were very close and treated me as one of them. That Gerit moved me to the house in back when he knew there was to be a *razzia* proved his uncommon bravery. As if I were part of his family, he kept me under his wing, knowing full well the consequences if he were caught.

For some reason unknown to me, the Dominee told me I was

going to Ternaard but not for a few days. So, the day after the raid, I thought I would say goodbye to Jacob and Katina. Nobody was home nor were they the following day. She had not been there during the *razzia*, for the rear door was broken and her house had been ransacked. The neighbors had nailed the door back in place.

Pieter Woudsma was buried on April 1, 1945, in Dokkum beside his brother. He had been arrested on March 27 and, as close as they could tell, was murdered on March 29, the same day his body was released to his family. I pitied Frieda, for she was out of her mind with grief. She was unable to attend the funeral so mevrouw Stielstra went in her place. Frieda's engagement ring was placed on Pieter's little finger.

The day I was going to leave Holwerd, Sjors told me he would say my goodbyes to Katina and Jacob. "I'll tell her that you love her," he teased.

"If you tell her that, it will be a lie and I'll break your neck!" I said. "Don't forget that! She must be looked after and remember, Sjors, she is a woman and she's alone, right?"

Sjors nodded his head in understanding. "Right, Jan."

My last stop before meeting Sjoukje was to visit Dominee de Boer. We talked personally, privately, and compassionately for the better part of an hour. After we prayed, I gave him the addresses of my family and friends in the United States that I could recall from memory. I told him I wanted to keep in touch and through him, I wanted to keep tabs on Greta's welfare. He promised he would let me know immediately if there were any change in her well-being. I was walking on air when I left him. The spiritual power he possessed was awesome.

Back at the Stielstras', I got into my blue dress, choked back the tears, and said my goodbyes. The morning patrol had headed east toward Ternaard fully an hour before. My hair, still uncut since before I had been shot down, eight months before, was down over my shoulders. My woman's attire still fit perfectly. My new sweater was in my suitcase, wrapped in mijnheer Stielstra's finest butcher paper and tied with string. Mevrouw Stielstra had washed and ironed my dress and Sjors had polished my shoes. According to Sjoukje, I looked more like a woman than most women did. We left hurriedly before I made an idiot out of myself and shed the tears trying so hard to come.

"We never saw a German patrol to flirt with," Sjoukje said as we pulled into Bertus Nauta's driveway.

"That's okay with me," I said.

I put the bicycle in the shed and closed the door. Tini greeted us with a hug, kissing our cheeks twice.

"Where's Bertus?" I asked, not seeing him anywhere.

"He is in Dokkum," she answered. "He will be home by dark."

Sjoukje, anxious to leave, said goodbye to us and left. "See you in a few days, Jan," she said cheerfully.

I removed my dress in the kitchen and hung it over the back of a chair. Tini poured tea for us and we sat down. She talked. "There is so much going on it's impossible to keep up with it. The Allies have crossed all the rivers that held them back and are steadily moving northward. I understand they are very close now. I think the war will be over and we will be free in three weeks' time. The underground has a name now, it's called the Nederlandse Binnenlandse Strijdkrachten, or NBS. There are twenty-five thousand armed members in Holland. I know you will only be here a day or two. Bertus will tell you more when he gets here. You know how he is. He wants to tell you himself. So, please listen to him, even if it is something I have already told you. I don't know where you are going next. The Boche are getting desperate now. They know they are on their last leg and are gathering all the bicycles and other transport they can. It will be difficult for the Allies to recognize the Germans for they are deserting, wearing stolen civilian clothing, and are more cruel than ever.

As I listened, I put my Luger in the hiding place.

I told Tini the story about the Austrian Grune Polizei with the big dog. She listened attentively with her hands over her mouth, unable to believe there were any good Germans.

"You mean the one with the big dog? The Grune Polizei?"

"That's the one!" I told her.

"Well," she said in disbelief. "Bertus should be told about this." She paused a moment. "We kept in touch with your welfare in Holwerd. We heard about your meeting with Greta. May I talk about it . . . should I?"

"It's all right," I said. "I thought the world of her, but it was her decision to marry Jan."

"Marry?" she interrupted. "Did she actually marry him?"

"Yes."

"What a waste!" she said. "She was forced into it by listening to those old Frisian crones. I heard he is so bad he can't even say his own name, let alone remember it. A doctor told me the German SS amputated all of his privates. He is a vegetable and will have to be helped for the rest of his life. Is she trying to be a martyr for the sake of his family? If she is, she's compounding her mistake." Tini looked at me. "She should have stayed by you as she wanted. God, I cannot respect her decision in this matter."

That was the end of the conversation as far as Greta was concerned, and I was glad. After I left Holland I would lick my wounds and never look back.

I told Tini all the things I did in Holwerd, mentioning I had played chess with Pieter Woudsma.

"Did you meet Pieter Woudsma?" she interrupted.

"Yes," I replied, "we became pretty good friends."

"He had a brother named Wijtse. Now he was the one! He did more hell-raising to the Germans than any other ten men in the Netherlands." She told me about some of his exploits.

I told her of the murder of mijnheer Peersma, how the two Germans had shot him down in cold blood.

"I would recognize those two if I ever saw them again and it would give me great delight to do the same to them," I said.

Tini refilled our cups with tea and sat back down.

"Remember the family who were taken away during the *razzia*?" she asked. "Their older children came here from Groningen and have decided to live in our village. They like Ternaard and the people like them. Of course, the man has to stay hidden because of his age, but this is going to be their home from now on."

She took a sip of her tea, reflecting. "We have never had any more trouble with the Germans. They feel they have cleaned out any problems they had here. Little do they know! I think we have at least two hundred rifles hidden in our small village." She laughed. "Many of them belong to the men you trained. You should feel a great deal of pride for the work you have done. They are ready to fight when the time is right!"

"When do you think we can actually fight the Germans?"

"Bertus says no more than two weeks and probably sooner."

"That soon?" I couldn't believe it.

Bertus came home at 8:00 that night and was genuinely happy to see me. There was a very dark-complexioned young man with him. He introduced him to me as Jon. He was about 6'2, very handsome, but poorly dressed and very unfriendly. He had a P-38 pistol shoved in his belt. He didn't acknowledge our introduction, but that was fine because I didn't want to know him either.

Bertus and Jon went into the front room and closed the door behind them. For the first time, as far as Bertus was concerned, I was an outsider. Perhaps, I told myself, there were some secret conversations between them. Again, I sat down with Tini.

"He's sure an unfriendly sort!" I said.

"Hij is een slecht zware jongmens (He is one bad, tough, young man)," she said. "I do not like him and I cannot stand to be around him but he is important right now." She took my hand and smiled. "Besides, he cannot repair clocks. Why don't you stay here after the liberation? Holland is a wonderful place to live during peace time. You should make the Netherlands your home, Jan."

I had been in Holland almost eight months. A lot of water had gone over the dam and it seemed I had been there much longer. In retrospect, my life in the United States was a fond memory, almost a dream. My life in Holland was my only life, my real existence. During my time with them, I never met a Dutchman I didn't like (besides the man with Bertus). And my life with these people wasn't over yet. Surely now it would just be a matter of coasting along until we were liberated, only two or three weeks more. I thought my time for getting involved with danger was over. But I was wrong.

"I'll come back to Holland some day when there is peace," I finally explained. "I have a home and loved ones who probably think I am dead. The United States is my home and I love my country just as you love yours. If I chose to stay here, after my discharge from the Air Force, there would be a tremendous opportunity. Of course there is the language barrier, and though I get by with grammar-school Dutch, it would be most difficult. Holland has to be rebuilt the same as the rest of Europe and must get back in the world marketplace. This will be done by Dutchmen. No, my place is in the United States with my own people, speaking my own language."

"I'll bet if Greta had not found Jan you'd stay," Tini said.

It was a cruel thing for her to say. I weighed her remark carefully. "No, I'd still have to leave. I am still in the Army Air Force and I will be until I'm released. I will report for duty as soon as I get with my own people. There are parts of my life I have to put back together again before I feel free to do as I please. Perhaps if all were well between Greta and me there would be reason to rejoice. Of course I would come back for her. We had already decided she would come to the United States. Unless something happens to Jan, it's over between us — and that's that. But you'll see me again. In America we have a saying, 'A bad penny always returns.' "

She took my hand. "Don't make it too long before you come back, Jan. We love you like you are one of the family."

The living room door opened. Bertus sat with us at the table and Jon went out the back door. He took over the conversation, speaking in Dutch.

"Jan, a lot has happened in the two months since you left here. My home has become headquarters for local activities. Many people come and go. It's not safe for you here. The day after tomorrow, Sjoukje will take you to a small village closer to Dokkum called Bridaard-on-Kanaal. It's not far and you will be with another family for a short time. Your shooting war will begin in Dokkum when you help with their liberation. Everything has been arranged. We are planning to attack the Germans in Leeuwarden. We hope the Allies are here to help us within two weeks. They are knocking on the door just south of here. This time, the Germans will know who they are fighting and there will be no reprisals against the civilian population. Later, when you go to Dokkum, you will stay with Dominee Visser and be reunited with Jim. We gave him his wish, and he has been able to sit out the war. If you had joined him, think of all you would have missed."

"I wouldn't have missed anything I've done for anything in the world. I know I helped a little in our fight." I looked at Tini. "I don't think I'll have enough time to repair any more clocks if I'm leaving in two days."

She laughed. "I'll save a clock for when you return!"

Bertus interrupted. "I want to thank you again, Jan, not only for myself but for Paul and Harry Wessels, who by the way is just fine. The people you have trained are now training others and they are ready to fight the Boche. You made a good lookout when we gathered in the weapons on so many dark nights. Only one thing more . . . I'm truly sorry about you and Greta."

He put his hand on my shoulder and squeezed it. Then he got up from the table and went to bed. I went to bed shortly afterward. A few minutes later, Jon came into the room, undressed, and jumped into the bed so recently occupied by Greta. I resented him all the more for that.

When I woke up in the morning, he was gone.

I spent the day with Tini. In the evening, I decided I'd clean my Luger since it would be the last chance I'd have.

It was gone! It wasn't in the hiding place.

266

"Tini," I asked, "have you seen my gun?"

"No, but I saw Jon looking at it this morning."

"When will he be back?"

"I don't know. Bertus will be back soon. We can ask him."

Tini was angry too. I was almost certain Jon had taken it. I had carried it with me all the way through Holland, and though I never once fired it, I didn't want to lose it to that jerk.

It was a good hour before Bertus arrived. I approached him on the subject immediately.

"Bertus, have you seen my pistol?"

"No . . . oh yes, I saw it this morning when Jon was looking at it. He said he would like to have one like it. He put it back, I think. At least he acted like he put it back."

He looked in the hiding place and saw the pistol was gone.

"Well," Bertus said, "if Jon has taken it let me handle it. I will get it back for you. He will be back here tonight."

"I hope so," I said. "When I leave tomorrow I'm going to have my gun, you can tell him that for me."

I stayed up quite late waiting for Jon to return. When it became obvious he would be late, I went to bed and never heard him come in. When I woke up he was asleep in bed. His clothing was strewn all over the floor.

I dressed, packed my suitcase, and took it downstairs, where Bertus and Tini were eating breakfast. The first thing I did was look in the hiding place. My Luger wasn't there. About an hour later, Jon came down, looking disheveled, black whiskers heavy on his face, his uncombed hair in his eyes. He sat at the table and Tini put some hot oatmeal in front of him. He slurped it down noisily.

Finally, Bertus asked about the gun. At first he denied taking the weapon, then said he would like to trade his P-38 for it. Bertus explained how I had come by it and carried it through Holland. Jon said he'd bring it back that night.

"Where is it now?" Bertus asked.

"I have it hidden."

"Go and get it. Bring it back here right now!" he ordered with a ring of authority in his voice.

A staring match ensued, with Jon losing out.

"Oh, I'll get one of my own!" he finally said.

He went out back to the shed. When he returned, he had the Luger, holster, and both spare clips of ammunition. The holster and spare clips had been in my suitcase, but I failed to notice they were missing too.

"There you are, American!" he said, dropping them on the table.

"Thank you," I said, genuinely glad to have them back.

Sjoukje walked in the back door. "Ready to go?" she asked.

"As soon as I dress like a lady," I replied.

I put on the dress in the front room and rolled up my pant legs, then put the Luger in my belt.

I said my goodbyes to Tini and Bertus. Jon was sitting at the kitchen table, slurping tea. I put on my coat and tied the scarf around my head. In the back yard, I tied the suitcase on my bicycle, waved at Tini and Bertus, and we were gone.

We headed south and went almost all the way to Dokkum. When the town was in sight, we took a right and headed for the town of Raard. We stopped at a shop where the proprietors, a kindly young man and his wife, took us into their home in the back of the shop and fed us. Immediately after eating we rode until we came to a crossroad. The sign indicated the town of Jislum to the right and Bridaard-on-Kanaal to the left. We made the left turn and came to a huge canal with several barges moored to the sides. Minutes later, we entered the village itself.

We rode down the main street beside the canal. A few blocks further, Sjoukje turned her bicycle into the walkway beside a two-story house. I followed her out back where a youngster, perhaps fifteen or sixteen years old, bounded through the back door and clumsily stopped short of knocking Sjoukje off her bicycle.

"*Dag,* Sjoukje," he said, panting.

"*Dag,* Raol," she replied with a look of discernment.

"Is this the American?"

"Yes," she said.

"Hello, Jan Veen," he said. "Come into the house."

The place was poorly furnished compared to most of the homes I had visited. Instead of the usual Dutch neatness, everything was a mess. Clothing, dirty dishes, and clutter were everywhere. A woman about fifty years old entered the kitchen. She looked tired.

"This is my mother, mevrouw Bokma, and I am Raol," the boy said, introducing them. He spoke very broken English but was proud of the way he was able to make me understand his words.

"*Dag,* mevrouw Bokma," I said.

"*Dag,*" she replied, handing us cups of tea.

Sjoukje, somewhat distressed at the condition of the house, walked over to where I stood and said quietly, "You will be here for the next week or so. It's a safe house but German patrols go down the street in the front. You will have to be careful."

"Where can I get rid of this dress?" I asked.

She spoke to Raol, who promptly took me upstairs. I was given a bedroom to myself. It had a double bed with a wrought-iron headboard. The paint was chipped badly. However, unlike the rest of the house, the room was clean. There was a wall closet, and I hung the dress in there. I kept the Luger in my belt under my sweater. Then I went back downstairs and joined Sjoukje for more tea. The boy went outside.

"When will you be back?" I asked her.

"I'm not sure. I know it will be in about a week. I am not supposed to say this, but I think Dokkum will be liberated no later than April thirteenth." She spoke in English and the woman of the house gave no indication she understood. "That is very select information and is secret, do you understand?"

I nodded in the affirmative.

"I will stay here until almost dark. I have a stop to make on the way and I don't want to arrive too early."

"Sjoukje, where do you live?"

She smiled. "I thought you knew. I live very near by."

"Aren't you going to tell me?"

"Since you don't know, I'll tell you the next time we meet. You know the Germans are getting ready to run, so there's no telling what they will do. We think very few of them will fight when the Allies come and they will surrender quickly. They want to save their own hides and they know there is no longer any hope. They may do one last outrageous act of cruelty, but we hope not. All the men from the underground are armed. They have their guns ready to do war with the Germans as soon as they are ordered. In fact, some of them have formed small groups and attacked the Germans with no reprisals. If the Nazis try anything, since the Allies are so close, the organization will attack them. The Boche know the Dutch would win. Of course, they know where the Allies are. It's only a matter of days. Put yourself in their place. Why die? It's even possible, some of us feel, the Germans might try to befriend us to soften the blow of defeat."

This was the wisdom of a seventeen-year-old Dutch girl.

Sjoukje left just before dark, leaving me in the hands of Raol, an irresponsible sixteen-year-old. He was a nice kid — but still he was a teenager.

"I want you to meet all my friends while you are here," he said. "As soon as it is dark, I will take you to some of them. They are anxious to meet you."

"Raol," I said, "nobody is supposed to know I am staying here except your mother and you. You're endangering all our lives when you tell you have an American at your house."

"Yes, but these people won't tell anybody," he answered confidently. "They are good people, just wait and see."

I hoped he was right.

In back of the Bokma house was a huge field. On the far end a row of houses had their backs to the field. I presumed a street or road was on the other side. On the right side of the field was another row of houses whose back yards also faced the field. The closest house to Raol's belonged to a Dutch family who obviously were a cut above the average. They had one son, twelve-year-old Hans, and three daughters. Karen was the oldest, Loty and Maria, the youngest. All the children had honey-colored hair and the bluest eyes I have ever seen. The girls graduated from high school and were waiting for the war to end so they could attend college. Their father insisted they get a college education. After Raol introduced me to them, it became evident we were going to be good friends. The girls had taken English in high school and wanted me to teach them perfect English in ten easy lessons. They were, like Raol, typical teenagers, giggly and flighty. The oldest of them, Karen, was more subdued and mature, but due to her close association with the younger members of her family, she hadn't consciously matured yet. The family's name was Borgham.

The first night I was there we were invited to the Borgham house. After the preliminaries, the lady of the house served tea in fine china cups and saucers. The talk was light and the girls insisted I speak in English. Since neither one of their parents spoke the language, I suggested we speak English another time. They were wonderful people and a very happy family. We were invited to their home the following night for supper. We accepted gratefully. Their home was furnished lavishly and sparkled with cleanliness. Oil paintings adorned the walls. The clothing the family wore was tasteful and expensive.

The next night at their house, we had a delicious supper and retired to the living room, which they had opened for this special occasion. We settled into chairs and the girls sat on the floor cross-legged,

270

facing me. They were dressed in fluffy dresses and had ribbons in their hair. Mijnheer Borgham asked me if I would, without divulging any names, dates or places, tell them what had transpired in Holland since the day I was shot down. He wanted me to tell the story in Dutch so he could understand. Again he repeated that I should not say anything which might affect the safety of another person. I explained I spoke Dutch very badly. But with their prompting, it was the first and only time I ever told my story to anybody in Dutch. It was fun, and the family said they understood me.

Because I related my experiences for over two hours, they could grasp how much of their language I knew. Thereafter, they kept their conversation in simple words which I could comprehend. I felt like this was my final examination speaking the language I had learned over the past eight months. Later, I discovered mijnheer Borgham was a psychologist from Amsterdam. He abandoned his practice three years before because of the German occupation.

I spent long hours with the girls, speaking English and Dutch with them. They had a very thick Oxford English accent but liked my American accent better and tried to copy it. We invented a word game where they gave me a word in Dutch and I would say the same word in English and then vice versa. It was fun and a good way to learn new words without forgetting them. When we tired of the game, the young boy said he wanted to give me a final word for the day. *"Geslachtsgemeenschap,"* he said, a real tongue twister. The girls giggled and almost broke down.

"What does that mean?" I asked and got no reply. All I got was more giggles.

I dropped the subject and talked of other things, but later I asked Raol. He started laughing again.

"Raol, what's so funny about *'Geslachtsgemeenschap'*?"

He rolled over with laughter the way I pronounced it. Finally, he whispered in my ear, "You know, when a boy gets on top of a girl and sticks his *mannelijk* into her *schede,* you know, her *vrouwlijk!"*

"Oh!" I said, finally understanding Hans's joke.

I noticed that Karen, the oldest daughter, often stared at me invitingly. She made certain she sat next to me, and once at the dinner table she took my hand in hers, squeezing it meaningfully.

We usually sat on the floor when we were playing the word-trading game. This was a bad time for me, for the girls always sat cross-legged opposite me, and Karen would expose herself. Loty, too, often exposed her bloomered crotch. Maria and Loty got up from the floor to get tea for us. I spoke to Karen.

"Do you know what you're doing while you're sitting there cross-legged like that?"

"Of course," she replied, looking straight into my eyes. "Are you frightened of it?"

"Not afraid, just amazed," I answered.

"Well, don't be," she said.

Her sisters came back, balancing four cups of tea on a tray. Karen excused herself and left the room, returning in a few minutes. She took her place on the floor opposite me and crossed her legs again. I couldn't believe it — she had removed her panties. She ignored my glances but moved her legs a little when I looked. She was a brazen young lady. Being as beautiful as she was, I couldn't understand it. It was difficult to keep my eyes in my head. Finally, it became too much for me to handle. I excused myself and went home to the Bokmas'.

An occasional German patrol came through town. They seemed more friendly than they had before. Mijnheer Borgham advised us that it meant nothing. They were not to be trusted.

I enjoyed Bridaard. Though I was twenty-seven years old (my birthday on March 12 had gone by unnoticed), I still felt I belonged to the same generation as these kids.

The day after Karen exposed herself to me, Raol and Hans went fishing. It was a warm day, so after they left, I went to my room and took off all my clothes but my shorts. I pulled the window up as far as it would go and let a rare warm breeze blow in on my body as I lay on the bed. The curtains were billowing gently. I heard footsteps on the stairs and, thinking it was the lady of the house, paid no attention to them. The door to my room opened. Standing there, framed in the doorway, was Karen.

"Hello," she said.

I didn't move from where I was lying on the bed. "Hello, what are you doing here?"

"I came to see you."

"Well, sit down," I invited.

She kicked off her shoes, sat on the bed, and pulled her feet up under her.

"Is this where you sleep?" she asked.

"Yes."

"It's a nice room." She pulled her feet out from under her and

272

then sat cross-legged, revealing herself as she had before.

"Do you know what you're doing?" I sat up on the bed.

"I hope so," she said. She smiled and put her arms around the back of my neck then kissed me until finally, breathing heavily, she pulled away. "Well?" she asked.

With her arms over her head she looked into my eyes. She finally got off the bed and removed her dress, the only garment she had on. She straddled me and bent over to kiss me, but said nothing. Our union was indescribable. After an hour passed, she got up and sat on the edge of the bed. She kissed me again, then put her dress back on. I dressed and walked her home.

While she was upstairs, I had a cup of tea with Loty. Fifteen minutes later Karen reappeared, looking none the worse for wear. She sat down beside me and put her hand on my leg, squeezing it, and whispered in my ear, "That's the best! It just doesn't get any better than that!" I didn't argue with her.

Later in the day, Raol returned. I was in my room, cleaning the Luger. He came in and admired the weapon.

"Lots of girls on the street!" he said, looking outside.

We went to his room, which overlooked the main street of the village and the canal beyond. There were many attractive young ladies and children walking. There were also a few men and boys, the same age the Germans were seeking. If a patrol came now, it would be tough for all of them.

Raol yelled to some girls. "Hey," he invited, "Come on up and see what we've got!"

"No, Raol," one of them said. "We know why you want us to come up there." They giggled and kept going down the street.

"I'm going to marry that one!" he said. "She is the best looking girl in Bridaard, and she's the smartest too."

We sat there for a long time, looking down on the street and the people. After talking to him, I found out he wasn't such a brainless teenager after all. He had a head on his shoulders.

A German patrol rounded the corner and came into view on the main street. There were three soldiers of the *veermacht,* not the Grune Polizei, thank God. There were, of course, still several young men on the street. Some of them disappeared between the houses, through doorways, and others seemed to evaporate into thin air. A few stayed on the street, knowing it was too late to try to escape. The Germans walked through the village and disappeared. This was a big change. Mijnheer Borgham was right!

The next day, Karen came to the house and asked me to go for a walk with her. We crossed the canal toward Jislum. There, we went to a beautiful old windmill and stayed an hour.

The following day we visited a canal boat, which was moored about a kilometer out of town on the canal.

The next day her sister Loty caught us in the bedroom. She looked at us for several seconds and smiled before closing the door without saying a word. It didn't bother Karen.

"She won't tell on us, but she might want to treat herself," she said.

I went to the Borghams' for supper that night. As always, her mother and father were most gracious. Afterward, we played our usual game. Loty kept looking at me as if to say, "I know about Karen and you!" but she didn't say anything. We had a good time and all three of the young ladies stayed respectable. We tired of the game and Karen served tea then sat down next to me.

"I told you Loty would want to," she whispered in my ear.

"Would want to what?" I asked.

"Treat herself to you."

"You mean, she wants to make love with me?" I asked.

"No, silly, she doesn't love you."

"Well, what then?"

"*Geslachtsgemeenschap!* That's all she wants."

"Oh," I said, "and what did you tell her?"

"That I would tell you."

"Okay, so you've told me."

"Well, will you do it?"

"Do I have to?" I asked, teasing her.

"If you don't she will make my life miserable."

"Well, tell her no."

Karen squeezed my hand tightly. "I'm glad," she said. "I don't want to share you with anybody. Not even Loty."

The following afternoon, Sjoukje stopped by the house, staying only a moment. She told me the Canadians were pressing northward through Holland. I was going to Dokkum on the evening of the twelfth. I walked out with her as she got on her bicycle.

"Oh yes, I made you a promise. I live in Holwerd. I was no more than two blocks away from you all the time you were staying with the

274

Stielstras. Surprised? See you in a couple of days," she called over her shoulder as I stood there with my mouth wide open.

That night, Karen and I stayed in the canal boat. We accidentally fell asleep and stayed all night.

Thursday was April 12. I got up early in the morning and packed my bag, including the dress, stockings, slip, and coat I was used to traveling in. Karen put a rubber band around my hair and I wore it in a ponytail. From then on, to hell with the women's clothes; I would travel as a man. When I put my cap on, I put the ponytail under it and looked masculine.

Karen stayed with me all afternoon.

"I hoped our relationship could turn into something more. I haven't fooled myself into thinking it could. Will I see you any more, do you think?" she asked. "I'm in love with you, you know."

"I'll see you again if you'll tell me where you'll be a few years from now."

She handed me a piece of paper. Her real name and her address in Amsterdam were written on it.

"I'm going to Dokkum to help with the liberation. Why don't you come when the shooting is over? You should find me okay."

"I'll come . . . I promise I will!" she said.

"I've never asked you before, but how old are you, Karen?"

She smiled. "Afraid I'm too young?"

"It's too late to be afraid of that now."

"Well, I'm twenty-two. Feel better?"

"Yes," I admitted. "And Loty?"

"Loty is twenty."

"You are the greatest!" I said honestly.

"I don't have to tell you this, Jan, but I will. You are the third man I have ever been with in my life. But you are the only one who was of my choice. I was forced before — "

I stopped her. I didn't want to hear any more about it.

She stayed until Sjoukje came. She helped me get the bicycle from the shed and tie my suitcase on it. I said goodbye to Raol and his mother and kissed Karen goodbye. Sjoukje was ready, so I hopped on the bicycle and we headed down the road toward Dokkum. I waved goodbye to the three of them as we left the village.

"I'll say this for you. You sure make friends with the good-looking girls in Holland. That one doesn't want you to leave!"

I still didn't answer her. But inwardly, I agreed.

"The Canadians are not very far. They have taken Zwolle and are near Meppel. You will be with them in two or three days. You can rely on my word," she said.

"I want to thank you for all your help, Sjoukje," I said.

"Just kill a couple of them goddamned Germans for me too."

Her language surprised me. I had never heard anybody other than Niko and George curse while I was in Holland.

I answered her, "You're goddamned right I will!"

FOURTEEN

The Royal Canadian Dragoons liberated Dutch towns from the Belgian border north through Holland. They liberated Meppel, Havelte, and Diever on April 13, 1945. The Royal Canadian Dragoons were a "wreckie" outfit, moving in front of the lines. They probed German defenses with fast, light, mobile-armored equipment. Even the troops were transported in heavy trucks. Their half-tracks mounted .75mm cannons and the armored cars had a .35mm cannon in their turrets.

As the Canadians headed north, the Nederlandse Binnenlandse Strijdkrachten (NBS) went into battle against the Nazi forces before they arrived. They did so for two reasons. First, they wanted their liberators to have somewhat of an easier job, and second, they wanted revenge for four long years of torment. Sometimes a stubborn nest of Germans decided to fight. This slowed the progress of the Canadians and they brought their heavier armament into play. But with their greater expertise they generally did the stubborn defenders in quickly. They were a brave, modern fighting army, with more guts than most. They had fought all the way through North Africa, Sicily, Italy, France, Belgium, Luxembourg, and Holland. Many of them survived the entire campaign all the way from North Africa. And now the end was in sight.

I arrived in Dokkum Thursday night, April 12. There were 200

German troops in the little town. Two men were waiting for Sjoukje and me on the outskirts of town. She put her arm around my neck and kissed me on the cheek. "Good luck, Jan, and God bless you!" She pedaled away quickly toward the north.

I was told to be quiet and keep up with them. We rode down streets and alleys, across canals and through the downtown area. I was taken to Dominee Visser's house under extremely hazardous conditions. We saw several Germans; some were on duty but they had all been placed on alert. Dokkum was a dangerous place to be because the enemy troops were considered to be diehards. They meant to fight the Canadians as soon as they were in range.

When I entered Dominee Visser's house, the first to greet me was Jim. We were elated to see each other, but he told me some bad news. President Franklin Delano Roosevelt had died that day of a cerebral hemorrhage. It came over BBC only minutes before I arrived. I will never forget. The end of the war was so near. It was a shame he didn't live to see total victory.

Jim had gotten his wish. He was bored to tears but he was alive. Nobody, German or otherwise, had disturbed his serenity. He had his own room with a hiding place in the attic which he never used once. The Dominee had provided him with innumerable books in English. The food had been exceptional. The preacher's wife kept his hair trimmed and his clothing in good repair. I noticed his new clothes. He laughed at my long hair.

"I thought you would have it cut by now. They won't allow weapons in the house," he said, noticing the Luger in my belt.

"Then I'll sleep in the barn! My gun and I stay together!"

Dominee Visser had been in another part of the house when I arrived. He entered the room and welcomed me to his home. When he saw the gun in my belt, I pulled my sweater down over it.

"Nine millimeter?" he asked.

"Yep," I answered.

"It's the best the Germans ever made. Had supper yet?"

I told him I hadn't. He called out to his wife to prepare some food for their new guest.

"Jim will show you where to wash. When you come down, we'll have tea while you eat. I want to know more about you and what you have been doing since Ternaard."

When I finished washing, we went down to the kitchen. I met

278

the minister's wife. She was a matronly blond woman, tastefully dressed in a pale green dress.

"Please sit here," she said, smiling, and placed me at the head of the table in the place usually reserved for the Dominee.

The meal was delicious. It consisted of the usual fare of boiled potatoes, cabbage, bread and tea. Near the end of the meal the Dominee joined us and I told him of my experiences. I told him of building the hiding place, being captured again by the Germans, the *razzia* in Holwerd and Ternaard, and about the Grune Polizei and his big dog. I talked about instructing the use of the weapons and getting weapons from the air. Jim asked about Greta, but I eluded the question. I also gave Dominee de Boer's greetings to Jim.

"Then you know Dominee de Boer also?" the pastor asked.

"Yes, very well. Jim and I both do. He is one of the finest men I have ever known."

I explained the feeling of God's spirit when we prayed and how it almost overwhelmed me.

Dominee Visser looked at me and was intently interested in what I was saying. "Hmm," he said thoughtfully. "I have heard that about him many times before. Strange."

When supper was over we excused ourselves and went upstairs. We shared the only bed. I dropped off to sleep at once.

The entire household was awake when I awoke in the morning. I got out of bed, opened my suitcase, and got my toiletries so that I could wash and shave. Then, dressed in clean clothes, I stuck my Luger in my belt and pulled the sweater over it. Downstairs, I walked into a kitchen full of men. It surprised me and I made a hasty retreat for the stairs. The Dominee called out, "Jan, Jan Veen! It's all right. You are welcome to join us."

I went back to the kitchen. Jim was sitting in a chair in the corner. He waved to me to sit in the chair beside him.

The Dominee put his hand on my arm. "Jan Veen," he said.

All six men shook my hand, but the one who really shook it vigorously was a man I had taught to use a Sten gun in the barn at Paul's farm.

"I will explain to Jan if none of you gentlemen have any objections. These gentlemen are the leaders of their groups in our village. Tomorrow morning, before sunrise, the NBS is going to attack the Germans. We are going to come out in the open, armed, and storm the prison where the Germans are billeted. We will either take them prisoner, or, if they resist, we will shoot to kill. We intend to free Dokkum and hold it till the Canadians arrive Saturday or Sunday. Since this is the only place where we can meet safely, you are welcome to sit in on the meeting. But I doubt if you will understand us."

One of the men who obviously was carrying a gun under his coat spoke to me. "I see you are carrying a weapon. Are you going to join us tomorrow?"

"It will be an honor. I want to be part of the liberation!"

"Good, good," he said. Then, looking at the others, he said, "We'll put him with Jan's group. He speaks some English."

The group continued to speak Frisian and I couldn't understand them. I poured a cup of tea and sat down in the corner of the room with Jim.

"Are you really going to volunteer to fight the Germans?"

"Sure," I replied.

"You're nuts. Here we are just a day or so away from being liberated and you're sticking your neck out on the last day. Suppose you get killed. All your efforts have been for nothing."

"Jim, I haven't been thinking about anything else since I was shot down. I'm not going to take any unnecessary chances. I just want to give them a hand. They've been giving me a hand for eight months."

When the meeting broke up, the men left singly at three- or four-minute intervals. When they were gone, we went out into the foyer and joined the Dominee, who was saying goodbye to the last of them. He closed the door.

"I hope they remember me in the morning," I said.

"Don't worry, I know their plans. You will be with them."

I spent the day with Jim, who finally stopped being negative about my going with the Dutchmen. I went into more detail about all that had happened since I last saw him. His particular interest seemed to be in my relationship with Greta, but I gave him no satisfaction except to tell him she was married and lived in Suameer. I told him of my escapades in Bridaard and his ears perked up at the mention of Karen.

"That's the only trouble staying here with the Dominee all this time. No ladies, no sex, no nothing — not even a kiss. The first chance I get, I'm gonna find a girl and keep her in bed for a month. I might even need two of 'em."

I laughed. "It was your choice, you know." I changed the subject.

"I wonder what happened to George and Niko. George is probably dead, but I can't understand why Niko never came back. I don't care about the watch, but I'd just like to know he's okay."

"I think he's with another group. If he's south of here, he's liberated by now," Jim said.

"One thing's for sure, Jim. I'm sure as hell glad I didn't stay in hiding like you. I met some wonderful people, did some interesting things, and I'm just as alive as you are."

He scowled at me. "Don't rub it in, you lucky bastard."

I probably shouldn't have lorded it over him but I couldn't help it. He wouldn't admit he should have stayed in Ternaard.

After supper a stranger came to the house and spoke to the Dominee in Frisian. I was in the kitchen and heard their conversation. I couldn't grasp all of it but got the drift of it.

The Dominee came into the kitchen, accompanied by the middle-aged man. "Jan, meet Jan," he said. "Jan would like for you to help him. You will be with him tomorrow anyway."

"Should I go?" I asked.

"Of course, he is one of my best friends. He has a problem and I think you can help him."

"What's the problem?"

"I think you had better let him tell you. It has to do with a big machine gun. We probably won't see you before tomorrow night. Don't worry about your personal things."

I went upstairs and got my two spare clips of ammunition. I put on my hat and coat. Downstairs, Jim said, "Take care of yourself," and shook hands with me.

Jan and I walked on the darkened street past the Dominee's. At the main street a bridge crossed the canal that ran beside it. Many bridges crossed the canal, some of them drawbridges. We passed the *magistraat* (city hall) and crossed a canal to the other side. Two blocks further, we came to a house which was one of many abutting each other. Jan removed a key from his pocket and opened the door. I closed the door behind us as Jan turned on a small, weak flashlight. We walked down a dark hall to the back of the house then went outside. There was a shed in back and he knocked. When the door opened we entered, and inside somebody lit a candle. There was a workbench in the middle of the dirt floor, with a .50-caliber machine gun lying on it. The pair of Dutchmen standing beside it looked at me in despair. It appeared they had tried to field-strip the weapon and couldn't get it back together again.

I laughed aloud when I saw the parts on the workbench.

"Right up my alley!" I said and went to work.

I finished field stripping the weapon. The Dutchmen frowned as I further disassembled it. I laid the pieces out in an orderly fashion. Field stripping this gun had been a part of my daily life since I went to gunnery school. It felt good to get hold of it once more. I checked the parts and put the weapon together, explaining where each part went and what it was for. Then I pulled the bolt back and released it. I depressed the trigger and heard the familiar click as the firing pin released.

"Do you have any ammunition?" I asked.

Jan took a candle to the corner of the room. There, in some make-shift boxes, were at least a thousand rounds of .50-caliber ammo. It included an assortment of lead, armor-piercing, and tracer bullets. The ammo belts were crudely put together and the ammo wasn't evenly placed in the metal links. The gun would have jammed if they had tried to fire it that way. I rethreaded some of the rounds, placed them in the receiver, and closed it. I pulled the bolt back twice, placing a round in the firing chamber to show how it was done. All I had to do was depress the firing mechanism and the gun would have fired. I lifted the cover of the receiver, pulled the bolt back twice to unload it, and removed the ammo belt. The .50-caliber that had been in the chamber went flying across the room and fell harmlessly.

"There, now you've got a good machine gun!" I said.

The Dutchmen had welded some pipe together and made a make-shift tripod to hold the weapon while firing it. It would be clumsy, but it was sturdy and adequate to do the job.

"Can a man hold the gun in his hands and shoot it?" Jan asked.

"No, no!" I said. "It has too much recoil and would be dangerous and not accurate. All you would shoot is the air. It must be on a solid mount like this tripod. Fire short bursts of eight or ten rounds at a time, then you will hit what you are aiming at. It is a powerful weapon and will do a lot of damage. When did you get the gun?"

"Two years ago from an Amerikaans Bommenwerper Flying Fortress shot down near Zwolle. We got one gun from each side. We got the bullets a little at a time, from Amerikaan Jagers [fighter planes], inside the wings. The Germans don't always look good enough in the wings when they strip them. We're taking the gun to Groningen. Our fight starts tomorrow also."

We talked some more and the men thanked me. They took the gun and the tripod out the door and disappeared in the darkness.

"Others will come back for the ammunition later on," Jan said. "I will personally see the bullets are belted so they won't jam in the gun. Thank you for repairing it."

We went back the same way we came. Once on the streets, we backtracked, crossing the canal once more and then down the road beside it. There were several shops, closed for many years, and off to the left, on one of the small streets, I saw the city *waag huis* (weigh house) in the middle of the square. It was the hub of activity in better times when the farmers brought their cheese to be weighed officially before sending them to market. I had seen pictures of former days when the round balls of Edam cheeses were piled high on pallets around the floor. We continued along the canal to some houses. We passed by several before Jan went into the yard of one of the larger homes. We went around to the rear and he opened the door.

There were three women and a man at the kitchen table, drinking tea. Six rifles were neatly lined along the wall.

"Jan Veen, *Amerikaaner!*" Jan shouted by way of introduction.

I shook hands with all of them.

"Jan knew how to fix the machine gun easily. Any of us can use it now!" He looked at me and nudged me with his elbow. "It's right up my alley, huh, Jan?" He completely slaughtered the words as he uttered them in English. I laughed out loud then helped him until he said the words right. They were really nice people.

We didn't go to bed. I went to sleep on a couch in the corner of an adjoining room. More people came to the house, drank tea, and talked about the liberation that was so soon to come. It was difficult to celebrate something that had not yet happened.

This day to these good Dutch people of Dokkum would end five long years of Nazi occupation. Four of them were years of tyranny and oppression at the hands of the heinous Nazi beasts. It was no wonder they talked all night. My dreams of seeing that first Canadian tank or armored vehicle coming down the road, with the knowledge they were my neighbors from north of the United States, were indescribable. What a sight it would be . . .

At 4:00 A.M. Jan shook my shoulder. I was wide awake in an instant. I slid into my shoes. Fifteen armed men carrying Sten guns or rifles slung over their shoulders were drinking tea. The women were busy making sandwiches. When I stepped into the kitchen, a cup of tea and a sandwich were shoved into my hand.

"Eat it, boy," Jan said, "it might be the last you'll get." I ate the sandwich even though I really didn't want it.

One of the women pinned a white armband on my coat. The black letters "N.B.S." had been professionally printed on a press. They were all wearing one. Another woman pinned a small piece of orange ribbon, tied in a bow on the bottom of the armband. She said, *"Oranje Boven!* (Orange above!)," the Dutch national color.

I finished my tea, loaded my Luger, and put it on safety. Jan smiled. "You'll need a little more than that pop-gun."

He reached behind the door and gave me a Sten gun with three extra clips of ammunition.

"These are yours," he said. "You will need this ammunition and maybe more for the job you have to do."

The move on the Germans was timed to the second. At exactly 4:20 we left the house and stayed in a group with our weapons ready. We crossed the canal and walked down a side street as quietly as possible. At the corner of the canal and another side street, the group stopped. Jan came back to me.

"Jan," he said, "this is your post. You will be our lookout. We need a good marksman in this position. There is a password we must use to pass this position. It is 'Bernhard.' Part of our master plan is to have a sentry posted here, so all members in the NBS know you are here after half past four. If you see a German in uniform, or anybody suspicious, shoot first and ask questions later. Remember, we are all wearing armbands. The NBS on it is our uniform. If they are not wearing one, shoot first or capture them. These are direct orders."

I nodded my head in the affirmative. "Yes, sir," I said.

"Remember . . . Bernhard!" He patted me on the shoulder and the entire group continued down the side street.

In the dim light, I made out the shapes of the buildings lining the canal. I stood with my back against a corner building where I couldn't be seen.

What went on that morning in the little town of Dokkum would be talked about by the Frisians for many years.

The Germans, expecting to fight the Canadians when they were within marching distance of the town, canceled all patrols and recreation. The German *kommandant* ordered his men to get a last good night's sleep. Their guns would be blazing the next day to teach those Canadian soldiers how terrible the fury of an enraged German soldier can be. As a result, they were sound asleep at 4:30. A soldier was on guard inside the unlocked door.

The Dutch patriots assembled quietly and, on a given order, entered through the unlocked door which they thought they would have to break in. They so completely surprised the guard he was unable to sound the alarm. The Dutchmen, by now 300 strong, went into the enemy stronghold and captured the entire German garrison, going about the job very quietly. They stripped and disarmed the enemy, then gave them back their uniform pants and nothing else. The Germans were locked in the cells they used as a dormitory. The few who awakened exchanged shots with their captors. Two Dutchmen and fifteen of the enemy were killed.

After I had been left alone at my post, I watched for a long time before I saw anybody. When I did, it was two German Grune Polizei pushing their bicycles. They were unaware of what was taking place and were headed for the prison.

I pulled back the bolt on the Sten and said, in my own Yankee language, "Halt!"

They stopped immediately.

"Put down your guns!" I shouted in English.

They dropped their rifles. One of them said in very good English, "Canadian?"

"Neen," I said, *"Ik ben een Nederlander!* (No, I am a Dutchman!)."

The German looked at me in disbelief. He said something to his partner. Both of them bent over as if to pick up their guns. I pushed the safety off the Sten and pulled the trigger. The little weapon spewed out ten quick shots before I could release it. I aimed to their left and into the canal where the bullets ricocheted off the water and chewed up the cement sides of the canal wall. One of the soldiers straightened up with a look of disbelief in his eyes. The other went for his rifle. I had no choice, so I shot him, knocking his legs from under him as he screamed to the top of his lungs, blood spewing from his leg.

"The next time I shoot to kill!" I yelled in English. "Now put your hands over your heads *right now!*"

They both reached for the sky. The wounded German was writhing in pain but I offered no assistance. I made the other one walk to the wall of the building with his hands on top of his head and stand where

I could watch him. Then I went back to the intersection to watch. Within seconds, six or seven of Jan's men came running with their guns ready. Once they saw the wounded German, they searched him, took all their bicycles and rifles, and marched the healthy one to the prison to join his comrades. Moments later two Germans, under guard, put the wounded German on a stretcher. I went to him.

"I am an American," I said.

"*Amerikaaner?*" he asked, looking at me in disbelief. Then he turned his head as they carried him away. He'd wonder about the *Amerikaaner* for a long time.

Jan came running up, looking relieved when he saw me. "I heard somebody got shot. What happened? Who was it?"

"I had to shoot a German Grune Polizei," I said.

"Good for you. Keep your eyes open, we're still not clear."

"Good going!" one of the men said as they departed.

The rest of my guard duty was uneventful.

Plans had been made months in advance regarding the local citizens. Anybody who wanted to stay in the safety of the town proper was to be there no later than 10:00 A.M. The series of canals flowing through and around the village formed an excellent defense. The drawbridges over the canals were raised. The canals became a moat and would have to be bridged to storm our defenses. It was a small fortress at best. Any of the local citizens not in town on time were unable to enter. Members of the underground were stationed around the perimeter. If the Germans attacked, they would run into a hornet's nest of small arms.

Soon after my encounter with the Germans, a considerable amount of small-arms fire came from the direction of the prison. I assumed they were still securing the place.

The streets began to fill with people — men, women, boys, girls, old and young alike — all of them reveling, happy, and very noisy. For the first time, they were free to walk the streets fearlessly. Everybody except the very young wore the armband. It was a wonderful sight.

Dokkum was free! Free before daylight on April 14, 1945!

Some of the people stopped at the place where I shot the German soldier and looked at the pool of drying blood on the walk. They tried to talk to me but spoke in Frisian and I couldn't understand.

At 10:00, Jan came by and relieved me. We went to a small coffee shop by the *waag huis* (weigh house). Several armed men and women filled the place. It was impossible to hear each other. I took a sandwich and a cup of tea and sat down.

"You did a good job. Everybody's talking about the American pilot who shot the German," Jan said.

He told me what happened inside the prison and how it was captured. They had overcrowded the prison since many Dutch collaborators were thrown in with the German troops. He explained how the town had become a fortress surrounded by a moat. He wanted me to take a position near the north main road into town and stay there until the Canadians came.

We finished our sandwiches and tea. We walked on the road beside the canal until we were opposite a huge windmill just across the canal. The drawbridge was up with slit-trenches on each side of the road, no doubt dug by slave labor.

I jumped down into it. It was only about three feet deep and perhaps fifty feet wide. Jan gave me two extra clips of ammunition for the Sten and left, saying he would be back to check on me later. In a few minutes, a stranger came by and gave me two extra boxes of ammo. I was loaded for bear!

The trench started filling with members of the Resistance. They brought blankets, food, and some things to help pass the time while we awaited our emancipators. Several women made an appearance, bringing food, tea, and tobacco. At supper time, we were served a hot meal while manning our defenses. We even had napkins and silverware. What a hell of a way to fight a war!

Okay, Dokkum is secure. Come on, you Canadians! I thought.

Later, more Dutchmen took up positions in the trench, making them crowded. The group leaders thought if trouble came it would come at night. The man next to me had taken part in the raid on the prison. He laughed.

"The Germans," he said, "were surprised to wake up looking down the barrel of an Enfield. Some of the bad Dutch collaborators were earmarked for this day and their fates had been sealed for a long time. We rounded up and executed the few we found before an NBS firing squad in the prison yard."

This explained the shooting I had heard after the prison was taken. They were still looking for others who were hiding.

"Today," he said, "justice has been served. Dutchmen who helped the Germans and caused much of our suffering are still lying inside the prison walls where they fell, their epitaphs written in their own blood in which they are lying."

287

I asked him about the girls who "serviced" the enemy troops.

"The women and young girls are going to be dealt with later after the Canadians come. The price they pay has been set but is not as rash as the firing squad. They will live amid their peers with their heads shorn of hair so everybody knows of their sin."

Occasionally, strangers would walk to the bridge from the other side of the canal to call out they had seen no Germans.

"They have all gone home!" they cried.

Later, there was considerable gunfire in the distance from across the canal. Those who only moments before proclaimed the Germans had run were now scurrying to the ditches and fields to take cover, for they were unarmed. We had no way of knowing from where the shooting was coming. Finally, as fast as it began, it stopped and all was quiet.

After the hot supper, there was no activity from the other side of the canal. The people left the streets. The Dutchman next to me put his finger up to his lips, signaling quiet. At the same time, we hunched low in the trench. In the distance we heard an engine misfiring and running poorly. It got louder.

The main road that crossed the canal disappeared into a curve about 500 meters beyond the bridge. We could hear the squeaky sound of an armored vehicle approaching the curve. It sounded as if it had water in its gasoline. When the armored car came into view, it stopped halfway to the bridge, its turret swinging back and forth, looking for a target. Then all hell broke loose.

From the other side of the canal, two bazookas fired at the same time. Small-arms fire, both automatic and rifle fire, peppered the vehicle. Small patches of paint turning to dust puffed into the air with each hit. It turned around and retreated in the direction from which it had come. It was probably the only time the Dutchmen ever fired a bazooka. Unfortunately, one shot caromed off the side of the turret and exploded several feet on the other side as the other shot skimmed on the back of it, exploding harmlessly just beyond the first. Neither shot did any damage. It was fully a half hour before the dust kicked up by the action settled, and by then dusk was settling in.

The armored car never left the area. During the night we heard the unmistakable sound of its clanking motor. I don't believe it had any ammunition, for it hadn't fired the cannon. I was fearful they would fire mortars or big guns at us, but they never put in another appearance. For that we thanked God.

288

We took turns leaving the trench long enough to relieve ourselves. As the evening light faded, there was no news of the Canadians except to say there were now two columns, one headed for Leeuwarden and the other in our direction. They had clear sailing, thanks to the efforts of the NBS. The Canadians were making certain the areas they left were secure before proceeding.

In the darkness we stayed in the positions to which we had been assigned, watching, ever alert. Twice during the night, the Germans started the motors on their armored vehicles and moved to different areas. There were two of them now in different locations. They were both operating in our end of the village.

The night was long. We tried to take turns sleeping but couldn't. I guess we were all excited over the importance of the hour, realizing history was being made. We smoked and talked quietly and listened and smoked some more. The women brought tea and sandwiches and provided us with tobacco when we needed it. We were careful when lighting cigarettes to shade the match.

When the sun came up, it brought with it the dawn of the Dutch people's first full day of freedom, and mine too. It was Sunday, April 15, 1945. I had been in Holland eight months exactly.

We were fortunate to have a pair of fieldglasses belonging to one of the men who willingly shared them. They reached out a goodly distance so we could watch the other side of the canal. Reports began to filter in that Drachten had been liberated the day before. Bergum, about twenty-five kilometers from Dokkum, was freed a little later on in the day. Greta was now free. I thanked God!

Further word came that the Canadians had stopped just short of Bergum for the night and were probably on their way to Dokkum. More information filtered through that we were to look for them before noon. The NBS was fighting in Groningen and was having a real battle with the Germans. However, more Canadians were on the outskirts of the city and the battle would be short-lived. The casualties were light on both sides and enormous numbers of the Boche were being taken. The Germans in Leeuwarden had surrendered without any assistance from the Canadians. I was proud of the fact that some of the people to whom I had taught weapons were a part of the Leeuwarden group.

I was relieved in the early morning long enough to take a leak and wash my hands and face. When I got back to my position, the women brought tea, oatmeal, and milk. It hit the spot.

The morning dragged on without further word.

Just before noon, an automobile full of men came bearing down on the open bridge from the other side of the canal. They stopped at the water's edge, jumped out, and started shooting at our defensive positions with their Schmeissers. Two of them wore German uniforms. The action took us by surprise. My Sten was the first to return the fire, and I saw one of the uniformed men fall. It was as if it was a signal to start shooting, for everybody opened up on them. After the dust cleared, two of the intruders lay dead and the rest were so stunned and badly wounded they lay beside the vehicle and threw their weapons aside, trying to hold their hands in the air to surrender. Much of their gunfire was directed at our trench, and bullets careened around us over our heads. Nobody was hit. I fired three clips from the little Sten and it was hot to the touch. I know I hit the man in uniform. The car was full of bullet holes.

It was over in less than thirty seconds. We watched as the people cleaned up the mess. They took the wounded and the captives to the side of the road and made them lie face down. The dead were dragged by their heels and thrown into the ditch beside the road. Later the bridge was lowered and the car brought into town. The prisoners and wounded were carried to the prison.

The Dutch had their own special kind of justice to deal out to these traitors, for the people in the car were all in the NSB (Dutch Nazi Party). These particular captured Dutchmen had been members since the start of the war and were well known. All of them, long wanted by the NBS, wouldn't survive for long; only their death would satisfy the NBS. Even their own families hated and detested many of them.

We reloaded our weapons with fresh clips, then reloaded the clips with fresh ammunition. We watched the action as the Dutch patriots shoved the car across the bridge and down a side street next to the *magistraat*. The drawbridge was raised again and things settled down.

At noon we took turns going to the toilet and getting something to eat and drink. I wondered what Jim was doing through all this. I hoped he was okay.

I walked to the *magistraat* and looked at the NSB car. There were more than 300 bullet holes in it. I wondered how many of them were mine. Articles of clothing lay inside and many papers were strewn about. Several boxes of ammunition lay on the back seat. Some of the bullets had spilled onto the floorboards.

I went back to the trench and the afternoon dragged. Word kept coming to us on the progress of the Canadians. It seemed they had bogged down just south of Dokkum, somewhere in the vicinity of Damwoude, a distance of five kilometers. They were fighting some stubborn Germans but it didn't last long and they were soon headed northward again.

Groningen had fallen, with the Dutch and Canadians winning a long, hard-fought battle. Some good Dutchmen and a few good Canadians had given their lives for freedom.

Again, time dragged on. At 2:00, 3:00, and 4:00 the sound of powerful gasoline engines came to our ears. A lot of engines. Next came the cheerful screaming from the hundreds of people welcoming their benefactors. The cheering could not have been louder if Babe Ruth had hit his fourth home run of the day in Yankee Stadium!

None of the men moved to go and greet the Canadians, for they didn't want to desert their post. I couldn't stand it anymore. I told the man next to me I had to meet my countrymen. I slung the Sten over my shoulder and got out of the trench.

A woman ran up to me and put a package of Avalon cigarettes in my hand. "From America for an American!" She disappeared immediately among the people headed for the *magistraat,* where the Canadian vehicles were assembling. I didn't even get a chance to thank her. I stopped in my tracks, lit one of the cigarettes, and put the pack in my pocket. It was delicious.

I crossed the embankment to another road and then to the center of town. The sounds from the engines had stopped but the cheering had not. It was louder than ever. When I got on the street beside the canal, I saw the armored vehicles in front of the *magistraat* and several Canadian uniforms milling among the people. There were fifteen or more Canadian trucks beside the canal. What a sight! What a beautiful, wonderful sight!

I broke into a run.

Almost rudely, I pushed my way through the throngs. It took five minutes before I could get to the nearest half-track mounting a .75mm cannon. A lone soldier was sitting in the driver's seat. I pulled myself up on the vehicle and he promptly pushed me off it, the same as he did everybody else.

"Hey!" I yelled as loudly as I could. "I'm an American!"

"You are?" he replied. "Well, get your ass up here, Yank!"

I climbed into the front seat beside him.

"How in hell long you been here, Yank?" he yelled.

"Eight months to the day."

He called to a soldier in back of the vehicle to join us.

"What'dya want, Johnston?" he asked.

"Go tell the major we got another bloody Yank pilot here!"

Johnston turned back to me. He had a handlebar mustache, a broad grin on his face, and eyes like Santa Claus.

"I'm Corporal Johnston, with a 'T'," he said. His beret sat at a jaunty angle. He reached under the seat and handed me a Hershey bar filled with almonds. Then he pulled out a carton of Camel cigarettes.

"Keep 'em, we got plenty."

I bit into the Hershey bar just as the major, the CO of the outfit, pulled himself onto the vehicle effortlessly. He sat in the back beside the gun. I started to stand but he pushed me back into the seat.

"We don't go on formalities here," he said, taking a small notebook and pencil from his tunic pocket.

"Can I have your name, rank, and serial number?"

"Harry A. Clark, staff sergeant, 19000426, sir."

He started to write the information in his notebook.

"Oh hell, Sergeant, write it down for me if you will." He handed the notebook and pencil to me.

"Anything else you want to know, Major?" I asked.

"Better write down the day you were shot down and your unit back in England."

When I finished, I handed him the pencil and notebook.

He thanked me. "We're going to billet here for the night. I'd suggest you stay with us from now on. Why don't you say all your goodbyes to your Dutch friends and report back to Corporal Johnston in the morning?"

He turned to Johnston. "The sergeant's your responsibility. He'll ride with you till we decide what to do with him."

He got down off the half-track. "Oh yes, Johnston. For God's sake get him something decent to wear. He doesn't look at all military in that get-up!" He walked away and shouted back to him. "I think he might do with a haircut too."

"There's another American in Dokkum," I told the corporal. "His name is Jim Moulton but I haven't seen him for a couple of days. I know where he's staying, though."

"Good, bring him with you in the morning when you return."

"Boy, you don't know how good it is to see you guys," I said. I had tears in my eyes as big as horse turds. The lump in my throat and the emotions I felt building inside made it difficult to speak.

"I'm free at last!" I said. "It's all over and I'll be going home. I can't believe it."

Corporal Johnston looked at me and said with much empathy in his voice, "Oh yes, I do, Yank. We've picked up a lot of you guys on our way up here. Especially in France. We had about twenty a couple of days ago in Meppel. You've been with the underground longer than anybody we've picked up as far as I know. But I know how you feel, buddy."

We sat there for another thirty minutes or so until the order came down to disburse the vehicles. We talked about the war and what had happened over the last eight months. He admired my Luger, gave me another box of ammunition for my Sten, and stuck a full box of Hersheys and the carton of cigarettes under my arm as I got down off the half-track.

"We'll be camping close to town and it'll be easy to find us in the morning. Generally, we loaf at night. If you want to come on back, I'll find a place for you to bunk. If not, we usually pull out about eight. You oughta get here early so we can feed you and get you in a uniform like the ol' man wants. Spread some of those cigarettes and candy around. We got plenty, so don't sweat us running out. See you in the morning, okay?"

The back of the half-track filled with soldiers and he drove off waving his arm.

I walked alone, my gun slung over my shoulder. It seemed impossible there were no longer any of the dreaded German patrols to worry about. The Dominee's house was locked, so I ate a candy bar and waited. Jim and the Dominee returned.

"Where have you been?" asked Jim.

I told him where I had been for the past two days.

"I couldn't even get close to the Canadians, they kept pushing me back," he said.

"Didn't you tell them you were an American?"

"No, I couldn't find an officer to report to. I guess they were in the city hall and nobody could get to them."

"I reported to them and have told them about you. We're going to meet them about seven in the morning."

"Where are they going?" Jim asked.

"To finish their drive to the North Sea, according to Corporal Johnston. Once they've done that, Holland will be a pocket and all the

Germans within its perimeter will be surrounded."

"You mean you're going to fight with the Germans again?"

"No, Jim, I'm going to fight against the Germans. And I'll do it every damned chance I get, okay?" I was provoked. "I don't think there's very much fight left in them, do you?"

"I don't know if I want to report to the Canadians yet. I think I'll catch up to them later, all in one piece."

"Don't be stupid, Jim. Nothing can happen now. Hell, the Canadians' vehicles are armored and they have bullet-proof vests to wear. Besides, Jim, you gotta report to them. Remember? 'Report to the first Allied troops we come in contact with after we're shot down.' These people are it!"

"Fuck the orders, it's my ass and I'm looking out for it! It'll be my decision and mine alone when I report."

With that, he went upstairs, leaving me alone at the kitchen table. I followed him upstairs. He wasn't in the bedroom but my suitcase was. I picked it up, went back downstairs, and left the house. I walked to Jan's house, where several people were celebrating. They were drinking beer and having a wonderful time. They welcomed me and after I drank two beers, I was half drunk.

The liberation of Dokkum was now complete. Drawbridges were lowered and traffic moved freely in and out of town. Only the Canadians had motor vehicles and the people brought their bicycles out of hiding and rode them without danger from the Boche.

The lives lost were but a drop in the bucket to the sacrifices the NBS was prepared to make. It was the very best of days. We were all happier than we could ever remember. Jan invited me to stay for the night. He gave me a room upstairs to sleep in. After it got dark, I went to my room, shaved, and washed in cold water. I found my last clean pair of underwear and put them on. After I pulled back the covers on the bed and lay down, somebody knocked at the door. A feminine voice, one I recognized, came from outside the door. I opened it for Karen.

"I told you I would come as soon as you were liberated," she said. "I didn't have any trouble finding you."

I was standing there in my underwear. Although the room was quite dark, I felt embarrassed. I started to put my pants on, but Karen took my arm.

"I'm glad you were going to bed. I'd hate to spend the evening

294

talking to strangers. We can be close and talk about the future. We've never been able to do it before."

"What do you want to talk about?"

"Well," she said, "when I'll see you next."

"Some day I'll come back to Holland and see you."

She laid down beside me. "How soon?" she asked.

"After I've gone back to America and see how things are."

"Well, how long . . . one, two, five, ten years?"

"I really don't know," I said. "But some day."

The sun was shining when I got out of bed. I dressed quickly and took one of the maps out of my escape kit and gave it to her. "Something to remember me by," I said, giving her a final lingering kiss. She had a serious look on her face.

"Jan Veen, I love you. Now don't go and get yourself killed!"

I bounded down the steps into the bright sunlight.

There were already a lot of people on the streets. I had no idea what time it was, but I thought it had to be around 7:00. The taste of freedom was sweet on the lips of the Dutch people. I crossed over the bridge where I had stood guard. The Canadians were just beyond the bend in the road, and within a few minutes I found Corporal Johnston.

I sat down to a breakfast of Spam and eggs. After I downed a plateful I got sick to my stomach and threw up in back of the half-track. I went back and ate some more and promptly threw up again. After the third time, I decided I wasn't used to the rich food and watched as Corporal Johnston and some of his pals had a good time at my expense, laughing at me. He was in hysterics, not because the food made me ill — "But because of yer bloody determination to eat the crap!" he said.

He took me to the medical sergeant, who told me to eat bland foods such as milk, eggs, and very little meat. Oatmeal with milk and sugar stayed down fine, as did toast and real butter. The hot coffee was scrumptious.

As I was eating, a sergeant came by and asked me my clothing sizes. In a few minutes he came back with some clothes.

"Here's underwear and socks. Sorry but I got no shoes that will fit you. Here's a couple a' shirts, some britches, and a tunic. Sorry, mate, but yer not a Dragoon so I can't issue you a beret. Best you wear a helmet anyway. It'll keep yer ruddy head from gettin' shot off!" He put the clothes on the mess table.

"Get 'em on, Yank!" shouted Corporal Johnston. "We're gonna shove off in a couple a' minutes."

I got out of the civilian clothes on the spot. I put on the issued clothing and put my holstered Luger on my belt. The ammo clips fit in a pocket. For the first time I didn't have to worry about shooting myself in the balls.

I slung the Sten over my shoulder and threw my civvies in the field. The only thing I kept was the armband on my sleeve, putting it in my pocket. I went to the half-track, where strong arms pulled me aboard. The gunnery sergeant rode in front with Corporal Johnston. Moments later, we were on our way, heading west out of Dokkum to hunt Germans. What a switch.

We were on the same road Sjoukje and I had ridden into Dokkum a few nights ago. We were headed in the direction of Bridaard-on-Kanaal. As we rode along in the half-track, one of the men spoke.

"Hey, Yank, I hear you been here almost a year, huh?"

"Yeah, over eight months now," I replied.

"I'm Mike. This here's Charley, that's Tommy, Terrance, Terry to you, Larry, Jody and that little fellow over there is Bobby." He pointed to each one as he called out their names. Bobby was at least 6'4 and weighed 225 pounds.

"I'm Harry," I said.

"We want no aliases around here!" he said. "We know yer a bloody 'Yank' and Yank's yer name in this outfit."

"Okay by me, Mike. You can call me anything you want."

All along the road to Bridaard-on-Kanaal people lined the road on both sides, waving to our convoy of armored vehicles and trucks along with Dutch flags in their hands. They shouted happily to us. The look of freedom showed in their faces and their actions showed their appreciation. We moved along at twenty-five to thirty miles an hour, then pulled into Bridaard. Another group of Canadians, of which I was not aware, was waging a battle with some Germans. Bullets whined through the air and 200 or so German troops stood in the middle of the road with their weapons lying on the side of it. Some of the Kraut troops were holed up in a farmhouse close to the edge of town, and the Canadians were lobbing .35mm cannon fire at it. The thatched roof caught on fire and the house started blazing from one end to the other before they came out with their hands over their heads. The Canadians marched them to where we were.

Once our convoy stopped moving and we observed the surrender of the farmhouse, we got off the vehicles. There were about twelve or fifteen young, attractive women in German uniforms who had been captured and were standing in the road. One of the Dutchmen went to the major and asked permission to separate the women from the soldiers. I followed along as the men took the women behind a barn and questioned each girl. They were Dutch girls who "serviced" the German troops in return for humane treatment and above-average living standards. These women, because of their status, had treated the regular population with cruelty and were detested as much as the Germans.

The girls were stripped naked then had their hair sheared off on the spot. The Dutchmen were not too careful with scissors and all of them were cut on their scalps.

One of them, a particularly beautiful girl, said she was in love with one of the Germans and they were going to be married. The women, heads shorn and naked — and lucky, in my judgement, to be alive — were marched past the entire column of German soldiers naked, then disappeared into the crowd of townspeople where the women took over. They would be punished and further embarrassed for many days. I never found out their fate.

As I stood there and watched, a single shot was fired from in back of the barn. I joined several Canadians running in the direction of the gunshot. Two Dutchmen came from the back of the barn, one of them sticking a .45 automatic in his belt. The one who wanted to marry the German didn't have to worry anymore. She lay on the ground naked, her head shorn of hair and a bullet hole in her forehead. The back of her head had disappeared where the bullet came out. Her body was jerking violently in death throes.

Disarmed, the Germans were marched back to Dokkum, guarded by the NBS. There, they joined their comrades and overcrowded the prison so much they were billeted outside in the prison courtyard.

I saw Raol, Loty, and Karen. She must have made a fast trip back, but she stood there with her parents in a crowd of people. We were leaving town when I saw them and they called out my name. I waved to them and threw Karen a kiss. She was crying.

Our convoy reversed itself, and we headed back toward Dokkum again. We took a different route to the north of town, using back roads and passing through small villages on the way. Again, people lined the roads, waving their flags, shouting and crying with happiness. In the villages, each of the windows flew the familiar red, white, and blue

Dutch flag. Where there were flagpoles, the tri-colors waved proudly in the morning breeze.

It was a joyous time. We passed through Rinsumageest, then north to Raard and Bornwird. We headed east again and skirted the northern boundary of Dokkum and went through Aalzum, Oostrum, Ee, and Engwierum, finally arriving at Dokkumer Nieuwezijlen. The NBS told of the German barges tied to the side of the canal. They were painted white with red crosses on the side of the hulls, indicating they were hospital barges, to prevent them from being fired upon by aircraft. The barges, according to the NBS, were loaded with German contraband. A mile from their location, we stopped and proceeded on foot, carrying our weapons. The Canadians also carried Bren guns and Browning automatic weapons as well as .30-caliber machine guns and bazookas.

When we came upon the barges, some 300 yards distant, the Germans opened fire with automatic weapons. The major called for the half-tracks with their .75mm cannon. At the same time that the .75s lobbed about ten shells into the midst of the barges, we all opened up with our own small-arms fire. There were only two direct hits and one of those was on the closest one to us — but that was enough. The Germans surrendered!

Most of what was on board was contraband. Millions of guilders in Dutch currency were confiscated, as well as beautiful oil paintings and other art objects. A couple of the barges really had wounded aboard and one of these was hit by a .75. The result was a mess. We lost no men, but there were German casualties.

"That's the way the old man wants it!" Mike, the gunnery sergeant said. "We're takin' too fuckin' many prisoners."

We stayed at Dokkumer Nieuwezijlen for the night.

I got a haircut there. Mike said I wasn't nearly as pretty after I got it. "But," he decided, "you look enough like a man now that you have been on the field of honor to wear the beret." Where he got it, I don't know, but it fit me. I wore it while I was with the Dragoons — and proudly too, I might add. To hell with the helmet!

We were surprised the next morning to find that none of the barges sank. Evidently, all our hits were above the water line. They were eventually towed to Dokkum with the Germans still on board. There, the Germans were placed in the prison, with the others really overcrowding it. The barges, their cargo still intact, were tied up in the town for a long time after the war was over. Dutch officials sorted out their valuable contents.

The "old man" got word there was a German column advancing along the North Sea road. It was the same road that went to Paesens, Ternaard, and Holwerd. The column was further to the east, somewhere near Eenrum. Later, rumor had it, the Germans were planning a surprise attack to recapture Leeuwarden. We headed north, traveling through Ezumazijl, Anjum, around the town of Lauwersmeer, and to the town of Lauwersoog. As before, the townspeople lined the roads in the villages. The word from the NBS was that the convoy was eight miles east and advancing rapidly.

We left Lauwersoog and backtracked four kilometers to an area north of Lauwersmeer. There was a farmhouse on the bend of the road with a haystack in the field close to the house. Johnston wheeled our half-track behind the haystack and put the nose of the vehicle into it slightly. Quickly, the crew removed just enough hay so that the barrel of the .75mm cleared it. The other armored vehicles and half-tracks moved behind the house and barn into the high brush of the fields where they couldn't be seen from the direction the convoy was coming. The troops who had been riding in the backs of the trucks hid themselves in the bushes or ditches in the fields.

"Hey, Yank, didja ever kill a Kraut?" Mike asked. Before I could reply, he said, "Yer gonna kill one now!"

He handed me the lanyard to the cannon. It was a piece of rope connected to the triggering mechanism of the weapon.

"Now, when I give you the word to pull on the lanyard, give it a good yank, Yank!" He laughed at his own joke.

Charley took a .75mm shell from the ammo box and set it on end. He adjusted the fuse on the business end to less than a tenth of a second delay. Terry opened the breech of the gun and Charley slammed the shell into the chamber. He set the safety on the weapon, took three more rounds of ammo, and set the fuses.

Quietly, then, we waited. There were no more progress reports coming in over the radio. We smoked a cigarette, keeping our eyes peeled on the bend in the road. Half an hour later, we heard the first distant whine of a motor. The sound grew louder and I recognized it as the sound the German armored car had made in Dokkum. I told Mike about it and he relayed the information by radio to the major. At last, perhaps a half mile away, we could see the German column moving our way, rounding a far bend.

There were three trucks leading the convoy, then two armored vehicles, followed by several more trucks in the distance. They had to come around a curve in the road, then head straight at our position before turning to the right on the bend in front of us. The dike was off to their right and open fields full of Canadians to the left. Charley told me we would wait until the convoy was in a line and headed straight for us.

"Just before they have to make the turn in front of us, when the trucks are all in a row, we'll blast 'em."

The first three trucks rounded the curve. Then two armored vehicles came into view and lined up with the others.

"Now, Yank!" Mike yelled.

I pulled the lanyard and the .75mm belched its missile toward the convoy. The haystack filled the air with pieces of hay, straw, and dust as the shell disintegrated somewhere beyond. Some of the hay was on fire, falling all around us. The half-track tried to back up from the recoil of the cannon and I'm sure the front wheels were airborne for a moment. I almost lost my grip on the vehicle but managed to hold on. What a noise it made!

"Now, Yank!" Mike yelled again, and I jerked on the lanyard. Once more the .75mm roared, shaking the half-track again.

Our first shell went through the first truck and exploded when it hit the second one. The second shell went through the third truck and both armored vehicles went up in smoke, their crews scrambling to escape. The convoy stopped and some of the trucks in the rear tried to turn around, but it was too late. The Dragoons had them surrounded.

Meanwhile, Corporal Johnston was backing the half-track away from the haystack, which by now was blazing.

After firing only a few rounds, it was all over and the Germans surrendered. Three hundred German troops — either dead, wounded, or captured — were lined up on the road. When the shooting died down, hundreds of Dutchmen began assisting the Canadians with the cleanup. Again there were no Canadian or NBS casualties.

I saw Germans die right before my eyes. I saw them blown to bits, heard their screams and moans. It was a heinous sight, but their finale was of their own choosing. I helped march some German prisoners toward Paesens only a half mile down the road. At least another hundred or so NBSers appeared and relieved us of our prisoners. One of them was mijnheer Visser. All we could do was wave at each other.

We stayed in Kruisweg that night. I had to clean the .75mm cannon. How was I to know that, "He who fires it, cleans it"? Another thing I found out about firing the big gun was that everybody puts their hands over their ears when it's fired, but the man who fires it can only put his hand over one ear. I didn't cover either one, and they were both ringing from the blast. I went after the job of cleaning the cannon good naturedly, and as a result the whole gun crew helped me.

That night, the radioman for the outfit sent a message back to the United States for me. He said it would be transmitted to England then forwarded to the United States by Canadian radio equipment. I sent two messages: one to my mother in California and one to my wife. I doubted if they would ever receive them.

This was my second night with the Dragoons and my supper stayed down. I felt I was on the road to recovery at last.

After I ate and the .75 was clean, I was sitting on the back of the half-track smoking a cigarette, thinking about how I would get home. The crew of the vehicle came over and sat down.

"Yank, you ain't such a bad bugger after all," declared the corporal. "I think the old man's gonna ship you down south tomorrow so we've decided to make a man out of you. When you joined us you were just a mascot, but now you've fired and cleaned our weapon so we decided to make it official!" Several of the Dragoons joined our circle to join in the friendly kidding.

"Yes, sir, we're gonna make you a Royal Canadian Dragoon."

He reached in his tunic and took out a small box from which he removed the silver pin of the Dragoons. He took my beret and placed the pin on it, then put it back on my head. He addressed the group that had gathered.

"We must be gettin' soft," he said jokingly, "makin' a damned Yank a Dragoon. Give that pin back!"

I flinched as he reached for it, but he took my hand instead and shook it. I got the addresses of several of the guys and found that most of them were from the vicinity of Toronto.

The next morning, Jim was eating in the mess tent. He looked funny in civilian clothes. I couldn't figure out why.

"Hi, Jim," I said, shaking his hand. "When did you pull in?"

"Last night. I rode in with one of the Canadians who was on his way here. It was so late when we got in and I didn't know where you were. The OD got me bedded down all okay."

"Well, I'm glad we're together again. We may be sent down south to our own people later today."

"How's it been? I heard you guys have been having all kinds of battles and capturing Germans left and right!"

301

It hadn't seemed tough at all. "This outfit has a hell of a good commander who has his head screwed on right. As a result, we get the job done without too much trouble and a minimum of casualties for his men," I added, really spreading it on. "Yeah, Jim, it's been real tough and just dangerous as hell. It's something to get shot at and hear the bullets whistling by your head two or three times a day. Consider yourself lucky you stayed with Dominee Visser."

"See, I told you so!" he said loudly. "I don't see why you keep sticking your neck out."

Corporal Johnston, sitting near us, was listening to our conversation. I had winked at him before I spoke. As I talked, he squeezed his nose with his fingers and got up from the table so he wouldn't have to spoil my spiel by laughing out loud. The quartermaster got Jim a uniform and brought it to the mess tent.

Reluctantly he put them on. "I don't think we should put on Canadian uniforms. We should wait until we get in American hands before we put on any uniforms at all. Don't you think so?"

"Just put the uniform on, Jim."

Later we were ordered to "saddle up." We boarded the vehicles. Jim rode in the back of a different half-track. I stayed on the weapons carrier.

"Our destination is Groningen," Corporal Johnston yelled over the noise of the vehicle. "We'll billet there for a couple of days to give our guys a chance to catch up." He was speaking of the regular Canadian army, following the wreckie outfit north. "We haven't had a chance to regroup for so damn long we forget we belong to somebody else."

Our route took us through the towns of Vierhuizen, Ulrum, Leens, Wehe den Hoorn, Eenrum, Mensingweer, Obergum, Winsum, Sauwerd, Adorp, and finally, Groningen. Actually, we set up camp closer to the village of Bedum than Groningen itself.

We had a major mishap that day. A lieutenant, the major's aide, riding in an open Jeep, was shot by a sniper from the steeple of a church. It infuriated the Dragoons, for the lieutenant was a particular favorite among them. A squad stormed the steeple, killed the sniper, and threw his lifeless body to the ground below. This angered the major as unnecessary brutality on the part of his men.

The lieutenant, shot in the thigh, was seriously wounded. The bone was broken. He was in a lot of pain and was sent by truck to a military hospital in the south. He took with him a beautiful Mauser 9mm rifle with a high-powered scope and hand-engraved stock. The sniper's gun was presented to him by the men who killed the enemy.

Jim was beside himself over the incident. "It could have been any one of us getting shot today," he declared.

"Shit," I said and went back to the gun crew.

Later, after we were billeted, Corporal Johnston said the old man wanted to see Jim and me. We reported to him at once.

"We've got a supply truck leaving for Brussels in the morning. I think you're probably anxious to get started for home, so we'll send you with it. The British are in Brussels and the Americans aren't too far away in Namur. Anyway, they'll see to it you get with your own people quickly. I'm glad we were able to liberate you and it's been a pleasure to have you with us. I understand you got on well with the men." He stood up and we shook hands with him heartily.

"Yes, sir," I said. "And sir, I just want to tell you I think you're a hell of a good commander. You've got the greatest bunch of guys it's ever been my good fortune to meet up with. I'm sorry about the lieutenant." I stood back and saluted him.

He smiled. "If you ever come to the Toronto area, give us a look see. They'll just stick a band-aid on the lieutenant and he'll be all right."

The following morning, after my goodbyes to the guys on the half-track, Jim and I were ready to go. With our familiar suitcases by our sides, we reported to the supply tent. But something was wrong with the supply truck and it wouldn't start.

The major came by as we were discussing the situation.

"We can't keep these Yanks forever. Give the keys to the lieutenant's Jeep to Sergeant Clark. He can drive it to Brussels and get some of the bullet holes plugged up and a new windscreen [windshield] in it." He looked at me. "Just leave it at the British Motor Pool, Sergeant." With that, he departed.

We drove the Jeep with a full tank of gasoline and two spare five-gallon "Jerry" cans full of gasoline all the way to Brussels. After we had gone twenty miles or so, we became part of a lot of military traffic. We had to detour through Metz, Germany, to cross the Rhine. It took us all day. We were never challenged once over our possession of the Jeep or for any other reason. All the troops we encountered were either Canadian or British.

Jim and I both felt we had earned the special privilege of having our personal transportation, even if it was only temporary.

303

T he beautiful city of Brussels was teeming with activity and military traffic. It was difficult to get directions to the motor pool or British headquarters. The trolley cars were back in operation. To add to the confusion, the foreign drivers of military vehicles in their Jeeps and half-tracks, luxury sedans and semi-trailer trucks, all speaking in their native tongues, shouted profanities at each other while trying to get to their destination. Half of them, like us, were completely lost, but each driver felt his mission was more important than his counterpart. The bicycles, motorcycles, civilian trucks, and automobiles added to the mass confusion, merging with the military traffic, which was the heaviest of all.

We came upon a British MP and asked him directions to the motor pool. Annoyed at our inquiry, and no doubt considering us to be aliens from a distant planet, he grudgingly pointed with a limp forefinger to a white marble building down the boulevard.

"In the rear," he said, a ring of arrogance in his voice.

"Thank you very much, sir!" I said with as much sarcasm as possible to the unhearing MP as I pulled away. Jim, whose eyes had been bulging out of his head, ogling flirtatious women, was silent. I drove around twice around a traffic circle with a huge statue in the center before I could clear the traffic to the direction I wanted to go. I saw a small sign in inch-high letters, on a driveway beside the building to which we had been directed: "MOTOR POOL — ENTER ONLY."

Driving down a concrete ramp to the back, I discovered a maze of military vehicles in a compound with a small building at the entrance. It was surrounded by an eight-foot, barbed-wire-topped chainlink fence.

I parked beside a small building which looked like the office and got out. As I entered the door, a British sergeant came out and said to me abruptly, "You can't park that here."

"I don't want to park it here, I want to turn it in," I said.

"Move that goddamned thing out now! Take it down the road!"

I got back in, started the motor, and put it in gear. I watched in the rearview mirror as I drove forward about a hundred yards and saw the sergeant's hulk go back inside the building. Then I pulled the Jeep to the side and parked parallel in front of the other vehicles, blocking them in.

"Wait here, Jim," I said and walked back to the building. I thought the sergeant was discourteous and very abusive. Inside, there were about ten sergeants and no customers. I didn't recognize any of them as my antagonist. A sign over a cage similar to a bank teller's read "MOTOR SERGEANT." A sergeant reading a book sat inside. I addressed the man on the inside of the cage.

"I've got a Jeep outside, damaged by sniper fire and belonging to the Royal Canadian Dragoons. I'm supposed to turn it in."

He ignored me. His book was too interesting. I waited for several moments and repeated my request.

"Number?" he asked.

"What number?"

"Number of the Jeep."

"I don't know."

"Gotta have a number before you can turn it in."

"Well, where do I find the number?"

For the first time he looked up from the book. "On the bonnet [hood] of the damned thing. Don't you Kanuks know anything?"

"I'm not a Kanuk," I said loudly, "but I'll get the number!"

I walked back to the Jeep, memorized the number quickly, and returned to the motor sergeant. I gave him the number.

"Okay," he said. "Now that wasn't too hard, was it? Bring it up beside the building and park it. I'll inspect it later."

"I was told not to park it here," I said.

"Well, I'm telling you if you want to turn it in, park it beside the

305

building." Now he was losing his patience.

"Shit!" I said aloud and stormed out the door.

I threw the Jeep in reverse and backed it all the way to the building and parked it where it was before. When I got out, I said, "Come on, Jim, this is as far as we're going."

I retrieved my suitcase from the back and literally pushed Jim ahead of me toward the building.

I went back to the window. The sergeant was reading again.

"I want a receipt for the Jeep," I demanded.

"Sure thing," he said and shoved a piece of paper toward me. It was a receipt for the vehicle. I couldn't believe my eyes.

As we left we met a British officer who was walking toward the motor pool. He stopped to light a cigarette.

"Pardon me, sir," I said, "can you tell me where we should report?" I told him our predicament.

"Yes. Right around to the front of this building. There's a desk inside marked 'New Arrivals.' They'll set you right."

We thanked him and headed for the front of the building. The magnificent edifice, an architectural masterpiece, was made of white marble and was eight stories high. The front of the immense structure ran the entire length of the city block. White marble steps, fully a hundred feet wide, went up to the colonnaded entrance of the building. On each side of the entrance stood a pair of twenty-foot-high white marble statues of Roman gladiators fiercely brandishing their swords.

We entered the foyer, which contained several desks. Each one had its own area with a small sign overhead held by a slender stick. We saw the one which read "NEW ARRIVALS." Two British soldiers were attending the desk. Each of them was sitting in a chair and looked at us when we approached. They had bored expressions on their faces. Neither of them gave any indication we were alive, but they both tried to outstare us. I finally lost the waiting game.

"We are Americans. Where do we report?"

"If you are Americans, what the hell are you doing wearing British uniforms?" he asked cynically.

My patience was wearing thin after my frustrating experience at the motor pool. His remark infuriated me.

"What the hell is it to you what uniforms we're wearing?"

He sputtered at my reply. "Listen here, Yank, stay right in that spot!" He got up from his chair, which I thought by now was glued to his fanny, and headed for the stairs. He walked a few steps and turned around. "And, if you leave here before I get back, consider yourself under arrest."

"Big deal!" I shouted at him.

He climbed the stairs two at a time.

I looked at the other soldier, whose chair, I was firmly convinced by now, was glued to his ass.

"How about you? Have you got some insulting remarks you want to throw my way?"

He ignored my inquiry.

"Let's go," Jim said.

"Hell, no," I replied. "This is where we're supposed to be."

"I told you we shouldn't put on these damned uniforms! We should wait for uniforms from our own people," Jim complained.

"Oh for Christ's sake, shut up!" I told him, thoroughly disgusted with his unfounded fears.

A few minutes later, the soldier came back, followed by a British lieutenant, pronounced "Left Tennant" (no disrespect for his rank, of course). He was a runt of a man, almost laughably so. He wore a canvas revolver holster with a lanyard running from the handle of the revolver through the epaulet on his tunic. The entire affair was so oversized for the little man, it made him look even smaller and gave him a comical appearance. He wore a solitary ribbon on his tunic. I smiled.

"Just what is the problem here?" he squeaked in a voice befitting his size.

I'll bet he's the soprano in the church choir, I thought. But aloud, I said, "No problem, sir, at least not with us. We're just doing what we were ordered to do by the commanding officer of the wreckie outfit in Holland who liberated us."

"Holland?" Squeaky asked questioningly. "What the hell was you up to in Holland?"

"We were both shot down eight months ago. The commanding officer gave us a Jeep to get to Brussels since it was damaged by gunfire and needed repairs. We turned it in to the motor pool in back of the building, sir!"

I waited for him to say something, but he stood there like a bump on a log.

"Here's the receipt for the goddamned jeep, sir!" I said, loud enough to wake him out of his stupor.

"We don't need that kind of language here," he said loudly.

"What are your names, ranks, and serial numbers?"

Jim and I both gave him the information and very slowly, deliberately, he wrote the data in his small notebook.

"Well done, soldier," he squeaked to the one who had come to fetch him. "Follow me!" he ordered, squeaking again. His voice turned to a high-pitched alto as he shouted. This time I did laugh.

I picked up my suitcase and accidentally bumped it so hard against the desk where the two soldiers were seated, I was afraid it would pop open. The desk moved a foot from where it had been. I looked the soldier straight in the eyes and gave him the finger as he turned beet red. I wanted to hit the chicken shit in the face as I looked up at him, with my face about an inch from his. I smiled and said quietly, "Fuck you, you Limey bastard." I fully expected him to punch my nose, but he didn't. I never looked back.

We followed the skinny little lieutenant up two flights of stairs. It left him wheezing like he had just run a four-minute mile. We walked down a long corridor. The carved walnut doors lining the hall were ten feet high. The rest of the walls were white marble. Finally, Squeaky stopped and struggled to open the massive door. Jim and I stood there, inwardly chuckling at his losing effort. Then, using both hands, he opened it a fraction of an inch and helping hands from within pushed it open.

The offices constituted the most disorganized mass of confusion I have ever seen. It was something I expected from his evident inexperience and lack of character. Filing cabinets were everywhere. Nothing was in its place. British soldiers and WRENs were trying to compete with each other to do clerical jobs. He led us to a small office at the far end of the mess. He had no trouble with the door since it was a standard size. We entered and discovered the office was paneled in walnut and had a huge teakwood desk. Squeaky sat down in his huge, upholstered chair, looking like a small boy sitting at his father's desk. There were about five steel folding chairs in the room.

"Sit down!" he ordered, but we had already taken seats.

"I'll be back shortly," he said, giving us a final arrogant glare which slid off the end of his skinny, long nose.

He was gone for over an hour. I was getting more unhappy by the minute. Jim was upset and worried because of the trouble I had gotten us into. I reminded him these weren't the Germans.

"The little bastard never asked us if we were hungry, wanted a cup of coffee, had to take a leak, or anything," I said. "I don't ever want to see the little bastard again. Let's go."

I stood up, but Jim stayed in his chair.

"Come on, Jim, let's get the hell out of here! An hour is long enough to wait for anybody, and I've got to take a leak!"

At that moment, the office door opened and Squeaky came in. Pompously, he lost himself in the chair behind the desk and said in his soprano voice, "Well, I guess you're who you say you are." He opened a teletype and laid it on the desk. Getting the information he wanted was probably why it took him so long.

"However," he continued, "I'm afraid before we can turn you over to the Americans in Namur there will be some serious interrogation for both of you."

"What kind of interrogation?" I asked.

He looked at me critically for interrupting him. "As I was saying, Sergeant, we have to know about your activities while you were in Holland. After all, you've been practically AWOL for over eight months. I want names, dates, and places you stayed. You were there for a long time and I must know everything that happened to you while you were evading capture. Everything!"

"Lieutenant," I had to pinch myself to keep from calling him Pipsqueak, "in the first place we were shot down, do you understand? Shot down! We parachuted behind enemy lines and evaded capture. I have never been AWOL and I resent your suggesting I was. Do you understand what I'm saying?"

"I didn't mean you were actually AWOL. I meant you haven't been in Allied control or supervision during the time you were evading. That's practically AWOL."

"I worked for the OSS most of the time I was in Holland. You can interrogate me if you want, but you'll have to have an American OSS man with proper identification here when you do!"

"Oh, now see here, Sergeant, I work closely with the OSS. I'm with MI9, British Intelligence, you know." ،

"No, I don't know. Meaning no disrespect to your rank, but I don't care if you're King George himself. I'll not answer another question unless my own people are here."

If the soldier downstairs had sputtered, Squeaky outsputtered him. He got up from the desk and opened the door.

"Sergeant!" he yelled.

A British sergeant in his fifties came into the office. "Yes, sir!" he said loudly, snapping to attention.

"I want these two men to stay in this office till I return. Do you understand?"

"Yes, sir, I understand. Under arrest, sir?" he asked with a twinkle in his eye.

"No, damn it, just make certain they stay here!"

He left the office sputtering. He was fuming, his face beet red and his eyes almost bulging out of his head.

The sergeant looked at Jim and me. He took out a package of Player's cigarettes and gave us one. We lit off the same match.

"He's a squeaky one, now ain't he?" the sergeant said, taking a long drag on his cigarette and settling himself in a chair.

He turned out to be a decent fellow and we talked until the lieutenant returned some twenty minutes later.

Again he lost himself behind his desk, glaring at us.

"My CO feels we don't have the time to interrogate you. Too many important things to do. We'll arrange for you to be transported to Namur, which is the closest American headquarters. I want both of you to know one thing. I'm making a full report of your insolence to your commanding officer in Namur, and further, I'm going to recommend you both be reduced to the rank of private for your insulting remarks. For a shilling, I'll recommend any punishment they deem fit to give you."

I stood up and picked up my suitcase. I looked the little man right in the eyes.

"And I want you to know something, Lieutenant. Since you're going to report me to my superiors anyway, it doesn't make any difference. If I had that shilling, I'd give it to you and call your bluff. All we did was come here and report to the nearest Allied forces. Those were our orders. I'm not so sure we did that. Who in hell's side are you on anyway?"

He started sputtering again.

I smiled at him. "You know, sir, I respect your uniform and your rank, but as for you personally, sir, you wouldn't make a pimple on a real British officer's ass! If you want to have me thrown in the guard house, get on with it. I've got more important things to do than stand here and argue with a pipsqueak." I had to call him that. It fit him so perfectly.

We stared at each other hard, but he made no move.

"If you're not going to arrest me, then stand aside because we want to get back with some real men, sir!"

310

The sergeant laughed out loud. The lieutenant gave him a demotion kind of glare if I ever saw one. The noncom shrugged his shoulders and walked out of the office still laughing.

He kept laughing as we followed him down the stairs to the basement of the building. We entered an office with a "TRANSPORTATION" sign over the door. A corporal stood behind his desk.

"Got two for Namur," he said, still smiling.

The corporal opened a book and checked some columns.

"Rail," he said, "train leaves at fourteen hundred hours. Be here at noon tomorrow for transport to the station. Got it?"

"Okay." We gave him our names and left.

We went down the hall. A sign read "TRANSIENT BILLETS." A corporal approached us.

"Got two for the night," the sergeant said.

"Right," the corporal replied.

From shelves on the back wall, he got sheets, blankets, towels, and a pillow case for each of us.

"Need shaving gear?" he asked. Without waiting for a reply, he handed us toiletry kits. Afterward, he sat back down at his desk without saying a word. We threw our blankets on some bunks and made them up as the sergeant stood by.

"Well, you're on your own, mates," he said, turning to go. "Oh yeah, how are you fixed for money? Have you got any?"

"Nary a sou," I said.

"The paymaster's just down the hall. Look for the sign. I'll tell him you're coming and he'll give you as much of an advance on your back pay as you want. But remember, even though you both got a lot coming, any draw you make on it will catch up to you sooner or later, so don't go crazy and draw too much. Have a good time in Brussels, Yanks."

"I hope you don't get in too much trouble with his majesty upstairs," I said to him.

"Don't worry about me. I eat bigger fish than him for breakfast. He's been told off before, but you . . . Blimey!" He started laughing again. "I'll try to intercept any nasty notes he sends to Namur." He laughed again and climbed the stairs.

We made our beds, showered, and shaved with *new* razor blades! The razor glided over my face with the greatest of ease. What a luxury. When we finished, we went to the paymaster's office. In just a matter of minutes, our pockets were stuffed with a hundred dollars worth of

Belgian francs. There was a canteen next door where we purchased new underwear and socks. We went back to our bunks and changed into them. The corporal took our suitcases for safekeeping.

On the main street we caught a streetcar. As we rode along, we saw what we were looking for — a small building with the word "MASSEUSE" written on the side. We were happy to find it was legitimate. The masseuse gave us both a massage and a bath with brushes and at least three inches of soapy lather. I felt clean for the first time in nine months. We were ready for the world.

"Lookout, Brussels, here we come!" said Jim.

We caught another streetcar and headed toward the center of Brussels. Some Canadians on the streetcar told us where to go for some good food and a good time. Ladies of the night frequented the place. After we ate a delicious meal, I proceeded to get plastered on just a few drinks.

Jim disappeared for a couple of hours in the company of two real fine-looking ladies, but I declined the offers of some pretty specimens because I was too drunk. When he came back we left the place and went to some other night spots and drank ourselves into oblivion. In the wee hours of the morning we finally went to bed.

It was a short train ride to Namur. When we got off at the station, American enlisted personnel directed us to our destination and provided us with ground transportation. We wound up at a huge, red brick building beside the railroad tracks. It looked like it had been a college at one time, but now it was headquarters for the American Forces.

Inside the building, we were directed to some offices on the second floor. I gave a pretty WAC sergeant our names and she informed me that we were expected. She steered us to an office where a full colonel greeted us. We reported, giving name, rank, and serial number.

"I understand the British gave you a hard time in Brussels," the colonel offered. "Well, you're not the first!"

He spoke to another WAC sergeant. "Will you please take Sergeant Moulton to Colonel Jamerson's office? He's expected."

When we were alone, he seated me across the desk.

"Yes, sir," I said, "I had the misfortune to run into a tiny lieutenant who wanted to interrogate us. That was okay. All I wanted was somebody from the OSS there."

He picked up a teletype from his desk and read it.

"Did you actually say 'Fuck you' to him?"

"No, sir. I said 'screw you, sir' to him. I also said many other things. In so many words, I told him that he defamed the uniform he was wearing. I also told him I respected his uniform and the pips on his shoulders but as a person, he wouldn't make a pimple on a real British officer's ass."

The colonel laughed. "This is, thank God, the only copy of the teletype." He tore it up and threw it in the wastebasket.

Still smiling, he pushed a button on his desk. An enlisted man opened the door. "We're ready now," he said.

A first lieutenant came in, followed by a WAC sergeant who was armed with a stenographer's pad and a handful of pencils.

"Sergeant Clark, this is Lieutenant Black. I'm Colonel Carter. We are both OSS. If you want identification, we'll gladly show it to you. I'll call you by your code name, then you'll know we're OSS." He looked in the file in front of him. "Here it is, you're 'Veen' radio and code name and have been working with the group in Friesland in Holland." He smiled as he waited.

"I guess you know who I am, all right," I replied.

"Now, I hope your chair is comfortable because I want you to tell me everything that has happened to you since you were shot down until you walked into my office a few minutes ago. First of all, I want you to relay any pertinent information regarding military operations which might help the Canadians."

I told him about the island of Schiermonnikoog and the defenses I knew to be intact. I also told him about the 250 Germans on the island with their .88mm flak guns. "The Canadians are aware of all this," I added, telling him how I had fought beside them and interpreted for them for three days.

Then we started. I talked for five and a half hours. We drank a million cups of coffee, it seemed. I left out nothing. I told about getting shot down, killing the two Germans, Paul in the woods, Pete and Mimi, my escapade with Sue, the Wig-Wam, Oom Joop, Franz and the others, Niko and George, getting captured, Hoornsterzwaag and the men there, the trip to Holwerd, Dominee de Boer, Visser and Teun de Jong, Paesens and Engelsmanplaat, the schoolmaster and his wife, the sister, my love affair with Greta, Bertus Nauta and Tini, Harry Wessels, being captured again in Ternaard, the Stielstras, Katina, the German Grune Polizei and his dog, the Bokmas, Karen, Loty, and Dominee Visser in Dokkum. I told of the bravery of Sjoukje

313

van der Hoop, Jan in Dokkum, and finally about the wonderful guys in the Royal Canadian Dragoons.

They asked many questions as my tale unfolded. The WAC secretary filled her pad and got another. We had to wait several times while she sharpened her pencils. It had been dark outside a long time when we finished.

"Unbelievable," the colonel said.

"If you were to render aid and assistance to any of these people, whom would you choose?"

I thought a minute. "All of them, sir. They all helped me so much that I'll give credit to every one of them for saving my life. But, of course, Pete and Mimi, Bertus and Tini Nauta, mijnheer Visser and Teun de Jong, George and Niko, the Stielstras in Holwerd, and Sjoukje van der Hoop are the ones who most come to mind."

We sat for another hour and tied all the loose ends.

"We're sending you and Sergeant Moulton home. You can have a few days R&R before you return. Paris, Brussels, London, anyplace at all, just name it."

"How about Paris, if Jim agrees?"

"Paris it is. Lieutenant, make the arrangements. Is there anything else you need?"

"Yes, sir, a couple of things. I'd like to know about the rest of my crew. What happened to them? I saw nine chutes. Did they all get out alive?"

"I don't know, but by the time you get back I'll try to have the answers for you. Sergeant, your story is one of the most interesting I ever heard from an evader."

"We'd like to get back in uniform. Is that possible?"

"That will be taken care of as soon as you leave here."

We shook hands and I left his office.

We were placed in a special category called "Project R," whatever that was. It referred to prisoners of war, escapees, and evaders. On all the orders cut afterward we were referred to as "Project R."

Jim had been through with his interrogation for about two hours when I left the colonel's office. I caught up with him in the canteen. He had been good enough to draw our bedding and fix us up with a bunk. He liked the idea of a few days in Paris.

It had been a long, hard day. I was exhausted from the interrogation and I still had a hangover from reveling the night before, so I went to bed. Jim stayed in the canteen, drinking beer.

314

At 8:00 A.M. a soldier woke us.

"Sergeant," he said, "the quartermaster is looking for you. I'd suggest you get over there. The mess hall's on the next floor. I'll tell him you'll be there in about an hour, okay?"

"Yeah, thanks," I said and put my feet on the floor.

I grabbed a towel and after I shaved and showered, I dressed and went upstairs. Jim was already eating breakfast.

Jim said he had gotten about half smashed on beer the night before and felt more like dying than cleaning up.

I got in the chow line and took a tray. German prisoners of war did the kitchen work. They couldn't speak English but were especially polite as they put food on my tray.

After eating, we went to the quartermaster and were issued new American uniforms — everything from the skin out. They had our sizes in everything they issued. I was given the ornaments for my uniform as well as chevrons for the sleeves of my blouse and shirts, Air Force and Eighth Air Force patches, a pair of Air Crew Wings, and all my combat ribbons. I was also given an A-2 leather flying jacket and a nylon flight suit. I didn't accept any of the rest of the flying gear offered. Best of all, I was issued a duffle bag to carry my accumulated gear.

"It would be nice if I had time to sew on all this stuff," I said to the quartermaster corporal who issued it to me.

"Just a minute," he said and left the cage. In less than a minute he was back with a German POW in tow.

"This Kraut used to be a tailor." He gave the German everything that had just been issued to me. "Take him to your bunk and he'll have them sewn on within an hour. If he does a good job, give him a candy bar or a couple of cigarettes."

I signed for the clothing and the German followed me to my bunk. He sat down and took a sewing kit from his pocket and went to work. I went down to the canteen to see what I could buy.

The first thing I bought was a wristwatch. It was a Benrus, exactly like the one I had been issued in the United States when I began flying. I hoped Niko was enjoying the one he got from me. I got some more razor blades, a pocket comb, a half dozen handkerchiefs, two cartons of Camels, several packages of gum, a dozen assorted candy bars, and a new Zippo lighter with fluid and spare flints. I spent almost $5 for everything except the watch, which cost $19.

The corporal who awakened me in the morning came into the

315

canteen looking for me. He told me that Jim and I were to leave for the airfield at 2:00 that afternoon. The quartermaster had our passes and wanted to give them to us. I bought him a cup of coffee and he sat down. He told me there were fifty to seventy-five POWs in the building and they did the Americans' bidding. If we needed a shoeshine, washing, bed made, ironing — anything at all — the POWs did it. They were lucky for they got good food, clean beds, and good treatment. Some of the guys were even friendly with them. The quartermaster said it was against regulations, but it was getting to be that way. After a while, he said he had some more chores to do and left.

I went back upstairs and found the German had finished sewing. He had also pressed my clothes and had them hanging on hangers. I gave him a carton of Camels and five of my candy bars. You'd have thought I gave him a hundred dollars.

I showered again and dressed in issued clothing. It all fit.

Jim came in and put on his uniform but hadn't made use of the POW's labors. "Who gives a shit about rank, anyway?" he said. "All I want is to get out and be a civilian."

We picked up our tickets and left our locked duffle bags with the quartermaster, who gave us a receipt for them. They were stored behind a locked cage, where they would be safe. I left my Luger inside it. We took only a few clothes.

The ATC C-47 landed at Orly. It was a short flight and our first ride in an airplane since being shot down. I thought I'd be nervous but I wasn't. Instead, I felt invigorated just being in the air again. After we deplaned, we caught a taxi into Paris. We had no idea where we'd stay. The people in Namur were willing to make arrangements for us, but Jim and I decided to shift for ourselves. We could always stay at the American compound.

"Where would be a good place to stay in Paris?" I asked the cab driver who picked us up at Orly. He spoke enough English to understand us and asked if we wanted an expensive or a small, money-saving establishment.

"Just a small, homey-type hotel where we can go sightseeing. In the middle of things, you know."

"I know of just such a place," he said.

He drove to the Hotel Tivoli. It was small by comparison. We paid the driver and took two rooms. After unpacking, we met in the

316

lobby. The desk clerk spoke excellent English and supplied us with a small prewar map of the "City of Lights." He gave us directions on how to get to the Arc de Triomphe, only a quarter of a mile away. Two blocks from the hotel we came to the Champs des Ellysees. To the right we saw the Eiffel Tower.

For the next three and a half days we were tourists in every sense of the word. We toured the city on foot, taking a cab back to the hotel because we were too tired to walk. We went to the Grand Palace, Place Pigalle, Moulin Rouge, Eiffel Tower, the Louvre, Notre Dame, the Opera House, and Mountmartre, among others. We walked along the Seine, visiting all the small stands along its banks, and watched the artists capture on canvas the vision they saw before them. We bought a few books and trinkets across from Notre Dame and looked at the thousands of statues adorning the city. We looked until we were exhausted admiring the wonders of beautiful Paree.

At the red light district we only looked — no souvenirs. We talked with people in English and tried to make them understand us. We were able, I don't know how, perhaps by sign language, to be understood. We ignored the ladies completely until the last night, when we met a couple of really nice girls at the hotel. They were touring the city and were from Marseilles. They both understood high-school English. We ate at a very luxurious restaurant. The meal came in so many courses I couldn't count them or tell you what was in the food. There was wine, revelry, and afterward, we took them to the Lido. To show their appreciation, we shared rooms with each other and they coaxed us to stay. The temptation was great, but we were able to resist it.

The French people were wonderful. They were helpful, courteous, and very friendly. Often, they wouldn't take pay for their services. *Vive la France!*

On the other side of the coin, the French soldiers had a lousy attitude toward Americans, the British, and anybody not living under the tri-colors. Why they felt that way toward soldiers of all Allied nations I'll never know. We helped them, giving our blood and money freely. I think the civilian population appreciated us, but the soldiers, whom the British called "Frogs," seemed to hate anyone foreign, especially American or British.

Back in Namur, we retrieved our belongings. My Luger was still in my duffle bag. Colonel Carter saw me and told me about my crew. Four airplanes from our squadron had been shot down near Havelte on August 15, 1944. He was happy to say that the gunners of the 466th

317

had shot down seven ME-109 fighters and were credited for the kills. He bade me success in my future life. Two hours after we arrived, we were on a train, with orders in our hands to ship us back to the USA. Our destination was Camp Lucky Strike at Le Havre, France.

We slept in tents. The troop ships were anchored offshore, waiting for us to board and take us back to the States. As soon as a convoy was made up, we would set sail.

The first thing they did when we got off the train at Camp Lucky Strike was to take all our clothes from us, wash and dry clean them, then delouse us by spraying DDT powder all over our naked bodies. Everybody coming to the camp got the same treatment, whether he was a general officer or a private in the last row. Our clothes were returned and we were assigned tents as we awaited transport. Jim and I were given complete physical examinations. The doctor said I was suffering from malnutrition. I was an even forty pounds underweight, tipping the scales at ninety-six pounds. I had weighed about 145 when I was shot down.

While we were there, we were interrogated again by intelligence people in the camp. They made a big deal out of our activities in Holland. We stayed until May 3, 1944, when we went by small boat about a quarter of a mile off the coast of Le Havre to the SS *George Washington,* an old four-stacker that would take us home.

Assigned bunks so deep inside the ship, it took us an hour to find and make our beds. There were 5,000 of us aboard the old liner, including the first shipment of prisoners of war released from *stalag luft* camps in Germany. I didn't know any of them. I never found a man from the 466th. There were hundreds of other GIs, mostly infantrymen, all of them hospital cases, paraplegics, with arms and legs missing. They were in bad shape, but their morale was higher than ours.

The SS *George Washington* sailed from Le Havre on the evening of May 3. After a short stop at Southampton for fuel, we set sail for the United States. Our convoy consisted of ten troop transports protected by four destroyers.

I met a man whom I shall never forget. We became close friends. His name was Ned Glass. He was part of a USO group who had been entertaining the troops overseas. The troupe was on its way home and gave nightly performances for the returnees. His wife, a part of the group, was Kitty McHugh and the sister of Frank McHugh, a well-known Hollywood comedian who appeared in countless motion pictures. Ned and I talked for hours about my experiences with the un-

318

derground. We made plans to meet when I got back to California after I got out of the service.

On May 8 the Germans officially surrendered unconditionally to the Allies. The war was over. Europe was still a beautiful country and had many beautiful people who survived the murderous Nazis.

I set foot on American soil on May 13 as the ship docked in the New York area. I was sent to Fort Totten, processed quickly, and sent home, arriving on May 18 — exactly nine months and three days after I was shot down.

Jim had a stroke of luck. On board the ship, he got in a big poker game, winning in excess of $2,000. He gave me $510 — our gentleman's agreement — to pay his gambling debt. He was glad to be alive to pay it.

I was glad to be alive too.

"Amerika Holland een Doel!"

EPILOGUE

I made four trips to Holland to do research for this book. In 1983, I went to the police station in Meppel and met Rob Ravensteyn, a police officer who actually found the whereabouts of Oom Joop and Peter van den Hurk. After that, with Pete's help, I was able to retrace my steps of 1944–45 and make this memory come alive for me. The people I knew, my "helpers," were mostly still alive as of 1989. The information I have on what happened to them follows.

True Love

True Love blew up in midair at about 5,000 feet altitude. The airplane's main structure fell into a farmer's field while the tail section fell onto the roof of his barn. I visited the exact location in 1985 and there is still a small indentation in the field where the plane crashed. The farmer has passed away but his son still farms the place. One day while plowing in his field, he saw something shiny in the field and picked it up. It was the identification bracelet belonging to Bob Lehman. With the assistance of the Eighth Air Force Historical Society, the farmer was able to get in touch with Bill Lehman, Bob's brother, and he returned it to him.

Jan Mennik, of De Wijk, a Dutch air historian and expert on the air war over Holland, took me to the exact spot where I was shot down.

He showed me the location of the runway for Vliegveld Havelte. The correct German name for the airbase was Steenwijk Vliegfeld. Our plane went down on the outskirts of Steenwijk. Beside the runway the revetments to house the Messerschmitts and Focke Wulfs are still in evidence, the same ones I had looked into forty years before. My thoughts were refreshed, recalling the fears I felt hiding in the forest. I was able to find the path where I lay down in the ditch and confronted the two soldiers.

According to Col. Arie P. de Jong, the official government historical expert on World War II in Holland, we did ourselves proud that day over Holland. We lost four planes but we shot down seven Messerschmitt ME-109Gs, a new series of airplanes equipped with JATO (jet-assisted take off) rocket units for extremely fast climbing. Our mission to Vechta was as perfect as a mission can get. All our bombs fell on the airfield. None fell on civilians. The airbase at Vechta was never used again.

John S. (Jack) Archer, Jr., *Pilot*

Jack was killed on the first pass of German fighters led by Major Goetz, according to Don McCarty, an eyewitness inside the plane, and the Dutch historians named above. I accidentally discovered that Jack's body was interred at Margraten American Military Cemetery in the province of Limburg in southern Holland. I saw several graves from the 466th Bomb Group and looked at the registrar of graves. He is the only member of our crew who is buried in Europe. I am grateful he lies in such a beautiful place. Others killed on the same mission are interred there.

Thomas L. (Tommy) Bell, *Copilot*

Tommy was mortally wounded on the second pass of German ME-109s led by Lt. Ernst Scheufele. Though near death, he was able to fly the B-24 airplane even after the fatal second pass by the Messerschmitts. His remains were sent back to the United States. He is buried in the Golden Gate Cemetery in Redwood City, just south of San Francisco, California. Although already dying, he heroically kept the B-24 on course as long as he could, screaming for the crew to bail out. We tried to get him decorated for his bravery. He died when the Liberator blew up in the air.

Norman (Norm) Peck, *Navigator*

Norm was killed when we were shot down. We believe he was killed on the first pass the German fighters made. His body was sent back to the United States and he is buried in New York.

Robert H. (Bob) Lehman, *Nose-turret gunner*

Bob was killed when we were shot down by the second wave of German fighters. According to Don McCarty, an eyewitness to the activity in the front of the airplane, he was killed when he called out the second time, "I think they are mad at us." His body was sent home and he is buried near Enid, Oklahoma. His brother Bill wrote to me in 1985 and told me about the bracelet. He really appreciated the farmer's gift to him.

Bart Philo, *Assistant engineer/Top-turret gunner*

Bart was killed instantly when the first wave of German fighters went through our formation for his badly shot-up body was sagging half out of his top turret. Don McCarty was a witness to his death. Bart's remains were shipped home and he is buried in Fruitvale, Michigan. He was the first to fire at the ME-109s as they flew through our formation and, undoubtedly, the first of our crew to die.

Donald (Don) McCarty, *Radio operator/Waist-gunner*

Don was a prisoner of war for nine months. He tried to bail out the bomb bays of the airplane but couldn't get them open, even by jumping on them. Finally, he ran through the wall of fire in the bomb bays and joined us in the rear just as we were bailing out. He parachuted to earth safely but broke his leg when he landed. The plane was already in a flat spin when he accomplished this feat. The Germans took him to the hospital in Leeuwarden, where they put his leg in a cast. Later, with other POWs he was sent to a *stalag luft* where his leg healed. He was liberated by the American Army in May of 1945. He returned to Terre Haute, Indiana, in June of 1945, got married, and raised a family. He became a radio announcer and later a local television personality before he opened his own advertising business.

William (Willie) Lowen, *Engineer/Ball-turret gunner*

Willie was a prisoner of war for nine months. He was severely wounded by exploding .20mm cannon fire. He spent a week in the hospital in Leeuwarden, where the German medics removed as much shrapnel from his body as they could. Willie said that during his months in the POW camp he picked small fragments of shrapnel from his body constantly. He went home to his wife and continued painting and paperhanging in Ponca City, Oklahoma. He is currently living on one of the Keys in Florida.

John M. (Johnny) Capps, *Tail-turret gunner*

Johnny was a prisoner of war for nine months. He was sent to Stalag Luft IV near Peenemunde, Germany, very close to the Polish border. (Ironically, Lt. Ernst Scheufele was stationed in Peenemunde before he was sent to Sachaeu, the base from which he took off the day we were shot down by him.) When the Russians started closing in on the area, the entire camp of POWs was marched for eighty-five days to another camp near Bremen, where they stayed until the camp was liberated by the Americans. During the time Johnny was in the camp, he grew a handle-bar mustache and still had it when he arrived in Dexter, Missouri, in June of 1945. He went into the automobile business. We visited twice after the war. Later, he married a local girl, Glenda, and raised a family. He was elected to the county clerk's office, a position he held until late 1985, and finally retired in 1987. I still consider him one of my best friends. I'll never forget I owe him my life. We celebrated the forty-third anniversary of being shot down together on August 15, 1987.

Lieutenant Leslie, *Squadron gunnery officer*

The lieutenant was a prisoner of war for nine months. The Germans mistook him for me for a long time. They threatened to kill him several times but he managed to get out of his predicament and made

323

it home okay. The Germans wouldn't believe he was only an observer along for the ride. His occupation was that of an actor, and he appeared in New York in several stage plays. He was liberated in May 1945.

Lt. Ernst Scheufele, *German ME-109 pilot*

I met the German pilot who shot our plane down on August 22, 1989, at Peter van den Hurk's home in Meppel, Holland. Three weeks previously, I received a letter from him stating he would like to write to me. I was coming to Holland for a meeting of the ESCAPE organization representing the Air Forces Escape and Evasion Society, so Peter arranged the meeting. I was nervous about meeting my former enemy, but once we were face to face, I discovered he was more nervous than I. We spent an entire day together, were interviewed by the press, and had a meeting with the *burgermeister* of Meppel. When the day was over, I was glad we met. He was just a guy doing his job the same as we were. I will continue to correspond with him.

Karl (Jan Berenda)

Karl lived in the village of Wittelte. Though I only knew the big man for three days, he has lived in my memory for forty years. He passed away in 1980. It is a strange thing, but Oom Joop knew him well and the two of them spoke of me often after the war was over.

Peter Jan van den Hurk (Pete)

A true hero of recent Dutch history, he was decorated personally by Prince Bernhard of the Netherlands for his bravery and giving unselfishly of himself for queen and country. He was credited with aiding over a hundred Allied airmen. He was decorated by the president of the United States, Dwight D. Eisenhower, for the assistance he gave American airmen. After the war he reported back for duty with the Dutch army and remained in the service as a captain for two years. In August 1945 he married his longtime sweetheart, Mimi de Jong, in Meppel. Today Pete is retired from the clothing business. In 1986 he moved from Amersfort back to Meppel, where he now resides. He and Mimi came to the United States and visited my wife and me in June 1987.

Mimi de Jong

Everyday she went to work for her German boss, but her most important job was helping the many men who were not in a position to help themselves. Mimi looks nearly the same today as she did forty years ago. There may be an attractive line or two in her lovely face and a little more silver in her hair, but she still has the wonderful smile I remembered so well. She stood proudly beside her husband as the medals were pinned upon his chest. And her husband stood just as proudly beside her as the same medals and honors were bestowed upon her.

Mevrouw de Groot

She returned to her home but not until the war was over in 1945. She lived there until her death. By opening her home to Allied flyers, she saved many lives. Her daughter, who escaped with her to the neighbor's house on the night of December 22, 1944, lives in Rotterdam with her family.

Jelly van Duren

Jelly married after the war was over. She and her husband lived for some time in the Netherlands, finally immigrating to Canada. Later they moved to Lakehurst, New Jersey, where her husband's employment took him. He is now retired, and they still live there. I saw them in Holland in 1985.

#51 Weerdstraat, Meppel

The house I stayed in with Mimi and mevrouw de Groot has been purchased by another family whom I met in 1985. They were good enough to allow us to go through it again. It was the first time either Pete or Mimi had been back since December 18, 1944. When I looked out the upstairs back window at the school yard, I could see Sergeant Major Fitzenheimer doing the "goose step"!

Gerit Temmingh (Policeman)

Temmingh almost lost his life in the war. He was captured because of the traitor who told about the Wig-Wam. The Germans sent him to Amersfort and he underwent severe interrogation. Then he was sent to the concentration camp at Bergen-Belsen, where he was put on a work detail even though he was condemned to be executed. He was liberated by the Americans on May 5, 1945, and was home on May 31, 1945 — a free man. His wife, Fenna, had given him up for dead. He is alive and well, residing in his beautiful home in Gieten, Holland.

Sue

Sue attended veterinarian school in France after the war, then did post graduate work in Germany. She is a wife, mother, and a well-known and respected veterinarian in a large city in Holland. I'm grateful to have known her as well as I did.

G. Koster (Oom Joop)

Saddened over the loss of his only son, Oom Joop went back into the painting business after the war. Most of the houses in Diever as well as some of the surrounding villages have a stroke of his brushes on them someplace. His wife passed away in the 1970s and his two daughters are happily married, one living with her family near Calgary, Canada, and the other with her family in Brisbane, Australia. He is eighty-nine years old and in reasonably good health. Oom Joop was not an underground fighter but he was the backbone of those with whom he associated. I am proud to be his friend. He was a very fortunate man to have visited with his wife the night the Germans raided and captured the Wig-Wam and its inhabitants. I am in constant communication with him. He travels frequently to both Canada and Australia. A street in Diever was recently named in memory of his son Franz, killed by the Germans.

Hermanus Vos / Geert Gernardus Koster (Franz)
Hilbert Gunninh / Chijs Egginh
Jan Egginh / Roelof Egginh (Dolf)
Thuis Gerhardus Drupsteen / Cebastian van Nooten

My eight comrades were captured by the Germans on November 21, 1944, and removed to Bergen-Belsen, where they lived out the final, short chapters of their lives before they were murdered by their Nazi tormentors. The location of their remains is unknown.

James Moulton (Jim)

Jim went back to Albany, Oregon, and married the girl who waited for him. I saw him in 1950 and met his wife and two children. He was working in a saw mill. I tried to keep in touch with him over the years, but we finally lost track of each other. My latest efforts led to a dead end until I finally received word he had passed away a few years ago. He told me when I last saw him that he wanted to forget all about our experience in the underground and since I was a part of that experience, that may be the reason he lost touch with me. I wish we had kept in closer touch with each other.

George (Pieter Bloom)

George's real name was Pieter Bloom. He worked for the Dutch government as a railroad switchman prior to the war. He despised and wanted to fight the Germans, so he worked for various underground groups in Friesland and did all the dirty work there was to do. He was a real fighter for their organization. His body was found in February 1945 on the island of Borkum, the northernmost Friesian island. He had a small hole in his head that could have been made by a bullet, except there was no exit hole where the bullet would have exited. It ruled out his being shot. He had three children and they all lived in Holwerd. His wife never remarried. I saw her and her grown children in 1985. She has remained in mourning for all her life.

Niko (Fjitre Wallinga)

Niko, whose real name I believe was Fjitre Wallinga, as he told me once, was a good friend to me. He helped me on so many occasions. My story will attest to that. According to another Dutch war historian, it was confirmed that he was a member of the hated NSB organization and may have even been a member of the dreaded SD. Hard to believe? In April 1945, after seeking him out, the Dutch Resistance executed Niko, believing, I think, that he had murdered George. He couldn't have been instrumental in George's death. I will always think George drowned and Niko was unjustly accused of his death.

Tini Mulder (Author)

Tini was one of the girls who brought the motorcycle to Horn-sterzwaag. She was also a fighter with the Dutch underground. After the war, she went to work as a journalist for a Leeuwarden newspaper and later became an author who wrote several books, both fact and fiction, about the activities in the underground. I saw her in 1984 and we had a long talk. She was decorated by the Dutch government for the work she did with the underground from 1940 to 1945.

Sjoukje van der Hoop Smit (Courier)

She was my little courier who took me everywhere. I discovered she was engaged to marry a boy from Holwerd, but he was captured by the Germans and never heard from again. Several years later, she married a Dutchman by the name of Tom Smit. They immigrated to the city of Chatham, Ontario, Canada, and raised a family. Both she and her husband are retired. I saw her in 1984 and the newspapers picked it up. There was quite a story with a large picture of us. She hasn't changed at all. I saw her father, Cornelis van der Hoop, in Holwerd in 1985 and had a long talk with him. He was also very active with underground activities. He has since passed away.

Greta Rusk (Fictitious name)

I kept track of Greta for over twenty years through Dominee de Boer. Shortly after the war was over, she and her husband moved to Rotterdam and she opened a bakery shop. It prospered, and according to the minister, expanded to the point where it was doing a tremendous business. Jan, her husband, recovered sufficiently to help her in the business, doing oddjobs and the like. He was just one turn higher than a vegetable but she remained faithful to him and tended to his needs. Of course, there were never any children and finally she sold the bakery business. Since that time, the country seems to have swallowed her up.

Dominee de Boer

We corresponded into the 1960s, not frequently, but occasionally. He left Holwerd not too many years ago. His wife lives in Leeuwarden, where, after his death, I believe he was buried. He never had to fight and remained a man of the cloth until he died. Never since have I felt the power of God as I did in this man's presence. I will never forget him.

S. Visser

Mijnheer Visser no longer lives in Paesens and is no longer a fisherman. He now lives in the village of Lekkum, in the province of Friesland. I was honored by the media in Paesens, where he acted as the host in 1984. His wife also attended and it was such a pleasure to see them again and talk about our walk in the water.

Teun de Jong

I saw my checker-playing friend in Paesens and again on the island of Schiermonnikoog in 1984 when I was honored by the *Burgermeester* of the island, Mijnheer Boekhoven. There, I was introduced to Air Commodore Paul de Jong. Joke Folmer arranged the reception. Teun and I did much reminiscing and is one of the people I would have recognized in an instant. Unfortunately, we didn't have time for checkers but he was fast to remind me I was the worst bicycle rider he had ever seen.

The Sister

She was an elderly woman even while Jim and I stayed with her. I wasn't able to find out anything about her at all.

Bertus and Tini Nauta

I found their house in Ternaard but there was nobody home. The neighbors had never heard of them. Through some exhaustive efforts, I found out they live in Grimsby, Ontario, Canada, about a hundred miles from Sjoukje van der Hoop. I contacted Bertus by telephone in December 1985 and went to see him in the summer of 1986. He immigrated to Canada in 1950, where Tini bore three children. He became a farmer for many years and in 1980 sold the farm and bought condominiums in both Florida and Grimsby. I spent an entire day with

329

them. Tini is still the same warm, wonderful person she was and still has the clock I repaired. We talked about the war years even though they were both reluctant to do so. They both suffer from cancer but still show their love for each other. My latest communications with them have been returned unopened.

Harry Wessels

Harry was given many military honors for the part he played with the Dutch Resistance. He went back to Groningen to the university as a professor of English. He has since passed away.

G. Stielstra (Butcher)

I went to the butcher shop in Holwerd in 1985. The whole place had changed. The shop is now a residence and the shed is no longer out back. Where the driveway was, a house has been built. I found Pieter Stielstra, who lives a few doors past the house where Pete Woudsma lived. He hardly remembered me at all, and was somewhat reluctant to talk to me. He said he did remember coming to see me at the church when I was there with Jim, George, and Niko. I discovered the Stielstras had both been divorced from their former spouses, each of them having custody of their three children. So when they married they had a family of six to start out with. I presume the other two children were with their other parent. Some of the real names of the Stielstra family are Freek Liestra, Omke Frerik, M. Teitsma, and V. D. Meer (deceased). G. Stielstra, the butcher, is believed to live in Dokkum at the present time. We also met an in-law who lives two doors from the old butcher shop. She was of no help to us.

M. Geerstma

M. Geerstma, the owner of the blacksmith shop where I was confronted by the big German and his dog, has since passed away. His son, however, remembers the incident as it was told to him by his father. He was glad to meet me.

Katina

I could find no trace of Katina. I found her house and it had been remodeled. Nobody could remember her or the boy.

Raol Bokma

I searched Bridaard for his whereabouts but couldn't find him. I found the house where he and his mother lived. His mother, I was told, was still alive and was living in a retirement home in the country.

The Borghams — Karen and Loty

After the war, they left Bridaard. I was unable to locate any of them, although I did find the house where they lived. I still have their address in Rotterdam but didn't look them up.

Dominee Visser

Dominee Visser passed away several years ago, in fact shortly after the war. His wife was very old but still alive in 1988 and lived with her daughter in Rotterdam.

Dokkum, Province of Friesland, Holland

In the *magistraat* building, they were kind enough to take out the picture albums of the day the Royal Canadian Dragoons liberated the town. There were pictures of the guys I served with and some pictures which I suspect are of me. There were also photos of the white barges with the red crosses painted on the sides of them tied up in the canal.

Ned Glass

Ned Glass has appeared in several motion pictures and television plays. I guess his biggest role was that of "Doc" in *West Side Story*, which starred Natalie Wood. After the war, he invited my wife and me to his good friend Moe Howard's house (one of the Three Stooges). We spent the day enjoying the pool and had dinner. I kept in touch with Ned for a long time but have been out of touch with him for years. He is still active in show business and has never aged at all.

331

Bibliography

Books

Ausweis voor Noord Oost Friesland. Dokkum, Netherlands: Schaafsma & Brower, 1965.

Bakker, W. *Bezetting en Verzet: 1940–1945 in Meppel en Wijde Omgeving.* Meppel, Netherlands: Boom-Pers, 1980.

Barbas, Bernard. *Planes of the Luftwaffe Fighter Aces, Bol. I.* Melbourne, Australia: Kookaburra Technical Publications PTY LTD, 1985.

de Haan, H., R. Ijema, and D. T. Reitsma. *Engelsmanplaat: geshiedenis van . . . en gebeurtinissen . . . een sandbank.* Moddergat, Netherlands: Stichting't Fiskerhuske, 1983.

Jansen, Ab A. *Sporen aan de Hemel: Kroniek van een Luchtoorlog. Deel III: Januari 1944–april 1945.* Baarn, Netherlands: Hollandia BV, 1980.

Rijnout, Bart M. *In Dienst van hun Naaste . . . : een Stuk Pilotenhulp in de Tweede Wereldoorlog.* Rotterdam, Netherlands: WYT Uitgevers, no date given.

van Kampen, L., and others. *Friesland 1940–1945.* Leeuwarden, Netherlands: Friese Pes Boekerij BV, 1980.

Woolnough, Lt. Col. John H. *Attlebridge Diaries: The History of the 466th Bombardment Group (Heavy).* Hollywood, Florida: Eighth Air Force News, 1979.

Interviews

Capps, John M. Personal interview. Dexter, Missouri, August 15, 1987.

de Jong, Col. Arie A. Personal interview, RAF Club, Schiphol Airport, Amsterdam, Holland, June 1985.

de Jong, Teun. Personal interview. Schiermonnikoog, Netherlands, June 14, 1984.

Folmer, Joke. Personal interview. Schiermonnikoog, Netherlands, June 13, 1984.

Koster, G. Personal interview, fourth. Diever, Netherlands, August 21, 1989.

Mulder, Tini. Personal interview. Moddergat, Netherlands, June 14, 1984.

Scheufele, Oberstleutnant, JG5 Luftwaffe. Personal interview. Meppel, Holland, August 22, 1989.

Temmingh, Gerit. Personal interview, second. Diever, Netherlands, June 20, 1984.

van den Hurk, Peter. Personal interview. Meppel, Holland, 1983, 1984, 1985, 1987, and August 1989.

van der Hoop, Sjoukje Smit. Personal interview, Chatham, Ontario, Canada, July 1984.

Johnny Capps, staff sergeant, tail-gunner.

Archer's crew. Author third from right in front row.

Photographs taken by underground for Harry Clark's identification card.

1st Lt. John Woolnough, leader of mission to Vechta.

Lt. Ernst Scheufele, Messerschmitt ME-109 pilot who shot down True Love *on August 15, 1944.*

One of a kind photograph of Hermann Goering and Gen. Adolf Gelland (right) taken by Ernst Scheufele over the wing of his ME-109.

Air photograph showing location of Vliegveld Havelte. Author came down 150 feet from the end of the runway on the east end.

Author standing in middle of runway of Vliegveld Havelte as it appeared in 1980s.

Havelte in 1985.

Peter van den Hurk in 1944, during the time he helped ninety-two Americans and six English flyers escape from the Nazis.

Mimi de Jong in 1944, when she was engaged to marry Peter.

Peter and Mimi van den Hurk (1989).

Gestapo Chief Frans Muller, the cruel Nazi who tortured Pete and Mimi. He sentenced them to face the firing squad on Christmas morning.

M. Demesmacher, a Belgian SS officer who was adept at torture. He was given credit for being the cruelest SS man in Meppel.

Oom Joop (G. Koster) and his family. Oom Joop is on the left with Franz standing behind him.

The policeman, Temmingh (1984).

Oom Joop and the author at the Wig-Wam as it looks today, a national shrine (1983).

Peter and Mimi van den Hurk (1989).

George (Pieter Bloom), who supposedly drowned on November 30, 1944, while coming back to the mainland from Engelsmanplaat for help. His body was not found until February 1945.

Bertus Nauta, schoolteacher and leader of a Resistance group in Ternaard for over two years. He now lives in Grimsby, Ontario, Canada.

Food ration book issued to the author.

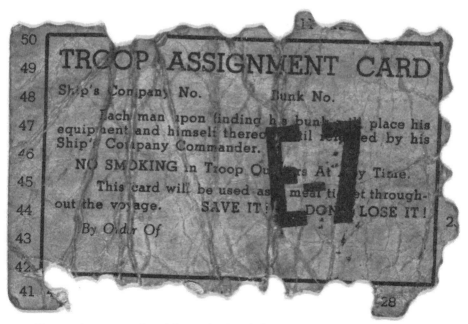

Troop assignment card used for meals aboard the SS George Washington coming home from Europe.

ORANJE
N.B.S.

NBS armband worn by author while assisting in the liberation of Dokkum on April 14, 1945.

In Memoriam

Petrus (Pé) Woudsma,

De oudste zoon uit het grote gezin van J. Woudsma te Dokkum.

Bij de laatste razzia werd Pé te Brantgum (bij Dokkum) gearresteerd, dat was 27 Maart 1945. Een week later werd deze jorge vaderlander door de Nazi-bloedhonden te Leeuwarden gefusilleerd......

Sedert 12 September 1944 was Pé ondergedoken, daar hij op dien datum door de Landwacht te Dokkum was gevangen genomen en nog dienzelfde dag, dank zij de spontane vaderlandse daad van agent Dijkstra (die ook met zijn gezin onderdook) kon ontvluchten.

Als koerier tussen de verschillende contactpunten heeft Pé waardevol werk verricht. Zijn activiteit inzake het verstrekken van brandstoffenbonnen was oorzaak, dat vele Joden en onderduikers 's winters niet in de kou behoefden te zitten.

Wijtse Woudsma (Rienk Prins)

De tweede zoon uit het grote gezin van J. Woudsma te Dokkum.

Na uit Duitsland te zijn ontsnapt, begon hij met het schrijven van een pamflet, getiteld: „Ik zag Duitsland", waarvan direct een duizend exemplaren werden verspreid.

Al spoedig trad Wijtse op als vaste koerier, die alle mogelijke en soms haast onmogelijke opdrachten sportief uitvoerde.

Ook nam hij deel aan de overval op het gemeentehuis van West Dongeradeel op 4 Febr.

Bouwe Jacob Nieuwenhuis
(Bob Visser)

Ongeveer half Januari is het een jaar geleden, dat Bob in Den Haag werd gearresteerd. Hij werd geboren in Hoogkerk. Gr., studeerde aan de Zeevaartschool en heeft als derde stuurman enkele reizen gemaakt naar Noorwegen, om vandaar uit te trachten Zweden te bereiken, teneinde zijn diensten bij de geallieerden aan te bieden.

Toen hem dat mislukte, gaf hij het varen er aan en kwam in contact met de „Groep Hein", waarvat hij een trouw en ijverig medewerker

Pete Woudsma, the author's chess-playing friend in Holwerd. He was picked up by the Germans in late March 1945 and murdered by the Germans on March 29, 1945, in Leeuwarden. His only brother, Wijtse Woudsma (left), was also murdered by the Nazis earlier in Leeuwarden.

Johnny Capps and the author in Dexter, Missouri, on the forty-third anniversary of their being shot down (August 15, 1987).

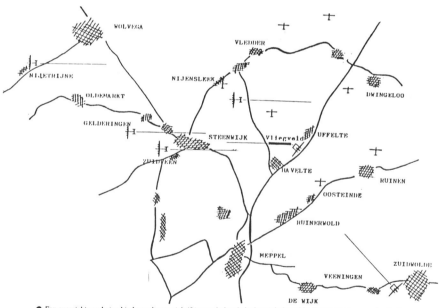

● *Een overzicht van het gebied waarboven zich 40 jaar geleden de luchtstrijd afspeelde. Hierop aangegeven de plaatsen waar toestellen van de strijdende partijen neerkwamen. De Liberators vlogen in westelijke richting, de Duitsers kwamen vanuit zuidelijke. In tweede instantie mengden de Lightnings van uit het westen komend zich in de strijd. Op het overzicht zijn de plaatsen aangegeven waar diverse toestellen en hun bemanningen neerkwamen.*

A map showing the disposition of airplanes shot down August 15, 1944, near Havelte, Holland. (4) B-24 Liberator bombers; (7) Messerschmitt ME-109s; (2) P-38 Lightnings.

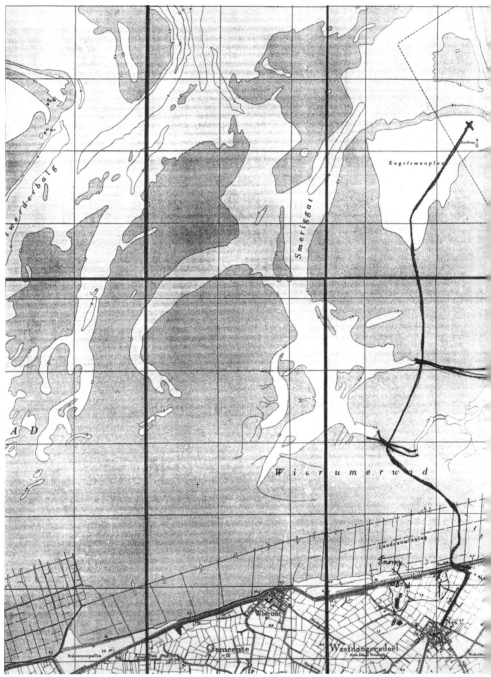

The actual route out to Engelsmanplaat taken by the author, Jim Moulton, Teun de Jong, J. Visser, Niko, and George on November 15, 1944, and the same route back on December 2, 1944, by Niko, Visser, Moulton, and the author.

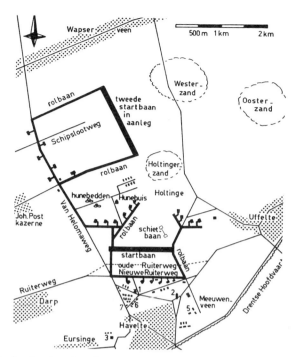

Actual map showing location of main runway and runway under construction (the one the author worked on). Vliegveld Havelte, Holland.

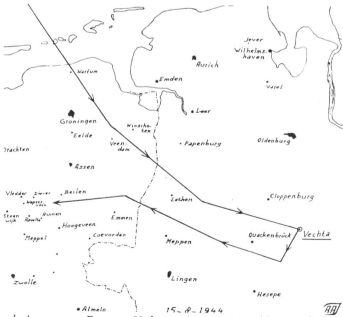

The author's route over Europe to Vechta on August 15, 1944. Note that it stops at Havelte.

Ernst Scheufele in 1944 (above) and in 1989 (below, left) shaking hands with the author.

True Love.

Major Gotz, commander of JG53 squadron of the Luftwaffe, who led his ten planes on the first pass at author's squadron, crippling some and shooting down others. Some of the crew were killed by his airplanes.

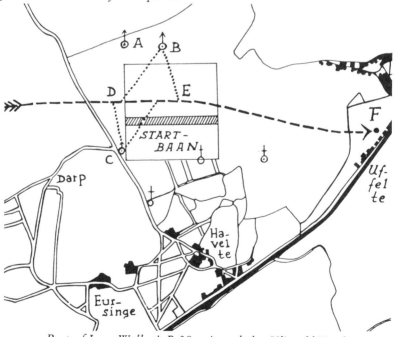

Route of James Wallace's P-38 as it crashed on Vliegveld Havelte.

Lt. Karl Lampen, ME-109 pilot of JG5 (Scheufele's squadron), was killed by crew-men of the 466th on August 15, 1944.

Peter van den Hurk.

AB A.JANSEN

SPOREN AAN DE HEMEL

Kroniek van een luchtoorlog 1943–1945

De strijd van de Amerikaanse luchtmacht tegen
de Duitse Luftwaffe boven Nederland

3

Cover of Ab Jansen's book showing his painting of True Love *being shot down.*

The only known existing photograph of the lifehouse on Engelsmanplaat. The submarine was not there at the time of the story but washed ashore later.

Vliegveld Havelte, 1989.

The two American airmen who were hiding in mevrouw de Groot's house for the Christmas holidays. They were taken as prisoners of war and sent to a stalag luft.

51 Weerdstraat, mevrouw de Groot's house and the first home in which the author hid when starting to evade.

(Back row) Mevrouw de Groot, Mimi de Jong, Pete van den Hurk.

The author and German pilot Ernst Scheufele in Meppel, August 22, 1989.

Sjoukje van der Hoop in 1944.

Sjoukje van der Hoop Smit in 1989.

rry,   12-4-'45

    This is to inform you that you belong to the fighting-group
kkum.and x so does your friend.
    They are busy with your "tobacco-box" and you will receive it
soon as possible.

*Actual message delivered to author in Bridaard. ("Tobacco box" refers to his Sten gun
and Luger.)*

*This German Messerschmitt (BF 109 G-14) was shot down near Kleinhau, Ger-
many, on December 3, 1944. The pilot was Oberleutnant Ernst Scheufele, who, 3½
months before, had shot down an American B-24 bomber, of which the author was a
crew member.*

— U.S. Air Force photo

Index

361